Cordell Hull

Secretary Hull with Sumner Welles, Under-Secretary of State

Cordell Hull

A BIOGRAPHY

BY HAROLD B. HINTON

WITH A FOREWORD BY
SUMNER WELLES

Doubleday, Doran & Company, Inc.
GARDEN CITY, NEW YORK
1942

RINTED AT THE *Country Life Press*, GARDEN CITY, N Y., U. S. A

Foreword

FROM THE TIME of the enactment in 1789 of the Constitution of the United States, the people of the United States have been served by forty-six Secretaries of State.

The list of American Secretaries of State comprises the names of very great men: men who have played a predominant part in the history of our country, and who have had a decisive voice in the shaping of the destinies of the American people.

Yet I believe the list of American statesmen who are entitled to recognition primarily because of their service as Secretary of State—because of the determining part they have played in the conduct of our foreign relations—is strangely small.

Towering figures in American history, such as John Marshall, James Monroe, Henry Clay, Daniel Webster, John C. Calhoun, and William Jennings Bryan, have held the office of Secretary of State, but in cases such as these their names are remembered chiefly because of their achievements in other spheres of activity.

During the one hundred and fifty-two years of our Constitutional existence I doubt whether it could justly be maintained that peculiar ability in the handling of our foreign relations had been demonstrated by more than a handful. In that category I believe there will be little question that there should be placed the names of Thomas. Jefferson, James Madison, John Quincy Adams, Elihu Root; and Charles Evans Hughes.

The overwhelming majority of the American people will also agree that to the list of select who have served as Secretary of State with outstanding distinction there can, with complete assurance, be added the name of Cordell Hull.

It is, of course, not easy for one who has served for so many years in daily contact with Secretary Hull, and who believes so implicitly in the value to the American people, and to the world at large, of the man himself, and of the policies with which his name will always be associated, to write this foreword without partiality. Such partiality would necessarily be felt by all of the officials of the present administration who have had the opportunity of close association with him.

Cordell Hull is the least self-seeking man I have ever known. One of the striking sidelights on the years of his distinguished statesmanship has been his willingness to stay in the background and to let others take the credit and glory. I know of several outstanding instances where Mr. Hull carefully diverted attention away from his own authorship or able sponsorship of a good plan so that some temperamental foreign government official might acquire merit in the eyes of his constituents at home as father of the proposal. Mr. Hull was content that the good idea should take root and flourish.

This may seem like a small attribute to bulk so large in a contemporary tribute to the Secretary of State, but it is a symptom of the inner sureness, the sound judgment, and the practical idealism which have made him the great man he is. He towers above his fellows in clarity of vision and refusal to be led astray from the main issue.

His chief contributions, during a period of world history which has been unparalleled in the gravity and in the number of problems presented in the field of the foreign relations of the United States, are well known and generally recognized.

His name will always be associated with the rapid building, on the foundation of justice and equality, of the new structure of inter-American cooperation; with the "Good Neighbor" policy.

The name of Cordell Hull will likewise always be remembered

as that of the untiring and consistent exponent of the principles of nondiscrimination and equality of treatment in international trade, which, had they been adopted and generally practiced during the decade after the signing of the Treaty of Versailles, would unquestionably have greatly diminished the probability that the world would have been forced into the maelstrom which has now engulfed the whole of modern civilization.

Throughout the period of mountainous tariff barriers, of the utilization of trade practices for political ends, of increasingly primitive barter deals and currency blocs, and of the thousand-and-one practices by which men and governments have stifled and thwarted progress toward the raising of living standards, and toward the increasing of employment, his voice has never faltered in proclaiming the imperative need for a return to those liberal trade practices which proved so powerful a force for human betterment, and for the maintenance of peaceful relations between peoples, in past generations.

No matter what the discouragements or obstacles have been—and at times they seemed insuperable—he has never wavered in his forthright advocacy of those policies. And fortunately today there is increasing recognition throughout the free nations of the world of the justice of the cause which he has made his own.

No one in the United States recognized earlier than he, or more clearly than he, the grave peril to the United States of the plans for world conquest on the part of the totalitarian powers. The policy of the United States as shaped by the President and Secretary Hull throughout the past nine years has been formulated with that danger always in view. Striving untiringly for the maintenance of peace so long as it was conceivable that peace could be maintained, the voice of Cordell Hull time and again has aroused the American people to the imperative need for the taking of those measures for self-defense which have now been adopted.

I have never seen him discouraged. During countless times, in these past nine years, when the situation seemed absolutely hopeless, he would try a new tack, evolve another formula, explore a new avenue. To him, no effort was too great, no mental searching too severe, to devote to the task of saving his country, and the world, from the horrors of war—for he knew that we could not hope to escape the consequences of another world war.

And at all times the emphasis of what he has said and of what he has done has been laid upon the need for what might be termed old-fashioned decency, justice, and fair dealing in human relations and in international relations.

He is a persuader rather than a leader. He relies on the ultimate triumph of reason to solve all human problems. He could not, if he would, coerce anyone into an intellectually repugnant course. His life, public and private, has exemplified that kind of democracy, governmental, intellectual, and spiritual, in which lies the future hope of the human race.

As this is written, our nation is engaged in a war brought upon us by those forces of evil which are attempting to conquer the whole world by the sword. No man can measure the suffering and unhappiness which have been, and which will be, brought to humble and unoffending people everywhere before sanity and decency once again govern our relations, one with the other. We, raised in the American way of life, want to live in a sane and decent world.

If this is the faith we are fighting for, Cordell Hull is one of its leading apostles. For years no man on earth has labored more diligently or more sincerely to perpetuate that philosophy and to prevent the retrogression to the level of savagery at which the world finds itself today. His name is written high, and will remain high, on the list of those who have kept alight the flame of civilization in the new Dark Ages which have come upon us.

UNDER SECRETARY OF STATE

Washington, D. C.
December 12, 1941

Contents

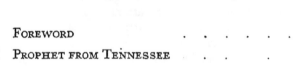

x   Contents

Illustrations

Cordell Hull

CHAPTER I

Prophet from Tennessee

THE S.S. *American Legion,* of the now defunct Munson Line,
was plowing its leisurely way through a choppy sea off the coast
of Uruguay one afternoon in the autumn of 1933. The vessel
needed paint and showed signs of the faltering financial status of
her owners, but she flew a gay and unusual pennon from her
foreyard.

The little flag that fluttered in the South American trade wind
was a blue rectangle with a white disk in the center, on which was
imposed the official coat of arms of the United States as adopted
by the Continental Congress on June 20, 1782. In each corner it
bore a five-pointed white star, with one point upward.

The display of the flag indicated the presence, aboard the ship,
of the Secretary of State of the United States. Its design had been
approved only a few months before by Congress (a previous flag
having been found faulty in heraldic significance), and this was
the second voyage on which it had been flown in honor of Cordell
Hull.

Mr. Hull was bound for his first adventure in Latin-American
diplomacy. He was traveling as the head of the United States
delegation to the Seventh International Conference of American States. He had with him a staff of experts, other delegates to
help him, and he had been well coached at the State Department

in the details of the problems which would arise, but he knew that the ultimate responsibility for this mission lay on his shoulders. It was a ponderous responsibility, coming so soon after the humiliating failure of the London Monetary and Economic Conference.

We were due at Montevideo the following morning. Mr. Hull had invited me to have a chat in his cabin before dinner, as I wanted to ask him some last-minute questions concerning the conference we were about to enter. Questions and answers did not last long, and the Secretary launched into an impromptu discussion of the state of the world, which was obviously preying on his mind. His simple and unaffected analysis of the world's difficulties made such an impression on me that I am able, even at this distance in time, space, and political development, to recall almost his exact words. They ran about as follows:

"Europe is finished. You and I will hardly live to see the day when Europe will be able to drag itself out of the pit it is now digging. The race of political and economic nationalism which has started in Europe will have to be run to its conclusion—to the impoverishment of its inhabitants—whether or not there is actual war.

"In our own interest, we must look to our relations with these countries down here. Among the Americas we may be able to find the answer. We ought to be able to work out a pattern of life which will inspire the whole world to follow our example when the present tumult dies down. Remember, we may not have as great a past as Europe, but we have a greater future."

These and other accurate predictions that Hull made privately and publicly at that time went unheeded. Adolf Hitler had been Chancellor of the German Reich for only six months. The Reichstag had just voted him the full powers with which he was to stamp out democratic life in Germany and in much of the world. Hitler was not feared in the outside world then as he came to be in succeeding years.

Hull himself was not concerned with Hitler or with any single individual. He saw, as few of us did at that time, that ideas were afloat in the world which gave promise of throwing all civilization back to the tribal life of the Dark Ages. He was more interested in the motif of the opera than he was in the performances of the heroes and villains playing the various parts. That is his usual approach to world problems.

Not that he underrates the human element. He knows how to make use of men, persuade men, cajole men, humor men, and yield to their little vanities, all for the purpose of advancing the cause or the idea he considers of importance. The democratic process involves relations between men as well as between ideas, and no one knows this better than Cordell Hull, veteran of fifty years as an officeholder and campaigner in most of the epochal political fights of this century in the United States.

At the same time he has a conviction that ideas will triumph over, or outlast, men. This is probably the measuring rod which has enabled him during all these years to calculate the future with an uncanny accuracy confounding to many a political foe.

Again, in 1938, just after the Munich "agreement" had lulled a self-satisfied democratic world into smug complacency, Mr. Hull gave me a shipboard dissertation on the world situation which prompted me to include the following in a dispatch sent to the New York *Times* from Panama:

Secretary Hull's conviction, which has been more strongly expressed privately than publicly, is that Europe is headed for a terrific smashup unless some new influence, not now in sight, comes into the picture, and that the United States and other American countries will suffer intensely, even if not directly involved. He believes that this view of the case is insufficiently appreciated in the United States, not to mention Latin America.

In the light of subsequent events it is easy to magnify examples of his accuracy and to forget his mistakes. There is plenty of public record, however, to attest the consistency of his judgment over the years. Now that the devastation of Europe has come to pass, he never says, "I told you so." He keeps to himself whatever recriminations he might wreak on those so-called leaders who counseled us that Europe's affairs are not ours and that we could hold ourselves aloof from the "age-old struggles" (the one which affects us most vitally right now dates only from 1933, when Hitler came to power) of the Old World.

One of the strangest estimates of Cordell Hull, which has gained a certain currency, pictures him as a dreamy idealist, his heart in the right place, but completely impractical in facing the brutal realities of today's world. On the contrary, he is probably one of the most matter-of-fact, feet-on-the-ground politicians and statesmen of our country in this generation. He is a Democrat in the partisan sense and a democrat in the philosophical sense.

Another misconception of him was shared by the impetuous young "brain trusters" and their disciples. This view pictured him as an economic determinist—one who believes that all human actions spring from economic motives and that all human ills can be cured by economic remedies. Their facile misjudgment failed to take into account the fieriness of his defense of human dignity in his dealings with Nazi atrocities. To him the violation of that innate dignity to which every human being is entitled far outweighed the material damage or physical violence the victim had undergone. His early protests to Berlin against mistreatment of American Jews by bullying Brown Shirts were models of diplomatic fury.

There are scores of Tennesseans who have helped mightily in the building of the United States, and Cordell Hull must be numbered among them. One cannot imagine him springing from other soil than that of his native state. The hard, turbulent conditions which surrounded its growth went into his make-up, and their influence accounts for much of him.

Hull came to man's estate in the lean days following the Civil War. The Nashville of his time, and the country surrounding it, had suffered a nearly mortal blow from which it has hardly yet recovered. He and his contemporaries found their opportunities circumscribed by the physical labor of procuring food and shelter in their impoverished surroundings. Theirs was an unpromising start in life.

The public and private problems of the time were threshed out in discussions around the general store, the post office, the church, the courthouse, and the other forums common to small American towns. Talk was the great educator in those days of poor and infrequent schools. Saturday afternoons were the favorite times of assembly at the store, when most of the men joined in the discussions and the boys listened. They paid especial attention to the theories and criticisms of the old Confederate soldiers, who occupied the center of the stage whenever they desired.

Cordell Hull's earliest political recollections are the memories of old soldiers, all of them long dead, disputing the details of public life in the small orbit they knew. The political officeholders were shining targets for them. They taught Hull a lesson he has never forgotten—that the democratic system, no matter how fine and apparently foolproof in its mechanism, must always be carried out through the medium of the fallible human being. No political or administrative machinery is any stronger than its weakest human component.

Because he never had any panaceas to offer, and because he never tried to remodel the whole United States at a single session of Congress, Hull did not attract the public attention he probably merited during his early days in Washington. During most of his time in Congress he sat on the minority side of the aisle, and his ideas could be offered only in opposition to overwhelming odds.

However, those ideas are preserved in the pages of the *Congressional Record,* and they make interesting reading these days. To most Americans Hull is a relatively new political discovery. They do not realize that he wrote the first of the series of Federal income and inheritance taxes which bear so heavily on us today or that he battled for the principle of taxation according to ability to pay at a time when the nation's conservative elements considered such talk to be little better than treason.

Hull was well in advance of the New Dealers in foreseeing the evils which would follow the period President Hoover described as the new era, with poverty abolished forever. At the height of the boom Hull told the House of Representatives that "we must visualize the nation as a whole—as one great financial unit, one giant productive plant with ever-increasing surpluses." We were then giving those surpluses away to foreign countries by lending them the money to pay, and Hull saw that this scheme was no good.

"If American plants today were loosed at full production capacity they would flood all domestic markets within ninety days, and many artificial parts of our economic structure would topple and fall," he said, in an estimate which was to be backed up by the Brookings Institution's studies, *America's Capacity to Produce* and *America's Capacity to Consume.*

"It is my individual view that these glaring facts and conditions soon will compel America to recognize that these ever-increasing surpluses are her key economic problems and that our neglect to develop foreign markets for surpluses is the one outstanding cause of unemployment."

There is a legend that Hull used to be a great poker player. It dates from his service as a captain of infantry in the Spanish-American War, when he is supposed to have kept his regiment cleaned out of funds by his prowess at the time-honored military indoor sport. It is probably based on fact, for even today he shows a poker player's caution by concealing his emotions and the plans he has in mind.

Nashville friends illustrate this trait by an anecdote concerning his service as a member of the state legislature half a century ago. Hangers-on at the state capitol were discussing the young legislator's agility in avoiding a direct answer to a question. One of them bet he could extract a direct answer from Hull. He stopped Hull as he was entering the capitol and asked him what time it was. Hull took out his own timepiece, looked at it, and shot back at his questioner:

"What does your watch say?"

The technique of making the other fellow say first is another heritage of his mountain upbringing. The mountain people still display considerable reticence in their dealings with strangers. They want to be completely satisfied as to the newcomer's business and motives before they get very far involved in a conversation.

President Roosevelt and Secretary Hull have never reached the close and warm friendship which Mr. Roosevelt has manifested for a few other members of his official family, but the two men have had a constant and common meeting ground in the broad outlines of the foreign policy they both believed the United States must pursue under the tragic conditions engrossing the formerly civilized world. One of their qualities in common is the capacity to make use of men, their abilities and their frailties, in getting things done. This is an asset which can be acquired only from long experience in practical politics, such as they have both had. Mr. Roosevelt acknowledged Hull's contribution to the success of his first two terms as President in various speeches during his campaign for a third term.

Speaking at Philadelphia on October 23, 1940, the Chief Executive said that "since last July hardly a day or a night has passed when some crisis, or some possibility of crisis in world affairs, has not called for my personal conference with the Secretary of State." Again, at Cleveland on November 2, Mr. Roosevelt told his audience that "it has been solely in the interest of peace and the maintenance of peace that your great Secretary of State and I have felt that we should both remain within easy distance of the national capital in these trying days."

Hull's mature life has covered the most interesting and probably the most important years of this country's history thus far. He has experienced every variation of the national life, from the frontiersman's existence he led as a child to the complexities of adapting the American way of life to a world dominated by the totalitarians. Not only political changes but all the dangerous paraphernalia of modern civilization have appeared at a bewildering rate ever since he has tried to cope with them in public life. Communications of all kinds, up to and including television, have been perfected within his lifetime. Mass production has become the keystone of the national economy. The habits and mentality of the entire population have changed radically.

Through all these metamorphoses Cordell Hull has believed that he has understood the few fundamental, guiding principles which would supply the answers to the new problems. The intuitive persistence with which he sticks to his basic ideas is no accident. It is the result of long years of training and practice. He has always favored the measured, reasoned decision over the flashy snap judgment which, coupled with a good deal of luck, sometimes wins for its possessor a reputation for brilliance.

The nation's foreign policy, during his time as Secretary of State, has been essentially his. With but few exceptions President Roosevelt has left the conduct of foreign relations to his prime minister. President Roosevelt dramatized the Good Neighbor policy in the matchless language of his first inaugural address, but Mr. Hull made it mean something more than mere oratory in Latin America. Mr. Roosevelt called for an equitable readjustment of the nation's foreign trade relations in words that wrung unprecedented powers from Congress, but it remained for Mr. Hull to give the whole thing substance by the painstaking negotiation of a score of reciprocal trade agreements. They have made an excellent team.

Without Hull's steadying hand on the tiller of the ship of state, there is no telling where the adventurous political impetuosity of President Roosevelt or the economic opportunism of Henry Wallace and the New Deal quick-fixers might have led the country's foreign relations. Hull has had the support of Sumner Welles, another steadying influence on the White House, in the main lines of foreign policy.

An outsider's estimate of Cordell Hull must be essentially superficial, because it must be based so largely on the public record. The Secretary of State is a man who does not talk of himself easily. He does not lend himself to build-up and glamour. He cannot, or will not, expose to the public view his inner self, his reasonings, his motives. The true and full account of his long career can be written only by himself—and he will probably never do so. He may publish his memoirs someday and is now considering doing so, but they will reveal little of the human side of the man.

He has never been able to reconcile himself to the supposedly exceptionless American tradition that the public servant's entire life is the business of the public. Hull's reticence about his official life is only slightly less profound than his shyness about his private affairs.

In the spring of 1917 Jesse S. Cottrell fell sick He is a veteran Washington correspondent for Tennessee newspapers and an old friend of Hull's. As Cottrell began to feel better, and had reached the stage of being bored at having to stay in bed, he ran out of reading matter. All he had at his bedside was the day's issue of the Washington *Star,* which he read through, even to the death notices and marriage announcements.

Suddenly he reached for the telephone and called John D. Erwin, an old friend and competitor in the Tennessee newspaper field (Erwin is now United States Minister to Honduras), and broke the news that they had both been scooped beyond repair.

"My God, John," Cottrell shouted into the receiver, "the Judge has gone and got himself married."

As a representative from Tennessee, Judge Hull was dependent on the writings of these two men for the formation of much

public opinion about him at home. In those days, of course, there
was no radio to serve the home-town needs of a member of Congress. Both correspondents had known Hull for years and had
chronicled his political career ever since he had come to Washington, and yet he did not think to tell them that he was going
to be married. He sincerely believed the public would not be interested, and it never occurred to him to make his marriage an
occasion to get his name into the papers in a favorable manner.

The marriage was a felicitous one for both Hull and his wife.
Mrs. Hull has been apart from, and yet a great part of, Cordell
Hull's career during the quarter of a century they have lived
together. Her conceptions of a wife's duties and a wife's contributions to her husband's career spring from the customs of the
Old South, where she was born and raised. She has literally loved,
honored, and obeyed her husband and is very proud of it. She
has made a career of it.

The *New Yorker's* cartoon showing two coal miners looking
up from their work in surprise as one of them exclaims, "For
gosh sakes, here comes Mrs. Roosevelt," could never have been
inspired by Mrs. Hull. She has never taken any but the most
casual and official interest in the economic and social questions
that have vexed the country ever since she married Hull. Her
interest in politics is purely subjective and concerns only the impact of current movements on her husband's welfare and happiness.

Mrs. Hull is a handsome, kindly woman with graying dark
hair and large brown eyes. She is in her late fifties, although she
likes to say she has forgotten how old she is. She has an excellent,
conservative taste in dress, which has stood her in good stead
among the acid-tongued women critics of the nation's capital.
This taste reflects her personality. She is never the first to take
up a new fashion, in clothes or in thought, nor is she ever the
last to put an old one away.

She was born in Staunton, Virginia, the birthplace of Woodrow Wilson, and for some years she has been head of a committee to raise funds for the restoration of the World War President's birthplace. She is one of eight children born to Mr. and
Mrs. Isaac Witz. Her father was a banker and small industrialist
in the Shenandoah Valley and left her a modest fortune, which

has softened the rigors of her husband's preoccupation with public life to the exclusion of making money. She grew up in the easygoing atmosphere of the little Virginia town, joining the Episcopal Church and graduating from Mary Baldwin College there. She led the usual life of the daughter of a well-to-do minor magnate and leading citizen.

When she met Hull, in the spring of 1917, her first marriage had recently ended in a divorce. It was for this reason that her wedding with Hull on November 24, 1917, was such a quiet ceremony, for in those days remarriage after divorce was still not quite accepted in the old-fashioned Virginia circles to which she belonged. She never mentions her first marriage, even to intimate friends, although she and Mr. Hull have never made any particular effort to conceal it. All reference books carrying biographical notes about the Secretary state that he married Rose Frances Whitney and not Rose Frances Witz.

She spent the winter of 1917 in Washington, where she had a brother, the late Julius Witz, and a sister, Mrs. William Woodward Cook. She stayed at the Cochran Hotel, which was a rendezvous for Southerners in the capital, including many members of Congress Some of the Virginia members, who had known Mrs. Whitney at home, introduced Cordell Hull to her. He also lived at the hotel, and they kept their home there for five years after they were married.

Hull was spending much of his time in Carthage in those days, and his bride fitted smoothly into the life there. Carthage reminded her of a smaller edition of her native Staunton, with its huge trees, attractive location, big houses, and spacious lawns sloping down to the banks of the Cumberland River. They "kept house" in the Bradford home on Carthage's Main Street part of the time and lived at the old Chapman House the rest.

It was here that Mrs. Hull learned to call her husband "Judge," which she does to this day when speaking of him to people she does not know well. He calls her "Frances" when speaking to her, or of her to personal friends. She got to know his old friends there and liked them. The Gardenhires, Mrs. Carrie Chapman, the McGinnesses, the Ligons, the Coxes, the Browns, and other lifelong admirers of her husband gradually took her to their hearts.

She became interested in her husband's political career, not only because of her natural pride and interest in his progress but because she absorbed from his backers in his own constituency the conviction that his continued officeholding was a good thing for the state and the nation and not merely a personal advantage. She worked around his headquarters in the Congressional campaigns of 1920, when she learned the bitterness of electoral defeat, and in 1922, when he was elected again to the House of Representatives. He took her to her first Democratic National Convention in San Francisco in 1920, to see James M. Cox nominated.

His succeeding campaigns for the House were not arduous, as he had established a lien on the seat from the Carthage district, and Mrs. Hull took no active part in them. In 1930, however, when he ran for the Senate, she toured the state with him, looking after his health, glad-handing the wives of important politicians, and otherwise making herself useful.

When they were in Washington they lived quietly. In 1922 they moved away from the Cochran Hotel, where they had met, to the Lafayette Hotel on Sixteenth Street. They kept their Washington residence there until Hull was elected to the Senate, when they moved into the Carlton Hotel. Having no children, they found hotel life the easiest and most agreeable mode of living in Washington. It left them free to commute to and from Tennessee as political exigencies demanded. It spared them the complications of running a house, with servants to be discharged and rehired every few months, their terms of office depending on the unpredictable longevity of Congressional sessions.

It was only after Hull was appointed Secretary of State that his wife began to regard Washington as their permanent home. During the nerve-racking interval between President Roosevelt's election and his decision to offer Hull the first portfolio in his Cabinet, she looked around discreetly for quarters which would be more fitting for the American equivalent of a prime minister. She selected a seven-room apartment in the Carlton Hotel, which could be kept up with a small domestic staff and which would provide her husband with larger and more comfortable working quarters. She had a premonition that he would be appointed and that his work would be tremendously enhanced in importance and volume.

Quiet as she was about her quest, news of it came to the ears of a few friends. Among them was Arthur Krock, head of the Washington bureau of the New York *Times*. He asked Hull about it and got the impression that the proposed new apartment was to be rented only in the event he became Secretary of State. Krock was able to scoop his rivals in announcing the appointment because Hull, after the first definite commitment on Roosevelt's part, casually said to him, "I guess we'll be taking that new apartment."

As wife of the Secretary of State, Mrs. Hull was plunged swiftly into an unaccustomed milieu. It is a tribute to her upbringing and her innate common sense that she brought it off so well. It was no longer possible for her to be so self-effacing and practically anonymous as she had been as the wife of a Tennessee representative and a Tennessee senator. She automatically became one of the senior hostesses of the national capital. By custom and by force of circumstances, she had to receive hundreds of resident diplomats who had hitherto played hardly any part at all in their quiet, simple mode of life.

The change in official status involved a decision. She realized that no halfway measures were possible. Either she and the Judge must resign themselves to the endless round of luncheons and dinners which makes up so-called official social life in Washington, in which event his work would suffer, or they must have none of it, so that he could continue his practice of meticulous study and reflection on the pressing problems of the moment in his spare time at home. The Secretary ordained the second course, and she loyally obeyed the edict.

Mrs. Hull let it be known that she and the Secretary would accept only official invitations and that their own entertaining would be only of the inescapably formal kind. This was a wise decision, as the Secretary's health would not have permitted fronting the illimitable expanse of Washington tablecloths which faces the complaisant Cabinet official.

Left to his own devices, Mr. Hull has effective gastronomic defenses against official banqueting. He eats a plate of white meat of chicken and salad and drinks a glass of milk before going to the official meal. At the banquet he converses amicably with his partners to either side but takes none of the dishes served to him. This is slightly disconcerting to those who are not familiar with his dietary habits, but it promotes his general physical welfare. As a further precaution against the evils of dining out, he never takes a drink outside of his own home. There he occasionally takes a little old rye (of which he is a connoisseur) with plain water, as rye should be taken, before eating his chicken and salad and setting out to a public function. After that, drinking is over.

Mrs. Hull accompanied the Secretary on his South American trips and widened her acquaintance among the statesmen of the Western Hemisphere. President Terra of Uruguay and President Benavides of Peru were among the leaders to show her the most honor, although neither of them could speak English and their dinner conversation had to be carried on through an interpreter.

Mrs. Hull liked the social side of the Pan-American conferences she attended, except that they were hard on her husband. To the Secretary the long, formal dinners lasting into the early morning hours were fatiguing chores. In South American official circles Spanish hours are kept, and the official banquets would be scheduled for 11 P.M., with the guests sitting down at midnight. Mr. Hull's idea of a normal evening is to have a light meal between six and seven, work until ten o'clock, and then go to bed. The round of entertainments at the conferences, which he could not avoid, always left him exhausted, but his extraordinary recuperative powers would come to his rescue on the homeward voyages and he would reach Washington in the pink of condition.

In Washington Mrs. Hull acts as her own social secretary. Most of the time she answers the telephone herself when a friend calls her apartment. The telephone operator at the hotel (they moved to the Wardman Park in the spring of 1941) asks the caller's name, and if Mrs. Hull wants to speak she responds herself. If she does not want to speak, the hotel operator says she is out.

Their evenings are spent quietly in their apartment, with the rare exceptions when unavoidable official dinners take them out. The Secretary brings home piles of papers from his office, or notes

for a speech, and works on them at his desk while Mrs. Hull reads
or writes letters or pastes up clippings in the enormous collection
she has amassed. It now numbers more than fifty fat volumes
and presents a complete newspaper picture of her husband's
activities since he became Secretary of State.

Old friends, most of them people without any particular
standing, drop in on them from seven to nine for the little visits
that are Hull's only relaxations these days. The favorite topic of
conversation on these occasions is political gossip, usually concerning matters which happened years ago. Hull enjoys exchanging reminiscences with other veteran Democrats who have seen
the party through its downs and ups of the past half-century. He
still takes a keen interest in Tennessee politics, although he does
not attempt to exercise any influence in state affairs.

Mrs. Hull's principal assignment as a hostess, of course, fell to
her when President Roosevelt asked her to accompany the Secretary of State to Niagara Falls in the spring of 1939 to welcome
King George VI and Queen Elizabeth to American soil. Although
Mrs. Roosevelt took over the principal duties of the royal entertainment when the party reached Washington, Mrs. Hull had her
share of the responsibilities and carried them off in good style.

She is popular with the women newspaper reporters in Washington because she is friendly and unassuming. She has never
followed Mrs. Roosevelt's example of holding press conferences,
because she feels she has nothing of interest to tell the press. She
always has time, however, to help some harassed society editor
who missed a party with the names of the people she saw there,
what the women wore, and those other details which brighten
the society columns of our metropolitan papers. As a result, she
herself always gets a good press. The society reporters vie with
one another in reporting how beautiful she was, how smart her
gown was, and how she was the center of attraction at the gathering. She probably has more uniformly nice things said about
her in the newspapers than any other woman in public life.

Because the Secretary will go only to official functions, she
tries to double up and make brief appearances at all the teas
and afternoon receptions by herself. Lately she has given up the
endless string of ladies' luncheons which she used to attend, pre-
ferring nowadays to have a quiet luncheon at home with the

Secretary. She discovered that he was having luncheon from a tray in his office or going without, and she insisted that he break his work long enough to come home for a substantial meal in the middle of the day.

She misses the croquet games which were the Secretary's only form of outdoor exercise before the war made such inroads on his time that he had to give them up. With her and two or three favorite opponents from the State Department, Hull used to play several times a week at Woodley, Secretary of War Henry L. Stimson's house, and at the home of James Clement Dunn, State Department adviser on European political affairs. It used to be said that Hull, who is an expert player, would send away an opponent's ball with a mighty whack, muttering sounds that suspiciously resembled the names of certain dictators with whom he was having trouble. The sounds would vary with the progress of events in the world, according to this legend.

This placid existence would probably be dull to most other women, but Mrs. Hull thrives on it. She insists that the Secretary wear his overcoat at times he thinks he doesn't need it, just as other wives do, and he gets annoyed, just as other husbands do. Their differences never seem to be more important than that, however. Their tastes and habits are similar enough so that they are constant companions, within the limits imposed by official demands on his time.

She has made a career out of seeing to it that her husband has been comfortable and in good health and happy through the quarter of a century she has lived with him. She is not ambitious for him in a worldly way and has repeatedly urged him to retire from public life. She appeared to be carrying the day before the present European war broke out. Hull was telling friends that he intended to resign after Roosevelt was elected for the third time, settle down in Washington, and write the memoirs for which he has notes and papers scattered in trunks and boxes over much of the country between the national capital and Carthage.

When the war came he decided that he would have to stay for the duration, and his wife interposed no objection. She knows the inflexibility of his will too well to oppose any reasoned decision of his, and at the same time she realized there could be no happiness for him on the side lines during the most critical fight he would ever see.

Thus her career continues along the same lines, assuming more importance all the time. She it is who persuades him to take those little vacation trips to Virginia or Florida which do him so much good. She wants him to be in good health for his own sake, but in pursuing that subjective goal she is also serving the general good. If there is such a thing as a dower right in a statesman's public heritage, Frances Hull deserves it.

CHAPTER II

A Lawyer by Profession

A MOTORIST driving south from Danville, Kentucky, would find himself rolling along the Cordell Hull Highway as soon as he passed the Tennessee line. If he turned west at Byrdstown, he would be following the Cordell Hull Parkway. He could hardly be unaware that he had entered the country which will always be famous as the region that produced the great Democrat who has come to be a legend in the district.

The country where Hull was born and raised is beautiful, striking, and varied. It lies just between, and combines the qualities of, rich, fertile middle Tennessee and poor, mountainous eastern Tennessee. It is situated in the foothills of the Cumberland Mountains and is only beginning to be readily accessible to the outside world. A good part of it completely missed the stage of development by railroad through which so much of the United States passed. Just as Japan jumped from rush lanterns to electric lights, Hull's part of Tennessee has skipped directly from river boats to automobiles.

Scenically, it is attractive throughout. Bee Rock, near Monterey, provides one of the finest vistas in the country, although it can be reached only over a mile of rough dirt road which is almost impassable in wet weather. It is a little promontory sticking out from the peak of an elevation, from which one gazes up and down a wooded valley rising to become an irregular and enchanting series of hills, each one higher than the one in front of it, stretching away to the horizon on both sides.

The landscape ranges from the knobby hills, covered with scrub trees and undergrowth, around Jamestown, where coal mines furnish the main cash crop of the inhabitants, to the gentle slopes of Carthage, on the west, where almost every agricultural product grows in profusion and where prosperity is well in evidence. A portion of it, around Cookeville, used to be called the "blackjack country" because it was covered with useless little blackjack oaks which had to be cleared away slowly and painfully before the land could be cultivated.

This upper Cumberland country was settled at the end of the eighteenth and the beginning of the nineteenth century. The settlers were of the same aggressive Anglo-Saxon stock which built up middle and western Tennessee.

Until the construction of the Louisville & Nashville Railroad in the late eighteen fifties, a main highway ran from Ohio, Indiana, and Kentucky through Tennessee to the south, passing by Livingston and Oak Hill in Overton County, thence through Sparta, McMinnville, and Chattanooga into Georgia. This highway was the main artery through which were driven huge quantities of mules and other livestock to Georgia and the cotton-growing section. The traffic brought considerable prosperity to the upper Cumberland region, and it was as advanced socially, culturally, and materially as any other portion of rural Tennessee in the early days.

The new railroad, however, paralleled the highway on a route through the valleys to the south of the Hull country and soon drained all of the profitable transient commerce away from it. As the years passed, the inhabitants became poorer and more backward, and the Civil War threw them into destitution.

Despite the general worsening of conditions in the region during the last half of the century, the tradition of the law as the profession for the ablest young men survived and increased. Tennessee had no abler or more noted lawyers than many of those who traveled the lonely mountain circuits of the upper Cumberland in the days following the Civil War. Among them were Major William H. Botts, Colonel John P. Murray and his son, G. B. Murray, of Gainesboro; J. W. McHenry and Judge Alvin Cullom, of Livingston; A. O. W. Totten, of Monroe, Overton County, who later served on the state supreme court from Memphis; Judge E. L. Gardenhire, also of Overton County; Benton and John H. McMillin, first of Celina and later of Carthage; Colonel H. H. Dillon and Captain Walton Smith, of Cookeville.

Because of the lack of travel and transportation facilities the cream of the young men of the region tended to gravitate toward Nashville in the lean years following the Civil War. Samuel J. Keith, of Jackson County, the Dibrells, the Bransfords, the Goodalls, the Fites, the Bolivar H. Cookes, the Tinsleys, the Cheeks, the Settles—these and literally thousands of others from the upper Cumberland and the foothills of its mountains migrated to Nashville and made their contributions to its upbuilding in every walk of life. For two generations the state capital recruited many of the more progressive citizens of the mountain district, along with their accumulated wealth.

There are practically no Negroes in the region. The present-day inhabitants are almost exclusively descendants of the Virginians who settled to the west following the Revolutionary War, encouraged by the generous land grants the Continental Congress voted to veterans. One detects, even today, a trace of Virginia accent (that indescribable but unmistakable pronunciation of the word "house," for example) in the conversation of people who have never been outside the county where they live.

Cordell Hull's first Tennessee ancestor, Allen B. Hull, was one of the adventurous former soldiers who decided to carve a fortune out of the wilderness. He brought with him his wife Syreana, and they are both buried in Nash Cemetery near Armathwaite.

These early pioneers found they had let themselves in for a difficult life. There were arable valleys (the mountaineers call them "coves") which could be cleared and made to provide sustenance for a few families, with the land's produce added to the apparently inexhaustible supply of game. But they could not get hold of any cash to pay their taxes or to buy staples and luxuries from the trading posts to the east. They could grow cash crops with great effort, but there was no way to transport their wares to the markets.

Cattle could thrive amid the underbrush on the uncleared hills, and grazing became a leading industry. Today splendid herds of Angus Aberdeens get a comfortable living off those same hillsides. But in earlier times the cattle raiser had to drive his animals on foot all the way to Virginia to sell them for three cents a pound or less as stockers. The cattle would be fed all summer on the pasture slopes, and the men would drive them away in the autumn, just before the bad weather made the primitive roads impassable. They would lose a certain number of cattle during the trip, and the remaining animals would shrink in weight under the hardships of the long march. It was a thankless and unprofitable business.

There was no river communication toward the east, but to the west the Cumberland provided a ready-made avenue in the spring, when it had enough water to be navigable. By a twisting, treacherous route it finally led to Nashville, the only important market to which there was any practicable access. Nashville had developed into a trading post of consequence, as it was a convenient starting point for expeditions into the frontier land further to the west. The arterial roads which were used by the settlers pushing toward the west missed the Hull country, however, passing it both on the north and on the south. His ancestors and their neighbors were out of the main migratory stream.

It was easy to convert the corn which grew in the clearings into whisky, but it was hard to raise the excises demanded by the Federal government. Nearly every man made himself a little corn liquor from time to time, and nearly every man would sell a gallon or two to a neighbor who had run short. None of them, however, would or could pay any taxes on the liquor. Every man's hand was against the revenue agent, and it was only the most daring and hard-boiled of these governmental representatives who would make even an effort to enforce the law. Of those who did try to carry out their enforcement functions, a goodly number disappeared mysteriously in the mountains.

The region made slow progress until the Civil War. By 1812 Carthage felt prosperous enough to afford a town jail, and a few years later an enterprising citizen opened a hotel. By 1833 William Cullom built a pretentious house, described in the *History*

of Homes and Gardens of Tennessee as "furnished in the manner
of the time, with carved rosewood, rich damasks, French china,
velvet carpets, real lace curtains, and unbelievable quantities of
silver hammered from silver coin." By 1850 Carthage had become a regional center for the activities of the Methodist Episcopal Church, and the first railroad train ran into the town, amid
appropriate ceremonies, in 1855. Then in 1863 the Federal
troops occupied Carthage, and the miseries of war gripped the
whole region. Prosperity and progress vanished, not only for the
duration of the war but for the better part of fifty years.

Carthage was then, as it is now, the little capital of the
most flourishing part of the Hull country. Cordell Hull was not
to know its comparative elegance until he was a grown man. His
father, William Hull, had been raised in the less affluent eastern
section of the region, and Cordell, the third son, was born in
a little farmhouse between Byrdstown and Willow Grove, two
miles or so from the Kentucky line.

The house still stands and is readily accessible by Route 53
out of Byrdstown. It is now occupied by a modestly prosperous
tenant farmer and has been somewhat enlarged since the Hull
family lived there nearly seventy years ago. It is a plain, substantial, one-story structure, and the various additions have
been constructed in the lean-to manner. At one end is a large
brick chimney, betokening an ample fireplace within. The rest
of the building is frame.

A stone retaining wall has been put in at the edge of the road.
The house itself stands back about twenty-five feet from the
road. Half of it is sheltered by a large grape arbor, and a front
porch goes across the other half. The railing of the porch is decorated with gay flowers growing out of Esso tins. The grass in the
front yard sometimes needs cutting, but in other respects the
home appears to be in good, habitable condition—a typical
house of the region, built for utility rather than beauty. While
less pretentious than some of the houses near the towns, it is
far from the humblest home to be seen about there. It might be
described as a lower-middle-class dwelling in that part of the
country.

By the time Cordell was born his father was about thirty years
old and had already begun to prosper in a small way. His father,

who became known all through that country as "Uncle Billy," had lived the average precarious existence of the young men of the region during the wild days of the Civil War and the Reconstruction. He had had an eye shot out by a marauder whom he killed, in revenge, several years later.

The section around the Hull home was hopelessly divided in its allegiances during the war. It suffered relatively little from actual battles between the regular troops on the two sides, but it was constantly ravaged by guerrillas who claimed, to cloak their depredations, that they were acting for one side or the other. Frequently the desperadoes met as rivals in trying to loot some desirable piece of property, and active fighting took place. These encounters gave rise to many of the feuds which were kept alive long after the war and the reconstruction period had passed.[1]

Having lived through these vicissitudes, William Hull decided he could afford to take a wife soon after the war was over and married Elizabeth Riley, who lived in Wolf River Valley in nearby Fentress County. Her grandfather, James Riley, was a Revolutionary soldier and had likewise come to Tennessee from Virginia.

[1] In Tennessee the old-time politicians say Sam Rayburn would never have become Speaker of the House of Representatives if it had not been for the troubled life there after the Civil War. Mr. Rayburn's father, who was a Confederate soldier, had his horse taken from him by some Yankee marauders as he was making his way to his home in the hills of eastern Tennessee after he had been discharged in Knoxville.

The local story is that the elder Rayburn brooded over this injustice so bitterly that he decided to move to Texas, to get away from it all, and this is how his son Sam got the opportunity to become one of the leading Democratic figures of the state and to work himself up to the Speakership.

Actually the local legend has only a kernel of truth. Sam Rayburn's father *did* have his horse stolen by hitchhiking Yankee soldiers trying to get back home after the Civil War. But his brooding, if there was any, must have been more than usually durable, for he remained in Roane County, Tennessee, at least long enough for Sam to be born in 1882. In other words, he probably stayed there twenty years or so after the horse was stolen before he decided to try his fortune in Texas.

In an attempt to reconcile the apparent discrepancy between the legend and the fact, I have come to the conclusion that the Tennessee politicians have unconsciously built up this imposing edifice on a slender foundation of fact because it offered them the only logical explanation they could devise to account for the departure of a man of such rare intelligence as must have been the father of Sam from such a fair country as Roane County, Tennessee. It probably covers an unrecognized sense of loss over the fact that Sam Rayburn is not from Tennessee, although he should have been.

The Log Cabin Where Cordell Hull Was Born on October
2, 1871, Still Stands on Star Point, Near Byrdstown, in
Pickett County, Tennessee

Mrs. Hull died in 1903 and is remembered by her neighbors as a quiet, beautiful woman who spent much of the last part of her life in a wheel chair as a result of inflammatory rheumatism. Like the other women of those mountain communities, she was seldom seen outside of her home, which is not surprising when one recalls the manifold and never-ending duties women assumed in those days.

She and her husband produced five sons in quick succession, Cordell's arrival occurring on October 2, 1871. The two older sons were Orestes and Senadius Selwin, and after Cordell, Wyoming and Roy were born. There seems to be no surviving explanation of the exotic names Mrs. Hull gave three of her sons, but the local legend has it that her third son was named for John M. Cordell, a state legislator for Scott County, to whom the Hulls felt indebted for some favor.

William Hull was a man of no formal education, but he had an innate shrewdness and industry which enabled him to get a little money ahead by working his 100-acre farm, and in a few years he was able to set up a crossroads store and post office a few miles to the west, which was called Hull, in honor of its proprietor, as was the custom. By this time, which was about 1883, the children were beginning to grow up, and their father determined they should have the schooling he had missed. The new Hull home was built to include a schoolroom, and a young man named Newton Staley was employed to instruct the Hull children and the children of the neighbors in the rudiments then believed necessary for the elevation of the youthful mind.[2]

[2] I am indebted to John C Meador, of Youngs, California, for a description of a visit to the Hull home at about this epoch. Mr. Meador does not recall the date, but I judge it to have been about 1884. He was taken to call at the Hull house by his father in the course of a visit to the neighborhood from the Meador home just across the Kentucky line.

"We arrived at Mr. Hull's home near noontime," Mr. Meador recalls, "and, true to Southern hospitality, we had to stay to lunch with them, and I remember Mr. Hull chided his wife for filling me up on buttermilk before lunch so I would go light on the spareribs and sweet potatoes. Mr. Hull had butchered a few hogs two days previously.

"I remember some lad (Cordell?) that was there, older and larger than I was, who boasted that he could outwrestle me or throw me. The only thing that I could do was to tell him if I had my pistol I could outshoot him.

"Mrs. Hull, to my way of thinking, was a real Southern lady and a woman

The store venture did not last very long, but it must have been profitable, as William Hull was able to sell it in 1885 and to buy a rich farm near Willow Grove—another move slightly to the west. The new farm was made up mostly of bottom land along the Obed River, as the maps list it, but which is called Obie's River by most of the people living in the section. Their version of it is probably correct, as it is supposed to have been named originally after Obadiah Terrill, a pioneer settler.

The stream is a tributary of the Cumberland, which it joins at Celina, where Uncle Billy Hull later moved his family into still greater affluence. It was at the Willow Grove farm, however, that William Hull got into the business of buying timber the farmers were cutting on their land and rafting it down the Obed into the Cumberland and on to Nashville, one of the principal lumber markets of the South. Here, at last, he had discovered a cash crop, and the family fortunes began an ascent which was vertiginous in those days. The boys were occasionally impressed into service to ride the log rafts down to Nashville in the early spring, when the swollen waters guaranteed swift and uninterrupted passage

Cordell was only an average log rider, according to the recollections of his childhood friends in the section. One of them expressed the opinion that he never made more than a dozen trips to Nashville in his life, riding the logs. That was enough, however, to etch a distinct memory on his young mind, for Hull often recalls those experiences as having been pleasant and valuable to him.

It is hard to gain an appraisal of Hull's character in boyhood by talking to his contemporaries who still live in that region. He has become a great man in their eyes (to their surprise, as two or three were candid enough to tell me), and they tend either to withhold comment, in that reserved, suspicious manner common to the older generation of mountaineers, or to launch into fulsome praises which could hardly be based on fact. The most probable description of him during his boyhood, fabricated by

that a boy of my age at that time would have been glad to call Mother. She had a very gracious, motherly, kind way about her.

"On our way home my father told me that Mr Hull was out in the woodland working on some building logs when he was shot."

winnowing out the implausible and averaging the rest, would go something like this:

He was an introspective, bookish boy who took little or no part in the fishing and swimming expeditions of the others. His outlook on life was serious, and he preferred reading to idling away the days as did most of the boys of his age. He paid no attention to the girls. In fact, he was slightly unpopular with the other boys and in all likelihood was held up to them as a model by their parents. When he went to Nashville on one of his log-riding trips he would take what money he had and canvass the secondhand bookstores until he found some lawbook he could afford. Ever since he can remember, he wanted to be a lawyer.

He made few intimate friends. In talking to a considerable number of men throughout the region where he lived for thirty-five years, I heard only two of them call him by his first name. One referred to him as "Cord" and the other as "Cordell." The rest called him "Judge," indicating that the first time they began to call him anything was after he was grown and had achieved political office.

Cordell was his father's favorite son from the time he showed interest in learning. The four other sons regarded their father's concern over their intellectual advancement as a cross to be borne as lightly and evaded as often as possible, but Cordell took to it.

When he was fourteen years old he made what he considers to be the most important speech in his life. In those days the mountaineer father of several sons (and most of them had large families) would select the one he considered most fitted for education as a lawyer, a doctor, or a preacher, and send him away to school. The family budget would be trimmed to permit this single pursuit of a professional career, but the sons who were considered less gifted were put to work on the farm to help support their more fortunate brother, since the father's financial ability usually would not permit the luxury of keeping more than one son away at school.

At this time Uncle Billy Hull had not quite made up his mind that Cordell was beyond doubt the one of his sons who ought to be chosen for a higher education. Cordell was attending the little school at Willow Grove and was invited to take part in a debate. He was to uphold the thesis that George Washington is entitled to more credit for defending America than is Christopher Columbus for discovering it.

Among the mountaineers, many of whom could barely read, speaking ability was rated as an infallible index to a man's general intelligence. A good speaker who came prepared to the platform, with his information marshaled in good order, and who was convincing in his argument, was to them a man possessed of a high intelligence quotient. A "speakin' " of almost any kind would draw an audience from miles around.

Cordell knew his father would be in the audience that would attend the school debate. He knew that he would be judged not only on his own performance but on his relative excellence compared to the rest of the debaters. He knew his father would ask the opinion of his friends on his son's speech. He knew that he wanted more than anything in the world to go away to school to learn to be a lawyer.

All of these premises summed up to a single resolve: he had to be the best debater on that fateful night. For a week he dug up everything he could find that had the slightest bearing on the subject. Fortunately for him, the county teachers' association was holding a convention in Willow Grove that week, and he gleaned many a fine point by buttonholing the delegates and presenting his problem.

His efforts bore fruit, for that night Uncle Billy decided Cordell was the son who should have the most schooling. He was sufficiently prosperous to afford a certain amount for all his boys, but Cordell was to be kept going as far as he wanted to go.

The debate led also to Cordell's first political speech, which he gave at a political rally in a cool beech grove near by, in the summer of 1888. He was sixteen years old. Excitement ran high at the meeting, but the program committee ran out of speakers. One of the neighbors who had heard Cordell perform on the subject of Washington versus Columbus pushed him onto the platform and told him to make a speech.

After all these years Mr. Hull can remember little about that maiden political oratory except that he was not frightened or confused and that he seemed to have plenty of facts at his command. As to subject matter, he can remember only that he was extolling the virtues of Grover Cleveland and that he was on a popular topic. Unfortunately, Mr. Cleveland's popularity throughout the nation that year fell considerably below the level displayed in Willow Grove, Tennessee.

Young Cordell's scholastic progress so delighted Uncle Billy that he decided to send him and his older brothers, Orestes and Senadius, who was always called Nade, to the Montvale Academy at Celina, the county seat. Since this was too far from home for them to walk back and forth every day, they were first boarded at a farm about two miles from the school, and then Uncle Billy rented them a house on the public square of the town, where they did their own housekeeping. They often walked twelve miles back to the farm on Friday nights to spend the week ends with their family and to help with the farm work, hiking back to Celina on Monday mornings.

It was here that the pattern of Cordell Hull's life began to set. Their teacher at the Montvale Academy (the main building of which still stands in Celina, although it has been moved from the site where Orestes, Nade, and Cord attended classes) was Joseph Simon McMillin, a man who is still remembered, although he has been dead forty years, as a fine character and an excellent teacher. As academic attainments went in those days in Tennessee, Joe McMillin was quite a scholar, a graduate of both the Philomath Academy and Burritt College. He taught his pupils whatever he thought they were capable of learning and seems to have instructed young Cordell principally in surveying, geometry, anatomy, and Greek—a curious mixture from the point of view of the modern pedagogue.

He displayed on the walls of the schoolroom, for the inspiration of his young charges, the motto: "There is no excellence without great labor." Cordell, who had already passed six feet in height and was possessed of the rugged health which has enabled him to lead the laborious life he has chosen for himself, took that saw very much to heart. From the start of his attendance at the Montvale Academy he was a star pupil, standing head and shoulders above most of the others, and endeared himself to Joe McMillin's proud heart.

All this might have led to nothing beyond an eventual job as Joe McMillin's teaching assistant, except for the fact that Joe was the younger brother of Benton McMillin, an active and suc-

cessful figure in Tennessee Democratic politics for half a century.
Joe had a perhaps exaggerated veneration for his distinguished
brother and inculcated in his pupils a species of hero worship for
Benton McMillin, Henry Watterson, the fiery editor of the Louisville *Courier-Journal,* and John G. Carlisle, a quondam Speaker
of the House of Representatives and Secretary of the Treasury.

Joe McMillin must have sensed in Cordell Hull's make-up a
latent flair for politics, for he brought the lad to Benton McMillin's attention. Cordell was a frequent speaker in the school debates, and his style of oratory was then about what it is now—
undramatic, relying on subject matter rather than rhetoric,
lengthy, and rather dull. Joe McMillin thought he would improve by taking Benton as a model and arranged for the boy to
drive the great man around to political meetings, to carry ban-
ners, and otherwise to associate himself with the machinery
of politics, which was then the major sport of that part of the
country.

He also encouraged Orestes and Cordell to spend a term or two
at the Normal School at Bowling Green, Kentucky, one of the
scholastic centers of the region. The brothers again kept house for
themselves, and Cordell now remembers that their living expenses in Bowling Green came to about four dollars a week each.
Joe McMillin then persuaded Uncle Billy to send them for a
year to the National Normal University at Lebanon, Ohio,
where they had relatives who looked after them.

By this time Cordell was eighteen years old and determined to
be a lawyer. A photograph of him taken at this epoch bears slight
but unmistakable resemblance to him as he looks today. The
striking black eyes and generally commanding appearance were
already distinctly in evidence. He is shown wearing a high standing collar decorated with an outsize bow tie of loudly striped silk,
his black hair parted and brushed in the same manner as his
white locks are arranged today. The assurance with which he
displays himself in the photograph bears witness that he was
then manifesting, to his own satisfaction at least, the unostenta-
tious care in dress which has always characterized him. He had
obviously donned, to have his picture taken, what the well-
dressed young man was wearing in Celina.

Uncle Billy had moved his family to Celina and was on the

way to becoming the local magnate. He bought a nice house, which now belongs to Mrs. David Egan, and enough land for his vegetable gardens, cattle, pigs, and the other appurtenances of a country squire, but he kept the bottom farm above Celina, and Cordell Hull still owns it. Cordell's brother Wyoming, who was mentally deficient and died many years ago, is buried on it.

There was nothing Cordell wanted to do that his father would not help him to realize, then as well as later in his career. Uncle Billy had already made up his mind that Nade should gradually take over the business side of his growing affairs and that Cordell should be given every opportunity to become the outstanding public figure of the family. Nade was only mildly successful in his part of the assignment, finally broke with his father, and died in San Antonio in 1940.

Cordell's decision to become a lawyer suited Uncle Billy down to the ground. He fitted the young man out with a little office on one corner of the square at Celina, where he commenced the process known as reading law. This meant studying Blackstone and a few other standard books, but also playing poker at the courthouse with the older lawyers and listening to their experiences and advice. The second part of the course was probably more useful than the first.

The prospective young lawyer became interested in the affairs of the outside world, which he hoped soon to enter. He was one of the town's few subscribers to the Nashville *Weekly American,* which arrived sometimes by steamboat only two or three days after publication in the state capital. On the day of its arrival Cordell's young friends (the boys, of course, for girls were not supposed to take any interest in such matters then, nor did they) would follow him from the post office to his office after he had collected his copy of the paper.

They would sit in an attentive circle while Cordell read aloud the items he considered of the most importance and interest. Then the paper would be divided and passed around the circle, each member studying each double page for any additional information he was seeking. Uncle Billy must have paid for the subscription, however. One of the boys absent-mindedly took a section of the paper to a little outbuilding on one occasion, where it met the usual fate of old newspapers and catalogues, before Uncle Billy had read it. Uncle Billy's blistering observations on discovering what had happened to his reading matter effectively prevented a recurrence of the mishap.

After his novitiate in reading the law in Celina, Cordell went through the same process in Nashville, first in the office of Pitts and Meeks and then with John H. McMillin, a brother of Joe and Benton. Then he decided he was ready to matriculate for the one-year law course at Cumberland University, Lebanon, Tennessee. Ever since the Civil War many of the greatest figures in Tennessee's legal and political life have had their principal training at Cumberland. Nathan Green, who was then its head, had carried forward the intensely practical methods of teaching the law which had been instituted by Abraham Caruthers and his brother before the Civil War.

Cordell obtained his LL.B. from Cumberland University in the spring of 1891, and Nade followed suit the following year. Cordell was admitted to the bar soon after graduation and before he was legally of age. He has never practiced law to any great extent because of his long public service, but he has kept alive in each succeeding issue of the *Congressional Directory* the statement that he "is a lawyer by profession." This respect for the law as the only field of learning and activity which would fit a man for public life was widespread over the South, of course, but it was probably more intense around Celina than anywhere in the country.

At least Cordell Hull felt that way when he hung out his shingle and began the weary wait for clients. Uncle Billy's increasing prosperity had emboldened him to construct a brick building on the square, which he rented out as offices. The bricks were burned in the pasture lot back of the Hull home, and the building is still standing. By his shrewd trading, farming, timber operations, and moneylending Uncle Billy had reached a financial status where his favorite son would never lack backing for any advancement he might seek, so far as his father was concerned.

The elder Hull was a picturesque figure in middle age and later life. He bore the reputation of a hard trader, but men in small towns who make money are always known as that. Their less monetarily successful neighbors assuage their own fiscal regrets by philosophically deciding that the town's rich man was a combination of Shylock and Scrooge during the years when they themselves turned their thoughts to the higher things of life.

Added to this reputation of hardness, however, was the legend of generosity in the case of William Hull. He is credited, in these days at least, with always having been willing to lend an ear to a worthy cause or a needy neighbor, once his own means had been stabilized, as they began to be about this epoch. He must have borne an increasing repute, for people all over the county fell into the habit of referring their disputes to him, in that informal system of arbitration which exists everywhere in rural districts and which makes for a smoothness and a sensible accommodation in life's uneasier moments such as does not prevail in the cities. It may be that Cordell Hull acquired the beginnings of his passionate attachment to the principle of pacific settlement by listening to neighbors he knew pour out their differences to his father and accept Uncle Billy's arbitral awards in lieu of fighting or litigating.

William L. Brown, the venerable and respected general storekeeper at Celina, who, of his surviving contemporaries, probably knew Uncle Billy best, has described Cordell's father as the best neighbor he ever knew. That was a likable and important quality for a man to have in those primitive days, and it still is. Perhaps there is some intangible but real connection between his early appreciation of this characteristic of his father and Cordell Hull's later philosophy about the relations of nations. The old neighbors of Uncle Billy are inclined to gloss over, or to be forgetful of, his youthful indiscretions. They remember him now as an interesting character, the richest man in the county, a devoted father to Cordell, and an intelligent man despite, or because of, his lifelong refusal to wear a collar. The only photograph of him in circulation shows the head of a rather stern-looking man, his blind eye minimized by an artful shadow, wearing a dark coat riding up at the neck over a white shirt held together at the throat by a collar button but ungraced by a collar.

There are several versions of Uncle Billy's one-man feud, which he pursued until he killed his man. At the time it happened, just after the Civil War, little attention was paid to it.

Now that Cordell Hull has become famous, various magazine writers have dug into his background and antecedents and have enlarged on Uncle Billy's shooting scrape by printing second- and thirdhand accounts given them by people who heard the story from parents or grandparents.

The most authentic and carefully evaluated edition of it is the one published in the Nashville *Banner* in 1940 by William E. Beard, associate editor of the paper, who is an old friend of the Hull family. Mr. Beard sifted all the information he could get and finally based his story on two principal sources. One of these was Lewis Hull, a surviving brother of Uncle Billy and an uncle of Cordell, who related the origins of the dispute. The account of its culmination was said to be Uncle Billy's own version of it, as told to a close but unidentified friend some years after it took place. The Beard story runs about as follows:

William Hull traded a cow to a neighbor, Jim Stepp, for a musket. The transaction took place in the latter days of the Civil War, when guerrilla bands were ravaging the upper Cumberland. Jim Stepp repented of the bargain and stole his musket back. William Hull went to his house and forced him to return the musket. In revenge Stepp informed some Yankee guerrillas who were operating in the neighborhood that Hull was trafficking with the Confederates and that he intended to give the gun to them.

The guerrillas tracked Billy and a friend of his named Alex Smith to the home of Cynda Lovelace, a widow who lived in Fentress County near the Kentucky line. They shot at sight, killing Alex Smith and shooting Billy Hull through the head. Mrs. Lovelace convinced the guerrillas that both men were dead, and they went away. She took Billy into her home and nursed him until he was well enough to be moved back to his father's house. The bullet had passed through his head, taking out one eye but missing the brain.

When Billy recovered he learned that the attack on him had been instigated by Jim Stepp and he set out to avenge it. This was considered perfectly natural under the rules of the community, and it is doubtful if even his own father tried to dissuade him. He heard that the Stepps had moved up the Cumberland above Celina. By the time he got there the family had gone over to Monticello, Kentucky. He followed that trail, only to find they had gone to the Far West, apparently beyond reach.

A few months later, however, Billy got the news that they had come back to Kentucky and had settled near Center Point. That was all he wanted to know. He loaded his pistol and crossed the Cumberland to Center Point. He went to the general store and asked directions. Some of the cracker-barrel patrons pointed to two men coming down the street, saying that one of them was Jim Stepp.

Hull walked up to them and asked if either of them was Jim Stepp, although he recognized his foe. He merely did not want to leave any doubt in the minds of possible witnesses that he had selected the right man. When Stepp acknowledged his identity Hull asked him: "Do you know me?" Stepp replied that he believed not, that he thought he had never seen the other man in his life.

"Look me over now and see if there is anything you recognize," Hull said, taking the bandage off his sightless eye. "I have come to do to you just what you tried to have done to me."

He emptied his gun into Stepp, killing him instantly. He related later how Stepp's dog, who was walking with his master, ran excitedly around and around the body as it lay in the street.

Billy Hull walked back to the Cumberland, crossed it, and returned to his home without interference from anyone or any legal complications to the end of his life. Occurrences of this sort were by no means uncommon in the border region where ·Uncle Billy lived. The bitterness of the Civil War and the guerrilla depredations, in which neighbors were pitted against neighbors, had left undying animosities which could be settled only by mortal combat under the code of the region.

Courts were slow and uncertain and were often in the hands of carpetbag judges. In Billy Hull's case he could have established nothing substantial against Stepp in the courts of Kentucky. He felt, and apparently the community at large agreed with him, that Stepp deserved to be killed and that he was the logical executioner. One of the residents of the district, to whom I talked about this affair, recalled that a Tennessee senator was interviewed in Washington some years after the Hull affair on the subject of lawlessness in that part of the state. He was asked why

so many killings went unpunished. The senator delivered the
following opinion, which ultimately led to his defeat in the next
Democratic primary, according to my informant, who would
not tell me the name of the unfortunate politician:

"In cases of homicide in my state, the first thing the jury wants
to know is whether the deceased deserved to be killed."

The same tolerance is displayed in regard to stories, which
have been printed, that Billy Hull made his first thousand dollars
selling moonshine liquor which he made himself. Tolerance
is hardly the word, for I found only two men who attached any
credence to the yarn. One of these was prepared to believe it or
disbelieve it, disclaiming any personal knowledge. The other
was inclined to believe it but went on to explain how everybody
engaged in this traffic in the Civil War days, even leaving the
inference that he might have tried it himself, although he is a
respected and staid citizen today. The great majority of the
Hulls' friends, however, deny the allegation with righteous indignation.

Whatever the merits of these and other legends of Billy Hull's
less praiseworthy qualities, they have little bearing on Cordell's
development. They are recalled only because they have often
been recounted, usually in the effort to paint the Secretary of
State as a self-made man who rose to the heights against every
conceivable kind of obstacle, including the influence of a bad
father. Even if all the uncomplimentary details which have been
published about his immediate family and kinsfolk were true,
they would have to be viewed in their proper proportion, and
there is little evidence to establish even a modicum of truth in
them.

So far as Cordell Hull is concerned there is only evidence to
demonstrate that Uncle Billy was a good father to him and encouraged him to educate himself and to seek advancement in the
world. The evidence I have gathered comes from the recollections of old friends and not from Hull himself, who has been so
deeply wounded at the disadvantageous portrayal in minor respects of his father, his brothers, his cousins, and his uncles that
he will not discuss those matters at all. No question of honesty
or integrity was ever raised about any of them

Uncle Billy's other sons disappointed him, and it is only

natural that he should have lavished his attention, affection, and material help on Cordell, the only one of them who seemed to have the capacity to appreciate and utilize the advantages he was trying so hard to give them. Orestes, the eldest, became a physician of fine promise but died when he was a comparatively young man. Nade, the second, never practiced law after taking his degree at Cumberland University. Wyoming was afflicted. Roy, the youngest, quarreled with his father, ran away and joined the army, where he rose to be a sergeant, and died a few years ago as the result of an automobile accident.

The probably correct judgment of Hull's early life is that he grew up under more, rather than less, favorable circumstances than the other boys in his neighborhood, that he lived the kind of life and underwent the kind of conditions which were almost made to order for the formation of his later character, and that he had the good sense to take every advantage of the opportunities that were offered to him. This may make him sound like a character taken straight from a novel by Horatio Alger, but it seems to be the right estimate.

The lack of outside interests, the limitless capacity for work, and the sturdy health which he had in those days have stayed with him. Whether they were born in him or were developed by his environment will always be a subject of speculation to those who are interested, including Hull himself. The qualities exhibited themselves so early and so consistently that they may have been innate, but there is no doubt that his father encouraged them in him as well.

By the time he entered the practice of law in Celina, at the age of twenty, he was a self-assured young man who had pretty definite ideas of what he wanted to make of himself and how he could do it. His first major decision was the most important one he ever made in regard to his own affairs, and he must often wonder at the temerity of it when he looks back from this distance. He decided to run for the state legislature, although he was not yet of age. On consulting the calendar, however, he found that he would be legally entitled to take his seat by the time the legislature met in 1893, provided he could persuade his proposed constituents to give him the job.

The serious obstacle of an older and better-known man to be

defeated in the Democratic primary did not daunt him. With his father's active encouragement and material help he began to campaign for the nomination. Although he could not have realized it, he was winding up his boyhood and its associations. The epoch of Olympus, as his birthplace was called, Willow Grove, and Celina was drawing to its close. He was about to try his wings away from the home nest, and they were never to bear him back except for rare and brief pilgrimages.

The family association with Celina continued until Mrs. Hull's death, a few years after which Uncle Billy moved to Carthage, but Cordell was to live there for only short intervals after he decided to go to the legislature. They buried his mother in a field behind the Hull house in Celina, under a simple marble shaft. A stout iron fence was erected around the plot, and she was left amid the scenes of her greatest happiness, where she had become sure that her third son would do well in the world and would be a credit to her.

Uncle Billy bought a fine brick house in Carthage, with a large garden overlooking the Cumberland River. He fell into the habit of paying frequent visits to Nashville, where he became a familiar figure around the Maxwell House. He was a little comical in the big city, with his shabby clothes and without his collar. He used to carry a cheap paper suitcase, the worse for wear, in which he was reputed to keep large sums of money. Later on, as he grew older, he went to Florida in the winter, wearing the same clothes and carrying the same suitcase.

He lived to see Cordell become a veteran member of the House of Representatives and chairman of the Democratic National Committee.

He helped his son in his electoral campaigns and thought his son was always right. His wide acquaintance in the eastern, and more doubtful, part of Cordell's Congressional district was of real value, old local politicians tell me.

Late in March 1923 Uncle Billy was taken sick in Florida. He felt it was a serious illness and he telegraphed Cordell to come to him from Washington. His favorite son was with him when he died.

Cordell telephoned W. F. Brown, son of the merchant and a boyhood friend of the Congressman, to prepare a grave next to

that of Elizabeth Riley Hull in the plot enclosed by the iron fence
behind the old home at Celina. Fay Brown agreed, of course, and
did not tell Cordell that the Cumberland was in flood. The burial
plot was almost under water. The grave was dug with the greatest difficulty, and pumps were kept running to bail the water
out of it constantly during the days it took to get the body there
from Florida.

On the day before the burial service the Cumberland, perhaps
remembering its long years of sympathetic cooperation with
Billy Hull, relented and subsided. Uncle Billy was laid to rest
beside his wife; a twin marble shaft was put in place, and the
iron fence closed once again. The shafts and the iron fence are in
excellent condition today and mark a pilgrimage spot for tour-
ists, who stop and ask to see the graves. Mr. Brown or his son
will always show the way, one or other of them accompanying
the visitor down the street toward the river, almost to the spot
on its bank where their store used to stand, and over three fences
to reach the back field, bordered by giant trees standing in an
orderly row, where the burial plot is to be found.

When they opened Uncle Billy's will they found that he had
left every cent of the $200,000 he had accumulated to Cordell,
except for a bequest of $5000 to a daughter of Nade. She was to
receive the income from that sum, to help her education, until
she was twenty-one, when the principal would go to her. Cordell
was to act as her guardian without bond until she became of age.

Although Cordell has discussed these matters only with his
most intimate friends, if at all, the general understanding is that
Uncle Billy felt that he was the only one of his sons who could
be relied upon to make wise disposition of the money, such as
their father wanted. It is supposed that he summoned his third
son from Washington to his deathbed to tell him what he wanted
done about Nade, Wyoming, and Roy, who were all living in
1923. These instructions, or wishes, were scrupulously carried
out, his friends are sure, for none of them can remember Cordell
Hull failing to live up to an obligation he voluntarily contracted.

Most of the real property his father left him Cordell Hull has
kept. Its management, which is supervised by Brad McGinness,
his personal lawyer and long-time friend, and the shrinking
number of old friends who still live in the Hull country are the

only ties which bind the elder statesman to the scenes of his youth. His greatest triumphs and honors came to him long after he had left them behind. He has newer and more influential friends scattered throughout the country and throughout the world. But to the end of his days Cordell Hull will continue to describe himself as "a citizen of the State of Tennessee."

CHAPTER III

Apprenticeship

Nashville had grown to be an agreeable provincial capital by 1890. It had become an important railroad junction after it had extracted the last dollar of profit to be made by outfitting the wagon trains headed west. Its situation, in the heart of some of the most fertile and most easily cultivated land in the United States, made it a natural marketing and banking center.

Life for the gentry was pleasant and easy. Their prudent investments in first mortgages, their inherited lands, and their cautious forays into the embryo industrialism of the region brought them incomes by which they could once again live almost the same life as had their ancestors before the Civil War. There were no slaves, of course, but the economy of middle Tennessee had not been bound to slavery for many years, and the Civil War found practicing abolitionists, who had freed their own slaves, among the leading citizens of Nashville.

Horses occupied most of the interest of the gentlemen of the region, as they had ever since Andrew Jackson had had such phenomenal success with his Truxton. Iroquois, generally considered to be the greatest American-bred horse that ever lived, was at the height of his fame. He had been retired to stud at the Belle Meade Farm, and his colts were fetching as much as $10,000 in auctions at Madison Square Garden in New York.

This amazing horse climaxed his active racing career with the

39

season of 1881 in England, when he won the Derby at Epsom, as well as the Newmarket Stakes, the Burwell Stakes, the Prince of Wales Stakes at Ascot, the Great St. Leger Stakes, the Newmarket Derby, and the St. James Place Stakes. He also finished second in the 2000-Guinea Stakes. He is buried near the present Belle Meade Country Club, which occupies much of the land that made up the famous old Belle Meade Farm.

Stage artists of such caliber as Joe Jefferson, Rose Coghlan, and their peers appeared regularly at the Vendome, which had no movie palaces as competitors to lure away the faithful box holders and constant patrons. Nashville was on the same theatrical circuit as St. Louis, Cincinnati, Louisville, New Orleans, and Memphis.

The best people still had their children tutored at home, to send them to Europe for the finishing touches, but there was an increasing trend toward using the schools closer at hand. The University of the South, at Sewanee, was just establishing a medical school in response to the increasing demand for professional education closer to home. Nashville was not as yet called "The Athens of the South," as later enthusiasts tried to label it, but the tendency to become a scholastic center for much of the South, which has grown with the increase in importance of Vanderbilt University, was beginning to manifest itself.

The cultural and social life of Nashville overlapped its political life at the state capitol. All Nashville lawyers and most businessmen were obliged to have pretty close contact with the state legislature. The legislature still elected the United States senators who represented the sovereign state of Tennessee at Washington. Those few male residents of Nashville who had reached the constitutional age of thirty and who did not aspire to be senators had ambitious friends whose cause they were pushing.

More important still, the state legislature had the power to grant or withhold franchises needed for the rapidly growing railroads as well as the acts of incorporation giving legal life to the manufacturing ventures which were multiplying. The Union Mills Company, for example, had just incorporated for $1,000,-000—a large enterprise in those days. While there may have been no more outright venality on the part of the state legislators then than there is now, it was nevertheless considered useful for a lawyer or a businessman to have his particular friends at the state capitol.

The politicians frequented Cherry Street, between Church and Union. This favorite block was about halfway between the county courthouse and the state capitol and served as a sort of open-air political exchange, where deals were made, alliances were formed and ruptured, shootings took place, and politics was rife.

The state capitol itself looked much as it does now. It sits on a commanding hill, with its best side facing the city and its nether portions shading off discreetly toward the red-light district, which was then wide open and licensed, conveniently placed for the state's solons and their visiting constituents. The capitol's ornate marble corridors, with the marble slightly tobacco-stained and chipped through the passing years, resounded to the tread of officials, legislators, favor-seekers, and mere hangers-on during each biennial session of the legislature then as they do now. Between sessions it was largely deserted except for the permanent state officials, including the governor and his immediate aides, who had their offices in the building.

This was the larger world in which Cordell Hull wanted to try his wings. Viewed from the Celina office of a young lawyer not yet old enough to vote, Nashville looked like a golden goal. If he could only get to the legislature he would not have to keep on reading laws—he could help write them. He could listen to the discourses of the greatest speakers in the state, learning law, oratory, and politics all at the same time. Joe McMillin had instilled in him a reverence and an ambition for these three branches of what was then the same profession.

Hull lacked political glamour. He was a handsome, upstanding young man, and his appearance was an asset, but his principal quality seems to have been a visible sincerity which lent conviction to his words, especially when backed by the accurate information he always had on tap before he spoke his mind on any subject. He could make people believe as he did, even though he was a rather tedious speaker, unskilled in the florid, loud-mouthed forensic technique of the epoch.

When Hull began feeling his way toward a campaign for the Democratic nomination as floterial representative (called a

"floater" in the political vernacular) for four counties, the nation
was just recovering from a severe depression which had lasted
for more than a year. These panics were believed to be cyclical in
character, arriving inevitably every seventeen to twenty years.
The bad times had encouraged the growth of the Populist movement, and "Alliance" (Farmers' Alliance, Farmers' and Workers' Alliance, and similar names were used by the organization
throughout the country) candidates were in the field for almost
every office to be filled the following year.

General James B. Weaver was the Alliance candidate for the
presidency. He and his party were feared by Republicans and
Democrats alike. Leaders of both major parties believed that the
economic depression had about run its course and that the fortunate faction which came to power in 1893 would earn the gratitude of the electorate in the recovery years that were bound to
follow.

His Tennessee constituents were urging Benton McMillin,
then an outstanding leader in the House of Representatives, to
secure speedy tariff reform as soon as the Democrats should capture control of that branch of Congress, and there was considerable indignant comment on the solicitation of Nashville manufacturers for ten-dollar contributions to the American Protective
League. Tariff and treason were still practically synonymous in
the vocabulary of Southern Democracy.

Nashville itself had weathered the panic fairly well and was
inclined to be self-congratulatory when it read of the 100,000
commercial failures in New York City during the troubled
period. J. R. Frith, of Dun's Agency, published his estimate of
the local situation in the Nashville *American* of October 2, 1891.
He told his interviewer:

We have not had half as hard times as we would have had if the
community had been spread out in speculation, carrying a large
number of purely speculative enterprises, such as railroads to this
or that point, land companies located here and there, whose only
justification were the surveys and the stones put up to mark the
corners of the lots.

Then again, none of our factories have shut down. There has
been no trouble with our laboring classes; they have all had work
to do. There has been little if any suffering in that way.

The comparative immunity from labor troubles vouchsafed to Nashville did not extend to the whole state. There had been a prolonged coal strike at Oliver Springs, near Knoxville, which the miners finally won by disarming the company guards and forcing the militia to surrender.

Young Hull had already had some experience in the machine politics of his section, and the early successes he made encouraged him to seek the seat in the legislature. When he was barely nineteen he was elected a delegate from his county to the state Democratic convention at Nashville. He faithfully attended all the sessions and listened to the big men of the state organization discuss Democracy's problems, which were principally to prevent Republicans from getting any state jobs. Toward the end of the convention his county delegation held a caucus, and an old Confederate veteran from the other end of the county nominated Hull to be chairman of the delegation. Apparently the youngest member's industry and aptitude had favorably impressed his fellow politicians, and he was elected by acclamation.

Heartened by the prominence this, his first, electoral victory brought him, Hull decided he could wrest the Democratic nomination for floater from Pickett, Fentress, Clay, and Overton counties from a man named Carlock, although his prospective opponent was much better known and had powerful machine backing. Hull maneuvered Carlock into submitting the nomination to a primary election. Previously the nominee had been selected by the Democratic committees of the four counties, meeting in joint session.

With the new procedure decided, Hull made an active speaking tour through Overton County, Carlock's own bailiwick, and beat him by sixteen votes there. He carried the other three counties by larger majorities. We have no record of how he won at the general election, but he was probably swept in on the general tide of Democratic triumph in the autumn of 1892.

President Harrison had been unpopular in Tennessee, and Grover Cleveland's election was hailed as a belated return to national sanity. A few months before the election, apparently hard up for grounds on which to criticize Mr. Harrison, the Nashville *Weekly American* seized on the diplomatic tangle with Chile, which gave rise, for a time, to talk of war. The paper's comment is of interest because it was Cordell Hull's favorite and practically only newspaper at this time and because it points out an aspect of Latin-American relations which Hull has been careful to avoid.

"Feeling against this country has been created in the breasts of the Chileans bitter enough to cause them to make an attack on our sailors simply because they are our sailors, and a prejudice has been created all over South America which for years will work against us in those markets for the flour, lard, and other products of our farms," the paper's editorial page, then in charge of E. W. Carmack, set forth. "The imitation of Jacksonian firmness given by little Mr. Harrison has not been a happy one."

An enormous torchlight parade was organized in Nashville to celebrate the Democratic sweep, which extended even to control of the Senate by forty-four Democrats to forty Republicans and four Populists. Delegations came from all over the state. The Chattanooga section of the parade was headed by George W. Ochs, who was to become editor of *Current History* for many years. One of the main features of the parade was a float made in the form of a coffin. Four pallbearers marched alongside carrying a banner on which was inscribed: "The Republican Party— Died, November 8, 1892. Never to be resurrected." The newly elected city council of Nashville called itself the New Deal.

The *Weekly American* took the same note in its editorial the following week, having this to say of the Republican party:

"It has fallen and will never rise again. We have not one word of sympathy to utter over its remains. We only hope that the history which is now being written may serve to warn our descendants against its like."

Not only did the Republican party stubbornly decline to stay dead, but the fight for the governorship in Tennessee engendered bitterness that was to provoke an incident which first brought Cordell Hull to public notice in the state. The Democratic state convention had drafted Peter Turney, a distinguished Confederate veteran who was serving as chief justice of the state supreme court, to be the party's nominee for the governorship instead of renominating the incumbent, Governor John P. Buchanan, who had turned Populist during his term in office. This started a feud which was to split the party wide open at the next gubernatorial election in 1894.

Hull took his seat when the Tennessee legislature convened on the first Monday in January 1893. He had attained his majority between his nomination and his election, so that he was legally qualified to take the oath of office when the legislature met.

The Tennessee legislature meets once every two years unless called into special session by the governor, and the sessions usually last only a few weeks. Hull was appointed to the chairmanship of the Committee on Enrolled Bills and to membership on the Committee on the Judiciary, the Committee on Municipal Affairs, and the Rules Committee.

The new member made frequent speeches, but they were not recorded. The journal of the Tennessee legislature is a highly skeletonized record of its sessions and contains no stenographic transcriptions of debate or procedure. Once, when I asked Mr. Hull what all these speeches were about, he told me he could not remember, adding that "people didn't have much to worry about in those days." The journal records only a single observation of his, which he asked to be placed there in explanation of his vote on an appropriation bill. It reads as follows:

"I am strictly opposed to some of the provisions of this bill, but rather than for the state to incur the expenses of its defeat I vote aye."

However, he was learning, and he was making friends. He had no trouble being elected again in 1894, and when he returned to Nashville he had risen in the esteem of the legislature's leaders. As one small mark of their approbation he was named a member of the committee to escort Speaker Tipton, whose election he had managed in the caucus, to the chair on Monday, January 7, 1895, when the lower house was engaged in organizing itself for the coming session. But bigger things were in store for him.

The wounds left over from the gubernatorial race of 1892 had festered in the body of the Democratic party in Tennessee. A. L. Mims had been nominated by the disgruntled Populist followers of Governor Buchanan and had drawn enough votes away from the Democrats to make it a neck-and-neck race between Governor Turney, who was running for re-election, and his Republican opponent, H. Clay Evans of Chattanooga. As a matter of fact, the election's returns were certified to the Speaker of the House of Representatives as 105,104 votes for Evans against 104,356 for Turney.

Governor Turney had the active support of such leading Democratic politicians as the two United States senators, Isham G. Harris and William B. Bate (against whom Hull had voted in the previous session of the legislature), Representative Joseph E. Washington, Frank P. Bond, W. A. Henderson, E. L. Bullock, Josiah Patterson, Robert L. Taylor, and others. These stalwarts were not disposed to see the Republicans capture the governorship by any such slim margin as the official vote indicated.

They decided to contest the election and secured the services of John J. Vertrees as counsel. Vertrees was a phenomenon of Tennessee legal life. He had never graduated from a college or a law school and yet he became the dean of the Tennessee bar, and his memory is still revered by all Tennessee lawyers old enough to remember him or his reputation. He impressed himself so much on William Howard Taft, when the future President and Chief Justice was sitting on the Circuit Court of Appeals at Cincinnati, that Mr. Taft afterward appointed him to represent Secretary Ballinger in the famous dispute with Gifford Pinchot. By that time Vertrees was old, and he failed to cover himself with glory.

In 1894, however, he was at the peak of his powers. He had already taken notice of young Cordell Hull because of the reputation for brilliance which followed him down from Celina and because of the young legislator's serious devotion to duty during his first term in the legislature. Vertrees arranged with the leaders that young Hull should have an important part in the contest they were cooking up.

Hull took the floor in the House, just after the reading of the journal on January 10, 1895, and presented the following petition:

I, Peter Turney, respectfully present this address and petition. I am sixty-seven years of age and all my life have been a citizen of Tennessee. I am eligible to the office of governor, and at this time am the governor of Tennessee. I was a candidate at the election in November last for governor and claim that I then received the highest number of legal votes and that I was then elected governor of Tennessee. Nevertheless, I am reliably informed that, on the face of the returns, it appears that the Hon. H. Clay Evans received the highest number of votes cast. I am also reliably informed that this result is due to gross and fraudulent disregard and violations of law and that an investigation will establish this fact.

I therefore pray your honorable body to take such steps as will permit me to appear before you when you assemble in joint convention to contest the returns and to show that I was elected and that said H. Clay Evans was not.

Respectfully,
P. TURNEY.

The salient point of the contest was that Governor Turney claimed to have received a plurality of the *legal* votes cast. The governor alleged that many of the voters whose ballots had been counted in favor of Evans had not paid their poll taxes before voting, in accordance with the newly enacted law of 1891.

The poll tax was then, and still is, a matter for bitter political debate in Tennessee. In principle the Republicans opposed it as unconstitutional because they held it violated the Fifteenth Amendment that "the right of citizens of the United States to vote shall not be denied or abridged by the United States or by any state on account of race, color or previous condition of servitude." It was the position of the Republicans in Tennessee that the poll tax, amounting to two dollars a year, of which one dollar went to the state and one dollar to the county for the improvement of the public-school system, was designed to "abridge" the voting rights of Negroes, few of whom could or would pay two dollars a year for the privilege of casting their ballots. It was, they insisted, a mere coincidence that Negroes voted the straight Republican ticket at all elections.

However, the new law was on the books, and the Evans partisans could not rely exclusively on constitutional grounds because an appeal on that basis would take at least two years to get through the various Federal tribunals which would have to pass on it, and by that time Governor Turney would have served the disputed term. They were under no illusions and knew that the Democratic legislature was going to count their man out if there was any chance at all.

Within a day or two after presenting Governor Turney's petition Hull put through a motion to defer indefinitely the official opening of the certified returns, which should have been done on January 15. Representative Jarvis introduced a bill to provide the machinery for legislative adjudication of the contest after an investigation. This was approved on January 24 by a vote of 53 to 43, and when the Joint Convention met on February 5, pursuant to Hull's original resolution, to open the certified election returns, the whole question was thrown into the lap of a joint committee from the Senate and the House.

The investigating committee was made up of Senators Caldwell, Scales, Beene, Hodges, and Jeffries and Representatives Hull, Waddell of Obion, Jarvis, Fitzpatrick, Rowan, Keeney, and Stone. It divided into subcommittees for the purpose of examining the electoral records in the various voting precincts in the contested forty of the ninety-six counties in the state. Hull was named chairman of Subcommittee No. 3, the other members of which were Representatives Jarvis and Rowan. This subcommittee held hearings, for the most part, in the mountain counties of eastern Tennessee, such as Greene, Unicoi, Carter, Johnson, Sullivan, Campbell, Morgan, Anderson, Scott, Roane, and Rhea, but it ended up in Davidson County itself, the seat of Nashville and the state capital.

For the best part of three months the various subcommittees took testimony. The printed record of their hearings occupies thousands of pages of about as dull and repetitious reading as is to be encountered anywhere. The burden of all the testimony, in support and in rebuttal, was much the same. A sample of the testimony, most of it unwillingly given, which the Democratic members of the committee wanted to elicit in support of Turney's allegation was that given by Gale Armstrong, twenty-nine years old, a trustee of Hawkins County. Mr. Armstrong testified that he had issued blank poll-tax receipts to the Republican campaign committee in his county, with the understanding that the committee would pay him subsequently for those that were used and return the others to him. The campaign committee, of course, would give away receipts to such citizens as promised to vote the right way, and the campaign committee would remit two dollars to Mr. Armstrong for each used receipt.

Asked why he lent himself to such dubious enforcement of the poll-tax law, Mr. Armstrong told the investigating subcommittee that he did it "to collect as large a school fund as possible for Hawkins County, for the good of my party, and for my own good." The last-given reason is probably the right one. Mr. Armstrong would not have remained in perfect health if he had declined to humor the Republican campaign committee of his own county, in all likelihood.

Hull and his subcommittee drew the toughest of the contested districts. It was for this purpose that John J. Vertrees had drafted the vigorous, fearless young member, knowing he would be competent to deal with the mountaineers he had to examine. His courage was soon needed, as the various lawyers acting on behalf of Evans began to try what Hull deemed dilatory tactics. They began to apply for subpoenas for countless witnesses, knowing that the committee had only a limited sum to spend on the investigation. Hull ruled that such subpoenas would be issued only when the contestee's counsel would pay the traveling expenses and witness fees involved.

At length the hearings were concluded, the majority report was signed by Senator Caldwell, chairman; Representative Fitzpatrick, secretary, along with Senators Beene and Scales and Representatives Waddell, Hull, and Jarvis, and the legislature met in Joint Convention on April 30 to consider the contest.

Preliminary parliamentary skirmishing showed that lines were closely drawn. On May 1 the Ledgerwood Resolution to limit debate to six hours a side was adopted by 66 to 63. The favorable side was made up of fourteen senators and fifty-two representatives, while the negative votes were cast by eighteen senators and forty-five representatives.

The next test came on a motion to substitute the minority report of the committee, upholding Mr. Evans' election, for the majority recommendation declaring for Governor Turney. This motion was lost by 71 to 56, thirteen senators and forty-three representatives voting "aye" and nineteen senators and fifty-two representatives voting "no." Argument of counsel on both sides was heard, and the committee's majority report was finally adopted by 70 (eighteen senators and fifty-two representatives) to 57 (thirteen senators and forty-four representatives).

Thus the state legislature decreed that 94,794 *legal* votes had been cast for Governor Turney against 92,440 for Mr. Evans and 23,088 for Mr. Mims. Governor Turney was installed in office and served his second term amid loud protestations from Republicans (and some mutterings from Democrats) that Mr. Evans had been outcounted. Three members of the legislature demanded that their misgivings be embodied in the proceedings.

"Believing that, under the rules of the committee, there has not been a full and searching investigation, as I think there should have been, I cannot vote for the majority report," stated Senator A. W. Stovall of Madison County. "I am reliably informed and verily believe that the people I have the honor to represent unanimously desire that I should support the majority report. This I cannot conscientiously do; but, in deference to the desire of those I represent, I respectfully ask to be excused from voting."

Representative W. V. Flowers of Hickman County inserted the following statement:

"I do not know that I can agree with all the holdings of the minority report; but I do not believe that the investigation has been as thorough as it should have been, and the proof before me does not justify me in voting to take an office from a man who has a prima facie title to it and give it to another, and therefore I vote no."

Representative R. C. Gordon of Maury County was the third dissenter to justify his opposition.

"I voted for the election contest bill with the hope and belief that the investigation by the committee would be characterized by thoroughness and fairness, for which it was enacted, but the rulings of the committee seem to me to have been so partisan that I am sorry to say that I believe justice has been defeated to the people of Tennessee and to this investigation," his statement said.

"Having voted continuously for thirty-seven years with the Democratic party, in no instance having deviated from the faith, and now, from a conscious duty I owe to myself and the solemn oath I have taken, I cannot do otherwise than vote for H. Clay Evans."

Regardless of the merits of this ancient controversy, it is easy to understand what marvelous training in human values, or practical politics, it afforded Cordell Hull. At the age of twenty-three he was thrown into a highly pragmatic study in democracy. Here was where he first learned that men, their strengths and their weaknesses, are the keystones of the political structure we have tried to build in this country.

He himself, of course, was not an important figure in the process. He was assigned to a certain duty, which he performed rather well. His not to reason why, he ventured into the hill counties which the more experienced members of the investigating committee had sense enough to shun. He conducted his cross-examinations under rules of his own making and produced a volume of testimony which was never shaken. The final objectives of the great maneuver were not his, and he probably understood them only dimly.

His interest in the matter (although occasionally, even now, he feels called on to attempt an explanation of the whole affair and then gives it up) was purely professional—that of a young lawyer attempting to establish a question of fact. In six weeks' time he gained more experience in examining witnesses than he would have had in a lifetime of ordinary court work at Celina.

If he suspected then, as he will not concede now, that the whole thing was a put-up job, it did not shake his faith in the Democratic party or in democracy in general. For present purposes it is enough to point out how this experience in the field sharpened the wits of the political neophyte and made him realize that men's motives and their testimony do not always coincide. Many a trial lawyer has gone to his grave without recognizing this truism.

To this young legislator the matter appeared in its elemental blacks and whites. What he had to find out was whether or not the poll-tax law of 1891 had been observed in the precincts which he was supposed to investigate. To the best of his knowledge and belief, based on the recurring testimony of hundreds of witnesses, it had not. The report of his subcommittee and his own personal influence on the final result hinged about that finding of fact.

In the case of the Turney-Evans contest the bona fides of the contestants is open to some suspicion by reason of a parallel situation which revolved about the election of a member of Congress from the Eighth District, which ran at the same time. P. H. Thrasher, the incumbent, was the contestant against B. A. Enloe who, according to the official returns, was the winner. Another investigating committee found for Mr. Enloe, in both majority and minority reports, and the alleged facts of the case were substantially the same as those which brought about the contest between Messrs. Turney and Evans. It can only be surmised that the Democratic leaders in the state attached considerably less importance to a seat in the lower house of the Congress than they did to the governorship of the state, and that is understandable.

There was a subsidiary issue in the gubernatorial contest about which no conclusion was reached, so far as can be judged from the records. It was alleged by the Turney partisans that unusually shaped ballots were provided in certain precincts to those who signified in advance that they wanted to vote for Evans. The Tennessee election laws had, and still have, a salutary prohibition against anybody marking a ballot for another voter or indicating to another voter how his ballot should be marked, except for exhibiting to him sample ballots in the same manner as is permitted in most states.

This prohibition is an outgrowth of the literacy requirement, which has long been a part of the Tennessee electoral code. In other words, if a prospective voter could not read a ballot well enough to mark it without assistance, he was presumably illiterate and not entitled to vote anyway. It was prescribed that all ballots should be printed on plain white paper of standard dimensions. The charge was brought that the Evans committees, in the mountain counties, issued larger ballots, unmistakable even to the unlettered and probably marked in advance, to those of their adherents whom they suspected of being unable to manage for themselves.

On both sides there was no illusion as to the intent of the literacy and poll-tax requirements. They were enacted into law by the "better classes"—the property owners and the descendants of the pre-war conservatives—to prevent the Negroes and the poor whites from voting. The Republicans opposed these restrictions because the Negroes and the poor whites voted the Republican ticket when they could. The Democrats put them through because they felt, still under the influence of the Reconstruction, that these elements of the population must be prevented from participating in the state's political life despite any Fifteenth Amendment or other Federal enactment.

Any modern reader can judge for himself how justified or unjustified were these precautions which the well-to-do white population of Tennessee felt obliged to take against political domination by the recently freed blacks and the carpetbaggers. The only point to be considered here is that they were part of the legal code of the state in 1895 and that Cordell Hull had to accept them as an integral portion of the politico-social structure of the only life he had known until then.

The moral to be drawn, in any judgment of Hull and his subsequent political morality, which is unquestioned even by his severest critics, is that times and customs change and that no contemporary statesman of his long years of public life can be judged now against the background of the forty years following the Civil War.

To anyone who would like to criticize Hull's part in the contest over the Tennessee governorship it would be interesting to cite the Hayes-Tilden presidential controversy. There the Congress of the United States decided it should not go behind the official returns as certified by the officials of the state of Florida. In the Turney-Evans contest the Tennessee legislature decided it should go behind the official returns as certified by the officials of certain precincts. In both cases history must bow to the verdict of the sovereign legislative bodies which made these decisions and hope that, in the long run, the wishes of the majority are for the best.

Hull was not particularly impressed by the outcome of the Turney-Evans contest. He finished out his term in the legislature, did not run again, and settled down to the practice of law in Celina. Those years were not especially notable. William E. Beard, of the Nashville *Banner,* records an instance where a prospective litigant took his case to the young lawyer, who by now had acquired considerable repute in his home town, only to have Hull tell him he had no case which could possibly stand up in court and advise him to arrive at the best settlement he could. Then, as now, this was unheard-of procedure for a struggling lawyer in search of fees, and it is to be hoped that the incident was spread by word of mouth to the benefit of the strange youthful attorney with such rigid ethics.

Celina was rocking along in a condition of modestly increasing prosperity. It was the market town for the region, but the men did the marketing. They rode their horses or drove their buggies into town every Saturday, while the women stayed at home and kept the household routine functioning. Mr. Brown, who was then the principal merchant, told me that the women came to town about twice a year to trade their butter, eggs, poultry, and the other produce which was their province for the thread, buttons, cloth, and other staples of their department. The men bought the flour, liquor, and such reinforcements for the inner man, usually on credit, on their weekly trips to town.

The courthouse was the center of the town life. The same one is still standing which occupied the center of the square when Hull lived in Celina. It was built about 1870 by a contractor who underbid his closest competitor by quoting a price of $9,999.99 instead of $10,000. An old resident told me, with a sly chuckle, how the WPA has just spent $12,000 in "restoring" it.

It is no architectural treasure, but it bulked large in the lives of the inhabitants—especially large in the life of a struggling lawyer who had no outside interests. Cordell Hull made it his civic center, listening to the older lawyers re-argue their famous cases and discuss politics.

I heard that he courted a girl named Bessie Green, but in such a halfhearted way that she married a man from Kentucky. Other old friends said that Bessie Green was a myth so far as Cordell Hull was concerned, and that the alleged courtship took place much later, with another girl, after the telephone was functioning. According to the second account, Cordell tried to press his suit by the new means of communication, unmindful of the workings of the party line. The young lady got so tired of hearing their most ardent conversations repeated to her, verbatim, the following day that she gave up the promising young lawyer and politician in favor of a more old-fashioned swain who wooed her in a buggy, with the reins wrapped around the whip.

Both girls, if they existed, were right. Cordell Hull at this point in his career had his mind on other things. His mental horizon had already begun to stretch far beyond the limits of Celina. The brief but colorful experience in Nashville had only whetted his appetite for more of the exciting, useful life which he believed could be his in a larger world.

The avenue of escape presented itself sooner than he expected and in a manner of which he would never have dreamed. The United States went to war with Spain—a conflict that was to have the profoundest effect on his country, and an effect which neither Cordell Hull nor the mightier men who engineered that war ever imagined.

He was to play an honorable though slight part in the turn of events which turned the eyes of the United States definitely outward. It was to start the nation on its path of accelerating world power, and Cordell Hull was to be one of the first pilots of that perilous voyage. Probably it was fortunate that the green young Celina lawyer could not pierce the mists of the future to see where that war (a very small war, as such things go nowadays) would lead him and his country.

CHAPTER IV

Latin-American Genesis

Long before relations with Spain reached the official breaking point the hardships of the Cubans were loudly and passionately discussed in the forums of the United States. Perhaps the young men of the country, who had not participated in the Civil War but who had grown up to the recital of its glories, were spoiling for a fight. Perhaps the Cuban situation appealed to that instinctive sympathy for the underdog which the American public has always manifested. Perhaps the country as a whole was ripe for an era of imperialism, and Spain was the readiest victim in sight.

The motives behind the impending struggle did not greatly interest Cordell Hull or Tennessee. What they wanted to know was whether this was a private fight or could anybody get in it.

The year 1898 opened with politics at boiling point in Tennessee. The state legislature was trying to fill the vacancy in the United States Senate caused by the death of Isham G. Harris, and the Democrats could not decide on their nominee. They had control of the legislature, so that their nominating caucus was, in effect, the decisive action to be taken.

For twelve days, through 145 ballots, the Democrats wrestled among themselves. The principal contestants were Benton McMillin and Robert Taylor, with Thomas Battle Turley, of Memphis, a bad third. As so often happens in those three-cornered political fights, when a stalemate has been prolonged, Turley was finally elected and poor Benton McMillin was again balked in his consuming ambition to go to the Senate.

Chastened but undespairing, he went back to the House, where he was a foremost leader, at the opening of the new Congress. War talk was running high. On March 9, during the debate on a $50,000,000 national defense appropriation bill, Mr. McMillin was impelled to utter a word of chauvinistic counsel.

"The American people do not want war with any other people," he told the House. "We were taught by our ancestors not to go out of our glorious path one inch to bring on a conflict.

"But the same wise ancestry also taught us not to go out of our path one thousandth part of an inch to escape a conflict where injustice was about to be done to the humblest American citizen or the great American flag.

"Coming from a portion of the South that was recently engaged in conflict with the Union, I think I speak the sentiment of every man and every boy, of every woman and every child in that section when I assure my distinguished friend from Massachusetts that, numbering about the same in population that his state, Massachusetts, does, if a conflict does come, Massachusetts will send no soldier to the bloody field who will not find one from Tennessee to keep step with him and to go with him, shoulder to shoulder, to the conflict."

Long applause interrupted the speaker.

"My friend from Texas, Mr. Cooper, has made a beautiful allusion to the Alamo," McMillin continued. "I want to tell him that if the conflict thickens and men's courage is tried again and new Alamos are to be consecrated, other Tennesseans as brave as that great Tennessean, Crockett, and his comrade, Travis, who made the Alamo immortal, will be there again to shed their blood and again to die for the glory of the flag, Mr. Speaker, which hangs over your head and the immortal principles that it emblemizes."

Mr. McMillin did indeed "speak the sentiment" of the people of Tennessee, who wanted to fight. Charles Sykes, adjutant general of Tennessee, wrote a hot letter to the adjutant general of the army demanding that the National Guardsmen of the state have the first chance to go to the war, if there was going to be any war.

"Not a day goes over now," he complained in his official letter, "that this office is not in receipt of letters from parties in the different sections of this state asking that they be allowed to raise volunteer regiments in the event there should be any trouble between this country and Spain."

The acting adjutant general of the army, Thomas Ward, soothed his Tennessee colleague by assuring him that the National Guard units would get the first chance to fill whatever troop requirements were to be asked from Tennessee, if an emergency arose.

There was already an emergency in Nashville, according to a critical writer in the *American,* as of January 25. The paper said:

The threatened war with Spain compels the Tennessee militia to keep on hand several hundred dynamite bombs, some thousands of cartridges, and a plentiful supply of gunpowder, and as the legislature has never made any provision for a state armory, these munitions of war are stored at the capitol of the state—a structure that will have cost over $1,000,000 (when it is paid for) and which may be a mass of ruins some fine morning.

Fortunately, this calamity never arrived. Whether the legislature belatedly supplied a state armory for the explosives or whether the state was just plain lucky is unclear from the record. The newspaper stopped its complaints, and in a few days a minor danger of this character was completely forgotten in the excitement of a great tragedy.

On February 15 the U.S.S. *Maine* blew up, or was blown up, in Havana Harbor. Almost at once it seemed inevitable that war would come. Public opinion had become increasingly critical of Spain as facts and alleged facts about the administration of General Weyler were published in the Hearst press, the New York *World,* and other newspapers and magazines, as members of Congress delivered denunciatory speeches from the floor, as lecturers exhibited escaped prisoners and recounted their horrible experiences, and as the whole publicity machine of the country was turned loose on the Cuban situation.

There were anxious, nerve-racking days while the navy's board of inquiry tried to decide whether the battleship's own magazines had exploded or the accident had been caused by a bomb or torpedo set off on the outside. President McKinley and his Cabinet exercised what caution they could under the circumstances and made every effort to keep cool until the inquiry was completed—so much so that they were criticized in many quarters for apparently temporizing over an insult to the national honor.

Once the experts reached the conclusion that the *Maine* had been sunk by an explosive charge set off outside her hull, matters moved quickly toward the emergency the acting adjutant general had had in mind. Congress passed a resolution on April 20 demanding that Spain withdraw from Cuba by the twenty-third. Before that ultimatum could be delivered to the Spanish government, however, the American Minister in Madrid was handed his passport, indicating that diplomatic relations were broken off. Congress replied by passing another resolution, on April 25, declaring that a state of war had existed between the United States and Spain since April 20.

There followed more anxious days, particularly for Tennessee, while President McKinley debated with his General Staff how many troops it would be necessary to call to the colors. Apparently every able-bodied man in Tennessee wanted to go to war, and many that were not so able-bodied.

Finally the War Department called on Tennessee to supply three infantry regiments. Governor Robert Love Taylor applied at once for a commission as brigadier general to command the Tennessee troops, on the ground that he could not ask Tennesseans to serve in any battlefield where he was unable to lead them. On learning that the three regiments would be separated and would not serve as a unit, the governor withdrew his application, prompting the Nashville *American* to include in an editorial the acid reflection that "the remuneration as officers will incite many to volunteer who like a little politics and coin mixed up with their patriotism."

In its issue of May 5 the *American* published the following squib:

Celina, May 5 (Correspondence): The people up here are manifesting the keenest interest in the pending war, and every bit of information available is seized with avidity by the eager populace.

Many are ready and willing to enlist for the war, now that there is a possibility of others getting a chance to go.

Cordell Hull has been actively at work for some days raising a company of volunteers for the war and hopes to have them ready when they can be used.

In Celina, as everywhere else in the state, a great many young men had been disappointed when the first three regiments were recruited completely and rapidly from the National Guard of the state. Their chance came when the War Department asked for a fourth regiment of infantry, confiding its command to Colonel George LeRoy Brown, a Regular Army officer of thirty years' experience, with Lieutenant Colonel Harvey Hannah as his second in command. The regiment was to be composed of twelve companies, and twenty-five companies were immediately offered. There were more heartaches during the elimination process, and these were reflected in two dispatches to the *American*.

"Celina, June 1 (Correspondence): The war excitement is getting high," commented the piece which appeared in the *American's* edition of June 4. "Hon. Cordell Hull has about completed a company of volunteers in this and adjoining counties and will be ready to move at any time when called for."

The *American's* correspondent in one of the "adjoining counties" took a less philosophical view of the delays and published the following in the paper of June 14:

Livingston, June 11 (Correspondence): Much disappointment is manifest among the boys who had prepared to enlist under the second call and hoped to be one of the companies of the Fourth Tennessee Regiment from Clay and Overton counties. About seventy have signed the obligation to enlist in Clay and about forty in Overton County.

Work was only commenced in Overton on Monday last, and boys were rallying fast. Cordell Hull had charge of the enrollment in Clay and W. R. Officer and G. E. Dougherty in Overton. In case a third call follows, a company will again be tendered the governor from these counties, and if necessary each county can quickly raise a full company.

At long last the organization of a fourth regiment was authorized and things moved rapidly. On June 21 Governor Taylor announced that Cordell Hull had been commissioned as captain of Company H of the new regiment.

The first constructive military step the Fourth Tennessee Volunteers accomplished was the recruiting of a magnificent band of thirty-five pieces. It decided (or someone decided) that it should be called "Taylor's Tennessee Tigers." The Knoxville *Journal,* a Republican paper, thought this was carrying things a bit far, although it approved the alliterative qualities of the title. It suggested that the new troops might better be called "Brown's Bloody Butchers," or "Hannah's Heroic Hornets," or "Tatom's Terrible Tomcats" (there was a Major Tatom in the outfit).

The Fourth was ordered to mobilize at Knoxville, and Governor Taylor went over to see his Tennessee Tigers on June 30, the day after Captain Hull and his forty-four men arrived. The young captain was not entirely without experience, according to the Nashville *American,* because he had undergone training at Cumberland University "where an army officer is in charge of the military department." He and his men were equipped and whipped into shape sufficiently to be mustered into the Federal service, with the rest of the regiment, on July 13.

Although these enthusiastic warriors did not know it at the time they were drilling and becoming military at Knoxville, what Woodrow Wilson was to describe three years later, in his *History of the American People,* as a "war of impulse" was nearly over. Dewey had destroyed the Spanish naval forces in the Philippines without losing a single man. Schley and Sampson had served the same medicine to Cervera when he tried to run his fleet out of Santiago de Cuba past the American blockade. Shafter's land forces had stormed El Caney and San Juan Hill and were demanding the surrender of Santiago. There remained only the pacification of Cuba, the occupation of the Philippines, and the reduction of Puerto Rico before Spain sued for peace.

The Fourth Tennessee was to draw, from among these assignments, the occupation of Cuba. With better luck than some of the other units called to the service in 1898, the regiment lost no men from disease in the camp at Knoxville. On November 28 it entrained for Savannah to sail for Casilda, while the peace commissioners of the two belligerents were meeting in Paris to settle the final terms of Spain's complete capitulation.

In 1938, on a ship en route for Lima, Peru, where Mr. Hull was to head the United States delegation to the Eighth Pan-American Conference, I happened to be standing with him on deck the day we rounded the eastern end of Cuba. Borrowing some field glasses, he saw, or thought he saw, the spot where his regiment landed forty years before. He had been in Cuba for only one day in the interim—a day spent ashore on his way back to the United States from the Montevideo Conference early in 1934.

The thirty-five-piece regimental band did its best by "Dixie" as Taylor's Tennessee Tigers sailed out of Savannah on the army transport *Manitoba*. According to Mr. Beard's account, the regiment sailed by Tybee, Watling, the Crooked Islands, through the Windward Passage past Santiago, on which portion of the voyage the soldiers were treated to a heartening view of the wrecked Spanish battleships beached along the coast where Admiral Cervera's men had been compelled to take refuge from the witheringly accurate fire of the American gunners.

Five members of the regiment died of spinal meningitis during the voyage, however, and Captain Hull was detailed to command their joint funeral when Casilda was reached. Regimental headquarters were established at Trinidad, some four miles inland from Casilda, the Spanish forces obligingly evacuating the town in time to prevent conflict. Mr. Beard reports that a Spanish soldier stayed behind for the purpose of enlisting in the Fourth's thirty-five-piece band.

After the unopposed landing and occupation of Trinidad the duties of the Fourth Tennessee Volunteers quickly developed a routine character. On December 23 Captain Hull was designated Inspector General of City and District, but his duties seem to have been that of regimental law officer for the town. He apparently discharged them efficiently, as he did the other minor military duties assigned to him.

For the first time in his life Cordell Hull was thrown out of his familiar environment under conditions of responsibility. Routine as were the military services of Company H, there were presented maintenance problems in a strange land which called for the judgment and ingenuity of its young captain. By all accounts he was adaptable and ingenious enough to solve them to the

satisfaction of his command. Under the rough-and-ready discipline prevailing among volunteer troops during the Spanish-
American War, there would have been plenty of open complaint
if the troops had considered their captain derelict in his duty.

Retrospectively speaking, the most important contribution
made to his future development lay in the awakening of Hull's
interest in matters far beyond the horizon of Celina and Nashville. Such things are subconscious at the time and make their
results felt only long after the event. Just as countless American
doughboys brought back with them a completely novel interest
in France after their army service there during the World War,
so Hull became interested in the great world which had previously been largely an abstraction to him.

Neither he nor the greatest statesmen in the country appreciated the epoch in the national history to which they were writing
the first chapter. Wilson was quite right in calling it "a war of
impulse." We can now trace, with more or less accuracy, the
causes which made the short conflict inevitable, but at the time
it appeared simply to happen. We can now see the unending
consequences of that sudden militaristic flare-up in the national
consciousness, but they were unrealized at the time.

Cordell Hull had a small part, but one which impressed the
situation on his mind, in this turning point in the history of the
United States. Years later he was to try to cope with the un-
foreseen results that the new turn of fortune would bring in its
train.

For one thing, the Spanish-American War marked the final
liquidation of legal disabilities growing out of the Civil War. Only
two years before its outbreak Congress had decreed that former
Confederates were eligible for commissions in the army or navy.
The result was that hundreds of Confederate veterans became
officers in the new war, and their participation on terms of
equality with Northern officers healed much of their wounded
pride and that of their friends.

The Spanish-American War was the first united national effort
since the Mexican War. Young and middle-aged men from every
part of the country served among the nearly 300,000 troops
called to the colors. The volunteer system, under which the President assigned quotas to each state, insured that the soldiers would

represent all sections, although it had the drawback, from the point of view of national unity, of keeping together the volunteers from the different states instead of mixing them conglomerately together, as was done in the A.E.F. during the World War and under the Selective Service and Training Act of 1940.

Even so, the mere moving of the troops about the country made for a new form of national acquaintance. The Third Tennessee Volunteers, for example, were ordered to duty in the Philippines. They stayed in San Francisco for months, awaiting transportation. In that time the men gained a personal knowledge of and interest in California which they would never have attained in the ordinary course of their lives at home. This sort of thing went on to a considerable extent, considering the relatively small number of men called to the colors.

Mr. McMillin's speech on the floor of the House, in which he promised Massachusetts that Tennessee would match every volunteer, was a symptom of the new trend. Probably no such promise could have been extracted under any circumstances from a Southern politician in the preceding years since 1840. The enthusiasm, hysteria, imperialism, or whatever it may be called, that was rising in the country was bringing a new concept of nationalism—a trend that Cordell Hull was to deplore and combat in his more mature career.

At the time, he benefited only imperceptibly from the emancipation from sectionalism which the Spanish-American War began. There are no recorded traces that Hull was ever a professional Southerner, although he undoubtedly held for many years that exaggerated regard for the Democratic party, per se, which used to amount almost to a religion among Southerners. I remember reading the newspaper obituary notice of some minor Tennessee politician of whom the editor said, as his culminating encomium, that the deceased had "lived and died in the Democratic faith."

Hull's early life in the border part of the state where he grew up was not as conducive to professional Southernism as was the upbringing of young men in the deeper and darker South. The almost complete absence of Negroes in his section of the state, and the consequent avoidance of the difficult adjustment involved in the freeing of slaves who far outnumbered their former masters, saved him from the racial prejudices which even yet mark older men in portions of the South. The absence of this trait is one of the negative but important phases of Hull's character.

When he was being mentioned as a candidate for the Democratic presidential nomination in the spring of 1940, a few professional politicians expressed the view that the Democratic party could never hold the Negro vote which had previously gone to President Roosevelt if it nominated a candidate from a state like Tennessee, where Negroes are popularly reputed to be barred from the franchise. Whether or not that was a valid reflection from the point of view of practical politics, it would have had no application to Cordell Hull. So far as I have ever been able to judge, there is no "Negro problem" to him, conscious or subconscious.

When we were traveling down to Montevideo in 1933 the Haitian delegation to the Pan-American Conference was aboard our ship. It is a commentary on inter-American communications that the Haitians found it quicker and more comfortable to sail north for five days to New York in order to turn around and sail sixteen days south to get to Uruguay. At any rate, Mr. Hull invited the Haitian delegation to tea in his cabin after the ship had been at sea for a number of days, just as he did other delegations which were aboard.

After this demonstration of diplomatic courtesy, which the Haitians repaid by a shipboard dinner party with much champagne and old liqueur rum, I attempted to joke the Secretary of State by telling him I could never square him with his friends in Tennessee if I let them know he had entertained Negroes.

"When they speak French, that's different," he replied, enjoying his own little joke to the utmost but not forgetting to add a homily on the essential democracy of inter-American relations which must take no account of racial, linguistic, or cultural differences—a policy which he has pursued to its logical conclusion in his dealings with the rest of this hemisphere.

To get back to the Spanish-American War and its implications, it put the finishing touches to a dying sectionalism in the Democratic party. The double election of Grover Cleveland, a New York Democrat, to the presidency had gone a long way toward convincing the Southern Democrats that they could successfully and happily make common cause with their political cousins north of the Mason-Dixon line. The mutual war effort finally wiped away any smoldering obstacles that may have existed, and the only constant philosophy which might be reproached to Cordell Hull as sectional is his lifelong devotion to the low tariff. Actually, his low-tariff convictions sprang from deeper motives.

Another by-product of the Spanish-American War was the emergence of the United States as a world power and as a potentially great naval power. The easy victories of the American battleships, due to the patient and thorough training their crews had received for many years from unknown and unhonored officers, were conducive to popular delusions of grandeur. No doubt those very delusions had much to do with the rising imperialism, which had an undoubted popular basis.

The Democratic party officially condemned this trend for years in its platforms, and Cordell Hull "went along" with the party. The overwhelming national urge was for expansion and greatness, and this urge was to cause many a headache to Cordell Hull in after years. The annexation of Hawaii and the conquest of the Philippines presented the unwitting United States with that spearhead to the West which was to involve the country more and more in the politics of the Orient and the entire Pacific area.

Captain Hull had as little realization of the future importance of the events in which he was participating as did the other young men who served in the Spanish-American War or the other wars with which the country has been afflicted. For the moment he was interested in doing the job in hand as well as might be. He was passing through that phase of military patriotism with which every young man is seized at one time or another in his life. I have the following estimate of his military service from S. L. Sinnott, a Richmond lawyer, who was a sergeant in Company H: "Although . . . Captain Hull had never had any previous military experience, he was quite studious, intelligent, and worked very hard, and before the regiment left for Cuba had become quite an efficient and well-trained officer. . . . The duties of the regiment in Cuba were mostly in aiding the Cuban civilian population, doing garrison duty, and marches into the interior. Captain Hull was very industrious, took a deep interest in his work, and held the esteem and respect of the entire regiment. As one of his sergeants I came into close contact with him and admired and respected both his character and ability. In addition to his duties as captain, he served as judge advocate."

The only official record of the Fourth Tennessee's service that I have been able to find is contained in a volume published by the Government Printing Office in 1902 with the imposing title: *Correspondence Relating to the War with Spain and Conditions Growing out of the Same, Including the Insurrection in the Philippine Islands and the China Relief Expedition, between the Adjutant-General of the Army and Military Commanders in the United States, Cuba, Porto Rico, China, and the Philippine Islands from April 15, 1898, to July 30, 1902.* It gives the following brief history of the regiment:

Organized and mustered into the service of the United States at Knoxville, Tenn , July 1 to 13, 1898, with 47 officers and 1274 enlisted men. Assigned to First Brigade, Second Division, First Army Corps at Knoxville, Sept. 7; transferred to First Brigade, First Division, First Army Corps, Oct. 7. Left Knoxville Nov. 29; arrived at Savannah, Ga., Nov. 29. Sailed from Savannah on Steamship *Manitoba,* Dec. 1. Companies A, F, G, H, K, and M arrived at Trinidad, Cuba, Dec. 6; Companies B, C, D, E, I, and L arrived at Sancti Spiritus, Cuba, Dec. 12, 1898. Sailed from Trinidad and Sancti Spiritus on Steamship *Dixie,* March 28, 1899; arrived at Savannah, Ga., April 1. Mustered out of the service of the United States at Savannah, Ga., May 6, 1899, with 46 officers and 1117 enlisted men. Casualties while in service: Officers—none. Enlisted men—died of disease, 16; killed by accident, 2; murdered, 1; deserted, 82.

Captain Hull's regimental commander, Colonel Brown, gave him a glowing recommendation on his record card after the regiment had been mustered out of the service. This card and the other papers relating to Cordell Hull's brief military career are filed in the Old Records Division of the adjutant general's office, just like the papers concerning every other officer of volunteers who has served in the United States army. These records have lately been moved to the Archives Building, where a section has been turned over to them.

Colonel Brown wrote "excellent" after three items on the card: capacity for command, professional zeal, etc., and conduct

and habits. He attested that the "condition, etc.," of the men
under Captain Hull's command was "very good" and that Hull
was qualified, mentally, morally, and physically, for all the duties
of his position. He added that Hull was "not addicted to the use
of stimulants" in answer to another question concerning the officer's general character.

After declaring that Captain Hull was "an exceptionally discreet and capable man of excellent judgment," Colonel Brown
added the estimate that "this is an officer of marked ability, conscientious, faithful, ambitious, and brave. He has had much experience in handling men and is thoroughly trustworthy."

Hull's original muster-in card shows that on July 8, 1898, at
Camp Poland, Knoxville, Tennessee, he was twenty-six years old,
five feet ten inches tall, weighed 155 pounds, and had brown eyes
and dark hair. This card gives his birthplace as Hull, Tennessee,
but another record, in Hull's own handwriting, says he was born
at Byrdstown. Both records give his residence as Celina at the
time of being mustered in and list William Hull as the person
to be notified in case of emergency.

Three months after he was mustered in Captain Hull asked for
leave of absence, and the original application, written in ink on
what looks like a sheet from a drugstore tablet of paper, sets forth
that the new officer wanted to visit Celina "in order to properly
arrange my legal business so as to place all of same in the hands
of other attorneys. This is extremely important to me."

Another document in the files is a copy of Colonel Brown's
order of December 23, 1898, at Camp Tennessee, Trinidad,
Cuba, which reads as follows:

Captain Cordell Hull of Co. H, 4th Tenn. Vol. Infty. is hereby
appointed Inspector General of the District of Trinidad.

At such times as he deems necessary, or under special instructions
from the military commander, he will make careful and thorough
investigation of any or all public offices in the city or district and
make full report thereon, making recommendations in regard to
each, looking to a wise, honest, and economical administration of
the government affairs.

Captain Hull's closest friend in the company was his first lieutenant and tentmate, C. B. Smith, who is now a circuit judge in

Birmingham, Alabama. Judge Smith has supplied me the following recollections of their military service together:

The Fourth Tennessee was purely a volunteer regiment and was recruited in the same way that the fathers of its company officers had raised their companies for the Confederate Army during the Civil War. Captain Hull personally secured the enlistment of nearly every man in Company H. They were raftsmen from the Upper Cumberland River, mountaineers, farmers, and miners.

He knew their parents and relatives, and they joined the army because Cordell Hull was to be their captain and they had confidence in him. That he retained their confidence and esteem after their period of service was over is evidenced by the fact of his election as a circuit judge and later as Congressman in his district where these men lived.

When the Fourth Tennessee was mobilized, 1375 men, the vast majority of whom, including officers, had had no previous military experience, were in effect dumped in the woods near Knoxville and told "to be a regiment." We had tents but no cots for the enlisted men, and they had to sleep on straw on the ground covered with cotton blankets.

Captain Hull, who had lived in the open, took a detail of men to the woods, cut down small trees and bushes, and out of them made cots off the ground for all of our men to sleep on. The colonel heard of this and ordered all his company officers to inspect our cots and build some for their own men. Because of incidents like this, our regiment had the marvelous record of not losing a man from sickness while we were in the United States.

Captain Hull did not know "right shoulder arms" from "about face" when we were mobilized, but when we returned from Cuba he could not only handle a company but a battalion and regiment as well. He even then had a wonderfully retentive mind, with the ability to concentrate on any given task or subject and thoroughly exhaust and digest same.

Our colonel evidently thought we were to annex and Americanize Cuba right away, and he assigned Captain Hull to the task of codifying and compiling the Cuban laws.

Judge Smith preserved for posterity the only known animal story about Cordell Hull in an article he contributed to the *Foreign Service Journal* in 1935, in which he recounted the history of Nig. Nig was a little black dog of mixed ancestry, about the size of a fox terrier. He was about a year old when he trotted into the officers' tent at their Knoxville camp one day and declined to leave.

He proceeded to clear the company street of all other dogs, being a fierce and efficient fighter to a point far beyond what his size led the men to expect. He was strictly an officers' dog and preserved polite but distant relations with the enlisted men. As between Captain Hull and Lieutenant Smith, Nig discriminated to the extent of loving the lieutenant and respecting the captain. On cold nights he would crawl into the lieutenant's bunk but never attempted such familiarity with the captain.

Both officers grew very fond of him. Hull was then a constant smoker of long black cigars, and Nig disliked the smoke. Sometimes, when the dog was lying asleep on the floor, Captain Hull would puff a lot of smoke around him. The fumes would wake him up; he would give a dignified snarl and stalk out of the tent to sulk a day or so before he forgave the affront.

When it came time for the regiment to leave for Cuba the two officers decided to take Nig along as a company mascot. He hated the train ride to Savannah but felt quite at home aboard the *Manitoba* when she put to sea. After Hull's portion of the regiment was established at Trinidad, Nig took charge of the situation as he had done at Knoxville and saw to it that other dogs kept away from his quarters. Judge Smith says the task was easier than it had been at Camp Poland, because the Cubans had eaten all the big dogs and Nig had only ones about his own size to tackle.

At the Cuban station Nig's fame spread and he became the pet of the entire regiment. In the poker games it was considered infallibly good luck for the player under whose chair he elected to crawl for his evening nap. If he would permit a player to rub his cards on his head before looking at the hand, it was believed to be a guarantee it would contain at least two pairs. Apparently, however, only Messrs. Hull and Smith enjoyed this privilege to any great extent, which may account for their legendary prowess in the poker games.

Lieutenant Smith used to entertain friends by throwing sticks into the surf, ordering Nig to bring them back. He would time his tosses so that the dog would be bowled over by an incoming wave. As soon as Nig had delivered the stick he would charge back into the water to fight each wave as it came in.

As part of his duties in the occupation of Trinidad, Lieutenant Smith was ordered to conduct classes in English at the high school. At the first meeting, attended by about a hundred boys and young men, the lieutenant was seized with stage fright to such an extent that he couldn't think of a thing to say to his prospective pupils. After an embarrassing silence Nig stood up and pawed the instructor, asking to be taken away from this dull gathering. That gave Lieutenant Smith an idea. He patted Nig on the head and said "dog" in a loud, firm voice, as if he had always intended beginning the lesson in this manner. A youngster in the front row got the idea and said *"perro,"* the Spanish word for dog.

As the sounds of "dog" and "perro" spread around the room Lieutenant Smith, who had never sampled the Berlitz system, realized he had found something. He wrote "dog" on the blackboard and motioned to the young Cuban to write "perro" beside it. Then he went on to other objects in the room—chairs, desks, and articles of clothing—and Trinidad's first English course was under way.

By the time the regiment was ordered back to the United States in the following spring, Nig was a full-fledged member of it. Company H marched out of Trinidad under the strictest possible orders from Colonel Brown that nobody was to be permitted to return to the town for any reason whatsoever. Just outside the town it was noticed that Nig had got lost. Captain Hull told Lieutenant Smith to take two men quietly back into the town to find the dog—the only known instance of his disobedience to orders.

The detail had hardly entered Trinidad when they came upon Colonel Brown riding around the streets, evidently on an inspection trip to see that all the men had left and that his orders were being carried out. They saluted stiffly, expecting a severe reprimand at least. Colonel Brown asked what they were doing, and when they told him they were hunting for Nig he ordered them to be sure and find him and rode off in search of other loiterers. Meantime Captain Hull had slowed the company's march so that they were able to catch up as soon as they found the missing mascot.

The regiment disbanded finally in Nashville, and Nig was presented with an honorable discharge in regular form. He went home to live with Lieutenant Smith at Pulaski, where he met a proper soldier's death a few years later. He was killed in a fight with a bulldog twice his size.

Thus ended the military interlude in Cordell Hull's career. Although he is probably as proud of his service in the army as any other veteran, he never talks about it. There are men who have known him for years who are still surprised to learn that he served in the Spanish-American War. Outside of listing his captaincy in his official biographies, I have never known him to make a voluntary reference to it except once.

This was at the consultative meeting of Pan-American foreign ministers held at Havana in the summer of 1940. At the opening meeting Hull arrived at the appointed hour to find the galleries packed to their capacity and about half the delegates sitting in their places on the floor. As he walked to his seat applause broke out in one gallery; other spectators took it up, then a few delegates joined in, and finally the entire company, spectators and delegates alike, rose to their feet and gave him an unprecedented ovation.

Demonstrations of this kind are frowned upon in Pan-American gatherings for fear they will arouse the sensibilities of some Latin-American delegate who might be overlooked despite his importance in his own country and in his own mind. At Havana, however, the incident was too spontaneous and genuine to be squelched.

After adjournment that day a friend of Hull's who had seen him at previous Pan-American meetings congratulated him on the applause and the pleasant character of the demonstration. Hull smiled shyly and deprecatingly as he replied:

"Oh, that was just some folks in the gallery. They must have heard I was down here in the war."

CHAPTER V

The Country Judge

TENNESSEE was on the make when Captain Hull and his comrades-at-arms got back from the war. Its population had passed the 2,000,000 mark, a gain of something like 15 per cent over the 1,767,518 inhabitants it had reported in the census of 1890. The general level of prosperity in the state was rising, as was that of the nation, toward the peak that was to bring on the panic of 1907.

The general upturn had affected Hull's part of the state very little, however. Oil wells in Overton County that had been discovered in 1865 were still capped because there was no way to transport the oil to a market. As it turned out, this was no great loss to the community, as efforts to exploit the oil deposits in the region, of late years, have showed them to be of such a low-pressure variety and of such limited individual yield that they are pumped only sporadically.

The returned soldiers took off their uniforms, told tales of their travels to anyone who would listen, and gradually resumed their lives where they had left off a few months before. Captain Hull reopened his law office in Celina but kept his eye out for a better chance. It was three years in coming, but he recognized and seized the opportunity when it hove in sight. On December 5, 1901, the Gainesboro *Sentinel* published the following item:

> Captain Cordell Hull of Celina will shortly move to Gainesboro to locate. Mr. Hull is a lawyer and young man of excellent character. He has formed a partnership with J. J. Gore, and they will occupy the office recently vacated by G. B. Murray and Son.
>
> To Captain Hull we extend a hearty welcome and hope that he may find Gainesboro a pleasant and profitable place to reside. For the firm of Hull and Gore, or whatever it may be, we predict success, for with two such worthy young men working together nothing short of success will be their lot. Here's to you, boys.

Captain Hull had selected a young Republican to be his law partner, exhibiting that nice political judgment which has always been his. John J. Gore served for many years as a Federal district judge until his death a few years ago. In later life he became an archconservative, and it may have been something of that trait in him, coupled with his Republicanism, which led young Hull to believe they would be a good team, each being the complete opposite of the other.

For all its promise of success and the good wishes of the Gainesboro *Sentinel*, the partnership was not to last long. Less than two years after it was formed Judge W. T. Smith, of the Fifth Judicial District, tendered his resignation to Governor James B. Frazier, wishing to re-enter private practice. His term had more than a year to run, and he recommended that Governor Frazier appoint a young lawyer named Hull, who was practicing in Gainesboro, to fill the vacancy.

Hull received the unanimous endorsement of the bar in nine of the ten counties in the judicial district and substantial support in the tenth, and Governor Frazier made the appointment. The appointee was filled with gratitude and felt himself under a political obligation which he was unable to discharge for years. Only in 1931, after he had been elected to the Senate, was he able to secure the appointment of Governor Frazier's son as United States Attorney.

The new job Captain Hull was undertaking was no light one. He had to sit in each of the ten counties for three terms in the year. Each term lasted a week or more. Adding his travel time to

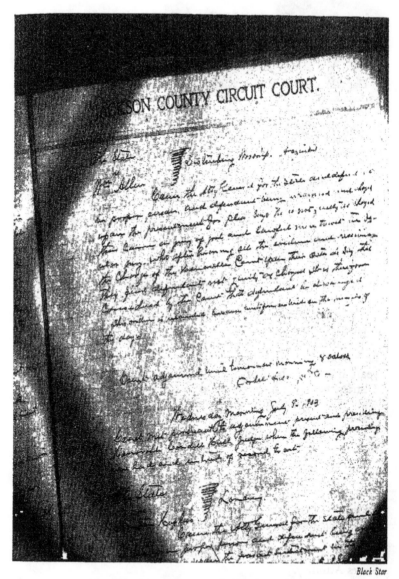

A Page from the Jackson County, Tennessee, Circuit Court
Record Showing One of Cordell Hull's Judgments

the actual sessions court, he found that the job required so much of his time that he spent little more than a month out of the year at home. He kept his residence at Gainesboro, which was about the geographical center of the judicial district, driving out to each county seat in a horse and buggy the day before a term opened and driving back to Gainesboro the day after it closed.[1] Gainesboro was within a single day's drive, although a long, hard day's drive through the mountains, from each of the towns where he had to hold court.

This was the usual life of the circuit judge. The judges seemed to like it, and many of them stayed on the bench for years. Judge John Fite, a former Confederate colonel, was a picturesque figure who spent some years on the circuit. An aunt left him a bottle of old French brandy with the proviso that he open it to celebrate his own one hundredth birthday, and toward the end of his life Judge Fite became more and more optimistic that he could carry out the terms of the legacy. Unfortunately, he missed it by two or three years. Many great and noted lawyers still rode the circuit as they did throughout the post-Civil War period.

There were compensations in the life of the circuit-riding judge. The terms of court were great events in the life of the region. The men rode in from the entire county, sometimes bringing their women with them for their annual purchasing sprees, for the opening day, and many of them stayed at the county seat for the whole term.

Not that they had any litigation before the court. They simply enjoyed listening to the arguments, especially when some big city lawyer from Nashville, or Chattanooga, or even farther afield, would put in appearance against some local star. They all had their favorite pleaders and would listen critically when their man was arguing. When court was not actually in session they stood around the square whittling, swapping horses, and talking politics.

---

[1]When he examined the state of his circuit the new judge found that the dockets in the ten county seats under his charge were all about a year in arrears, and he set out to bring them up to date. Often, if he had a week or two between regular terms of court, he would drive to a place where the docket was in the worst shape and hold an extra term, trying all the cases that were ready. Expeditions of this kind, added to his regular work, would occasionally keep him away from home weeks at a time.

On the whole, the cases were tried in a friendly atmosphere. The lawyers knew each other too well to attempt any sharp practice or short cuts in favor of their clients, except for an occasional outsider who would come in on a case and try to overawe the local bar with his metropolitan mannerisms and experience. They did not get very far, for the run-of-the-mine lawyers practicing before the circuit courts of Tennessee appear to have been thoroughly grounded in the law that was ordinarily invoked in the relatively simple cases that came up.

The circuit judge cleared up the criminal docket first and then turned himself into a civil court. The civil cases consisted mainly of disputes over coal and timber rights as well as clouded land titles springing from the uncertain surveys and ambiguous terms of the original Revolutionary grants.

I attended such a court a few months ago at Jamestown, which was one of the points on Judge Hull's circuit. It seemed to me that it must have changed very little since his day. Jamestown is noted for its Mark Twain Hotel, which occupies the site of the home of the writer's father, who was circuit court clerk for many years before moving to Florida, Missouri, where Samuel Clemens was born.

On this day the court was sitting in chancery. The case before it concerned a land title. The complainant was a poor farmer who had deeded some property to a large company but had repented of the bargain before payment was made and was trying to void the contract of sale. The twelve jurymen were all clad in overalls, as was the complainant, and were obviously lifelong friends of his. I was utterly unable to follow the involved testimony (the complainant was on the stand), but the members of the jury nodded wisely and understandingly at frequent intervals as the farmer unfolded his story and attempted to counter the thrusts of the defendant's lawyer, who also knew the farmer well.

Perhaps two dozen spectators at a time occupied the hard, uncomfortable seats in the bare, dusty little courtroom. They would wander in and out, joining their fellow citizens in the square when they tired of the forensic qualities of the tribunal. To the casual passer-by there was a reassuring aspect to the whole procedure. Knowing nothing of the merits of the case, I nevertheless got the feeling that justice would be done by the twelve simple farmers sitting on the jury. It gave a new meaning to the expressions "equity" and "common law."

The criminal cases, in Judge Hull's time, were the difficult part of the judicial work. When he was appointed to the bench in 1903, crimes of violence were still prevalent. There had been little serious effort in that part of the country to re-establish the sense of law and order which had been lost in the days of the guerrilla bands during and after the Civil War. Men were still wont to settle their differences by fighting and killing. Drunkenness, of the old-fashioned, violent sort, was common.

In the Nashville *American* of January 26, 1890, I found the following complaint in an interview with John Miller McKee:

"It seems almost incredible that in this land of civilization and written laws a deliberate murderer can escape the punishment of his deed, and yet that very thing occurs almost daily."

Matters had improved but little when Cordell Hull began to ride his circuit. Judge Smith, his predecessor, while a most able judge, was bighearted and had been an easygoing arbiter, tending toward leniency. He was a little loath to inflict severe punishment.

C. G. Black, clerk and master at Crossville for the past forty years, who remembers Hull as a judge in his court, recalls the turbulent conditions the young judicial officer had to face. As a matter of fact, Mr. Black sometimes recalls rather wistfully the character of the criminal dockets he used to prepare for Judge Hull.

"In those days," he told me, "the offenses were matters of fist and skull."

He drew a comparison, unflattering for the contemporary delinquents who come before his court, which described present-day crimes as limited to petty larcenies, bootlegging, automobile thefts, and other offenses which he links with the generally softer and, to him, more contemptible failings of the movie-mad generation he sees growing up around him.

Judge Hull opened his first term of court at Sparta in the spring of 1903. Almost at once the lawyers realized that a new judicial deal was in the making. Those who were inclined to be supercilious with the young judge soon found themselves put in their place. The bench would listen patiently and attentively to argument and then make his ruling. If one of the lawyers tried to persuade him to change his mind, he got scant attention and was usually cut off curtly:

"The court has ruled."

Judge Joe McMillin Gardenhire, a nephew of Governor McMillin and of Cordell Hull's instructor at the Montvale Academy, succeeded Hull on the fifth circuit and remains today one of his most intimate friends. Judge Gardenhire retired from the bench a few years ago and is now Nashville manager for the Reconstruction Finance Corporation. He remembers the trials of the young solon as well as the admiring legends he heard about him when he began to follow him around the circuit. To his mind Hull displayed in those days on the bench a trend of character which he considers is a fundamental trait today.

"He never starts anywhere unless he knows where he's going, and he never turns back," Judge Gardenhire told me in summing up the driving force behind Hull's career.

County courthouses in Hull's part of Tennessee are sparsely furnished today, and they were certainly no better when he was riding the circuit. He would carry a few lawbooks with him in his buggy, but he would have to throw himself on the hospitality of the most prominent lawyer in each county seat to get access to a law library. This was willingly granted, of course, not only to Hull but to any circuit judge.

Since dockets were always crowded, Judge Hull opened his courts at eight o'clock in the morning, to the accompaniment of much grumbling from the lawyers, court officials, witnesses, and principals. He would run straight through until late in the afternoon and then sit up most of the night reading up on the law likely to be involved in the cases on the next day's docket. That capacity for uninterrupted work and concentration is another quality which has lasted him all these years.

His influence on the public, as distinct from the reluctant admiration he won from the older and more distinguished lawyers who appeared before him, sprang from the impartial severity of his sentences on those found guilty of criminal offenses. Before he tried his first case he determined to be a vigorous enforcer of the law, showing no favoritism and living up to his oath of office in every respect.

This was not as easy as it sounds. In his early days on the bench he was often threatened by bullies for sentences he had passed on them or their friends, and the technique he developed in dealing with these worthies is precisely what he used in his policy toward the totalitarian dictators later on. He neither hunted trouble nor avoided it when he heard that some convict of his jurisdiction was vowing vengeance.

He was especially hard on those whom the juries found guilty of public drunkenness, for the drunks of that region often ended their celebrations by shooting up the town. Their high spirits seemed to be inseparably linked with danger to the innocent public. Instead of considering this was just good, clean fun, as most of the other circuit judges had done and were still doing, Hull decided he would make that form of entertainment too expensive to be popular.

L. A. Ligon, veteran lawyer and former mayor of Carthage, tells how Hull discovered early in his judicial career a flaw in the Tennessee criminal code covering public drunkenness. As the law stood, the grand jury could bring no indictment against an offender unless there was a prosecuting witness who would file a formal complaint. In nearly every instance, after the excitement had died down, there could be found no prosecuting witness willing to go through the necessary formalities before the grand jury, and the expansive drunk escaped trial for his misdoings.

Judge Hull called this situation to Mr. Ligon's attention just before the Carthage lawyer was to take his seat in the state senate at Nashville. He so impressed Mr. Ligon with the need for amending the statutes that the new senator secured from the legislature, with scarcely a dissenting vote, a modification of the law which permitted grand juries to institute inquiries into public drunkenness on their own initiative and to make presentments to the court where they felt the facts justified, without the appearance of any prosecuting witness.

Convictions for gambling were likewise sternly punished by Judge Hull, to the pained surprise of culprits with whom he had often engaged in a light riffle of poker in earlier times. His old friends now say that Hull never took a drink and never played a hand of poker while he was a judge, to the end that he might be able, in good conscience, to sentence any wayward friends of his who might come before him for sentence after conviction of those misdeeds.

His tactics began to attract the favorable attention of the better elements in his circuit, and he had no difficulty in securing election for a six-year term in 1904. He continued along the path he had marked out for himself, and a number of little legends survive to illustrate his mental struggle to enforce the law and yet indulge his humanitarian instincts.

One of these has it that a woman came to him to ask clemency for·her son who was about to be sentenced for some offense. She told Judge Hull that she was the woman who had taken Uncle Billy into her house when he had been shot and left for dead by the guerrillas. The judge thanked her for what she had done, went into court, and fined her son fifty dollars—a stiff sentence in those days. Then he gave the woman the fifty dollars to pay the fine.

James N. Cox of Cookeville, another old-time friend of Mr. Hull, tells of two old lawyers who were nearly always on opposite sides of cases and who prepared their briefs by getting good and drunk together the night before the trial. The first time they came before Judge Hull they developed an interminable wrangle between themselves, and it looked as if they were going to use up the better part of the day arguing with each other without getting down to the business in hand. The judge listened only so long, however, before he realized that the distinguished members of the bar were suffering from outsize hang-overs which they had alleviated by several hairs of the dog. He banged his gavel and said to the sheriff:

"Handcuff these two lawyers together and take them down to jail until they sober up."

Incidents of this character, added to a few well-placed fines for contempt of his court, established the discipline Judge Hull felt was necessary to the proper conduct of the state's business, and he began the laborious task of clearing the cluttered dockets. His success on the bench is attested by the unanimity with which he is still called "Judge" by the people of the region he used to serve even thirty-five years—a whole generation—after he resigned his legal post.

During the terms of court the most distinguished lawyers would usually have their meals together at the town hotel, and Judge Hull spent a good deal of his spare time with them. As one old friend of his expressed it to me, "He was always picking his company to improve himself." He learned much about the law and about human nature from these older men, and they took a liking to the young judge.

During the three years he rode the circuit he built up quite a following among the more serious people of the region. They admired his firmness on the side of law and order, his obvious mental integrity, and his quiet determination to get ahead in the world. This intimate connection with people and their troubles was probably the best training he ever had for his subsequent political career.

In the state, and in the nation, new things were stirring. Improvements in the design of coal-oil lamps had popularized them, and newspaper advertisements were reminding the people of Tennessee that anyone could now enjoy lighting facilities in his home that would have been the envy of the most luxury-loving Roman emperors. The new lighting increased the demand for crude oil (no one dreamed of the petroleum industry the automobile would create), and Hull's district benefited. The wells in Pickett, Overton, and Fentress counties increased their outputs. J. B. Killibrew, writing on the natural resources of Tennessee in the Nashville *Banner* of March 7, 1903, reported the following:

"In 1901 the Kentucky-Tennessee oil field was producing less than 200,000 barrels per annum. It is now producing ten times that amount."

At Nashville the state legislature got its mind off the dry subjects with which solons ordinarily deal long enough to take up a bill offered by a solemn representative from Lauderdale County. The proposed measure would have prohibited kissing within the confines of the sovereign state of Tennessee. The lower house amended the original draft so that it would apply only to its sponsor and his successors in office and then passed it.

In Washington President Theodore Roosevelt had invited Negroes to the New Year's Day reception at the White House, and the South was outraged. The *Banner* dared the President to run in 1904 with a Negro as his vice-presidential candidate. The

Republican party in the South broke into two factions which survive to this day—the Lily Whites and the Black and Tans.

Carthage, where Hull was to move some years later and which he lists as his home to this day, was trying to get a bridge built across the Cumberland River. The town council agreed to raise $15,000 if the county would supply the remaining $45,000 needed to complete the structure. The massive structure of steel and concrete which now spans the river there must have cost many times what the Carthage fathers had in mind in those days.

Wall Street had suffered something of a slump in 1903, but Tennessee itself seems to have staggered through the year in fair shape. In Hull's part of the country five companies were operating coal mines around Crossville and five others were reported about to start operations. The Nashville *American* said that the state capital had suffered little from the Wall Street declines because "the speculative public in Nashville made very little on the rise of the New York stocks and consequently lost little on the decline." However, such local favorites as Gray and Dudley Hardware (still one of the leading firms in Nashville) declined from 112 to 100, although its earnings were down to only 11 per cent in 1903 instead of 12 per cent as in 1902. Bon Air Coal and Iron Company was quoted at 80 instead of 91, even though its dividend rate had been maintained.

The stock of the First National Bank had risen from 135 to 147 and that of the Fourth National from 174 to 185. In the boom days of the nineteen twenties these two institutions were to be merged. The Cheek-Neal Coffee Company felt sufficiently encouraged to increase its capital stock from $42,000 to $100,000, mainly because it was doing so well with its sales of Maxwell House Blend in one- and three-pound tins.

President Roosevelt's maneuverings during the "revolution" which separated Panama from Colombia, coupled with his message to Congress urging immediate ratification of the canal treaty with Panama and a start on construction, were viewed with considerable suspicion in the South. The Democrats in the Senate were forming a bloc to oppose ratification.

Senator Carmack, then Tennessee's outstanding national political figure, wanted the treaty blocked and an attempt made to negotiate for the alternative route through Nicaragua, unless

The Courthouse in Carthage, Tennessee, Where Cordell
Hull Presided as Judge

mutually satisfactory arrangements could be worked out with Colombia which would avoid recognition of the conveniently conjured Republic of Panama. He called President Roosevelt's message "the most flimsy and dishonest piece of reasoning ever issued from the White House—the sophistries are so thin as to be perfectly transparent and do not for a moment conceal the truth."

The Chattanooga *News*, on the other hand, thought the Southern Democrats were taking a narrow, partisan view of the whole matter, overlooking their own interests.

"Its construction means more to the South than it does to any other section of the country," the paper's editor wrote. "It will make of the South the market street of America. It will put us in easy reach of the markets of the Orient and produce a big revival of industry in all the Southern states."

Nearly a quarter of a century later Cordell Hull was to rectify an injustice Panama claimed under that famous treaty and to make considerable progress toward the final reconciliation with Colombia where all was forgiven, if not forgotten.

The controversy over the Panama Canal tended to attract public notice toward Latin America in general. The *Banner* gave considerable space to an article by Stephen Bonsal in which the writer said that the German population in southern Brazil "manifests a sense of superiority over the natives, with whom they come into contact, and instead of becoming assimilated into the body of the people, as has been largely the case with their compatriots who have come to the United States, they have become a dominant factor bringing the natives who live among them into their manners and habits of thought and life."

Stephen Bonsal's son Philip is now chief of the Division of American Republics of the State Department, wrestling with the implications of the problem his father saw so clearly in 1904.

Amid these whirlpools of international intrigue and politics local life in Tennessee pursued its even tenor. Some idea of the judicial problems Cordell Hull had to face on his circuit may be gleaned from the account sent to the Nashville *American* on January 19, 1904, by its correspondent in Cookeville, one of the county seats where he presided.

"Circuit court met today," the correspondent reported. "Several important cases will be tried at this term, among them that

of Glenn E. Flemings vs. W. T. Cooper in a damage suit of
$10,000 for false imprisonment, and Lee & High against Jas. H.
and Walter Lee, a damage suit for $10,000."

There may have been some hint of the new circuit judge's
beneficial influence on the customs of the region in the journal-
ist's closing sentence, which read as follows:

"For the second time in several years [the italics are mine—it
was Hull's second year as a circuit judge] no murder cases are
on the docket."

Either the social customs of the region were changing for what
we now consider to be the better or the standards of journalistic
taste were evolving toward what we now consider the proper
thing. A few years before, the local newspapers were filled with
the most lurid sex stories of various kinds that have ever been
printed in this country. It would appear, from reading the newspapers of the period, that the editors either searched out at least
one of these accounts every week or that one torrid occurrence
a week was the normal expectancy in that part of Tennessee.

The accounts ranged from rape cases, in which no physical
detail whatever was omitted (most of them sounded like testimony
before a coroner's jury), to spicy tales of a brother from the country seeking his wayward sister in the brothels of Nashville or
Memphis. He usually found her, with the direst results to the unfortunate young blood whom she happened to be entertaining at
the moment.

During Hull's incumbency on the circuit bench, however,
rural life in Tennessee was described in much more sedate
fashion. For example, the ubiquitous, though anonymous, Cookeville correspondent reported to the *American,* on the same day he
told of the opening of the circuit court, the following picture of
the inhabitants' extralegal activities:

The Pierian Club met with Mrs. N. J. Finney this afternoon.
A Comedy of Errors was the study. . . . Mrs. Fred White gave a
dance last evening. About nine couples were present, being chaper-
oned by Mr. and Mrs. Harry Keirsey. Doughnuts and peanut balls
were served.

A few days later the *American* recorded the following bit of
current history from Cornersville:

Mr. and Mrs. C C. L. Glenn entertained two miles east of here on the Yell road in honor of their son Eligie, who left here about fifteen years ago for Texas a poor boy but who returns on a visit a rich man. Refreshments were served.

The mere presence of the new young judge on the bench could not have achieved these miraculous changes in the mores of the Tennessee hills. There was a trend toward the more sedate living which characterized most of the country at the turn of the century, as a reaction from the Civil War and Reconstruction days. It must be said of the young judge, however, that he took full advantage of the drift of public opinion to hammer home his never-changing conceptions of respect for law and order, peaceful settlement of disputes, and a general "live-and-let-live" philosophy of life. He has tried ever since to press for this sensible mode of living among individuals and among nations whenever he thought people would listen to him and many times when he knew they would not.

The industrialization of the South, which had started about 1886 and had slowed down during the panic of 1893, was on the march again, although it had not yet reached Hull's part of Tennessee. Managers of Southern textile mills were boasting that they paid dividends three or four times as large as those earned by New England establishments, making no mention of the comparative wage scales, of course. Southern-made iron was being turned out at such low prices that it could undersell the iron of the British and German masters in their own ports.

In Nashville the state legislature was considering reducing the tax rate because the treasury enjoyed a surplus of $700,000 which no one knew how to spend. An early example of the punitive tax, or the tax with a social purpose, was the proposal by Representative I. N. Rawls, of Dyer County, to impose a tax on bachelors— a levy which would have hit the young circuit judge of Gainesboro. An indignant reader of the *Banner* wrote a letter to its publisher sensibly suggesting that the state would make a great deal more money by imposing a progressive tax on divorces—$500 for the first, $1000 for the second, etc. There were some complaints about the cost of living, and an investigating legislator told the representatives that he found turkeys to be selling as high as

sixteen cents a pound in the Nashville markets, chickens at fourteen cents a pound, and eggs at twenty-five cents a dozen.

Governor Frazier, in his second inaugural address delivered on
January 24, 1905, called for an end of sectionalism in the nation's political life, pointing to an evil which was far more prevalent in those days than it is today. It was carried sometimes to
ridiculous lengths. For example, the *American's* Washington correspondent reported that a storm was brewing in the national
capital over a proposal by Senator Scott of West Virginia to
abolish five regiments of cavalry in the army and to replace them
by five regiments of coast artillery. This could be interpreted only,
the correspondent went on, as another attack on the South.
Southerners were traditionally excellent horsemen, and Southern
officers tended to rise to the high ranks in that branch of the
service. The move to substitute coast artillery could mean only
that Northerners were plotting to get those high posts for their
own men. To support his contention he quoted, as follows, an
anonymous Southern officer then serving in the army:

"I would no more serve as a coast artilleryman than I would
serve in a prison. Let them get machinists and professional strong
men."

On the floor of the House of Representatives, Mr. Bartlett of
Georgia was offended when Representative Smith of Iowa rose
to deny a statement the Georgia orator had just made.

"A better man than you denied Christ once," was the crushing
retort Mr. Bartlett made.

The *American* was inspired to publish an editorial mildly re-
buking Southern public men for their intransigeance in Washington. It said:

"Southern senators and representatives belong to a losing and
therefore an objecting party, which places them at a disadvantage as constructive statesmen. They are expert objectors and
excellent critics, but the tendency of such a critic is to become too
intense as a partisan and too much of a scold."

By this time Hull had come to believe that he did not necessarily belong to "a losing and therefore an objecting party." He
had reached the conclusion that Theodore Roosevelt, for all his
hard words about "malefactors of great wealth" and "swollen
fortunes," and for all his threats to enforce the anti-trust laws,

was really fighting a rear-guard action to stem the tide of liberalism which Hull thought he saw rising in the country. He believed that the President realized a great economic and social revolution was about due and that he was trying to stall it off until the Republican party could awaken to the march of events and remodel itself in time to keep the Democratic party from sweeping the country.

Cordell Hull, today, has as little sectionalism or factionalism in his make-up as any man in the country, but he still remembers with unmitigated bitterness the evils into which he considers the nation fell during the almost uninterrupted sway of the Republican party from the end of the Civil War until Woodrow Wilson's election in 1912. He still thinks that the United States was kept on a narrow course, with heavy handicaps steadily increasing, and that it was saved only by the revolution of 1912 when the American people turned the Republicans out of office.

As he pictures that period to himself he sees it as a sort of nightmare in which, after the Civil War, the monied and other special interests seized the Republican party and used it to obtain every kind of special and unfair privilege for themselves. The protective tariff, the land grants to the railroads, the anti-labor injunctions issued by Republican judges, and the opposition to income taxation were among the signs he saw. He resented the Republican tactics of staying in power by inciting the Middle West and the growing Far West against the South by recalling the Civil War—"waving the bloody shirt," as it was called.

The national scene began to beckon to him, ever more imperatively. He tired of the judgeship, which he had accepted in the first place only after Judge Smith had asked him three times to take the appointment. The dockets on the circuit were in good shape. The early excitement of a difficult assignment had begun to wear away. It was a hard life, driving over almost impassable roads in all kinds of weather, and it held little future for a hard-thinking and rapidly developing young man who had always been attracted to active political life.

Besides, Hull had always wanted to be a lawyer in active practice. Even today he sometimes regrets that he never found time for more active law work. He is a good lawyer and would have preferred to try his mettle in actual combat in the courts.

He began to lay his plans to retire from the bench and re-enter active politics. On February 2, 1906, he appeared in Nashville to testify before a mass meeting called to advocate improvement of the Cumberland River. The *Banner* gave the following account of his appearance:

Judge Cordell Hull of Gainesboro, Tennessee, said . . . that if the government of the United States were to discontinue improvement of the fertile Cumberland Valley waterway and isolate its hundreds of thousands of people an injury and loss would be worked that could not be estimated

Little effort would be made to build up towns or construct factories, etc , along a railroad that would run only six months in the year and be very irregular at that. The people of such a country could not be expected to remain in it and develop it without some assurance of a market and the resulting betterment of their condition.

Under present conditions on the Cumberland River the market might be entirely changed before a shipment could be made. It was well-nigh impossible for the upper Cumberland people to compete with others in business. Much of the isolated land was worth from $75 to $100 an acre. He did not think the government could afford to inflict on the people of the Cumberland so irreparable an injury as the abandonment of the improvement of the river.

River improvement is one of the prerogatives of Congress. Anyone so ardently desiring to increase the navigability of the Cumberland River would know that the matter would have to be presented to Congress in order to get any action. Judge Hull was fully aware of this, and a possible explanation may be found in the following article that the *Banner* had published the day before, which was February 1, 1906:

Cookeville, Tenn., Feb. 1: The formal announcement of the candidacy of Judge Cordell Hull of Gainesboro for the Democratic nomination for Congressman from this, the Fourth Congressional District . . . will appear in the Democratic newspapers of the district this week. Judge Hull has, of course, been a candidate for several months, and the action of the committee in calling the primary for May ushers the contest into immediate prominence and it is supposed that within a few weeks all the candidates will begin a vigorous presentation of their campaigns.

And so the die was cast. A new member of Congress was in the making. Across the Atlantic a young member of Parliament was about to be elected for Manchester and was engaged in a hot campaign in which his mother, an American woman, was giving him active aid, just as William Hull was helping his son Cordell. Of the British candidate the *Banner* had this comment to make, and Cordell Hull must have agreed with it many times in the years that followed:

Young Winston Spencer Churchill seems to have inherited the strong qualities of his very capable parents and is forging successfully to the front. He is unquestionably a man of much greater force and promise than his first cousin, Charles Richard John Spencer Churchill, Baron Spencer, Earl of Sunderland, Marquis of Blanford, and Duke of Marlborough. The eldest of the male line in England gets titles and estates galore but not always brains and character.

CHAPTER VI

The National Scene

WHILE Hull was completing his apprenticeship to public life by riding the judicial circuit in Tennessee the foreign relations of the United States were growing rapidly in scope and intricacy, as a consequence of the victory over Spain. Many of the problems with which Hull was destined to struggle years later already existed in the embryo, notably in the Latin-American field.

The whole episode of 1898 had awakened apprehensions among the Latin-American republics. These were not allayed by subsequent developments between the United States and Cuba and were fanned to white heat by the revolution which separated Panama from Colombia and made possible the immediate construction of the Panama Canal. There was considerable feeling among our neighbors to the south that the United States had driven Spain out of Cuba only to make the island an American dependency, as had been done to Puerto Rico and the Philippines. The imposition of the Platt Amendment, giving the United States the right to intervene in Cuban internal affairs for the purpose of preserving order, lent color to that suspicion.

President Theodore Roosevelt's conduct at the time of the Panamanian revolution and the alacrity with which he concluded a canal treaty with the new regime in Panama engendered the belief that he and his agents had fomented the revolution for this very purpose. The United States navy had displayed considerable activity around Colon while the coup was being engineered. The *Dixie,* the transport which brought Cordell Hull and his regiment back from Cuba, was one of the vessels ordered to the Atlantic port of Panama for the avowed purpose of insuring "free transit" across the Isthmus in the event there should be disorder. The Latin Americans, for the most part, subscribed to the view that the ship movements were intended to overawe the Colombian authorities if they attempted to assert their control over the troubled province of Panama.

There was some public opinion in the United States which disapproved not only of the Panama treaty but of the administration's budding Latin-American policy in general. Senator Tillman of South Carolina made a speech in Atlanta predicting that the Senate would not ratify the treaty and slinging some charges at President Theodore Roosevelt which sounded very much like some thrown at President Franklin D. Roosevelt during the campaign of 1940.

"President Roosevelt wants to be re-elected," Mr. Tillman said. "He is trying his best to provoke a war. He wants to be a war President because it has been the history of our country for some time that it is impossible to defeat a war President."

President Roosevelt's New Year's Day reception at the White House at the beginning of 1904, the traditional state function in honor of the diplomatic corps, which has been discontinued of late years, was attended by no diplomatic representative from Colombia. The New York *Times,* in its review of the events of 1903, included the following items which suggested the future perils lying in wait for Cordell Hull when he was to become Secretary of State:

If it would now appear that the disposition we showed in the Alaskan settlement (the arbitration of the boundary with Great Britain) has not guided us in our relations with the Republic of Colombia, there still remains ground to hope that even in that embroilment we may come to decisions more acceptable to the whole body of the American people. That we ought to mend our conduct is, we presume, the belief of a majority of right-thinking Americans, although for the present the ardent desire to have the canal built obscures the popular perception of what has been hasty, reckless, rough, and wrong in our procedure. The Isthmian canal is not a matter of life and death to this nation; our peace and safety are not involved. It cannot be asserted, therefore, that we are justified in breaking treaty obligations or invading the rights of a friendly nation, even though that nation may be weak and not always well-behaved. . . .

Tardily and in a somewhat halfhearted way we have performed our "plain duty" to Cuba. The treaty of reciprocity has been mutually ratified and is in effect. It is not all that we ought to do, either from the point of view of our own interest or from that of the interest of Cuba, an island which is in a large measure under our protection and should be the object of our fostering care. Our relations to the Cuban people will be of increasing interest and importance as the years roll by. We ought to be just to them. We should be very foolish if we did not go beyond the line of mere obligation and encourage them to maintain with us profitable trade relations. . . .

Upon the Continent of Europe the most remarkable and positive tendency that has developed during the course of 1903 is the growth of Socialism. It is an incident to the growth of democracy, which was powerfully and increasingly manifested during the nineteenth century. It may, perhaps, be called an episode of that growth. But it is an entirely natural development in any country in which the common people are at once conscious of the increase of their power and are in the habit of relying, for the things which they desire to have done, upon highly centralized and "paternal" institutions of government. . . .

Russia has been pursuing her career of expansion with that unhasting, unresting development, and that complete absence of scruple, which has marked the whole of her eastward development across Asia. Russian unscrupulousness has been particularly marked in the breaking of Russian promises, given primarily to the United States.

The young circuit judge, driving from Gainesboro to Celina, to Jamestown, to Carthage, to Cookeville, to Crossville, and to the other county seats on his beat, was to have to deal with Cuban economic and political relations, with the whole problem of intervention in Latin America, with the broken promises of Russia to the United States, and with National Socialism in Europe.

In the following year there were heard the rumblings of the New Deal with which he was to be associated a quarter of a century later. The Supreme Court handed down its famous 5 to 4 decision in the Northern Securities case, branding a holding company which tried to vote the controlling stock of two rival subsidiaries as a violator of the Sherman Antitrust Act. President Roosevelt urged that railroad rates be fixed by a government commission, and there were administration advisers who demanded Federal charters for all corporations engaged in interstate commerce. These and other upsetting ideas which were in the air prompted the editor of the New York *Times* to predict that "the year 1904 will long be remembered by students of the constitutional history of the Union as that which marked the beginning of the effacement of the States."

Abroad, King Edward VII established the foundations of the Entente Cordiale between England and France, and the French Republic broke with the Vatican. American public interest was centered on the Russo-Japanese War, and sympathies were as one-sided in the country as they were to be in the World War of 1914 and the World War of 1939. The New York *Times* was pleased to report the public conviction "that a Japanese victory is a victory for humanity, and civilization is a proposition which, fortunately, does not now need arguing in these United States." It continued, however, on the following note of warning:

It is quite possible that the future historian may find the internal changes in Russia the most important consequence of that war and by far the most important event of 1904. The common people of Russia have "waxed exceeding bold" under the encouragement that has been offered to them by the demonstration the war has furnished that the ruling classes of Russia did not know their business and were not trustworthy trustees of the interests of the Russian people.

The next year, 1905, was chiefly notable as a boom period. Business in the United States had responded favorably to the ending of the Russo-Japanese War, and Great Britain was beginning to recover from the Boer War depression. The riots and domestic troubles in Russia that followed the defeat in the Far East were viewed sympathetically but remotely and were not regarded as of prime importance to the safety of this country or of the world.

The boom continued into 1906, building the classic background for the depression of 1907. The President was recommending income and inheritance taxes to an unwilling Congress. The United States had undertaken an intervention in Cuba to preserve order, and the move had not been an unqualified success. Elihu Root had made a "good-will tour" of South America following the Pan-American Conference held in Rio de Janeiro. The relative tranquillity of domestic and foreign affairs, however, did not deter the New York *Times* from recording its apprehension over the "drift toward State Socialism" which it saw mounting in the nation. It had the following to say, and the casual reader must bear in mind that it was said about President Theodore Roosevelt at the beginning of 1907 and not about President Franklin D. Roosevelt at the beginning of 1940:

Mr. Roosevelt's advocacy of a large and always larger measure of government control over the country's business, his continual formulation of new plans for interference and regulation, and his evident belief in the virtue and efficacy of centralized power have accelerated this "drift." It would hardly be too much to say that they gave the initial impulse. We must not lose sight of the truth that active discussion of reforms and remedies usually proceeds from the existence of evils Evils there were, and considerable ones, but another mind than Mr. Roosevelt's might have prescribed other cures. Unquestionably he has won to himself a great following in the discussion and for the action he proposes.

These national and international events had little repercussion on the Fifth Judicial Circuit of Tennessee, except as they were chronicled and discussed in the weekly newspapers read by Judge Hull and the more thoughtful residents of his part of the state. The local philosophy about national political life was fairly simple, although not so elementary as that which Senator "Cotton Ed" Smith of South Carolina, now dean of the Senate, counsels to all young aspirants to Congress from a Southern state. Mr. Smith tells them they need to stand for only three things: states' rights, tariff for revenue only, and the supremacy of the white race.

When Judge Hull reached his decision to run for Congress in 1906 he had more in mind than those fundamentals. He was encouraged, by the friendships he was making and the support that was being offered to him as he drove around to his various terms of court, to believe that he might fill the Congressional seat occupied for twenty years by his early preceptor, Benton McMillin. Mr. McMillin had retired six years before. C. E. Snodgrass of Crossville and Morgan C. Fitzpatrick of Hartsville had been elected, in the order named, to succeed him, and the latter was succeeded by M. G. Butler, of Gainesboro, for the next two years.

From what Judge Hull heard around the judicial circuit, his fellow townsman, Mr. Butler, was by no means unassailable. After consulting his father, who promised him the unfailing financial and moral support that was always forthcoming for his favorite son, the Judge took the plunge. He resigned his judgeship and announced his candidacy to represent the Fourth Congressional District of Tennessee in the House of Representatives.

The same informal sort of primary system to select the Democratic nominee for the Congressional race existed as had been in vogue when Hull won the Democratic nomination to the state legislature fourteen years earlier. As a matter of fact, the system had been extended to cover the whole state, so far as concerned the selection of a Democratic nominee for the Senate, and the same primary which Hull was to enter was to register the choice of Tennessee Democrats between Edward W. Carmack and former Governor Bob Taylor for the Senate, so that a heavy vote could be expected.

In his judicial travels Hull had made many friends. Whether by accident or design, the serious, hard-working young judge had gradually attracted to himself the law-abiding and influential citizens of the counties where he held court. His judicial circuit, however, did not include the two largest Democratic counties in the Congressional district, and he had to face the handicap that both Butler and a third candidate, James T. Miller of Hartsville, were better known than he was in the Democratic strongholds of the Congressional district. He had, of course, the advantage that these two might cut each other's throats (as actually happened) in the more heavily Democratic sections, while he piled up a plurality in the half-and-half part of the district.

The constituencies on which he had to rely were of the sort that the late Nathan L. Bachman, veteran Tennessee politician who ended his career in the Senate, once described to President

Roosevelt. It was after the Democratic landslide of 1936, and Mr. Roosevelt asked Nate why there were so many Republicans in eastern Tennessee. The President complained that, no matter what avalanches of Democratic votes were started in other parts of the country, eastern Tennessee faithfully returned its same Republican members of Congress.

Nate explained how the schisms of the Civil War, the influence of Andrew Johnson and Parson Brownlow, and the influx of Northerners during the Reconstruction had left a Republican imprint on that part of the state which it was impossible to eradicate.

"I will admit, Mr. President, that we are not numerically strong in eastern Tennessee," he said. "But, qualitatively speaking, we have some of the staunchest Democrats in the country up there in those hills. Now, you take the time Hoover spoke at Elizabethton in 1928. There must have been thirty thousand people turned out for the meeting. They rode in from those hills all day long, until I never saw so many Republicans in one place in my life. It was a mighty fine speakin'.

"Well, sir, the next week they had a rape case on the criminal docket. The young woman said the crime took place in the bushes on the edge of this meetin'. The defense attorney decided to make that the strong point of his attack on her credibility when he came to cross-examine her.

" 'Young woman,' he shouted, 'you don't mean to tell this intelligent jury that such a horrible crime could take place right by this enormous crowd, within earshot and rescue distance of some of the finest citizens in this state, and not a man among them all would lift a hand to save you from this terrible fate?'

"The judge began to get interested. He adjusted his spectacles on the end of his nose, leaned over the bench, and interrupted the proceedings.

" 'Yes, young woman, what have you got to say to that?' he demanded. 'Are you trying to tell this court not a soul responded to your cries for help?'

" 'Oh, your honor,' she replied, 'I didn't make a sound. I was afraid they'd think I was hollerin' for Hoover.' "

Convinced Democrats of this description came to the support of Hull in his Congressional race, and the final results of the primary showed that he had secured 6298 votes to 6283 for Miller and 3103 for Butler. This margin of fifteen votes was too close to suit Mr. Miller, and he threatened a contest on the ground that Republicans had voted in the Democratic primary in one precinct of Fentress County. Judge C. E. Snodgrass, a mild-mannered man who was a former member of Congress, acted as Hull's attorney and announced to the state Democratic Congressional Committee, which would have had jurisdiction over the contest:

"Let 'em contest and we'll give 'em a bellyful."

That seems to have ended the talk of a contest over the primary, but Hull had then to face a hard election. He had a Republican opponent who ran him neck and neck and a Socialist rival who polled twenty-eight votes. However, he was returned as the winner and beat Miller two years later in the Democratic primary by nearly twelve hundred votes, thus permanently annexing the Democratic nomination for the district.

After he had recovered from the excitement of his two narrow escapes from defeat and was somewhat accustomed to the role of winner, Hull decided to move to Carthage, which he has called home ever since. Carthage, today, is as attractive a town of fifteen hundred inhabitants as can be found in the United States. It is built on a small hill in a bend of the Cumberland River, crossed by a fine new steel structure known as the Cordell Hull Bridge. On the other side of the river are larger, wooded hills which seem to tower as guardians above the neat little county seat and market town.

The view of the town as one drives in over Route 25 from Hartsville is reminiscent of an English village in the Cotswolds. The hills are decorative rather than severe. The houses are more prosperous in appearance than those to be found in most of the Hull country. They are well painted and their gardens show the unmistakable signs of constant care. The large brick house that Billy Hull bought when his favorite son wanted to move to Carthage is the first large place on the right as one enters the town from Hartsville. It is an imposing-looking place, with a large garden in front of it, screening it from the road, and another which slopes down toward the river behind the house.

The Congress to which Hull was elected was to be controlled

by the Republicans, although their majority in the House of Representatives was cut down to fifty-six. William Jennings Bryan went so far as to interpret it as a great moral victory for the Democratic party, but actually there was little general interest in it, being an off-year election.

Probably the most exciting contest of the elections of 1906 was the race for the governorship of New York, in which Charles Evans Hughes, later Chief Justice of the Supreme Court, narrowly defeated William Randolph Hearst, the newspaper publisher. Only the lukewarm support given to Mr. Hearst by the Tammany Hall organization prevented his election. Had Tammany gone all out, as it usually does for a Democratic nominee, Mr. Hearst would have been New York's governor and would have started on the road to the presidency which he had marked out for himself.

Tammany's lack of enthusiasm for Mr. Hearst was not based on moral and ethical grounds, as was most of the opposition to him, but on Mr. Hearst's outspoken antipathy for a number of years, expressed in season and out by his newspapers, toward the Fourteenth Street wigwam. Richard Croker, the retired chieftain of Tammany, cabled from his home near Dublin his complete astonishment that Tammany had permitted the nomination of Mr. Hearst. Asked about this political aberration, Charles F. Murphy, the contemporary leader of the organization, could only say that, "I don't like Mr. Hearst any more than Mr. Hearst likes me." He explained that Tammany had merely bowed to the wishes of the upstate Democrats.

Even President Roosevelt took a hand in the campaign. He authorized Elihu Root to issue a statement condemning Mr. Hearst's journalistic and political qualities and recalling that President McKinley's assassin had testified that he was "inspired" to his crime by reading the Hearst newspapers.

On the whole, the newspaper-reading public seemed to be more interested in the trial of Chester B. Gillette for the murder of Grace Brown, which Theodore Dreiser expanded into his moving novel, *An American Tragedy*, in Enrico Caruso's difficulties at the Yorkville police court on charges of molesting women at the monkey house of the Central Park Zoo, and in the fruity details of Evelyn Nesbit Thaw's testimony during the trial of her husband, Harry K. Thaw, for the killing of Stanford White, the architect.

Under the system which prevailed until the Twentieth Amendment to the Constitution was adopted, Hull did not take his seat in Congress until more than a year after he was elected. During that time he got himself settled at Carthage and engaged H. B. McGinness, a young local lawyer, to act as his secretary for his first term in Washington. Mr. McGinness served only one term, after which he was succeeded by Miss Will Harris, who is still Mr. Hull's private secretary. After the two years in Washington Mr. McGinness went back to Carthage to handle the Congressman's political and private business there, which he still does.

The "lameduck" session of the expiring Congress got under way with little enthusiasm and without the prospect of accomplishing much. President Roosevelt, in his annual message, advocated "a graduated inheritance tax and, if possible, a graduated income tax," but seemed to take for granted that nothing would happen to advance these executive wishes toward legislative enactment. He reversed his "trust-busting" attitude to a minor degree by asking amendment of the anti-trust laws in order to permit combinations of capital where it could be established that they would not be used for purposes improper to the public interest. Andrew Carnegie, the steel magnate, was so mollified by Mr. Roosevelt's concessions in the trust field that he gave an interview in which he approved of an inheritance tax while opposing any form of income tax.

The President was trying to obtain the widest possible use of the simplified spelling he used himself. He began to use such words as "thru," "tho," "dropt," and similar phonetic abbreviations in his official communications. After a series of wisecracking speeches by its more orthographically conservative members, the House of Representatives tucked into an appropriation bill a prohibition to the public printer to use any of this spelling in public documents, and the President gave up.

The agitation for revision of the copyright laws which springs up periodically and vainly was again being discussed in Congress, and Mark Twain delighted the national capital by wearing his white flannel suit through a near-blizzard to have a conference on the subject with Speaker Cannon.

James Bryce was appointed His Britannic Majesty's ambassador to the United States, to round out the career which was chiefly notable to Americans for *The American Commonwealth*, a description of this country's governmental machinery. While ambassador, Bryce compared his book with the operations he saw every day and took notes for the revised edition which most of us know. Mr. Bryce's advent was hailed in the American press principally because he had declined a peerage on the occasion of his appointment. The new ambassador felt that a commoner could more appropriately represent the British Crown in a country which had constitutional prohibitions against titles.

The pure-food law came into effect, with the Secretaries of the Treasury, Agriculture, and Commerce and Labor charged with its enforcement. It was regarded as a great innovation and was viewed with alarm in many quarters as another example of the spreading power of the Federal government over matters which had formerly been considered of exclusively local concern.

American music lovers were thrilled over a visit to this country by Giacomo Puccini and felt honored when he consented to attend a performance of his *Manon Lescaut* at the Metropolitan Opera, starring Caruso. The Italian composer announced that he was seeking an American theme for a new opera he intended to write but that he barred Indians because their costumes would be too much trouble for the producers to provide. He expressed his admiration for the works of Bret Harte. This quest resulted in *The Girl of the Golden West,* one of the least successful of his operas.

Among the little-noted events which were to have a bearing on the nation's future was the election, on January 15, 1907, of William Edgar Borah to the United States Senate by the Idaho legislature. Mr. Borah defeated his Democratic rival by more than three to one.

The national political situation was already becoming unsettled. Friends of Theodore Roosevelt pictured him as preparing to run for the Senate as soon as his term as President expired. He was said to admire the example of John Quincy Adams, who made a brilliant career for himself in the House of Representatives after retiring from the presidency. Less amiable descriptions of the President's frame of mind had it that he was fearful of the Republican party's chances of success in 1908 because of the uncertain state of public opinion, which John Sharp Williams summed up to his Republican foes in the House by saying: "The country is tired of you and afraid of us."

Relations with Japan were slowly worsening, largely because of the restrictive laws enacted in California, which found little sympathetic response on the Atlantic seaboard. President Roosevelt wanted Congress to amend the immigration laws so as to prevent the entry of coolie labor, to which the principal objections in California were addressed, in the same manner as had been done regarding Chinese immigration. These requirements had been not too sorely resented by the Chinese, although a boycott of American goods had reduced exports to China by 40 per cent the previous year. While that suggestion for Federal action was in abeyance he got the Attorney General to file suit against the State of California to force the admission of Japanese children to the public schools.

There developed a minor war scare which was of sufficient magnitude to prompt the New York *Times* to cable Viscount Hayashi, the Japanese Foreign Minister, for a declaration on the subject. On February 4 Viscount Shuzo Aoki, the Japanese ambassador in Washington, conveyed the following reply to the paper, which printed it prominently on its front page the following morning:

"The New York *Times* having addressed a telegram directly to the Imperial Government to ascertain the attitude of Japan, you are authorized to make a categorical declaration of the absolutely pacific intentions of Japan."

The projected Panama Canal remained the President's favorite vision, and he declined to be swayed in his judgment by the pessimistic predictions of some scientists, after the earthquake disaster at Kingston, Jamaica, that the same fate would befall the canal if it were ever constructed. In a speech delivered at Harvard University on February 23 Mr. Roosevelt summed up the events of the preceding decade, reserving most of his time for the accomplishments of his own administration. He said:

The last ten years have been years of great achievement for this nation. During that period we have dealt and are dealing with many different matters of great moment. We have acquired the

right to build, and are now building, the Panama Canal. We have
given wise government to the Philippines. We have dealt with exceedingly complex, difficult, and important questions in Cuba and
Santo Domingo. We have built up the navy, our surest safeguard
of peace and of the national honor.

We are making great progress in dealing with the question of ir-
rigation and forestry, of preserving to the public the rightful use of
the public lands and of the mineral wealth underlying them, and
with that group of vital questions which concern the proper super-
vision of the immense corporations doing an interstate business, the
proper control of the great highways of interstate commerce, the
proper regulation of industries which, if left unregulated, threaten
disaster to the body politic.

We have done many other things, such as securing the settlement
of the Alaska boundary. We have made progress in securing better
relations between capital and labor, justice as between them and as
regards the general public, and adequate protection for wagework-
ers. We have done much in enforcing the law alike against great
and small, against crimes of greed and cunning no less than against
crimes of violence and brutality. We have wrought mightily for the
peace of righteousness, both among the nations and in social and
industrial life here at home. Much has been done, and we are
girding up our loins to do more.

In all these matters there have been some men in public life and
some men in private life whose action has been at every point one
of barren criticism or fruitless obstruction. These men have had no
part or lot in the great record of achievement and success, the
record of good work worthily done.

The President's remark about "girding up our loins to do
more" gave rise to the same kind of speculation as to his future
political intentions as filled the press in the spring of 1940 about
Franklin D. Roosevelt's aspirations. The New York *Times* commented on March 1 that "the renomination of Mr. Roosevelt
is probably expected by some millions of his fellow citizens; they
look to see the convention run away with its leaders and take
Mr. Roosevelt in spite of his disclaimers."

The Fifty-ninth Congress expired at noon on March 4 to the
tones of the still-powerful voice of Senator Carmack of Tennessee, who was engaged in a filibuster against the ship subsidy bill
which the House had once rejected and then adopted on recon-

sideration. The principal achievement of this session of Congress appears to have been the appropriation of more than $1,000,-000,000 for one year's expenses of the government—the first time this total was reached in the nation's history. The editor of the New York *Times* viewed this phenomenon with a melancholy eye in one of a series of comments on the passing of the unlamented Congress. He wrote:

Nobody need be frightened by mere largeness of totals. It is the cause of the largeness which is, or ought to be, cautionary. Too much of it is honest graft, traceable to a generosity with the funds of others which the givers would not exercise in their own affairs, nor in their trust capacity, if there were any sense of responsibility, or any fear of publicity, in detail. A disproportionate amount is also due to military expenditures in times of peace, and a very large aggregate is due to the exercise by the national government of functions traditionally and properly local. In this encroachment by Federal upon state administrations, the citizens of each state suffer a diminution of their control over the government. This tendency of government is as obnoxious as the increase of expenses. We can pay the bills, but we cannot foresee whither we are being hurried by Federal activities which have sprung up like mushrooms and which are not of the wholesome variety altogether.

The paper's editorial page had the following caustic comment to make on the actual closing session:

Of all the incidents that marked the end of the Congressional session those upon which the contemplative mind will dwell with deepest satisfaction, it seems to us, are the waving of the flag of our Union by all the members of the House just before adjournment and the remarks of Senator Gallinger of New Hampshire, who declared with lionhearted fortitude that so long as he remained in public life he should continue to offer and to work for subsidy bills. There you have it—the old flag and an appropriation. Patriotism that plants itself upon these unshakable foundations can with entire security appeal to the country and evoke applause.

The concrete accomplishments of the sessions were summed up in the following language:

It is due, we believe, to the President's forbearance that the session has been so uneventful. He has refrained from urging upon

Congress any further measures for the reorganization of the business of the country, easily perceiving that a short session would afford insufficient time for the wrangling and turbulence which are now always expected to be the result of his attempts to bring Congress to his way of thinking. Next winter, we are told, his further great measures of policy will be brought forward, and he will attempt to extend, though we suppose he never expects to complete, his work of making industry and trade answerable to Federal commissions. It is understood that the next session is going to be interesting.[1]

The members of Congress had hardly reached their homes when the stock market succumbed to a mighty crash. The original slump on March 14 was followed by alternate falls and rises, with the net average going lower each time, suggestive of the process which started in September 1929. The newspapers and the experts blamed each succeeding drop on the dissemination of false reports by the "bears," whereas it was accelerated, if not caused, by the difficulties in which the railroads found themselves. These were in part financial and resulted from over-capitalization, or "stock watering," during the great contests between the financial giants to secure control of different systems, and in part were due to labor relations, which were becoming acute.

Early in the stock-market stage of the depression, before the public, or even the experts, generally realized that the stock gyrations, in which call money would be quoted at 3 per cent one day and at 25 per cent the next, were merely symptoms of deeper difficulties ahead, Wall Street leaders cabled J. P. Morgan, who was traveling in Europe, and he agreed to join any reasonable plan they could devise to steady the stock market.

Amid the financial gloom aviation was already beginning to attract widespread attention. Dr. Alexander Graham Bell, inventor of the telephone, announced in a press interview in London that he had been conducting some experiments, based on the Wright brothers' demonstrated theory of flight, which led him to believe that airships would one day enable a passenger to have his dinner in America and his breakfast the next morning in Europe—a prediction that might by now have been fulfilled if

[1]Compare predictions made at the end of 1940 about President Franklin D. Roosevelt's third term

two European wars had not intervened. Dr. Bell, however, tempered his forecast with an almost ghastly preview of the future.

"My expectation," he told his interviewers, "is that an airship will be perfected capable of making 150 to 200 miles an hour. My opinion, however, is that the next step in aerial flight will take the form of such improvements as will make possible the creation of aerial battleships."

The genial inventor went on to urge upon America the early development of these "aerial battleships" which, he said, would undoubtedly revolutionize methods of making warfare throughout the world.

Despite such martial talk the nations of the world were sending their representatives to The Hague in an attempt to codify international law in relation to war and to agree on principles to govern the treatment of neutrals in time of conflict. Among the troublesome concepts with which the international jurists had to contend was one which Secretary Hull has often encountered in his dealings with Latin America. Dr. Luis M. Drago, a delegate from Argentina, was pressing his own doctrine that the collection of public debts by force is wrong. This was an extension of an earlier theory advanced by another Argentinean, Dr. Carlos Calvo, that no claim against a government by a foreign citizen or a foreign government is valid and that the collection of private claims does not justify armed intervention by a government. In Hull's time at the State Department the Mexican government has been the steadiest adherent to these ideas.

The big development while Hull was waiting to take his seat in the House of Representatives, however, was the deepening financial panic. By the end of May gold exports had started, and Wall Street was alarmed at reports that $775,000 worth of bullion was to be shipped to Paris. The drain of gold grew in volume as the months went on. The familiar phenomena began to present themselves. The banks reported heavy surpluses which were in the nature of excess reserves, the public preferring to leave its bank accounts in liquid form until the storm had spent itself. At first there was little public discussion of the situation, but by June 21 Frank A. Vanderlip, vice-president of the National City Bank, felt obliged to warn the Virginia Bankers' Association, meeting at Jamestown, that "the railroads are curtailing expenditures, bankers are inclined to exercise caution in extending accommodation."

In August came Judge Kenesaw Mountain Landis' historic fine of $29,240,000 against the Standard Oil Company for alleged acceptance of illegal rebates. The judge, in his Federal district court in Chicago, arrived at this huge penalty by assessing the maximum fine of $20,000 on each of 1462 counts of which the Standard Oil Company had been found guilty.

Henry Seligman, the New York banker, was traveling in Europe that summer and gave a press interview in Paris in which he said that "the alarm caused among genuine investors by the government's anti-trust policy accounts largely for the drop in prices" on the stock exchange.

"It is not merely a speculators' scare," Mr. Seligman said. "The government has created a feeling of uncertainty which reacts not only on the corporations but on the immense number of people with small incomes, possessing a limited amount of capital invested in trust concerns and other business enterprises. They feel that the government's policy is antagonistic to their interests as people seeking to obtain a good return on their investments."

The conservative press began to speak of "the Roosevelt slump," and on August 17 the New York *Times* devoted its leading editorial to the general subject of the President's responsibility for the business reaction. The editorial said:

It can no longer be doubted that great numbers of the businessmen of the country, certainly a majority of the chief businessmen of the country, would regard the election of Mr. Roosevelt to another term of the presidency as a national calamity. . . . It is not merely his policies but the even harsher policies of his countless imitators that cause apprehension. . . . Mr. Roosevelt is not only a determined man, obdurate in adherence to ways he has chosen, but he is as little likely as any man in the country to be influenced by the menace or the presence of business calamity. He is untrained in business, has had no experience, does not know what it is to lose money or risk losing it in personal ventures. He has been in public office all his life, and such mistakes as he has made have been paid for out of public funds.

The national proving ground for Cordell Hull's embryo economic theories was in process of formation. The representative-elect spent the summer and fall getting his affairs in Carthage sufficiently in shape to permit him a prolonged absence. He understood the hazards of a political life, but he had a strong hunch that Washington would claim him for the most part of many years to come. Soon after Thanksgiving he packed his bag and unostentatiously set out for the national capital.

CHAPTER VII

The Man behind the Scenes

THE SIXTIETH CONGRESS met for the first time on Monday, December 2, 1907. The House of Representatives, being composed entirely of newly elected members (two thirds of the Senate, of course, were serving out their elected terms), was called to order by its clerk, Alex McDowell.

Its chaplain, the Rev. Henry D. Couden, D.D., prayed God that the present Congress, "however great and illustrious have been its predecessors, may rise superior to them all in the wisdom of its resolves and enactments."

After the prayer the roll was called, as is the custom, to see whether a quorum had arrived for the transaction of the nation's legislative business. To this roll call, 385 members answered their names.

Among those responding "present" was a new representative from the Fourth District in Tennessee—Cordell Hull. The first business on which he had to make up his mind was the election of a Speaker, to which the House proceeded at once. Hull dutifully cast his vote, along with 161 other Democrats, in favor of John Sharp Williams, the Democratic floor leader, but 213 Republicans snowed them under to re-elect Joseph G. Cannon of Illinois. "Uncle Joe" signalized the third of his four elections as Speaker in a neat little speech before inviting the members to take the oath of office.

"The principles of the past may help us to the extent of showing us the points of the compass," he said, "but beyond that we must depend on our own wisdom, our own constancy, our own industry, and our own fidelity to duty."

The new member from the Fourth Tennessee District was thirty-six years old. He contributed the following biography of himself to the *Congressional Directory:*

Cordell Hull, Democrat, of Carthage, was born October 2, 1871, in Overton (now Pickett) County, Tennessee; was graduated from the Law Department of Cumberland University, Lebanon, Tennessee, and is a lawyer by profession; was a member of the lower house of the state legislature two terms; served in the Fourth Regiment, Tennessee Volunteer Infantry, during the Spanish-American War, with the rank of captain. Later was appointed by the governor, and afterward elected, judge of the fifth judicial district, which position was resigned during his race for Congress; was elected to the Sixtieth Congress, receiving 11,961 votes to 10,132 for J. E. Oliver, Republican, and 28 for J. T. McColgan, Socialist.

Hull's colleagues in the House included a number of men whose names were to become better known. There were Charles A. Lindbergh of Minnesota, father of the distinguished airplane pilot; Gilbert M. Hitchcock of Nebraska, who was to lead the fight in the Senate for the League of Nations; Albert S. Burleson of Texas, who was to be Woodrow Wilson's Postmaster General; Nicholas Longworth of Ohio and Henry T. Rainey of Illinois, both of whom were to become Speakers of the House; Andrew J. Volstead of Minnesota, whose prohibition-enforcement law was to plague his fellow citizens for a decade; James E. Watson of Indiana, who was to become one of the most influential figures of the Republican party; Frank O. Lowden of Illinois, a future aspirant for the Republican presidential nomination; Oscar W. Underwood of Alabama, whose faithful supporters were to help deadlock the Democratic National Convention at Madison Square Garden in 1924; Joseph T. Robinson of Arkansas, destined to be fatally stricken while fighting, as Senate majority leader, for President Roosevelt's plan to reorganize the Supreme Court in 1937; Edwin Denby of Michigan, who was to serve President Harding as Secretary of the Navy; John Sharp Williams of Mississippi, a great orator and long-time power in the

Democratic party; George W. Norris of Nebraska, a lifelong liberal whose impact on American political life has yet to be assayed; Carter Glass of Virginia, father of the Federal Reserve System; John Nance Garner of Texas, a later Speaker of the House, twice Vice-President of the United States, and half-hearted candidate for the presidency in 1940; Morris Sheppard of Texas, author of the Eighteenth, or Prohibition, Amendment; Adolph J Sabath of Illinois, who was to outlast them all in consecutive service in the House.

The members of the new Congress had had their salaries obligingly increased, by the "lameduck" session a year earlier, from $5000 to $7500 a year. What little criticism had greeted the step was by now forgotten, and the newcomers felt conscience-free to enjoy the windfall without having to justify it to their constituents.

The new member from Tennessee went through the usual initiation of a Congressional neophyte. During his first four years in the House he drew nothing better in the way of committee assignments than membership on the relatively innocuous organizations dealing with pensions and reform in the civil service. In the Sixty-Second Congress, which opened its deliberations on December 4, 1911, he was assigned to the Ways and Means Committee—a development which was to pave the way for his cumulative influence on the nation's economic legislation.

The state of the nation when Hull took his seat in the House of Representatives was bad. The country was in the throes of what was then called a panic—a disagreeable condition of affairs which was later to be known as a depression. In those days the politicians thought almost exclusively in terms of money when they tried to legislate hard times out of existence. The leaders under whom the young Tennessean began his service talked volubly and vaguely of "currency reform" as the panacea which would deliver the country from the doldrums.

Compared with more recent economic disturbances, the panic of 1907 was not a very serious affair. Comparatively little mention of it was made in the newspapers of the period. The metropolitan papers were publishing pages of pictures illustrating the recent visit of state paid by the German Emperor to the King of England One of them portrayed a remarkable luncheon held at Windsor Castle. The guests of King Edward included the German Kaiser and his Empress, the Queen of Portugal, King Alfonso XIII of Spain, who was then unmarried, and the Queen of Norway. This group of royalty was photographed along with the hostess, Queen Alexandra. The result was on the hazy side but was published with great pride by American editors above an explanation that it was taken indoors under an arc light. This was a photographic triumph in those days.

The *Mauretania* was just sailing from New York on the return portion of her maiden voyage. On her passenger list was the Duchess of Marlborough, whose mother, Mrs. O. H. P. Belmont, went to the pier to see her off. Stuyvesant Fish and E. H. Harriman were fighting their epochal battle for financial control of the Illinois Central Railroad.

New York was leading a normally tranquil life. Victor Moore was playing at the Knickerbocker in *The Talk of New York,* and May Robson was appearing at the Garden Theater in *The Rejuvenation of Aunt Mary.* The Boston Symphony Orchestra was playing at Carnegie Hall with Paderewski as its soloist, and Walter Damrosch was conducting the New York Symphony Orchestra, supporting Josef Hofmann's piano playing. *The Merry Widow* was running at the New Amsterdam, with seats selling seven weeks ahead. John Drew was playing at the Empire in *My Wife.* Elsie Janis was performing at Wallack's in *The Hoyden,* and Nazimova was playing in Ibsen's *A Doll's House* at the Bijou.

In Washington the political scene was as relatively normal. Senator Foraker had announced that he would contest William Howard Taft's aspirations for the Republican presidential nomination the next spring, but this threat did not appear to alarm the public seriously. It was taken for granted that Mr. Taft would coast in under the blessing of President Theodore Roosevelt. "Uncle Joe" Cannon, the tyrannical Speaker of the House, came out foursquare for "currency reform" in a press interview granted just before the Sixtieth Congress began its labors, adding that the nation's prosperity could never be served by "tariff tinkering."

President Roosevelt, in his message on the state of the Union, urged Congress to require Federal incorporation of railroads and other large corporations and to demand the fullest publicity concerning their doings. He wanted the monetary laws revised to include "emergency currency" and he favored enactment of income and inheritance taxes. He called for four new battleships with coaling stations and docks in the Pacific, as well as a postal savings-bank system and conservation of the country's natural resources, but he also opposed any uprooting of the protective tariff.

The New York *Times* treated Mr. Roosevelt's communication to the Congress with something less than the objectivity it employs today. Its lead on the message story read as follows:

President Roosevelt's message was received by the Senate and House with interest and some show of amusement, but the amusement seemed to outlast the interest.

There were other familiar phenomena in the Washington political scene. The New York *Times* reported that Senator Aldrich and Senator Crane were summoned to the White House to discuss monetary legislation with President Roosevelt. The account said:

It has been some time since the senators have been honored with an exclusive audience with the President Two years ago they were called in a few times to confer in regard to the rate bill, but the President did not fancy their views then, and since that time they have been chary of offering them. . . . That the President believes the administration will reap more profit getting on the good side of these legislators is generally believed. That he does not want them to go ahead without his help and draft a bill acceptable to the banking, manufacturing, and business interests of the country and thus obtain the credit for a restoration of confidence is certain.

In Chicago an automobile show was under way, and the management proudly announced that the exhibits attained a value of two million dollars. The big show of the year, of course, was held in Paris, and one newspaper correspondent devoted most of a column to the amazing temerity of an American manufacturer called the Ford Motor Company in venturing to show its products on the same floor with the superb French automobiles. Incidentally, Mr. Ford was the only American exhibitor at the Paris show.

It was in this sort of national setting that the representative from the Fourth Tennessee District took his seat in the house. He busied himself with the usual minor duties that a member of Congress has to perform for his constituency. The first bill he persuaded the House to pass granted permission to the Nashville and Northeastern Railway to build a bridge across the Cumberland River.

He tried to push a number of other projects supposed to be of aid and interest to the dwellers in and around Carthage. These included a bill to construct a public building at Cookeville, which became a law; another to build an observatory for the Weather Bureau on Crab Orchard Mountain; another to improve the Cumberland River; another to erect a public building at Dayton; and one to reimburse his alma mater, Cumberland University, for a claim it held against the government.

However, his legislative projects were not all limited to such local matters. He proposed legislation to repeal the tariff duties on agricultural implements, to levy and collect an income tax, to investigate campaign expenditures, and interested himself in other questions of such a character as must have branded him a near-Socialist to the conservative public of the day. The ideas that were behind them, however, have come to be long-accepted reality by now.

The Tennessee senators were James B. Frazier of Chattanooga and Robert Love Taylor of Nashville, the former governor who had issued Hull's commission as a captain in 1898. His brother, Alfred A. Taylor, had remained in the portion of eastern Tennessee from which they came and was a Republican. In 1886 they ran against each other for the governorship, and Bob won, largely because of his superior fiddling ability. Before coming to the Senate, Bob had been governor of Tennessee three times and had served in the House from the eastern Tennessee district which his father and his brother had represented before him. Alf got a belated revenge, long after Bob's death, by being elected governor of Tennessee in the Republican landslide of 1920, in which Hull was defeated for the only time in his life.

Cordell Hull had little to do with them, although he was on good enough terms with them. Senators, in those days, were elected by the state legislatures and felt themselves immensely superior to the poor representatives who had to present themselves dutifully every two years to the whimsies of the electorate.

As a matter of fact, the new representative made friends slowly in the strange environment of the national capital. He went to live at the Raleigh Hotel, which was second in splendor only to the fashionable Shoreham, instead of the Congress Hall, where most of the politicians lived. He took no part in the high jinks there or at the club in I Street where "Uncle Joe" Cannon, Nick Longworth, and the other bloods of Congress held their poker games and stag evenings.

Young Hull was faithful in his attendance on the floor of the House and followed the debates attentively. Even when he retired behind the rail, in the space between the actual House floor and the Democratic cloakroom, to smoke one of his innumerable cigars, he continued to listen to the floor proceedings instead of joining in the chatter of the other Democrats standing there, undecided whether they would desert the dull session or remain where they could be counted in case a quorum was questioned.

His colleagues soon found Hull to be a serious, thoughtful, and very hard-working new member. He spent most of his spare time studying up on the projects before Congress, and the newer members soon dropped into the habit of asking him for information or advice on pending legislation.

The national situation gave him plenty of scope for mentally testing his budding economic and monetary theories. As the session wore on, the panic was accentuated. Money ceased to circulate, and ordinary business was transacted almost wholly by means of clearinghouse certificates that the banks gave out themselves.

The American Academy of Political and Social Science devoted its annual meeting to speeches offering various remedies for the existing difficulties the current system of banking and money had brought on itself. Frank A. Vanderlip, who presided at the meeting, introduced the subject in the following language, which sounds strangely familiar to all who went through the bank holiday of 1933:

I believe there has never been a time in our political history when there was a greater necessity than there is now for a broad educational movement relative to financial affairs. The causes of this re-

markable disturbance are more or less obscure; at least men who
are expert in finance are not agreed upon them.

Some attribute it to the policies of the President, others to the
gamblers of Wall Street. The truth lies in neither of these extremes,
nor, indeed, between them. It is broader and deeper than either.

As the panic spread, the Democrats throughout the country
lost no opportunity for blaming the hard times on the Republicans, who had been uninterruptedly in power for twelve years.
Some of the Republican political chiefs, particularly those in the
Southern states, became genuinely alarmed that they would be
turned out of office the following autumn if they allowed to go
through the generally accepted plan for the presidential nomination to go to William Howard Taft, the Secretary of War, at the
Republican convention at Chicago the next spring.

They started a movement to draft Theodore Roosevelt to run
again, using the argument that this would create no third-term
issue since the incumbent had been elected only once, in 1904,
and that his succession on McKinley's death ought not to be
counted against him. He had done only what the Constitution
required of him, they contended.

This kind of talk reached the ears of Henry Watterson, and
he thundered in the Louisville *Courier-Journal* against "the failure of the President to make any sign or utter any word touching a third term for himself in the White House," finding this
omission particularly surprising "in the case of a man so wedded
to the theatrical and so loving dramatic effects."

Whether or not he was moved by Marse Henry's clarion call,
Mr. Roosevelt found it expedient to repeat, a few days after the
editorial had appeared (while his daughter, Mrs. Nicholas Longworth, was undergoing an operation for appendicitis in the White
House), the pledge he had given upon his election in 1904. At
that time he had said:

"The wise custom which limits the President to two terms
regards the substance and not the form, and under no circumstances will I be candidate for or accept another nomination."

He must have regretted those words many times as they were
thrown in his teeth during the Bull Moose campaign of 1912.
At this epoch, however, he concluded his statement by saying

that "I have not changed and shall not change the decision thus announced."

Heartened by this clarification of the principal problem that had been bothering him, Mr. Taft undertook to defend Mr. Roosevelt's fiscal and monetary policies before the Merchants' Association in New York City, absolving the President from all blame for the panic. Mr. Taft had just returned from a triumphal tour of the Philippines, which may account for a certain oracular quality in his definition of the current economic disturbance.

"Expenses of operation and wages increase," he told the eagerly listening merchants, "and the profit from the new enterprises grows smaller. The loanable capital gradually changes its form into investments less and less convertible. Much of that which might be capital is wasted in unwise enterprises, in extravagance in living, in wars and absolute destruction of property, until the available free capital becomes well-nigh exhausted the world over."

The presidential crown prince, as Taft then was, had good reason to try for the best impression possible in New York, both for himself and his party, for there a movement of some importance was gathering to boom Governor Charles Evans Hughes for the Republican presidential nomination. The New York *Times* took this movement seriously and wishfully enough to publish a large photograph of the governor sporting a broad smile above the caption: "Proof positive of the governor's genial side." The photograph showed the governor wearing exactly the same beard (though it was darker in color) as is now worn by the former chief justice of the United States Supreme Court.

In addition to the third-term issue another political controversy which was to shake the country to its foundations was in the making. This was prohibition. Georgia, Maine, Kansas, and North Dakota were already dry, but the bishops of the Southern Methodist Church were to have to wait another four years before they could persuade Hull's Tennessee to follow in that same path.

Already the situation was so serious that John A. Roebling gave up his house in Asheville, North Carolina, where he had lived for ten years, when the town voted for prohibition. He

deeded his $500,000 estate to the Presbyterian Church and shook
Asheville's dust from his shoes with a parting blast at the political idiocy and presumption of the state in trying to tell a gentleman whether he should drink or not.

Divorce, another social problem which has plagued politicians
for many years, was on the increase as the Supreme Court in
New York was grinding out uncontested decrees at the rate of
one every ten minutes. Clubwomen viewed this development
with the greatest alarm as they debated the merits and morals
of Elinor Glyn's *Three Weeks* and, indeed, those of the author-
ess herself.

The repercussions of the panic spread overseas and inspired
Henri Rochefort in Paris to write in *Le Figaro* a humorous piece
which was meant to carry a modicum of truth. He reported:

France is anxious. She likes Americans. She awaits them as a student awaits a letter carrier who ought to bring him funds from
home.

Every day, jewelers, picture dealers, gamblers, and, let us confess it, fair ladies consult the list of *voyageurs* disembarking at Le
Havre.

Yesterday an American was finally perceived crossing Paris in an
automobile. In his rapid rush he knocked over a pedestrian, but so
glad were Parisians to see him that no one paid any attention to
this insignificant adventure. He was immediately surrounded by all
the merchants in the neighborhood. Diamond merchants, antiquari-
ans, automakers, tailors, and a host of others fought for this legitimate prey, which has really become too rare.

I can't swear that this is so, but I understand this American's
mail the next morning was also filled with perfumed notes declaring
the affection of the correspondents for the sister republic.

In the House of Representatives the Democrats, as usual,
could not stand prosperity. They were the minority party by only
fifty-odd seats, meaning that a gain of less than thirty in the
next election would give them control. With the panic as a ready-
made issue, they appeared to have a good chance. The Democratic members of the House fell out through the process of
counting such electoral chickens long before they had a chance
to hatch.

John Sharp Williams, of Mississippi, was the minority leader.

He was unpopular with many of his supposed followers, including Hull, because of his close friendship for Speaker Cannon. Most of the Democrats smarted under Uncle Joe's barely concealed tyranny in dealing with the minority.

David Albaugh de Armond, of Missouri, was a great rival of John Sharp Williams—so much so that they had a fist fight on the floor during Hull's first few days in the House. De Armond had tried to beat Williams for the leadership. Now, when Williams was about to go to the Senate, he thought he ought to get the coveted post, which would lead to the Speakership if the Democrats should get control of the House, but Williams and other old heads were planning to select Champ Clark, also of Missouri, as his successor.

Moreover, many Democrats resented the maneuvers of William Jennings Bryan to secure the next party nomination for the presidency, after having been its unsuccessful nominee twice before. The Great Commoner was telling friends that he was the logical heir to Theodore Roosevelt's progressive administrations and that the public would not fail to recognize that alleged fact. Bryan went so far as to endorse, and to ask Congressional Democrats to vote for, the Aldrich bill to expand the note-issuing powers of the national banks by $500,000,000, which would almost double the amount of currency in circulation. Hull was dubious of this too-ready-made remedy, although he took no part in the floor debates. On the first occasion it came before the House, in the form of the Vreeland bill, he was content merely to vote "present," but when the House considered the Senate substitute, which was the Aldrich bill, he voted "no."

On March 18, 1908, he delivered his maiden speech in Congress. In those days the first speeches of new members attracted more attention than they do nowadays. The neophyte bided his time until there came a lull in the legislative business of the House or the Senate and then arranged with the leaders to take the floor. He tried to stage his first appearance at a time when there was likely to be a good audience in the chamber, and he asked the leaders and his friends to pass the word around the cloakrooms. Many members would stay, largely out of curiosity, and the newcomer would be judged severely, but fairly, on his first speech.

The forthcoming test recalled to Hull his feelings before the speech at Willow Grove on the respective merits of George Washington and Christopher Columbus. He took the Congressional speech just as seriously and worked just as hard on it, and the results were just as gratifying. The speech attracted attention to him from older men who would not otherwise have noticed him for years, and it was a factor impelling the invitation from Kitchin, Hughes, and Hay to help in the reorganization plan. In addition to urging the immediate enactment of an income tax, Hull made the following principal points in his first speech:

1. He castigated what he called "government by injunction" —the process under which large corporations could hamper the work of regulatory governmental agencies by securing serial injunctions from friendly judges.[1]

2. He favored compulsory arbitration of disputes between employees and employers engaged in interstate commerce.

3. He urged more stringent Federal control of railroad and steamship rates.

4. He inveighed against paternalism, especially condemning a recent statement by President Theodore Roosevelt that "we need, through executive action, through legislative, and through judicial interpretation and construction of law, to increase the power of the Federal government."

5. He accused President Roosevelt of despotism, adding that "his contempt and utter disregard for the plain mandates of the Constitution have become proverbial."

6. He charged that the Republican administration's threats to enforce the anti-trust laws were mere bluffs and demanded "suppression of lawless combinations and proper curbing of corporate wealth."

7. He reproached the Republican side of the House that "on the subject of taxation this party has always stood for the doctrine that taxation is a blessing to the poor but a curse to the rich."

[1]Among these he numbered William Howard Taft who, when sitting on the Circuit Court of Appeals at Cincinnati, had granted injunctions preventing the men of the Northern Pacific Railroad from striking and, in the same year (1894), had granted an injunction against the Pullman boycott. Hull told the House that the forthcoming Republican candidate for the presidency had "thus rammed the rod of judicial oppression, as a red-hot iron, down the throat of American labor."

After the turn of the year the panic grew worse. Suicides of ruined stock-market traders were announced in increasing number as 1908 began. One speculator came up to New York from South Carolina to beg his broker to carry him, without margin, for a little longer until he could make back the $75,000, everything he had in the world, which he had lost. When the broker declared himself unable to do that, the trader killed him and then shot himself.

The Seaboard Airline asked for receivers, and there were threats of a Congressional investigation of its activities and finances.

In contrast to the mounting evidences of economic distress, the newspapers were able to announce that Miss Gladys Vanderbilt was to give Count Laszlo Szechenyi a wedding present of $5,000,000 to mark their marriage at St. Patrick's Cathedral, although she prudently kept title to the principal, bestowing only the income on her bridegroom.

The Episcopal Church felt called upon to pour balm on the wounded spirits of its members. Bishop Paddock of eastern Oregon, preaching at Christ Church in New York, told his congregation that God "calls some men to make money—a million it may be in one case, a thousand in another.

"Whatever difference there may be between the men who make these two sums is God-given," he added, by way of comfort, "and the million man should realize that fact and live accordingly."

Life went on, even if cash was scarce. Mary Garden sang *Louise* for the first time in the United States at the Manhattan Opera House as a proud presentation of Oscar Hammerstein, and Mr. Taft made it known that, in his opinion, it was "highly beneficial and entirely lawful for laborers to unite in their common interests."

People's habits were changing. The New York Board of Aldermen, egged on by Tim Sullivan, passed an ordinance making it unlawful for the proprietor or manager of any public place to permit women to smoke therein. The measure did not specify how the unfortunate proprietors or managers were to enforce the ban. Women arriving from Europe, where they had learned to smoke publicly or privately, announced they would pay no attention whatever to the New York law, and apparently didn't.

Cordell Hull, busy with his legislative duties down in Washington, was totally uninterested in this New York experiment at enforced propriety for the frail sex. His own state legislature, under the scourge of the Southern Methodist bishops, whose headquarters are in Nashville and who were to keep Tennessee's nose so tightly against the prohibition grindstone, had outlawed cigarettes for men, women, and children alike. When I went to college in Tennessee it was unlawful not only to sell cigarettes but cigarette papers as well. As late as 1920 Miss Anne Morgan was requested by the manager of the Hermitage Hotel in Nashville to retire to the ladies' rest room to smoke a cigarette she unthinkingly lighted in the public dining room at the end of a luncheon given in her honor.

A small cloud appeared on the foreign horizon—the forerunner of a storm Cordell Hull was to be forced to ride out more than thirty years later. The Imperial Japanese government rejected informal American suggestions that it voluntarily limit Japanese emigration to the United States in a diplomatic effort to forestall an exclusion act by Congress. The Japanese government, which was then building a naval base six hundred miles from Manila, considered any such step as incompatible with the national dignity.

Bent then, as now, on the establishment of a "new order" in Asia, the Japanese were busy "organizing" Korea. A French writer named Leo Byram visited Korea and was moved to publish a lyrical volume on the subject of little Japan becoming great. He wrote with awe and admiration of the efficiency of the Japanese administration which was so thoroughly "organized" that Korean mandarins dodged hastily to the side of the road when the humblest Japanese coolie came past.

Another portent of the future was the almost incredible report sent from France to automobile editors, telling of more than a hundred "movable dwellings," or "automobile residences," that were being used for living quarters. One picture of this ancestor of the ubiquitous trailer of today looked exactly like the caboose of a freight train and may have been one with a gasoline engine concealed inside.

Congress was by no means completely unaware of the technological progress that was beginning its swift movement. Toward the end of Cordell Hull's first term in Congress his namesake and senior, Representative Hull of Iowa, who was chairman of the House Military Affairs Committee, called on President Theodore Roosevelt and urged that the army purchase an airship for experiments in aerial cooperation with ground forces. Mr. Roosevelt was unconvinced and succeeded in talking the representative out of his project. In the administration, however, Secretary of the Navy Metcalf recommended that Congress enact legislation to give the government control of wireless telegraphy.

More than usual signs of unrest were discernible in Europe. King Carlos and the Crown Prince were assassinated in Portugal. The latter's son ascended the throne as Manuel II but ruled only by the kind permission of the real copyright owner, Joao Franco, the dictator. In Poland the nationalists were demanding a plebiscite on the question, "Do you consider that the Prussian government treats unjustly the Poles within its jurisdiction?" To the south of us things were looking brighter as four Argentine cruisers and one Chilean cruiser gathered at Punta Arenas to give a hearty welcome to the United States fleet, the irritation between this country and Chile, about which Tennessee Democrats complained so bitterly in the time of President Harrison, apparently having been forgotten and forgiven.

At the opening of his second term in Congress, Hull offered a few pro forma bills and resolutions. Among them were a bill to repeal the tariff duties on antitoxin and diphtheria serum, another to prepare a roster of the armies of the United States, another to improve the Obed River where his father's log rafts used to be assembled, and a resolution calling for an inquiry into the nation's diplomatic and consular service to determine why men from the cotton-growing states could not get jobs therein.

But his principal interest lay in the enactment of income and inheritance taxes Like many other Southern Democrats, he had never been able to swallow the Supreme Court's decision in 1895 which nullified the existing income-tax law and had prevented enactment of another. He attacked it from the floor of the House early in the session of 1909 in language that was very like that used by New Dealers during the Supreme Court fight of 1937.

"No decision of any court of last resort has been so universally condemned or its soundness so generally questioned as has this one," he told the House, adding that, "I would suggest that no court of last resort in any other country undertakes to veto or nullify a solemn enactment of the legislative branch."

He was all for having Congress raise the issue again by passing a new law and throwing it into the Supreme Court's lap, reminding his colleagues that "judicial interpretation and construction is sometimes affected by new judicial philosophy and by new and changed conditions in the social and economic world."

Hull had introduced, at the beginning of the session, a resolution seeking an investigation into the wages and manufactures of foreign countries and their income taxes. This was in the nature of a preliminary step toward the serious consideration he desired for his income-tax bill which he had drawn to avoid the objections the Supreme Court had raised to the 1894 act. One of the features of Hull's proposal was a flat tax rate of 3 per cent on the incomes of American citizens residing abroad.

In his fiscal reasoning, income and inheritance taxes were the more essential the higher Congress boosted the tariff, the operation of which, Hull reasoned, was always in the direction of further concentration of wealth in the hands of the favored few whose industries were protected against foreign competition. From the point of view of supporting the financial needs of the government, Hull contended that the tariff had been raised so high that it produced no revenue but merely acted as an insurmountable trade barrier, and he urged the income and inheritance taxes as means of supplying this deficiency.

"Formerly the revenues kept pace with expenditures," he said on the floor on March 20, 1909, "but during recent years our administrative policies have been so extravagant as to cause the government expenditures to rise rapidly, to go up by leaps and bounds, so that our revenues have failed to increase proportionately."

In support of the philosophy of an inheritance tax, he said:

"The right to transmit property is not a natural one but is more in the nature of a privilege granted the citizens by law. The citizen who amasses great wealth is protected in both his personal and property rights by the laws of the state and Federal government while he is engaged in so doing. In return for such protection it would be but a mild condition imposed upon the transmission of swollen and other fortunes to lay a reasonable tax thereon."

Hull and his fellow Democrats were on the popular side of the income-tax debate, and the Republicans suddenly decided to jump on the band wagon. In June President Taft sent a message to Congress urging that an amendment to the Constitution, specifically authorizing the Federal government to levy an income tax irrespective of apportionment according to the population of the various states, be offered to the legislatures for ratification.

Senators Bailey and Cummins collaborated on what is now the Sixteenth Amendment to the Constitution, and their proposal passed the Senate. When it came before the House, Hull was suspicious. He voted for it but took the floor to place his misgivings on record.

"During the past few weeks," he said on July 12, "the unexpected spectacle of certain so-called 'old-line conservative' Republican leaders in Congress suddenly reversing their attitude of a lifetime and seemingly espousing, though with ill-concealed reluctance, the proposed income-tax amendment to the Constitution has been the occasion of universal surprise and wonder."

He reminded the House that the statutory ratification of a Constitutional amendment would take a long time (the Sixteenth Amendment was finally ratified and proclaimed in 1913) and urged that his income-tax bill be immediately enacted so that the Supreme Court could have a chance to see whether it had changed its mind since 1895. He recalled that he had hoped to propose his bill as an amendment to the Payne tariff bill but that "the peculiar and ironclad rules of the House" prevented. The Democratic side of the House, in moving recommittal of the bill, had tried to instruct that an income-tax amendment be inserted (Hull had persuaded Champ Clark to include this section in the motion to recommit), but the majority had voted that motion down. In the Senate a corporation tax had been added as a sop to circumvent the movement for an income tax.

Unmoved by this appeal, the Republican majority proceeded to put through the Constitutional amendment, despite its "ill-concealed reluctance," and ignored Hull's bill for an immediate income tax. Neither he nor the Republicans realized they were giving him the opportunity, four years later, to draft the first un-challenged income-tax law the country ever had.

After the Democrats captured control of the House in the off-year elections of 1910, Hull began to reap the reward of his first four hard-working years of Congressional service. He had at-tracted the attention of some of the real liberals in the Democratic ranks, and these men were planning to reorganize the lower branch of Congress from top to bottom, in line with the party pledges that had been given so often and so vainly in past platforms. They were determined, for a start, to curb the power of the Speaker, which "Uncle Joe" Cannon had exercised so despotically, and to make more flexible those "peculiar and ironclad rules" about which Hull had complained. Actually, his bad experience in try-ing to offer his income-tax amendment to the Payne-Aldrich bill sprang merely from the arbitrary rules of recognition which Mr. Cannon made up as he went along. The Speaker simply would not recognize the gentleman from Tennessee (Mr. Hull) for the pur-pose of offering an amendment.

Soon after the short session of Congress convened, following the elections of 1910, Hull was approached by three Democrats who were quietly fomenting a parliamentary revolution to take place when the newly elected House, which would have a Demo-cratic majority, should start to work a year later. These conspira-tors were Claude Kitchin, of the Second District of North Caro-lina, who never held public office until elected to Congress ten years earlier; James Hay, of the Seventh District of Virginia, who had served as commonwealth attorney for twelve years, as a member of the House of Delegates for six years, and as a state senator for two years before coming to Congress fourteen years before; and William Hughes, of the Sixth District of New Jersey, who had served in the Second New Jersey Volunteers in the Spanish-American War and had been in Congress for six years.

All three of them had been in the House longer than Hull, and they appreciated the difficulty of the task they were setting them-selves. They knew they could count on Hull for lots of hard work, if they could convert him, and they knew they could count on his discretion. For his part, he was thoroughly in sympathy with what they had in mind but was doubtful whether the four of them could put it across. He asked for a day to think it over and tactfully approached Champ Clark and Oscar Underwood, the outstanding leaders of the Democrats in the House. By this time it was pretty well understood that Clark would be Speaker, and Hull wanted to know whether the Missourian was opposed to trimming the power of that office. If he was, the fight would be harder than ever, as all the old-line Democrats would rally behind their leader, Mr. Clark.

Hull found both Clark and Underwood noncommittal but definitely unopposed. He got the impression they preferred to sit on the side lines until the bulk of the Democratic membership should make up its mind and then go with the winners.

He told the other three he would join them, and they began a long series of meetings behind locked doors. They wanted first to make their own plans watertight before they approached other members. Having decided on the limitations they wished placed on the Speakership, they found that the power to make appointments to committees, which they were going to take from the Speaker, would have to be lodged somewhere. They considered all sorts of plans, and finally Hull's suggestion that the committee assignments be entrusted to the Ways and Means Committee carried the day.

This would make the Ways and Means Committee the steering committee of the House, which it remains to this day, and their next concern was with the membership of that powerful body. They wanted a steering committee which would appoint to the key committee chairmanships men who were in sympathy with and who would push forward the various reforms they believed the Democrats in the House could pass at the next session. This, they felt, would focus public attention on the reforms, even if the Senate refused to adopt them, and they could be taken to the country as ready-made issues in the presidential campaign of 1912, which they had high hopes of winning for the Democratic party.

They considered nearly every Democrat in the House, weighing merits and deficiencies. They decided that Edward William Pou, of the Fourth District of North Carolina, who had been in Congress for ten years, would have to be put off the Ways and Means Committee because he was suspected of having favored a protective tariff on lumber. With tariff revision one of the principal goals they had in mind, there would be no room for a Democratic protectionist on their slate.

When they had drawn up a list of the Democratic members of the Ways and Means Committee which they thought would be satisfactory they began the consideration of possible chairmen of the other standing committees, taking special care in considering possibilities to head the labor and banking committees. Far-reaching reforms in these fields were also in their minds. Toward the end of the session they took others into their confidence. They interviewed some of the men they were considering for the chairmanships and secured pledges from them as to the policies they would follow in relation to the burning questions the four Warwicks wanted to settle.

The result of this patient, hard work was that they had a practically complete program to recommend to the Democratic caucus which met the following December to decide how it would organize the House, now that it had control for the first time in so long. The old-timers had no alternative to offer, and the caucus accepted the plan to make the Ways and Means the steering committee. The same situation prevailed when they offered their slate for that committee and when the committee itself began the consideration of assignments to other committees. As each point came up, Hull or one of the others had a carefully thought out suggestion to make, and it usually carried the day.

This was Hull's first experience in work behind the scenes, and it made an indelible impression on him. He learned what a determined, hard-working small group can accomplish in a parliamentary system. He learned that most members of the House, for example, are glad enough to endorse desirable moves but few of them are thoughtful or industrious enough to conceive or execute them. His hability in taking this kind of unseen leadership, permitting others to receive the public glory, has stood him in excellent stead at the various international conferences he has attended since he became Secretary of State. He learned the technique in 1910, working with Kitchin, Hay, and Hughes.

A few weeks later the House attempted to amend the cotton schedule of the Tariff Act, and the Republican minority proposed an amendment advocated by President Taft to make permanent the Tariff Board which he had appointed, as an advisory agency, under rather vague authorization contained in the Payne-Aldrich Act. On July 29 Underwood yielded an hour to Hull to attack this project, and Hull took a position diametrically opposed to the philosophy which he advocated so eloquently twenty-three years later when, as Secretary of State, he secured Congressional authority for the limited modification of tariffs under the Reciprocal Trade Agreements Act.

At this point he held that the Republican insistence on a permanent Tariff Board was nothing but "premeditated hypocrisy and aggravated false pretense," intended to defeat all tariff reduction by the Democratic majority.

"Their perfidious game of tariff revision by a permanent tariff commission must now be worked overtime," he told the House, amid loud applause from the Democratic side. "This claptrap must be belched forth from the throats of every Republican in a tone of sincerity. Protectionist Caesar calls for Tariff Commission Cassius to help him or he sinks."

President Taft had vetoed the revised wool schedule, on the recommendation of the Tariff Board, and Hull declared that "the President was confessing to his own incapacity and lack of intelligence" by following the Board's advice.

"My contention is that 438 representatives of the American people, clothed with the power, duty, and responsibility of legislation for their welfare, know more about the tariff than five gentlemen comprising a Tariff Board," he concluded.

Bigger things were in the offing, however. The large progressive element in the Republican party had already tired of President Taft's hesitating administration. The left-wing Republicans were already making overtures to Theodore Roosevelt, trying to overcome his barely visible reluctance to accept a nomination for a third term in the White House, and the Bull Moose movement was on its way. This split in the Republican party, bringing on the three-cornered presidential contest of 1912 which resulted in the narrow victory of a Princeton professor named Woodrow Wilson, was to be the avenue for Cordell Hull to start on his way to national prominence.

CHAPTER VIII

Father of the Income Tax

Like all the younger and more liberal members of the Democratic party, Hull was tremendously drawn to President Wilson. He liked his new party leader's personality and his principles. He approved of the Jeffersonian simplicity that Wilson brought to the White House and was pleased when the President declined the customary honorary membership in the Chevy Chase Club and decided not to give an inaugural ball.

In the field of ideas the Tennessean felt even a closer kinship. As early as 1902 Wilson had said, in his inaugural speech at Princeton: "A new age is before us in which, it would seem, we must lead the world," carrying one step further William Jennings Bryan's declaration in his acceptance speech in 1900 that the United States was "a republic gradually but surely becoming the supreme moral factor in the world's progress." That theme is one which Cordell Hull has constantly played since he became Secretary of State.

In his *Constitutional Government in the United States* Wilson had expounded the theory that "the initiative in foreign affairs, which the President possesses without any restriction whatever, is virtually the power to control them absolutely," and this was another tenet which Hull defended vigorously both before and after the Supreme Court's sweeping decision to that effect in the Curtiss-Wright case in 1937.

"The place where the strongest will is present will be the seat of sovereignty," Wilson had told the Economic Club in New York during his preconvention campaign the previous spring. "If the strongest will is present in Congress, then Congress will dominate the government. If the strongest guiding will is in the presidency, the President will dominate the government."

Here was a philosophy which Hull was destined to see tested during the terms of both President Wilson and President Franklin D. Roosevelt. Wilson repudiated "dollar diplomacy" in relation to Latin America and favored upholding the new Chinese republic against Japanese aggression—two other principles which Cordell Hull was to follow to the letter when he attained a position of sufficient power.

The new President was likewise attracted to the tall, serious, studious Tennessean. Ray Stannard Baker, in his *Life and Letters of Woodrow Wilson*, in the volume dealing with the period of 1913–14, has the following to say:

Wilson was fortunate in having an unusually able group of Democratic congressmen to deal with, men who were, moreover, determined, now that the party had come to power, not to allow dissensions to defeat its objectives. Such leaders as Glass of Virginia, Rainey of Illinois, Fitzgerald of New York, Kitchin of North Carolina, Cordell Hull of Tennessee, Palmer of Pennsylvania, Stanley of Kentucky, Clayton of Alabama, all of whom had been long in public service, were men with whom Wilson could work on terms of complete understanding. . . .

He also took a keen interest in the new income-tax provisions of the bill which were being drafted by Mr. Hull of Tennessee, making clear his interest in exempting "all persons receiving less than $3000 a year income from the necessity of making income returns at all, in order to burden as small a number of persons [as possible] with the obligations involved in the administration of what will at best be an unpopular law.

But what really delighted Hull's heart was the alacrity with which President Wilson sprang to the task of tariff revision. His call for the special session of Congress to meet on April 7, 1913, placed the tariff at the head of agenda which included currency and related problems.

Wilson was just as convinced a champion of low tariffs as was his Tennessee disciple. Speaking before the Southern Society of New York in 1908, Wilson had defined the existing tariff structure as "a vast body of economic expedients which have been used, under guise of taxation, for the purpose of building up various industries, great and small," and added that "it is the present general conviction that our more recent tariff legislation has been a doling out of certain privileges on the part of the government and that certain protected interests have been built up with no particular regard to the interests of the nation as a whole."

So intent was the new President on pushing through prompt and thoroughgoing tariff reform that he wanted to purge highly placed Congressional Democrats who had failed to follow the party line on the tariff issue. First among the proposed purgees was Senator Simmons, of North Carolina, who had voted for the high schedules of the Payne-Aldrich bill on the theory that, if other states were going to get protection, North Carolina might as well share in the spoils. Mr. Wilson wanted the administration leaders on Capitol Hill to keep Mr. Simmons out of the chairmanship of the Finance Committee, which handles all tariff and other revenue legislation. He was dissuaded by Josephus Daniels, according to Ray Stannard Baker, who sums up, as follows, the line of reasoning Mr. Daniels advanced out of his long political experience:

If powerful and experienced Democrats in the Senate were repudiated, would it not mean a bitter factional quarrel, endangering all other measures Wilson had determined upon? And supposing, having begun the fight, he should fail to dislodge Simmons? In a factional party quarrel such as this he could, of course, expect no help from Republican progressives, no matter how sympathetic they might be with the objectives for which he was contending. In short, he would have lost the battle, tactically, before he had really begun it. He might, indeed, win out here and there by carrying the fight into the home states of obstreperous senators—as he did in certain instances at a later time—but the method presented obvious, indeed insurmountable, difficulties. While it might solidify progressive sentiment among the people and in the long run, by clarifying the issues, build up a movement that would be irresistible in the long struggle with privilege, its implications led away toward a new party, and the problems that Wilson was facing were urgent.

One cannot help wondering whether Cordell Hull remembered this sage bit of advice and offered it to President Roosevelt during the Supreme Court fight of 1937 and the disastrously unsuccessful senatorial purges in the elections of 1938 or whether Mr. Daniels himself, from his ambassadorial listening post in Mexico City, proffered these counsels again to his new chief.

In the House of Representatives President Wilson was more confident of his own leadership. Although Champ Clark, his principal rival for the Democratic presidential nomination at the Baltimore convention, had been elected Speaker, and the gulf between the two men was as unbridgeable as it proved to be all the rest of their lives, his next nearest rival at the convention, Oscar Underwood, was chairman of the Ways and Means Committee and appeared to be completely friendly.

To dramatize the importance he gave to tariff revision and currency reform Mr. Wilson decided to violate a tradition of 133 years' standing by delivering his message to the special session in person. His appearance before the joint session on April 8 aroused widespread comment in Congress and among the public at large. Senator John Sharp Williams, a staunch Democrat, disapproved, while Senator Henry Cabot Lodge, the Republican who was destined to wreck Wilson's dream of a League of Nations, thought it was the right thing to do.

The new President was by no means overawed at the presence of the entire Congress or at the thought of shattering precedent. He launched into a denunciation of the existing tariff on the ground that it had become "a set of privileges and exemptions from competition behind which it is easy by any, even the crudest, forms of combination to organize monopoly; until at last nothing is normal, nothing is obliged to stand the tests of efficiency and economy, in our world of big business, but everything thrives by concerted arrangement."

Hull and his colleagues of the Ways and Means Committee set to work at once, under Mr. Underwood's chairmanship, to pave the way for the first general downward revision of the tariff since 1857. During those hearings Hull got his first taste of and distaste for lobbyists. This aversion has stayed with him to this day, and he seldom makes a tariff speech without some sarcastic, biting reference to those representatives of special interests who are paid to temper the wind of tariff reduction to the shorn lambs of industry.

The Washington *Star*, in reporting the local scene in Washington on the eve of the tariff hearings, had the following to say:

Washington is fairly seething with tariff today (April 9, 1913). Hotels are crowded with businessmen from all over the country, attracted by the pendency of the tariff legislation. Wool men from as far west as Montana, fruit men from California, beet-sugar men from the West and cane-sugar men from the South; New England manufacturers, Southern cotton-goods manufacturers, woolen men from Pennsylvania, and representatives of many interests are on the ground to look after their own.

This roll call of lobbyists will sound familiar to anyone who has had occasion to follow subsequent attempts to modify the tariff. Under Republican regimes they bent their efforts toward "logrolling" combinations which would get tariff boosts for them all. When the Democrats were in power they turned their efforts to forming similar blocs to prevent reduction of the tariff rates affecting their interests.

The temper of the Congress, and of the country, was extremely partisan. The circumstances surrounding Wilson's election were not such as to lend themselves to the theory that the people had given the new administration a "mandate," and the conservative elements were profoundly concerned and resentful. There was no talk of "national unity" such as Wendell Willkie asked after his defeat in 1940. Wilson, as governor of New Jersey, had curbed corporations and instituted reforms which were considered highly radical moves at the time. The Republicans in Congress were determined that the new administration should accomplish as little national legislation tending in this direction as possible.

During the "lameduck" session of Congress which preceded Wilson's inauguration the current political confusion had been illustrated by the helter-skelter legislative projects which were considered and which nearly all failed in the deadlock between a Republican Senate and a Democratic House of Representatives. The Senate, for example, passed a prohibition law to forbid the transportation of liquor in interstate commerce, but the House let it die. Both houses passed a bill to prohibit the white-slave traffic, and President Taft vetoed it. The House voted appropriations for one battleship, the Senate raised the ante to two battleships, and the conference committee settled for one.

A number of the subjects debated have a familiar ring today. The Senate received a bill to enlarge the membership of the Supreme Court; the Senate approved a Constitutional amendment to limit the tenure of office of any President to a single term of six years, but the Democratic House, fearing it might be ratified in time to curtail Wilson's regime, declined to pass it; both houses considered the necessity of creating a National Defense Council; a prohibitive tax on short sales on all stock exchanges was debated in the House.

The army was attacked for having the weakest military aviation in the world, and Congress raised the pay for flying officers. Colonel George P. Scriven, new chief of the Signal Corps, of which the aviation section was then a part, promised Congressional committees that he would build armored airplanes—a promise that began to be fulfilled only some twenty-three years later.

The positive achievements of the "lameduck" session included the approval of a Lincoln Memorial, on the walls of which was to be inscribed the Gettysburg Address, and the creation of a separate Department of Labor. Commerce and labor had previously been confided to the care of a single member of the Cabinet.

While these legislative high jinks were going on President-elect Wilson had kept out of the melee, adopting much the same attitude as did President Roosevelt between his election in 1932 and his first inauguration in 1933. For one thing, the Mexican situation was going from bad to worse, and it was suggested to Mr. Wilson that he might do well to consult with the Secretary of War to insure the pursuit of a military policy which he could carry on when he came to power. This Mr. Wilson declined to do, and the Secretary of War he snubbed was named Henry L. Stimson—the same Secretary of War with whom Cordell Hull now deals daily.

Before his inauguration Mr. Wilson considered for appointment to various offices Democrats who have been familiars of Cordell Hull during his time in the Roosevelt administration. Joseph E. Davies was being considered for ambassador to Italy but ended up as Commissioner of Corporations in the Commerce Department. He has been ambassador to the Soviet Union and to Belgium in Hull's regime. Daniel C. Roper was under examination as a possible First Assistant Postmaster General. He later became Hull's Cabinet colleague, as Secretary of Commerce, for six years. Wilson was thinking of appointing former Governor Alva Adams (now senator from Colorado and an inveterate foe of the New Deal) as Secretary of the Interior. He was thinking of finding a Cabinet place for George W. Norris of Nebraska, the veteran liberal who has been one of President Roosevelt's mainstays in Congress.

No secret was made of Wilson's intention to make a clean sweep of Republican officeholders as soon as he got his hands on the patronage. His guides in dispensing the rewards to the faithful, after the Democrats had suffered in exile for nearly twenty years, were Colonel E M. House and Joseph Tumulty, who became his permanent secretary. The Republicans charged, and apparently with some reason, that the bulk of the presidential patronage would be withheld until the projected tariff revision had passed Congress, so that the promise of jobs for constituents, or threat of failure to secure jobs for them, could be held over the Democratic members of both houses.

Hull was ready for the tariff fight well before the new Congress met. He needed no inducements or threats on the patronage side to push him into the thick of the fray. He had drawn the assignment, by common consent of his colleagues on the Ways and Means Committee, of drafting the section of the tariff bill which would impose an income tax in accordance with the newly ratified Sixteenth Amendment to the Constitution. He set to work as soon as Wilson reached his decision to summon an extra session to convene immediately after his inauguration. All major countries of Europe, except France, already had income taxes, so that there was a considerable body of material from which to work, in addition to Hull's own ideas on the subject.

The Washington *Star* ran a Sunday article on April 20 telling how the proposed income tax was an effort to make the rich pay the taxes. At the top of the page it published a picture of "Representative Cordell Hull, who is responsible for the income-tax legislation." The article's description of Hull's responsibility ran as follows:

Representative Hull is a youngster just turned forty-two and has been in Congress four years already. When he came to Washington from the village of Carthage, in the black land of Tennessee, he brought with him one all-absorbing idea, and this was that the income tax was the one great and good and just manner of raising public funds Not only did he have the idea, but he had compiled a vast array of facts to back up his arguments, and, after arriving in Washington, he studied hard and steadily increased that array of facts. Whenever, in the deliberations of the House, there was a perceptible pause, Representative Hull arose and addressed that body on the subject of the income tax.

The old heads told the young man from Tennessee that legislation of this sort, being class legislation, was unconstitutional. The Supreme Court of the United States had so declared in 1894. Mr. Hull remained unconvinced. He reminded Congress that this country had had on its statute books a perfectly good income-tax law levied during the Civil War and operative until 1871. Through all those years taxes had been collected under it. If the law was unconstitutional those taxes were unlawfully collected and should be refunded. Hull introduced a resolution refunding all those taxes amounting to $346,000,000. Nothing came of the resolution, but these tactics kept the matter alive.

Finally the time arrived in 1909 when the Payne-Aldrich tariff bill was being fought through Congress in the early days of the Taft administration. One night young Hull found himself on a sleeping car with Senator Bailey, the one bound for the quiet village of Carthage and the other for his horse farm in Kentucky. The younger man told Senator Bailey his fervid tale of the income tax, garnished with all the earnestness of a great conviction. Bailey saw in the situation presented an opportunity to harass the Republicans, who were already in a very delicate position with reference to the methods of raising revenue.

So, in the midst of the deliberations of a Republican Congress upon a tariff bill that afterward was used as a club to mercilessly hammer that party, Senator Bailey introduced an amendment providing for an income tax.

The *Star's* writer forgot to mention the sentimental reason that had kept Hull so attached to the cause of the income tax during his career thus far in Congress. This was the recollection that Benton McMillin had been the author of the income-tax law which the Supreme Court threw out in 1894 by a 5–4 decision. Neither McMillin nor Hull had ever been able to accept the legal reasoning of the majority opinion in that case, and Hull felt about the income tax as Sir Galahad felt about the Holy Grail.

On the whole, the country did not appear to be too shocked by the threats of "radical" legislation which the Democrats were openly breathing. The New York *Times,* voicing the qualms of the conservatives, published an indignant editorial denouncing Vice-President Marshall's "remarkable excursion into the field of constitutional and natural rights, in which he announced that the right of a living man to determine the distribution of his property after his death was dependent on the action of 'the state' and was the creation of statute"—a legal thesis which would hardly arouse even a desultory argument among lawyers today.[1]

The administration went ahead with its projects while Congress was wrestling with the tariff bill. Postmaster General Burleson announced, after six months' trial of the parcel-post system, that he believed the government would shortly carry all small packages in the nation's commerce—a prediction which drew a hot rejoinder from express-company officials intended to demonstrate that this was little better than socialism, and impracticable in any case.

Other familiar phenomena were in the air and other familiar names were coming to public notice. Even women's fashions were enjoying a trend we have seen quite recently, to judge from an advertisement published by Saks & Company.

"With the low-bust corset in vogue," this company announced to its prospective feminine customers, "the brassière was never so indispensable as now. It is more than indispensable, it is imperative."

Aviation was being talked on all sides. Christopher J. Lake, the submarine designer, announced that he had discovered the

[1]Hull had made the same point four years before in his first speech in the House of Representatives. At that time he said that "the right to transmit property is not a natural one but is more in the nature of a privilege granted the citizens by law."

design for an airplane with "inherent stability" and told press interviewers that "I believe the day will come when men can walk about with perfect safety while flying in airplanes."

Lieutenant John H. Towers, U.S.N., was visited by Secretary of the Navy Daniels while he was recuperating at Annapolis from a fall into Chesapeake Bay—an accident in which the officer flying with him had been killed. Mr. Daniels told the young aviator that he would get three months' leave and a soft job as a reward for his suffering.

"I don't know what I should do with three months' leave, and that job wouldn't suit me at all," he told Mr. Daniels. "Mr. Secretary, I want to go back to flying."

"The man who shows such pluck and courage certainly is the sort we want," Mr. Daniels commented, and he must have been right, for Lieutenant Towers has now become Rear Admiral Towers and is chief of the Bureau of Aeronautics at the Navy Department.

Lieutenant Henry H. Arnold, U.S.A., wrote an article in the *Infantry Journal* on the possible uses of aviation in war. He declared:

The actual damage that can be done to objects on the ground from an airplane is very limited. But if 200 or 300 bombs are dropped in or around a column of troops, there will be some confusion and demoralization, even if the damage inflicted is slight. Seven out of fifteen bombs have been dropped in a space 25 by 50 meters from a machine at an altitude of 2500 feet, moving at a speed of fifty miles an hour. It is certain, therefore, that some damage can be effected by dropping explosives from airplanes.

This officer has revised his estimates upward any number of times during the quarter of a century following, during which he rose to be commander of the army air forces.

In London the First Lord of the Admiralty, Winston Churchill, was the occasion for a good deal of grumbling—not because of his political activities but because his American mother, who was the daughter of Leonard Jerome of New York, was divorcing her second husband, Captain George Cornwallis West, and wanted to resume her former married name of Lady Randolph Churchill. The divorce was one of the early ones of that pattern which has come to be considered collusive in England, where the erring husband is not compelled to divulge the name of the corespondent nor is the corespondent cited by name by the complainant. Gossip had it that the future Prime Minister had brought the pressure of his official position to bear so that the then unusual procedure was permitted by the court.

In Washington the Ways and Means Committee struggled with the tariff schedule and finally reported a bill including Hull's income-tax section. Wearily Oscar Underwood, chairman of the committee, kept the general debate running, with the House often sitting at night. The income-tax section was reached relatively early in the debate, and it was Hull's job to pilot that much of the bill through the House. On April 26, 1913, he delivered a long speech from the floor in explanation of his brain child and defended it against countless antagonistic questions. Among the influential organizations which had expressed opposition to some or all of his proposal were the Equitable Life Assurance Society, the New York Life Insurance Company, Allied Real Estate Interests, the Massachusetts Realty Exchange, the Omaha Real Estate Exchange, and the Investment Bankers' Association.

"A glance at the fiscal history of all countries shows a constant struggle on the part of the wealthy and more powerful classes to shift the chief weight of government taxation to the shoulders and backs of those weaker, poorer, and less able to protect themselves from the injustice and oppression inflicted by disproportionate tax burdens," was Hull's reply to this kind of opposition when he took the floor for the first time in the income-tax debate. "This conflict has been and is today being waged in the United States.

"The American people have completely learned that they are not being taxed either fairly or honestly; they are demanding that the inequalities, abuses, and injustices of our present system of high tariff taxation shall be eliminated and that a new system of taxes, fair and equitable, embracing a strictly revenue tariff and an income tax, shall be devised. The experience of all countries with respect to every form of taxation has resulted in the universal conclusion that the fairest and most just of all taxes is that which is levied upon the citizen according to ability to pay and that this result can best be accomplished by imposing a tax on net incomes."

Both President Wilson and Hull believed that an income tax was fiscally necessary, as well as politically desirable, to offset the loss to the Treasury of the tariff revenues which would inevitably result at first from the reduced rates they proposed to put into effect. Wilson went further than Hull in demanding currency reform (the movement that led to the founding of the Federal Reserve System) as an additional safeguard against economic depression from adjusting the tariff schedule downward.

Hull told the House that he had calculated his income-tax rates to yield just the $70,000,000 which would be lost to the Treasury from reducing the customs duties. He estimated that the application of then existing British income-tax rates would yield the Treasury $400,000,000.

"Under the present high tariff system," he said, "a poor man with a large family pays more taxes than a rich man with a small family. Hence the man of wealth who is too selfish and too unpatriotic to pay taxes will vigorously oppose the imposition of any just tax, as will any creature of class or privilege taxation."

Later in his speech he undertook to answer one of the favorite arguments against an income tax.

"The objection is also offered," he continued, "in a tone of injured innocence, that the proposed tax would be sectional in its effects. This measure certainly is not sectional in its terms, and should it be sectional in effect it would be due to the fact that wealth has first made itself sectional."

The debate dragged on through the spring, with Hull offering a whole series of perfecting amendments to the income-tax section. The House finally adopted the tariff bill on May 9 and sent it to the Senate, where pressure from lobbyists became so strong that an investigation was launched on a motion of Senator Cummins. The House also undertook an inquiry. The bill was amended in many particulars in the Senate and sent to conference with the House, which lasted for weeks, but finally the bill became law, including the first constitutionally unassailable income tax the country had ever had.

Soon after the first of the year, late in January 1914, Hull was invited to explain his income tax before the New York State

Bar Association, and his speech on that occasion was probably one of the finest legal expositions he has ever made. He explained that the comparatively high exemptions of $3000 for unmarried persons and $4000 for married persons had been written into the law so that the tax would apply to relatively few persons at first, enabling both the public and the tax collectors to become accustomed to its workings gradually. At any time it was desired to raise more revenue, he pointed out, the exemptions could be lowered, bringing more citizens within the income brackets liable to the levy.

He spoke at some length in defense of one of the most controversial features of the income-tax law—a feature that has been largely discarded in the United States, although it has been maintained in Great Britain and elsewhere. This was the collection of the income tax on corporate dividends at the source. Hull told the New York lawyers that this system of collection was desirable because of the tendency of personal property, such as income, to conceal itself, an experience which the states had suffered during the entire tax history of the country.

Hull told his audience that "a Kentucky law imposing a tax on dogs yields a larger revenue to the state treasury than that derived from the entire bank deposits," relating that the sworn bank deposits declared to the Kentucky tax collectors amounted to only $12,846,868 for the previous year, whereas the banks themselves reported that their total deposits amounted to $133,339,871. The speaker was insistent that 30,000 wealthy Americans, some of them with incomes in excess of $500,000 a year, must not escape American taxation just because they chose to live in France.

He jumped on the sectional issue, which he knew was rankling the minds of the New Yorkers, with both feet. He said:

I am well aware that in the past the greatest opposition to an income tax in the United States has come from the eastern section of the country upon the theory that it would unjustly contribute more taxes than any other section. From this view I respectfully dissent, for the reason that New York, for example, is the great center of commerce of the nation. It is a great distributing center. Hundreds of thousands of citizens of other states come here to reside. Her great incomes are drawn from all sections of the country. These concentrated profits are chiefly the product of the great industries throughout the nation. I deny the right of wealth to segregate itself and then, upon the plea of segregation, to exempt itself from its fair share of taxes. The people of other sections do not envy New York and other states similarly situated their good fortune. It is only asked that, while enjoying these and other superior blessings, their people shall cheerfully acquiesce in a tax law everywhere conceded to be just and fair.

Meantime President Wilson had appointed Benton McMillin, Hull's boyhood idol and political sponsor, as United States Minister to Peru to round out the Tennessean's long public career. A relative of his summed up McMillin's career to me by saying, rather ruefully, that "he devoted his entire life to the public and died without a dollar." His widow is now a member of the Civil Service Commission.

In the spring Hull nearly got into a fist fight on the floor of the House. An unwary Republican, not yet having plumbed the depth of anger and action which underlies the calm, courteous exterior of the Tennessean, tried Hull beyond his strength and was almost well beaten up in the process.

The House of Representatives on June 26 was engaged in one of its periodic idiocies, debating whether or not the Vice-President of the United States should have a new automobile. Mr. Marshall was then riding in a snappy 1909 model, and the Senate had added to the Legislative Appropriation Bill an amendment to provide funds to buy him a new one. There was a roll call on the Senate amendment, the result of which was announced as a tie, 127 to 127. This would have meant that the amendment lost.

Administration floor leaders, who favored the amendment, demanded a recapitulation. This means, under House procedure, that the reading clerk calls off the entire roll, giving the vote of each individual member, so that all members can be sure their votes are recorded the way they meant them to be cast. When the clerk came to Hull's name he announced that the Tennessee representative had voted "no." Hull rose and stated that he had voted "aye." The switch of that single vote would mean that the amendment was adopted.

Representative Farr, a Pennsylvania Republican, protested that he had been standing close to Hull and had clearly heard him vote "no." Hull sternly insisted to the clerk that his vote had been wrongly recorded. Mr. Farr shouted his charge again, and Hull started after him. Much as Hull's Democratic colleagues would probably have liked to see Mr. Farr get a good punch in the nose, some of them caught Hull and hustled him to the cloakroom until he had cooled off. Vice-President Marshall got the car.

At this point in his career Hull's taxation theories were based exclusively on the government's need for revenue. He accepted the thesis that government taxation should be assessed according to the ability of the individual to pay, and this was a premise by no means universally in favor at that time. It has since become so entwined with Federal and state taxation systems as to be practically noncontroversial, and we should consider Hull's philosophy of taxation as a highly conservative one now.

He was willing for tariffs to be levied against any imports if the customs duties would supply needed revenue to the Federal government. He had no sympathy with the protectionists for two reasons: first, he felt that protective tariffs were highly lucrative privileges voted by the Federal government for the benefit of a few, enabling them to make huge profits at the expense of the body of the population—a process which he considered to be the negation of democracy; second, he realized that protective tariffs, to accomplish the ends sought by their sponsors, would have to be high enough to bar all imports and hence would produce no revenue.

Therefore, when he proposed lowering tariff duties in favor of increasing the international trade of the United States, he urged the enactment of an income tax to compensate the Federal government for whatever loss of revenue might ensue temporarily, although he believed that lower duties would bring in imports in sufficiently larger volume to make up for the loss, given time.

His income tax was a revenue measure. It was not intended to redistribute the nation's wealth, to make the accumulation of large fortunes impossible, to punish anybody, or to accomplish any of the other "social ends" which the younger pilots of the early New Deal sought to accomplish under the revenue powers granted by the Constitution to the Federal government.

The same considerations governed his approach to the inheritance and estate taxes which he advocated. After considerable reflection he came to favor the estate tax over the inheritance tax because it yielded more revenue with less effort. From the point of view of social justice the inheritance tax is more fair than the estate tax, which is still levied by the Federal government. Hull was not interested in fine distinctions. To him the estate tax meant that the government would get the most money with the minimum of effort, and therefore it was the proper tax to apply.

This practical side of him is a yardstick against which most of his public actions are to be measured. He has strong emotions, powerful likes and dislikes, but he tends on the whole to keep his rational side forward in dealing with governmental business. This aspect of his character showed itself more and more at the State Department, when he had to deal with policies which had emotional appeals from every side.

In the summer of 1914, however, the Sixty-Second Congress was droning away with little thought of these niceties. It was pursuing its usual routine and highly partisan debates on relatively unimportant matters when the outside world was shaken by an event which aroused little interest or attention in much of the country at the time: the assassination of Archduke Francis Ferdinand, which led to the outbreak of the first World War in Europe.

CHAPTER IX

Enlarged Horizon

Iɴ ᴛʜᴏsᴇ ᴇᴀʀʟʏ ᴅᴀʏs ᴏꜰ ᴀᴜɢᴜsᴛ the European war found little reflection in the debates of Congress. The main concern in the minds of the members appears to have been the threatened strike of 55,000 railroad workers in the West and the drastic proposals in the Senate to extend the scope of the pending Federal Trade Commission bill.

By August 3, however, when it was obvious even in Washington that a general European war was inevitable, President Wilson gave to newspapermen at his semiweekly press conference a warning which sounded very much like what President Roosevelt had to say to their successors when the next European war broke out in 1939.

"I would urge you not to give currency to any unverified rumor, to anything that would tend to create or add to excitement," Mr. Wilson told the reporters. "I think that you will agree that we must all at the present moment act together as Americans in seeing that America does not suffer any unnecessary distress from what is going on in the world at large."

Rev. J. L. Kibler, chaplain of the Senate, seems to have been the first to mention the tragedy on the floors of Congress. On that same day he included the following in his opening prayer:

"Grant that there may be a tranquil and just adjustment of

difficulties among the nations abroad. May peace and prosperity and commercial enterprise be established and be maintained everywhere, and may our influence and example be such as to favor righteousness to the ends of the earth."

The following day, just after President Wilson had issued his official proclamation of the nation's neutrality, John Sharp Williams made the Senate sit up and take notice as he started the first real war speech that had been heard.

"Mr. President," the Mississippi orator thundered, "while the United States Senate is talking, and talking in extenso, and while very many senators are participating in the debate at unusual length, the whole world outside of the United States seems to have gone insane. The insanity, the idiocy, and the stupidity of war prejudice has seized the entire world, and, in the providence of God, it is thoroughly impossible for any part of the world to be engaged in devastating warfare without damaging the utmost other part of the world."

After this promising start, however, it developed that Mr. Williams was merely going to introduce another merchant-marine bill. There were several pending before the Congress, but the proposal of Mr. Williams had the value of complete novelty. He only wanted the government to purchase a lot of ships, man them with sailors and officers from the navy, and sail them from the ports of the Gulf of Mexico laden with the South's cotton destined for European ports. He dared any belligerent to tinker with such a vessel navigated by such a fearless crew.

On the serious side, Congress hastily appropriated the $2,500,-000 President Wilson asked to aid American refugees in Europe to regain their homes here, after carefully inserting the proviso that all American citizens thus aided should reimburse the Federal government for all cash expended on their behalf. It likewise rushed through the Aldrich-Vreeland bill, increasing the note-issuing powers of the national banks to $1,000,000,000, in the belief that this added elasticity in the currency would prevent the threatened drainage of gold toward the export market.

On August 6 the capital was thrown into mourning by the death of President Wilson's first wife, the former Ellen Louise Axson.

In the lull that followed that tragedy Senator James Hamilton

Lewis of Illinois, Democratic whip, let it be known that President Wilson wanted Congress to remain in session indefinitely until it was seen whether the Japanese declaration of war on the side of the Allies would mean that Japan and Germany would clash in military combat near the Philippine Islands. On the House side, the majority members of the Ways and Means Committee, of whom Hull was one, prudently decided not to recommend any new taxes until after the November elections.

On August 10 the first Federal Reserve Board was sworn in, with Charles H. Hamlin of Boston as governor.

Hull took no part in the war debates, which increased in frequency and vigor as the weeks wore on, until September 25. He was stung by Republican charges that the Underwood tariff would now prove the nation's fiscal undoing because it was obvious that imports from Europe would be smaller and would, therefore, yield next to no customs revenues at the reduced rates the Democrats had insisted on establishing. Hull dared them to propose the repeal of the Underwood tariff bill, including his beloved income tax, and the re-enactment of the Payne-Aldrich tariff. He said the Democrats would ask no better issue on which to face the country in the Congressional elections the next November.

"From the farthermost countries of the world we are getting daily information that the people are in a state of terror as a result of this awful European conflagration," he told the House; "that business is suspended everywhere, and, of course, our international commerce is almost entirely paralyzed. Both our international credit and exchange have broken down."

At the outbreak of the war, he estimated, the United States was doing business with Germany, Belgium, Austria, and European Russia at the annual level of $7,000,000,000, and that its enforced curtailment had caused the loss of $60,000,000 a year in customs receipts, about which the Republicans were complaining. The loss would have been even greater, from the budgetary point of view, had the higher Republican tariff rates been in force.

"Furthermore, any person who gives consideration to our existing conditions knows that while England and France had on hand a surplus of goods with which they had been supplying us constantly before the war, and that after thirty days, and when the ocean became cleared of the enemy's vessels, they shipped to us as much of this surplus as they could, this was chiefly to fill orders received before the war," he pointed out.

"But since then virtually all of the factory workers in France have gone to the war. Stocks of raw materials are rapidly disappearing, such as France and England procured from Germany and Belgium and other warring countries, with the inevitable results that our imports from Europe must naturally fall off so long as the war continues, and no one can prophesy that it will end within any short time."

Here was his first attempt to chart international trade dislocation due to war—the only condition, he believed, against which his formula for the well-being of the world was not proof. It is interesting to notice how, in the days preceding the second European war, Hull drew on the memories of that first bitter experience and how much better equipped he was to grapple with the probable dislocations at once. At this point in 1914 he saw the evils clearly enough but as yet had no remedies to propose.

Up to this time Hull's tariff theories had been based on his belief that protection was a domestic evil. As he saw it, the protective tariff tended to create monopoly and to enrich the few at the expense of the many. He considered any such system to be incompatible with the free economic enterprise in which he believed.

The World War and its dislocations of world trade, which impressed him especially because he was called upon to explain why the Democratic tariff system was allegedly adversely affecting the nation's budget, brought him his first conception of high tariffs as trade barriers stopping commerce and friendship between nations and, therefore, preventing durable peace. This idea grew upon him as the war progressed, especially after the United States became a belligerent and American statesmen began to think they could dictate the peace that was to follow. By the end of the war his whole tariff philosophy had undergone a vast expansion and had become the foundation of his political creed.

His preoccupation with domestic issues up to this point was not only natural but healthy. The Democratic party's mission was just what he had deemed it to be when he was thinking of running for Congress in 1906. It must justify itself to the electorate, now that it had the power, by reforming the abuses which had become so thoroughly entrenched during the preceding half-century of Republican control. The political front was the domestic one. Foreign problems were of little moment in comparison to the home ills which he and his fellow liberals considered to be crying for remedy.

At this time, after nearly two years of Democratic control of Congress, and with a great liberal like Woodrow Wilson in the White House, Hull felt that these evils were on their way to correction. His mind began to occupy itself to a greater extent with the problem of his own country's relation to the rest of the world. The war had brought home to him that the United States could not avoid being affected by untoward developments abroad, even though it had no hand in generating them and attempted nothing toward their settlement.

His painstaking research into European tariffs, income and inheritance taxes, and other fiscal problems had made him aware of the sameness of the difficulties confronting all democratic nations and their citizens. He felt that the United States had much to learn from the experiences and practices of foreign countries and never hesitated to say so on the floor of the House, where he could quote an authentic foreign precedent for any suggestion he had to offer.

By October 24 Congress considered the war situation well enough in hand to adjourn until the short session that was to begin on December 7. Already there were speakers to take the floor in both houses to urge that the United States stay clear of the conflict. It was in the midst of one of these debates in the new session, on February 26, 1915, that Hull gave a résumé of the difficulties the European war had brought automatically in its train, and many of the references he made to contemporary suffering sound as if they had been said about the state of the world at the beginning of 1941. He said:

Mr. Speaker, one of the surprising facts relating to the existing European war is the entire failure of so many intelligent citizens of the United States to realize and appreciate its tremendous effects upon finance, commerce, and industry throughout the world; indeed, they do not grasp the real scope and extent of the war itself.

Little do many people, especially in the peace countries, realize that we are passing through the most momentous epoch in the history of the human race.

The world population is about 1,620,000,000. A majority of this, or 925,000,000 persons, resides in the countries and colonies directly involved in the war. The total area of the globe, not including the polar regions, is about 52,000,000 square miles. The countries engaged in the war comprise an area of 28,500,000 square miles. All five continents are more or less involved in the actual fighting. The awful tide of militarism is at full flow.

He was addressing himself to a series of speakers who had been expounding the theory that no economic considerations could possibly justify the participation of the United States in the conflict, on the assumption that this country could avoid the consequences of war merely by holding aloof and minding its own business. Hull was not as yet an advocate of American participation, but this easy dismissal of the world's profound economic dislocations as having no effect on the United States was repugnant to his growing philosophy of the interdependence of all the world in the economic sphere. Some of the citations he made in this 1915 speech concerned problems with which he had to cope, in the concrete, in 1940. He told the House:

The rich Argentine republic is in the throes of a severe business depression. Since the war began it is estimated that there were more than 80,000 idle persons in one city alone, and a corresponding proportion of unemployed in other parts of the country. Not only has her international commerce, which has been chiefly with Europe, greatly declined, but the failure of Europe, on account of war necessities at home, to furnish large supplies of capital, as heretofore, has left both the people and the government almost prostrated.

Many of her railroads and factories have greatly curtailed operations for lack of fuel and certain other supplies. The shipments of her cereals have been largely cut off for the reasons I have heretofore stated. The government itself is in financial straits. The deplorable conditions of Argentina, which is the richest country in South America, well illustrate the unfortunate plight of all South American countries under European war conditions. Some of them can not even borrow money to pay interest on their public debts. They are almost in a general state of moratorium.

The fact is beyond controversy that the disastrous effects of the European war are world-wide. If we go to the Scandinavian countries, we find that Sweden, for example, is severely suffering from the stress of the war. . . . It is useless to recount the terribly acute conditions of privation, high prices, and commercial distress existing in countries like Holland and Switzerland. . . . Spain is likewise in the grasp of a severe commercial and financial depression and has her full share of unemployed.

At this time Cordell Hull had never been outside of the United States, except for the brief excursion to Cuba, and yet he appears to have been as well informed on world affairs and their fundamental importance as any member of Congress. His grasp of foreign problems was due to unremitting study and application, far beyond anything usually displayed by a member of Congress, especially in a subject which does not fall directly in his province. Hull's interest sprang, originally, from his preoccupation with tariff revision and income taxation.

He was making his weight felt more and more on the Ways and Means Committee because of the breadth of his technical knowledge of taxation in all its forms and because of his unlimited capacity for work.

On December 15 Representative Claude Kitchin of North Carolina, the majority floor leader, told his colleagues that the "war taxes" enacted on October 22, 1914, to expire on December 31, 1915, would have to be extended, as the Federal Treasury would continue to need the extra $80,000,000 a year they were designed to yield.

"When it was passed," Mr. Kitchin explained, "the House considered that the European war would last only, or not as long as, a year."

So when Congress recessed for the Christmas holidays Hull was appointed by the Ways and Means Committee to stay behind in the capital and work out methods of raising even greater additional revenue. He spent the entire holiday period working on the problem. One of the proposed schemes was to jack up the income-tax rates on the incomes in the higher brackets. Hull also drew up an analysis of various European inheritance taxes and their yields, in the hope that this might influence Congress to adopt his favorite tax. Other revenue suggestions his col-

leagues threw in his lap before going home to celebrate the holidays included a gasoline tax, a tax on pig iron and fabricated
steel, and an excise tax on munitions. He discarded these plans as
bordering too closely on class legislation, which might be held
unconstitutional by the conservative Supreme Court of the time.

Already there were current apprehensions over the expenditures that the European war seemed to be forcing on the United
States. Since the Civil War the expenses of the Federal government had been modest, measured even by the standards of the
times. Hull saw that increasing revenues would be needed, as
time went on, and began to form long-range plans for raising
money. After his studies over the Congressional recess he proposed to amend the income-tax law by raising its rates, so that
it would yield $185,000,000 to $195,000,000 a year instead of
the $85,000,000 to $90,000,000 a year it was then yielding. His
plan aroused the indignation of the New York *Times,* which
printed the following comment on January 27, 1916:

This is the law which was passed in order to give the nation the
power of taxation in case of war or other compelling necessity. It is
said that the discriminations which are lawful are popular, and it is
thought that more votes will be made than lost by making the
rich pay for preparedness. That is the politics of it.

The universality of a tax is nowadays a reason for rejecting it, for
unpopularity. The fact that few will pay commends a tax above all
other considerations. The test of popularity is not principle, but
selfish interest. Always there are those thus influenced, but now their
number is discouragingly large. The cure will come in time, with a
change of issues rather than with a change of citizenship, for the
people are better than their representatives and need only leadership to rally to the cause of public morality.

Newton D. Baker was asking for $8,000,000 to defray the ex-
penses of General Pershing's troops on the Mexican border. It
was obvious that military expenditures of one kind or another
would keep on mounting and the Treasury would face a financing problem of the first magnitude. Hull was ready with another
plan, which the New York *Times* described as follows on March
24:

Representative Hull of Tennessee, of the House Ways and Means
Committee, who has kept in close touch with both President Wilson

and Secretary McAdoo in regard to revenue raising, said today there need be no concern as to means of providing any necessary funds. He explained that there were sources open without further legislation—the 3 per cent Panama Canal bonds, long term, of which $240,000,000 may yet be issued, and the $200,000,000 of 3 per cent certificates authorized under the Dingley tariff law. Mr. Hull also called attention to the fact that the Treasury probably received this year the largest revenue yield in its history.

More and more Hull was becoming recognized as one of the outstanding fiscal experts in the House. His contact with the Treasury increased and he was on his way to becoming the official liaison between Fifteenth Street and the Ways and Means Committee. By May the Democrats had decided to revise the revenue laws, and the New York *Times* again mentioned Hull's leadership. It reported on May 22:

Representative Cordell Hull of Tennessee, who wrote the income-tax section of the Underwood tariff law, is the committee expert in charge of that portion of the forthcoming revenue bill relating to the income tax and a levy on inheritances. Amending the existing income-tax law is a comparatively simple process, but an inheritance-tax law is something to which Mr. Hull has devoted several months' study.

Mr. Hull has examined the inheritance-tax laws of several states and has delved into European systems for taxing inheritances. For a time doubt existed among the members of the Ways and Means Committee regarding not only the political wisdom but the constitutionality of an inheritance tax. A decision has been reached, however, that such a tax is expedient and will not conflict with the Constitution.

The decision had been reached largely at Hull's insistence. For years he had been dinning into the ears of his colleagues on the committee, as well as the general membership of the House, the merits of that particular form of taxation. Now he was wise enough to seize on the wartime fiscal requirements for more money in the Treasury to drive home his point. On the floor of the House during the summer, when the new revenue bill was under debate, Hull defended the tax innovations for which he was responsible by saying that "we are preparing now against possible war debts of the future."

By the end of the year he began to fear that deficit financing would run away with the administration as monetary requirements of the government kept on mounting. He formulated a system of double bookkeeping for the Treasury which reminds one of President Roosevelt's double budget in the early days of the New Deal and in the first months of the gigantic rearmament program of 1941. The New York *Times* had the following to say in its issue of December 30, 1916:

Representative Hull of Tennessee, author of the income-tax law,[1] outlined today a plan he has drafted for consideration of the Ways and Means Committee for separating preparedness accounts from the ordinary expenses and receipts of the government. He estimates that ordinary expenses this year and next will be less than the ordinary receipts and that special taxation and bond issues will be needed only to cover excess disbursements for various purposes, including army, navy, and fortifications extensions.

Mr. Hull's plan contemplates the issuance of $125,000,000 of Panama Canal bonds for army and navy expenses, $70,000,000 under the shipping act and for the proposed nitrate plant, and $25,000,000 to pay for the Danish West Indies, or a total of $220,000,000.

He was not having things all his own way, of course, and the same issue of the newspaper reported one of the counterproposals that was being advanced.

Treasury officials today said that the plan of Representative Garner of Texas, to be pressed by him in committee, for a 10 per cent ad valorem duty on all imports now free and a 5 per cent increase on all articles now dutiable would add $268,639,895 to the revenues for the period between March 1, next, and July 1, 1918, provided imports continued at the present rate. Strong opposition to this plan is already apparent.

The "strong opposition" was headed by Cordell Hull within the confines of the committee He considered the future Vice-President's plan, and others like it, as objectionable from two points of view: first, a trend in the direction of increasing tariffs would run counter to all the policies and promises of the Demo-

[1] He was not to be permitted to live that down.

cratic party and no emergency would excuse it; second, the higher rates would tend to cut down imports, which were becoming increasingly uncertain at best, and would thus be self-defeating from the point of view of raising revenue. Ever since 1910 he had been pointing to the utterly unpredictable yield of revenue from customs duties in an effort to win public opinion away from this facile and relatively painless method of raising public funds.

Four months later the United States was at war and all questions of fiscal prudence went by the board. Hull threw himself into the thick of the financing work. He made a speech in favor of each of the series of war loans, but only after his behind-the-scenes work on them had insured to his mind that they were necessary and well devised. He read up on English war financing as far back as the Napoleonic Wars. He studied the methods both France and Germany had used thus far to finance their war efforts since 1914. Out of all this study and reflection he had come, by the autumn of 1917, to a concept of the financing methods the United States should use (and which were, as a matter of fact, employed) which may be summed up as follows:

Small wars can be financed by taxation, but the present conflict was beyond doubt a great war of unpredictable duration. As much of it should be paid from taxes as could be provided by levies which would not cripple or even impair the nation's productive system. For the rest, money would have to be borrowed from the public.

The borrowings would have to be divided into two categories: first, the funds to be lent to the Allies would be secured by the sale of bonds bearing such maturities as the Allies themselves thought they could meet, since all of this money would eventually be paid back by the borrowers; second, the money needed for this country's own prosecution of the war, above what could be drawn from current taxes, would be borrowed on short-term obligations—something about five years.

His reason for advocating the short-term obligations was his conviction that interest rates would fall materially after the war was over. Accordingly there was no point in the government saddling itself with a long-term debt at the ruinously high rates of interest prevalent during the war when it was obvious it could not refund this debt at a later date on more favorable terms. He believed it would be wiser to risk the earlier maturities on the probable chance that the government could pay off the high-interest bonds, at the end of five years, by selling others of like principal amount but at half the carrying charges. He favored boosting the income and excess profits taxes to rates where they would yield $1,000,000,000 a year each and the estate tax to where it would yield $200,000,000 a year. These increases in revenue would pay part of the estimated expenditures of $10,-500,000,000 which he foresaw for the fiscal year of 1918.

Hull by no means lost sight of the larger issues of the war in his technical concern over the finance problem. On October 6, 1917, he described the course of the conflict in words that he might have used in 1940. He told the House:

From those early days of this great conflict when Germany, pretending only to threaten Russia, proceeded instead to mobilize her chief forces on the French border, on the opposite side of the German Empire from Russia, the outstanding fact, now beyond dispute, that the German government had suddenly embarked upon its hitherto secret plan of world conquest and world dominion became apparent. Both at the beginning and for a long period thereafter many other nations looked on in horror and hoped that they might be able to remain out of this awful conflict with honor and safety.

Strange as it may seem, one peaceable and peace-loving country after another has been drawn in, under circumstances impossible to avoid without such sacrifices of honor and of God-given rights as no country could make and long endure.

In this same speech he advocated tightening the income-tax law in order to prevent what he considered to be avoidances. He thought the exemptions for charitable donations were much too liberal, citing how a man with an annual income of $10,000,000 a year could give $1,500,000 to a charitable institution without paying any tax on that amount.

"The effect of this transaction," he held, "would be that the government would really donate 60 per cent and the taxpayer only 40 per cent, but the taxpayer would get the entire credit for the donation while the government would suffer the loss of $900,000 war taxes."

He saw no reason why Federal judges should be exempted

from paying Federal income tax. He supposed that the exemption had been written into the law out of deference to the Constitutional provision that judges' salaries could not be diminished during their terms in office. He contended that this was unreasonable and that the Constitutional inhibition would apply only "if Congress should classify the salaries of Federal judges and lay a different tax than that imposed on all other salaries of like amount."

By early 1918 he had reached the conclusion that "we have become a great creditor nation and will continue to be." Had his appreciation of the revolutionary change which had crept unperceived into the national economy been more widely accepted during the succeeding decade, the United States might have taken precautions which would have cushioned the shock of the world depression of 1929.

He also warned the American public that "if any citizen cannot see that world conquest and world dominion are and have long been the deliberate plan and purpose of German militarism, such citizen is indeed living his life to little purpose and will later realize, when it is too late, his utter failure to grasp and understand the certain objects and inevitable trend of this world-wide war"—a prototype of the earnest counsels he spread so patiently among the appeasers, isolationists, and middle-of-the-road men of the country in 1940 and 1941.

As the war went into those critical days of 1918, Hull fell into the habit of interlarding his highly technical speeches on financial topics with exhortations to greater war efforts. For example, a speech in favor of the war-revenue bill, delivered on September 10, 1918, two months before the Armistice, contained the following prophetic denunciation of the German war leaders:

The most ignorant person is now familiar with the uncivilized, savage, and barbarous methods employed by the German government in waging this unholy, outrageous, and unspeakable war of conquest. For brutality and inhumanity, for duplicity and false pretense, for rape and robbery, for piracy and fiendish cruelty, for the malicious destruction of innocent lives and property, for the deliberate violation of the inalienable rights of both nations and individuals, for the utter and contemptuous disregard of every vestige of right, justice, honor, fair dealing, and moral sense, the conduct of the German overlords, from the day they plotted and precipitated this world war, has been without parallel and without comparison and has brought upon their heads a universal judgment of criminal infamy which a million years of atonement cannot remove.

Loud applause from both sides of the chamber interrupted the speaker. He went on:

Talk about "a peace of negotiation." How can you negotiate any question with scoundrels and villains, with assassins and free-booters, with highwaymen and desperadoes? They must first either be killed or disarmed, and then let honorable men speak and act for their nation at the peace table.

Although he did not know it, the curtain was starting to fall upon this act of Cordell Hull's life. The Armistice was shortly signed, and Woodrow Wilson was first repudiated by the American people in the November elections of 1918, when a Republican House of Representatives was returned as a rebuke to the President's plea for another Democratic majority to insure successful conclusion of the war and the negotiation of a just and durable peace. The Democratic party was going into an eclipse that was to last until the Congressional elections of 1930, and Hull's ideas were to share that eclipse.

While his service to his country during the critical period of the World War was by no means limited to his financial wizardry in the House of Representatives, that is the portion of it which is engraved most durably on the public record. The debates of the period showed that Hull attracted the interested attention of all shades of opinion in the House when he spoke. Time after time, members who announced they were in total disagreement with the policy he was advocating asked him questions for the sake of information and expressed themselves as certain of the accuracy of his answers. There was a widespread recognition of his ability as a student and analyst and of the dependability of the facts he dug up.

There is no question that he was one of the principal authors of the economic and financial policies which characterized the two Wilson administrations. His income-tax law, as drafted in

1913 and as revised in 1916, has been estimated to have yielded $15,000,000,000 to the Federal Treasury in the crucial six years from 1914 to 1920. His borrowing policies contributed much to the orderly marketing of government securities during the war, and his insistence on applying surtaxes to the interest on Liberty bonds prevented them from gravitating into the hands of the extreme rich after the war, for purposes of tax evasion.

From the point of view of his own development, however, the most important result of his war experiences was the growing conviction that the tariff was more than a mere domestic issue of whether the few should extort tribute from the many. He became convinced that trade barriers between nations cause wars and that a lasting peace could be accomplished only by their gradual abolition.

There was a preliminary exposition of the advanced position he had reached by this time in his speech of September 10. He was interrupted by Representative Green of Iowa, who asked him if "he does not think it would be possible after the war to increase the revenue we derive from customs?" Hull replied that he did believe so and added the following:

Individually I have never shared in the persistent advocacy of the "war after the war" of which we have read so much during the past two years. Economic wars are but the germs of real wars. Trade retaliation and trade discrimination, from boycotting down, inevitably produce friction and irritation between nations and have, in fact, been one of the chief underlying causes of most wars in the past.

Should the present German rulers control the affairs of Germany as heretofore, I should, of course, favor economic and every other kind of warfare against them in the future, but our success in the present war, which is certain to come within a year, presupposes the elimination of these overlords and the lodgment of power in the hands of the people. Believing as I have that the best antidote against war is the removal of its causes rather than its prevention after the causes once arise, and finding that trade retaliation and discrimination in its more vicious forms have been productive of bitter economic wars, which in many cases have developed into wars of force, I introduced a resolution in the House of Representatives during the early part of last year which would provide for the organization of an international trade-agreement congress, the objects of which should be to eliminate by mutual agreement all possible methods of retaliation and discrimination in international trade.

This course should tend greatly to diminish the dangerous possibilities of economic warfare and to promote fair and friendly trade relations among all the nations of the world.

Dealing with the question of competition through the tariff is another and different question. In my judgment the country that will prosper greatest after the war will be that country which develops the highest state of utility and efficiency in its production; that country which encourages invention and scientific and industrial education and training in the largest measure; that country in which capital and labor in a friendly spirit mutually work out a relationship just and fair to both with respect to each important industry. Antiquated machinery, worn-out methods, and inefficient management will have to be abandoned.

These observations, which were interjected into a speech on quite another subject, might have served as a foreword for his speech of February 21, 1919, which Mr. Hull still considers to be one of the finest and most important he ever made. When he took the floor in the House on that day Woodrow Wilson was in Paris, commuting between the official Peace Conference at Versailles and the unofficial center of negotiations he and his adviser, Colonel Edward Mandell House, had established at the Hotel Crillon in Paris.

The American President was at the very zenith of his career. He had been received as a very savior and monarch of the world on his triumphal tours of France, England, and Italy. His Fourteen Points had been accepted by the Central Powers, even if not unreservedly by the Allies, as the basis for a just peace. The common people of the world believed that he and his country could and would fabricate a new order of peace, justice, prosperity, and happiness. Their representatives, however, as gathered around the tables in the Château de Versailles in the persons of "Papa" Clemenceau, David Lloyd George, and the others were more "practical," in their own minds, in that they were satisfied that peace, justice, prosperity, and happiness were not present in the world in sufficient measure to go around. Regretfully, therefore, they felt that it was their task to see that their own people got the largest possible share of the limited supply of these insufficient intangibles.

Far from the scene where clashed altruism, selfishness, idealism, nationalism, good faith, insincerity, and all possible other combinations of opposites, Hull envisioned the possibility of a lasting peace for the tortured Europe he had never seen. He spoke his piece to a Congress which was soon to be turned over to his opposition—the House of Representatives by a wide margin and the Senate by a majority of two votes.

Hull recalled to the House his proposal of 1917 to convoke an international trade conference in Washington at the close of the World War. He quoted the third of Wilson's Fourteen Points, which called for "the removal, so far as possible, of all economic barriers and the establishment of an equality of trade conditions among all nations consenting to the peace and associating themselves for its maintenance," saying that the adoption of this program was the only hope for "the permanent peace and friendship of nations." In answer to Republican criticism of such a program Hull reminded the House how President Wilson himself had explained on October 28, 1918, that each nation would be free to determine its own tariff policies but that whatever tariffs were adopted would be applied equally against the produce of all foreign countries. Wilson's idea was that "weapons of economic discipline and punishment should be left to the joint action of all nations for the purpose of punishing those who will not submit to a general program of justice and equality."

From this springboard Hull jumped into a sweeping description of the economic war germs he saw lurking about the world, observing that "this is undoubtedly a stage at which every commercial nation might well begin with a clean slate." Already he feared that "economic alliances established here and there by certain groups of commercial nations are calculated to arouse suspicion, hostility, retaliation, and ultimately economic war"—fears which were only too thoroughly realized in the next two decades.

"The verdict of history, in my judgment, will be that Germany finally did go to war to gain greater control over markets for her home products and over larger sources of raw materials she needed for manufacture at home," he said.

Trade discriminations between sovereign nations as well as between mother countries and colonies (and he cited numerous examples of both) are both dangerous and shortsighted, he told the House. In addition to tariff preferentials he listed subsidies, bonuses, drawbacks, rebates, etc., as forms of discrimination which tend to bring on economic warfare. He pointed to what he considered the weakness of the British colonial preference scheme then in effect, chiding the Canadians for condemning themselves to pay higher prices for the goods they purchased in the United States. He was especially scathing in his attack on "concessions" won by bribing officials of backward countries with "loans," and his principal illustration of this process was a surprisingly accurate forecast of what the American public came to fear Germany would do in Latin America. He said:

The acquisition of German Southwest Africa illustrates this class of international commercial depredations. A German merchant established a trading post in this territory and later ceded it to the German government. The government thereupon pretended to effect "treaties" with the natives for territory embracing 322,000 square miles and at once sent an army there to maintain German "rights."

German traders soon after the year 1886 pushed their way into the Pacific Islands and, of course, promptly demanded protection by the home government. German battleships were soon on the scene, with the final result that Germany acquired an area of 100,000 square miles in the Pacific Islands which German armies and war vessels have been guarding from that day.

The result in each instance cited has been a complete monopoly of the valuable raw materials and the trade of these localities by Germany. Force, stealth, and bribery have often been found in these territorial acquisitions. These helpless localities have first been placed under commercial tribute, and this has been followed by political and military domination. By similar methods Germany plundered parts of Poland, the Ukraine, and other small or defenseless countries.

It still causes one to shudder to recall how commercial nations, bantering, jockeying, and threatening each other in the course of strenuous trade conquests, have so often approached the very verge of a general war. Different terms have been used to define the various degrees or steps pursued by the strong nation in its efforts to secure new territory The terms "controlling influence," "spheres of influence," "protectorate," and "colonies" mark the successive steps from the beginning of the encroachment until the designing country secures its prey.

Here, for the first time, was disclosed the mature Hull. Here was the developed philosophy, in essence, which has won for him the admiration and esteem not only of his own country but of much of the world. The low-tariff Democrat from Tennessee had broadened into a great liberal internationalist, his horizon no longer limited to the memories of Republican rascality after the Civil War or the predatory operations of special privilege against the whole people of his country but enlarged to include the vision of a permanently happy, prosperous, and peaceful world. That horizon has never narrowed as the years have passed.

CHAPTER X

Rebirth of the Democratic Party

THE WAR WAS OVER. The stricken Wilson was unable to carry the double burden of the normal revulsion of the American public from the psychology of the war period coupled with his own political ineptness. When he was forced by illness to retire from active participation in the presidential campaign of 1920 the Democratic party's fate was sealed, as it might well have been in any event.

The defeat of the proposed peace treaty with Germany, embodying the Covenant of the League of Nations, in the Senate on November 19, 1919, and its final rejection by six votes on March 19, 1920, made it inevitable to a man of Wilson's temperament that the coming presidential election should be in the nature of a plebiscite on the issue of whether the United States should become a founder member of the League. The Democrats were obliged to seek far for a candidate who would accept the Wilsonian gage of electoral combat and finally nominated Governor James M. Cox of Ohio, an able man but one little known in national affairs.

Democratic leaders, such as Charles F. Murphy and Alfred E. Smith of New York, thought it would be a close election but believed the Democrats could win. They hoped that Governor Cox

could carry Ohio against the Republican nominee, Senator Warren Gamaliel Harding of Ohio. Whoever could win the forty-
eight electoral votes of that state would be the winner of the national contest, it was reasoned.

Soon after the Democratic convention, which was held early
in July, the Democratic high command set about organizing the
campaign which was to put Jimmy Cox in the White House and
the United States in the League of Nations. The Democratic National Committee, of which Hull had been a member since 1914,
was called to meet at Columbus on July 20 to prepare itself for
the fray. Homer S. Cummings, who was then chairman, had declared that he would not head the committee any longer, although he was willing to take a speaker's part in the campaign.
Judge E. H. Moore, Cox's preconvention manager, who would
have been a logical choice to succeed Cummings, said he would
not accept the chairmanship.

Thus it was obvious that a complicated fight was brewing in
the committee itself on the eve of a critical campaign. Some of the
party leaders conferred in Chicago prior to the Columbus gathering, and they conceded that Cordell Hull would be elected chairman. They described him as "one of the silentest statesmen we
have." They were full of confidence about the outcome of the
election, and Judge Moore told the press:

"Cox will carry Ohio without a doubt. The reaction to the
nomination has been wonderfully favorable throughout the
West."

Governor Cox, as a candidate, behaved somewhat as did
Wendell Willkie in 1940. He made little effort to propitiate the
old-line politicians. When the National Committee met at Columbus he let it be known that he demanded an Ohio man as chairman. A subcommittee, of which Hull was a member, was appointed to consult with him and with his vice-presidential candidate, whose name was Franklin D. Roosevelt, on this subject.
They brought back to the committee meeting the recommendation that the chairmanship be voted to George H. White of
Marietta. White had served several terms in the House of Representatives, and Hull, far from displaying any disappointment at
developments, issued a statement praising the new chairman
for courage, intelligence, honesty, and energy, adding that he

had gained this impression through service with White in Washington.

The November landslide to Harding blasted the Democrats out of the White House, out of both houses of Congress, and out of many state offices. Tennessee broke away from the Solid South to vote for Harding and elected Alf Taylor as governor—the first Republican in many years to carry that office.

Hull himself was one of the orphans of the storm. He was defeated in the Fourth Congressional District by a Republican named Wynne (known to his political intimates as Windy) Clouse. This was the only electoral defeat Hull ever had to suffer in his long career of offering himself to the whims of the voters.

Throughout the country the Democratic party was pulverized. It appeared doomed for another half-century of exile from national power. It bade fair to becoming again "a losing and therefore an objecting party," as the Nashville *American* had described it in 1906. Its high command split into many factions during the year following the campaign, most of which were united only in their dislike for Chairman White. Champ Clark was White's leading backer at this point, and William Gibbs McAdoo headed the movement to depose him. White himself declined to call the committee for a reorganization meeting, or to resign, until the dissident elements had agreed on a successor to the chairmanship.

The party was faced with a large financial deficit inherited from the catastrophic campaign, however, and its leaders realized, after the first coma following the knockout had passed away, that they must be up and about their business if the organization was to survive. Finally, pressed from all sides, White called the committee to meet at St. Louis on November 1, 1921. Again Hull seemed to be the favorite for the chairmanship. His closest contender was Breckenridge Long, who suffered under the handicap of not being a member of the committee. For him to be eligible to the chairmanship it would be necessary to persuade Edward F. Goltra of St. Louis, the Missouri committeeman, to resign so that Long could be elected to the vacancy and then nominated for the chairmanship. Goltra cleared up the whole situation by refusing to resign, and Hull became the unopposed compromise choice.

The new chairman, in a graceful acceptance speech, said that he would promote decentralization of the party organization so as to bring the county and local organizations more closely into the work of rebuilding the shattered ranks of the Democratic party and that he would seek above all to see that Democratic women voters were adequately represented. This was taking a leaf from his own bitter book, because "Windy" Clouse had been able to persuade the Republican women of the district to turn out and vote for him, while the Democratic women thought it was too much trouble to go to the polls and vote for Hull. This was the first election in the country's history where women were able to vote in every state, Tennessee having been the thirty-sixth state to ratify the woman-suffrage amendment to the Constitution shortly before the election.

Having elected Hull to what appeared to be a thoroughly thankless task, the St. Louis meeting broke up after adopting a resolution to the effect that "the Democratic National Committee expresses its gratification at the assembling of the disarmament conference and further expresses hope for its complete success." This was a reference to the Washington Conference on the Limitation of Naval Armaments, which had been convoked by President Harding, upon the urging of Charles Evans Hughes, his Secretary of State, as the Republican party's first step toward constructive international statesmanship now that it had saved the country from the League of Nations.

The following day Hull gave to the Associated Press an outline of the policies he intended to pursue as chairman of the Democratic National Committee. He announced, with characteristic directness and practicability:

The first step in administering the affairs of the committee will be to pay off the present indebtedness and create a good atmosphere in which to work. We shall try to pay all debts at an early date.

We shall also proceed at once with the establishment of a systematic and thorough organization in the various states and counties. In this connection we shall strive to maintain an efficient publicity bureau to get unbiased and accurate facts relating to the shortcomings of the Republican administration before the average citizens.

People have been fed up on a vast amount of misrepresentation, misinformation, and falsehood concerning the true record of the Democratic administration, covering the period since 1918. Subsequent events and daily happenings have exploded a vast number of these falsehoods, which at times were very dangerous. We shall make every possible effort to develop the Democratic National Committee into the most militant and efficient organization within our power to do so [sic].

The "efficient publicity bureau" mentioned by the chairman was soon established in two small rooms in a Washington side street. It was manned by Hull himself, Miss Will Harris, the secretary he brought from Tennessee in 1908 and who still presides over his secretarial work at the State Department, and Dick Buchanan, a run-of-the-mine newspaperman who was paid $25 a week. The Democratic National Committee now maintains, at its general headquarters in the Mayflower Hotel, a publicity bureau of seven permanent employees headed by Charles Michelson at $25,000 a year, with the lesser lights paid in proportion. Frank Kent, of the Baltimore *Sun,* who covered the publicity office frequently in those days, told me he thought Hull's organization was just as efficient as its larger and more expensive successor in the days of the party's prosperity.

The New York *Times* thought Hull's choice as chairman was a happy one. It commented:

Fortunately the long-smoldering attempt to promote discord and squabbling in the National Democratic Committee, turn it from its proper function, make it the agent of a particular candidate and not the general agent of the Democratic party, has been put out at St. Louis. Judge Cordell Hull, sometime an able judge in Tennessee and later a distinguished member of the House of Representatives, chosen chairman as a compromise candidate, has no part in the premature ambitions of any Democrats who are casting sheep's eyes at the White House. He has it in his power to do the Democratic party a considerable service. With the political events of 1924 the committee has nothing to do. Its instant task is to do what it can to elect a Democratic House in 1922.

Along with these bouquets the paper could not resist the temptation to take a little dig at Hull's taxation theories, which had been exercising its editors for years.

"What sober and responsible taxation scheme have the Democrats?" the writer demanded. "It is hard to find out from their drifting, leaderless, haphazard votes and opinions in Congress. Some of them talk like old Populists or contemporary Farmer-Laborites. The Democrats are not going to carry the next House by showing an inclination to chastise business with scorpions after the Republicans have chastised it with whips."

Chairman Hull made good on his promises to the nation's Democrats. He dug the national committee out of debt, using $30,000 of his own money to pay off the most pressing obligations. He traveled about the country exhorting and encouraging organization leaders everywhere, not neglecting to start his own campaign for re-election to the House of Representatives. The formal opening of his campaign came at a dinner given in his honor by the Tennessee State Democratic Committee in Nashville on December 28.

He opened his speech by advocating relief for farmers, aid for veterans, and reduction of taxes—all safe stand-bys for campaign purposes. He lay the blame for the existing economic depression on the Republicans—another sure-fire campaign issue.

"The burden of our public debt should be adjusted so as not to be oppressive to the American taxpayer laboring under panic conditions," he said. "The states, rather than the Federal government, should be urged to deal, by a uniform policy, with the growing evil of local tax-exempt securities."

Of the debacle of 1920 he said:

"It was not so much the Democratic party, it was the American people who have suffered the colossal and incalculable losses that resulted from Democratic defeat. It is beyond the power of wholesale abuse, falsehood, and detraction long to dim the glory of the eight years' unparalleled achievement of the national Democracy. The work of constructive, patriotic statesmanship accomplished by that party will stand out in clearer perspective during the coming years. The Democratic party emerged from that almost superhuman ordeal with flag untarnished, with doctrines sound and pure, with a record of undying fame, and with cheerful hope for the future."

The Tennesseans topped off their banquet by sending the

following telegram to Woodrow Wilson, who was a very sick man at his S Street home in Washington:

The Democratic Executive Committee of Tennessee and hundreds of leading Democrats from every county in the State, met to pay honor to Hon. Cordell Hull, Chairman of the National Committee, send heartiest greetings and felicitations on the occasion of your sixty-fifth anniversary, with sincerest wishes that you may enjoy many more such days—day by day gaining in health and strength as you are in love and affection in the hearts of your countrymen.

The Congressional elections of 1922 bore witness to the efficacy of Hull's political activities. In his own race he easily defeated "Windy" Clouse, who had probably been more surprised than anyone else at his victory in 1920. On the national scene the Democrats reduced the Republican majority in the Senate from 22 to 9 and in the House of Representatives from 170 to 18. This was a notable comeback for a party that had appeared to be thrown into permanent outer darkness only two years before.

It was extremely heartening to Hull. He felt that long-range ideas of the Democratic party, of Woodrow Wilson, and of all liberal elements in the country had received an encouraging endorsement His own thoughts at this epoch can be gleaned best from a campaign handbook which he had compiled and much of which he wrote himself. It called the Democrats "the party of sound principles and policies," and Hull interpreted the Congressional gains as meaning that the public agreed with this description.

The handbook attacked the results of the Washington Naval Conference as far more dangerous to the future of the nation than any feature of the League of Nations would have been, charging that the Republican party, after repudiating the League, had been willing "to write into some of the treaties the vicious and war-breeding policies of the counteralliance or the separate alliance which always contains the germs of future wars." This was an obvious reference to the Four-Power Pact "with its serious omissions and its compound mixture of contradictory and dangerous policies and principles, leaving Japan supreme in the

Pacific," as it was characterized at another place in the hand-book.

This was the only accomplishment of the Republicans in the field of foreign affairs, the campaign literature set forth, except that they had been able to block the Democratic program which would have "provided for early disarmament by all important nations, not as to a few major battleships merely, but on land, on the sea, under the sea, and in the air" and would have "provided for such economic cooperation with our European customers and such financing of our exports as would maintain sound, reciprocal market conditions to the end that the producers would have ready markets at prices fixed by the law of supply and demand."

"Every nation, great or small, has a right to live its own life, to determine its own policies, and to carry out its own ideals," the Democratic doctrine set forth. "But no nation, great or small, has the right to interfere with the life of any other; and any aggression, any interference from the outside with the domestic concerns of other nations, or any dispute between nations which may lead to war, is a matter in which we and in which every other peace-loving country of the world must be consulted *before* any outbreak. We must be consulted because our commerce reaches every corner of the globe, because any world convulsion affects us directly and indirectly, and because our influence, known by all the world to be unselfish and disinterested, is the greatest existing moral force for peace."

These utterances of 1922 were the fundamental principles on which Hull conducted the country's foreign policy from 1933 forward, when he became Secretary of State. The dangers of the Far Eastern situation as a result of the naval limitation came to be realized by all, but only in the next decade when it was too late to do much about it. The total disarmament pledge he tried to carry out at Geneva in 1933, when he got President Roosevelt to authorize Norman H. Davis, American ambassador at large, to promise the Disarmament Conference that the United States would never take action tending to defeat collective punishment of an aggressor, provided all nations disarmed and provided the United States concurred in the judgment as to the aggressor. This was the most sweeping promise of American participation in world politics that any authorized representative of the country has ever made, and Hull was prepared to live up to it had the European powers agreed on disarmament.

The economic portions must have been dictated by Hull, for they reflect in every phrase the path he followed without deviation until the outbreak of the European war in 1939 put an end to world sanity. The non-intervention principles he embodied firmly in the fabric of inter-American relations, laying countless old ghosts and disarming suspicions of long standing. The estimate of the importance to the United States of "any world convulsion" was amply borne out in the trying days of 1940 and 1941.

The next summer, on a hot day in early August, President Harding died in San Francisco after a visit to Alaska. The country entered on one of the most curious periods of its history under the leadership of one of its most curious Presidents— Calvin Coolidge. It was to be a period of complete eclipse for the Democratic party and for Cordell Hull.

Harding, the friendly country newspaper editor, the good fellow, the easygoing senator, had not been up to the job of President. The dangerous indiscretions of his Ohio friends and their friends came to light only after his death. The real leaders of the old-line Republican party breathed sighs of relief that the Lord in his inscrutable wisdom had seen fit to take Harding away before his sins of omission were visited upon him and set to work to build a new façade on the foundation of the unimpeachable Coolidge. The old Harding gang was quickly liquidated, some of its members ending their careers in jail, and the Coolidge era set in.

It was to be an era of old-fashioned horse sense, the Republican strategists decided. They sedulously disseminated quips of the new President which showed him in a good old New England light—thrifty, earthy, shrewd. His alleged remark about the war debtors that "they hired the money, didn't they?" was hailed as an evidence that the country's affairs from then on would be in the hands of any old-fashioned Yankee horse trader who could be relied upon to get the better of any bargain he drove on behalf of the United States.

Coolidge is inexplicable to this day. Beneath the dour, silent exterior he displayed to the world he took a boyish delight in being President. A day or two after he took up residence in the White House the secret-service chief showed him a button hidden in the molding at a particular point (it may be there now, so no particulars will be given) and explained to him that if he was ever in danger he had only to press it and a general alarm would sound, sending every available man in the White House to his assistance. He tested it so often and at such unexpected hours that the secret service quietly placed it somewhere else without notifying the Chief Executive of the change. They say his face was a study the first time he fumbled about the old spot and couldn't find any button, but he never let on that he knew of the trick they had played on him.

With all his idiosyncrasies, Calvin Coolidge was the logical choice to be the Republican party's standard-bearer in 1924. The Democrats were in far different shape. Aspirants for their nomination could be counted by the dozen, and there was little evidence of any particular leaning toward any of them. As a matter of fact, Cordell Hull had his first presidential boom in this period of confusion. A resolution was introduced in the Tennessee legislature reciting his merits and urging the Democratic party to nominate him. State legislatures often go through this complimentary procedure in honor of their favorite sons, but under the circumstances Hull felt called upon to discourage it. He wrote the Speaker of the Tennessee Senate a letter on March 16, 1923, which contained the following:

My first and highest duty is to so conduct the affairs of the Democratic national organization as will best safeguard and advance the interests and welfare of the Democratic party of the nation and make as certain as possible Democratic success in 1924. To this end I have consistently pursued the policy of making the party organization an agency in fact, as well as in name, for the entire party membership and of keeping it strictly aloof from elements, groups, factions, and individual contests for party nominations. To this course I have every disposition to adhere most scrupulously in the future.

Waiving, for the moment, consideration of my own limitations, of which I am fully conscious, I am sure that Democratic legislators will agree, in the light of the foregoing statements, that the Democratic National Headquarters must not even be suspected, though it be from the expressions of home folks in terms of a personal compliment, of the slightest participation in individual rivalries for such an important party nomination as that referred to in the resolution.

He was quite sincere in his estimate of the duties and functions of a chairman of the national committee. He was proud of the renaissance of the Democratic party under his aegis and he wanted not even the slightest taint of reproach to obscure the final discharge of his duties in that capacity, for by this time he had determined to give over the reins of office immediately following the national convention. He was tired and his own affairs were not in very good shape. He had devoted too much time and money to his work as chairman and felt that he was entitled to retire in all honor.

The Democratic convention which he called to order in Madison Square Garden in New York on a blistering July day in 1924 was a gathering of the leading lights of the party—a tribute to the renewed hope he had helped to infuse in the organization since the disastrous beating four years before. The delegates included sixteen governors, twenty-one senators, and more than one hundred representatives. They all believed the Democratic party had a chance to win the presidency the following November.

But they could not agree on the best man to head their ticket. The two-thirds rule was still in force, of course, and a deadlock appeared as soon as the balloting for the presidential nomination started. Day after day, night after night, the exhausted delegates answered the roll call by states, Alabama invariably starting off by casting all its votes for Oscar W. Underwood.

After the seventy-seventh ballot, with William Gibbs McAdoo and Alfred E. Smith locked in a hopeless battle to the death of both their aspirations, there was renewed talk of Hull as a dark-horse compromise. Senator Joseph T. Robinson of Arkansas was another possibility who was discussed in the corridors.

Hull was too astute a politician to fancy very seriously his own chances for the nomination, although no doubt he would have accepted gladly had it been tendered. As it was, he served on a committee appointed to find some way out of the impasse which looked as if it would last all summer. The committee's activities were carried on in the smoke-filled rooms so common to all political conventions, and there was no public announcement of what it recommended, but on July 8 McAdoo released his delegates. On the one hundredth ballot John W. Davis, who had had few votes up to that time, took a long spurt forward and continued to gain on each roll call until he was nominated on the one hundred and third ballot on July 9. The unnerved delegates nominated Charles W. Bryan, brother of William Jennings Bryan, as the vice-presidential candidate on the first ballot and adjourned.

Whatever may have been his opinion of the convention's wisdom, Hull maintained his role of impartial chairman and made no public comment. He arranged with Mr. Davis and with the national committee to turn over the duties of the chairmanship to the man who was slated to be his successor well in advance of the successor's election, and on July 19 he issued the following statement:

Clem L. Shaver of West Virginia will perform the duties as chairman of the Democratic National Committee for and instead of myself from this date.

I am greatly pleased to know that my successor as chairman is an exceptionally able man with much successful political experience. The management of the coming campaign could not be placed in abler or safer hands. Mr. Shaver is a man of great energy, fine judgment, and is scrupulously conscientious. I confidently predict for Mr. Shaver a highly satisfactory administration and for the Democratic party a sweeping victory under his guidance as official head of the party organization.

It is a source of satisfaction to me to be able to turn over the organization free from all debt, which includes the payment of some $235,000 of old obligations. A balance of several thousand dollars is on hand. There is also some pride in the knowledge that I am able to turn over to him a highly developed organization which is ready to function in each essential line from this day forward.

After stepping aside in favor of Shaver, Hull took only a normal part in the campaign on behalf of Davis. He ridiculed Senator George Wharton Pepper's praise of what the Pennsylvanian described as the "tiptoe diplomacy" of the Coolidge administration. Hull called it "the sort of diplomacy by which the urchin sees a ball game by peeking through a knothole," making it plain that he believed the United States should play a more positive part in world affairs. However, Mr. Coolidge was re-elected in no uncertain terms, and Hull had to settle down once again to minority membership in the House of Representatives.

He became worried at the taxation policy which he feared President Coolidge, with Secretary of the Treasury Mellon to guide him, would follow. He believed that the national debt (then considered staggering) of some $20,000,000,000 ought to be paid off at once, as well as the state and municipal indebtedness of $11,000,000,000, but he feared that the administration would flinch at maintaining the existing high tax rates and would seek instead to reduce the levies bearing on the richest elements of the population in favor of taxes which would have a more general distribution.

Entering the general debate on the new revenue bill on December 9, 1925, he reminded the House that "our government was able to do what no other government on earth had ever done" when it financed 44 per cent of its war expenses out of taxes during the World War. Even counting in the loans to the Allies, which had begun to look like dubious assets, as legitimate war expenses of the United States, the government had paid 32 per cent of its cash expenditures by taxes. This pay-as-you-go policy must be continued in peacetime, he contended.

Instead of the haphazard methods under which the Federal government, the states, the counties, and the municipalities each taxed the same sources without regard to the incidence of other burdens their taxpayers had to bear, Hull recommended a permanent division of fields of taxation within which the various authorities should have jurisdiction. The reforms he suggested have never been adopted, although they are resurrected from time to time during tax debates. He offered the following division of tax labor:

1. The Federal government should raise its revenue (some $3,000,000,000 was needed for the current year) from the income tax as its principal source and from customs duties, tobacco and estate taxes, excises such as were being levied on alcohol, oleomargarine and other articles, and small stamp duties

to be adjusted so as to balance the yields of the more important taxes.

2. The states should derive their revenues from gasoline, license and other auto taxes, inheritance taxes, income taxes with a flat rate of 1 or 2 per cent, special assessments, license, occupation and other minor taxes.

3. The municipalities should seek their income from real-estate taxes, along with sales taxes and minor business levies.

He closed his speech with a general attack on the administration's fiscal policies.

"The Mellon-Coolidge leadership shouts for tax reduction in order to aid business and reduce living costs, but they carefully exclude the heavy tax burdens arising from existing extreme high tariff rates and insist that even the conceded tariff excesses must remain untouched," he said to the accompaniment of applause from the Democratic side. "In other words, 'tax reduction' means to lower internal and raise tariff taxes.

"Most Democrats look on this partial and contradictory view as rank duplicity and hypocrisy. They earnestly believe that comprehensive and honest tax relief must embrace the elimination of excessive tariff-tax burdens, the existence of which no one seriously denies."

While it might be inferred from this speech that Hull had reverted to his original view of the tariff as a matter of purely domestic concern, he was actually more convinced than ever that permanent world peace depended on the abolition of unreasonable trade barriers. At this epoch, however, it looked to most Americans as if world peace was an established fact. Prosperity seemed to be mounting. American loans were beginning to flow to Europe, a surprising amount of them ending up in Germany, which had not been materially damaged by the war. What was actually happening, although it was not yet generally understood, was that the private citizens in America were lending the German government the money to pay the reparations it had promised to France. The United States was entrenching itself as the creditor nation Hull had proclaimed it to be a few years before, but its financial and political leaders were giving no thought to this change's long-range implications in the nation's economic life.

Hull had attacked the Italian debt settlement, for example, on the ground that the Funding Commission had decided it was easier to reduce the principal of the obligation rather than to accept goods in payment of interest and principal alike. He would have preferred to lower tariffs to a point where Italian goods could be sold in the United States for enough dollars to pay the interest and principal of the debt. The New York *Times* said he was wrong in this but described him as a man "who has great prestige as an economic expert in Congress."

He had not forgotten his early abhorrence of high tariffs because of the domestic evils he believed they fostered, now that there was little public interest in his conception of liberal international commerce as a prescription for world peace. He attacked President Coolidge for telling the farmers of the country that the Fordney tariff rates were helping them. He said:

No mere rhetoric or eulogy can remove the great blanket of mortgages, aggregating from $7,000,000,000 to $10,000,000,000, from farm lands everywhere or raise the purchasing power of the farmer's dollar to a point within sight of the dollar received by the manufacturer who sells him all the clothing, household furnishings, farm implements, and most of the things he must purchase to wear or use.

The only purpose of the tariff is to raise prices, and if it fails to raise prices it is a deliberate fraud. The farmer now must know that it has not and cannot raise the prices of most all his staple products which constitute the chief value of our annual agricultural production such as cotton, tobacco, corn, wheat, oats, rye, hay, meats, and lard. The President suavely attempts to solace the farmer with the assurance that he should be entirely content with the home market.

The President is on wholly unsound ground when he tells the farmers that their only tariff losses are on the few imports which come in over our high tariff walls.

Hull's ideas and actions at this period, however, were far from being purely partisan in their nature. For example, he introduced a resolution to carry out a suggestion by Herbert Hoover, Republican Secretary of Commerce, that an international trade organization be established to promote fair and friendly trade relations between nations, although he coupled this with a proposal to revise the American tariff downward, thus insuring, from a practical point of view, that his plan would get no consideration in a Republican Congress. He also endorsed a move by Representative Tilson, a Republican from Connecticut, to investigate the British combination which controlled the marketing of rubber and the Brazilian plan for supporting the price of coffee. Hull estimated that the American public was paying the British combine $670,000,000 a year too much for the rubber it bought and that the Brazilians were charging the American people $80,-000,000 too much every year for their coffee, little dreaming that he would sponsor a somewhat similar Brazilian coffee-marketing agreement in the desperate days of 1941.

"The American people have undoubtedly suffered sufficient losses to arouse them to the importance of throwing off preconceived, provincial, or archaic notions," the *Congressional Record* quotes him as saying, "and to resolutely face the world economic situation as it actually exists today. Our continued failure to do so will bring swift and unerring penalties, whereas the pursuit of the sound program proposed will make America the world leader in finance and commerce for generations to come."

These words and others of the same purport which he uttered from time to time in those years brought little attention to themselves or to their author. The Great Era was well under way. The stock exchange's modernized equipment could not keep pace with the public's purchases of securities at ever-mounting prices. A new formula had been found, and old-fashioned warnings such as Hull had to offer were completely uninteresting to a public which had only to take a tip from someone who knew a waiter who had overheard a luncheon conversation of tycoons in Wall Street in order to get rich overnight. Hull kept on warning just the same.

President Coolidge's current term was coming to its close. Many people wanted him to run again, in the feeling that, with him in the White House, the stock market could never break. As the preconvention maneuvering got under way in the spring of 1928, Hull made his first radio broadcast in an effort to arouse public opinion.

"The end of eight years of Republican leadership and rule finds the American people less attentive to governmental duties and tasks than at any time in the nation's history," he said into the microphone on the evening of May 15. "There is a hopeless confusion about fundamentals. The spirit of our institutions—the spirit of America—is at its lowest ebb."

This turned out to be something of an understatement in view of the developments of the succeeding years. At the time, however, his auditors did not believe him. When President Coolidge finally told newspaper reporters that he did not choose to run the Republicans proceeded to nominate Herbert Hoover on the assumption that he would carry on exactly as had his predecessor, letting well enough alone, and that the market quotations for securities would continue to rise until every citizen in the country was a millionaire—on paper, at least.

The Democrats awaited the outcome of the Republican deliberations at Kansas City and then assembled at Houston, faced again with the difficult task of selecting a nominee who could unseat the party in power. As early as April, Hull had been mentioned as a vice-presidential possibility, but by early June he had captured the North Carolina delegation as their presidential candidate after a hot fight with the forces booming Governor Alfred E. Smith of New York

It was apparent that the Democratic party would suffer defections in the South if Al Smith were nominated, at least in the sections where he represented Rum and Romanism, if not Rebellion. He was an "all-out" advocate of repeal of the Prohibition Amendment, and the Southern states were in general the citadel of the drys. On the other hand, repeal was a popular issue in the East and the Middle West, which the Democrats would have to carry if they were to win the presidential election.

Hull was an acceptable, though not a fanatical, dry. During the state-wide fight for prohibition in Tennessee in 1908 he had prudently stayed outside the state. He took no active part in subsequent prohibition campaigns, but the Anti-Saloon League certified him as being at least a nominal partisan of its cause. That situation, added to his growing national reputation as an expert on government finance, brought him the North Carolina delegation.

The triumph heartened some of his Tennessee friends into thinking he might be built into the party's presidential candidate, although Hull himself appears to have taken the boomlet not too seriously. They prevailed on the Tennessee Congressional delegation to pass the following resolution:

The Democratic members from Tennessee in both branches of Congress unanimously and enthusiastically direct the attention of the Democrats of the nation to Hon. Cordell Hull as the most suitable and logical man for the Democratic nomination for President. During Judge Hull's twenty years' able and patriotic service in Congress he has become generally regarded as a deep student of domestic and world problems, a sound, broad-visioned, liberal, and constructive statesman, an outstanding authority on revenue, fiscal, and economic problems and well versed in all governmental affairs. Judge Hull's counsel was freely sought by President Wilson and other party leaders. He was one of the principal authors of the economic policies and otherwise played a large part in the formulation and enactment of the marvelous constructive program during the Wilson administration, both in peace and war.

Democrats will recall that in 1922, with the Congressional elections approaching, our national committee was without a chairman, was beset with factionalism and discord, and was deadlocked and inactive. Finally the committee unanimously called Judge Hull to the chairmanship, he being the only member upon whom all factions could agree. When he took charge the affairs of the Democratic party were at a low ebb and the national committee was burdened with a heavy debt left over from the previous campaign. Judge Hull gave freely of his time, means, and talents. He traveled throughout the country and effected national, state, and district organization and harmony. He directed an unparalleled campaign of education on all the vital issues. The result was that in the November 1922 elections the Republican majority in the House of Representatives was reduced from 170 to 18 and the Republican majority in the Senate was reduced from 22 to 9.

Not content with this splendid victory, Chairman Hull carried on. He continued to maintain active headquarters of the Democratic National Committee. He continued to direct a matchless campaign of education.

When Judge Hull turned over the party affairs to the Democratic National Committee in the summer of 1924 the committee was out of debt, an efficient nationwide organization existed, Democratic victory in the following fall elections seemed apparent, and the Republicans were extremely apprehensive and on the defensive.

With such qualities of statesmanship and leadership, with a public and private life without blemish, with an abhorrence of every form of corruption, with prestige, esteem, and confidence national in scope, in the prime of vigorous manhood, we consider this great Democrat an ideal candidate, upon whom all members of the party can unite and behind whom they can march to a harmonious and glorious victory for democracy.

Armed with this testimonial, the Tennessee delegation moved on Houston. Hull was to be placed in nomination before the convention by Harvey H. Hannah. A skeletonized list of his accomplishments was prepared for distribution among such delegates as were not familiar with his political career. It listed the following points in his favor:

1. One of the principal authors of the economic and financial policies of the Wilson administration.

2. Author of Federal income-tax system, 1913, and revised act of 1916, which tax method yielded a revenue, chiefly from war profits, of $15,000,000,000 during the six-year period.

3. Author of Federal estate or inheritance tax system, 1916, which is designed, by affording uniformity, to aid the states in developing tax systems that will yield three to four hundred millions, thereby displacing a like amount of vicious general property taxes on farms and other property.

4. The first to advocate a surtax on interest of Liberty bonds to prevent them, after the war, from gravitating into the hands of the extreme rich, who would thereby escape their fair share of taxes.

5. Author of House resolution, in April 1917, providing for a world trade-agreement congress at the end of the war, to eliminate, by mutual agreement, economic barriers and the harsher methods of discrimination and unfair practices in international trade and commerce.

6. Presided over a board in the Treasury Department in 1917 which prepared regulations to make the war tax laws workable and more equitable. Most of these regulations were later incorporated as a part of the revenue act of 1918.

7. Author of law of 1920 to continue the importation of wood pulp and newsprint paper free from duty.

8. Earnestly insisted to the President that Congress remain in session in May 1918, instead of adjourning, and enact a comprehensive war-tax measure rather than finance a correspondingly larger amount of war expenses with bonds This was supported by an exhaustive analysis of the entire revenue, financial, and eco-

nomic situation. Such revenue act was taken up and passed in February 1919.

9. Author of original bill to stabilize the value of Liberty bonds.

10. Immediately after the Armistice in November 1918 proposed and strongly urged the enactment of a comprehensive sinking-fund law for the wise handling and payment of the war debt. Such a law was enacted during the winter following.

11. Member of the Democratic National Committee since 1914 and chairman of that committee 1921–24.

12. Voted to submit the Eighteenth Amendment to the states. Voted for the Volstead Act and all amendments designed to improve or strengthen it.

These two minor documents are of interest chiefly because they are so obviously autobiographical. If Hull did not actually write them, they were composed under his direction and with his complete collaboration. Taken together, they present an accurate picture of what he thought of himself and his career at that point. If he were asked today to select the principal landmarks in his Congressional career, he would cite the same events.

When the Democratic convention was called to order at Houston it was fairly clear that Al Smith would be the nominee. However, when the procedure reached the stage of placing candidates before the convention, Mr. Hannah summoned his best oratorical efforts to back the outside chance that a revolt might be started which would oust Smith and might eventually direct the lightning to the head of Tennessee's favorite son. He shouted at the delegates:

Tennessee does not offer merely a favorite son candidate, to be given a complimentary vote, but a candidate who measures up to the needs of the hour. Tennessee does not offer you a sectional candidate but a man who belongs to the entire nation.

He is, by his great ability and achievements, greater than any section or faction. He is a national figure. He is probably regarded as the highest authority in America on the question of taxation and national finance. It is doubtful if there is a man in public life more skilled in or better acquainted with our international relations. It was his all-powerful judicial mind that drafted the income-tax law that has stood the acid test of the courts.

Tennessee's candidate proved his matchless ability when he sat at the elbow of his great chief, Woodrow Wilson, and helped him to formulate laws and measures to finance the World War and save civilization from lapsing back into medievalism.

Mr. Hannah carried on in this vein, throwing in a few well-chosen references to another Tennessean named Andrew Jackson, until the perspiring delegates and spectators in the galleries began to boo in unmistakable evidence of boredom. Mr. Hannah paused and gave the prearranged signal to his fellow Tennesseans.

With alacrity and a semblance of spontaneity they picked up their standard and started the usual parade around the hall. The North Carolina delegation fell in behind them. Shortly the delegates from Alabama, Florida, Oklahoma, and South Carolina joined the procession. When they reached the Mississippi delegation several paraders tried to persuade the Mississippians to join, and for a moment it looked as if they would. Then they settled back in their places and the Hull demonstration was practically over. In all, it lasted about five minutes, which is not remarkable for a political convention.

When the first roll was called, which resulted in the overwhelming nomination of Al Smith (who had been placed before the convention by Franklin D. Roosevelt), Hull received fifty votes. He was fourth on the list, preceded by Senator George of Georgia and Senator Reed of Missouri.

The next day the newspapers carried columns of congratulatory messages addressed to Governor Smith from Democratic political figures all over the country. None of them achieved the economy of verbiage and sentiment embodied in the telegram signed "Cordell Hull," which said:

I SINCERELY CONGRATULATE YOU ON YOUR NOMINATION.

CHAPTER XI

A Conservative Senator-Elect

THE STOCK MARKET fell off after Hoover was nominated, as the in-and-outers cashed in their little profits, and it stayed relatively quiet until after the Democrats had concluded their deliberations at Houston. Then it resumed its almost vertical ascent. The Great Era was hastening toward its finale.

Hull took only a nominal part in the campaign that autumn of 1928. Al Smith's nomination had made prohibition repeal the paramount issue, especially after Hoover declined to plump for repeal and spoke of prohibition as "the noble experiment." Translated into practical politics, this meant that the dry Southerners were of no particular use to Al Smith in his national campaign and that they did not want to associate themselves any more closely than necessary with an issue which was unpopular in their own states. So Governor Smith surrounded himself with advisers such as Jouett Shouse, chairman of the Association against the Prohibition Amendment, John J. Raskob, and thinkers of like philosophy, and the Southerners, including Hull, concentrated on their own political fences.

Their political judgment was sound. Most of the Southern Democratic members of Congress were re-elected, including Hull, while seven of the ten states in the Solid South went for Hoover by way of protest against Al Smith's wetness and other characteristics. Tennessee flopped into the Republican column again, as it had done in 1920, and was joined this time by Florida, Kentucky, North Carolina, Oklahoma, Texas, and Virginia.

Al Smith found the going too hard for him. When it was announced that Hoover had beaten him by 444 to 87 electoral votes and by a popular vote of about 21,000,000 to 15,000,000, the New York veteran declared he would never run for public office again—a vow he has kept. The bitterest blow of all, of course, was his repudiation by his own state, where he had been considered invulnerable. While Hoover was carrying New York's presidential vote Franklin D. Roosevelt managed to get himself elected as a Democratic governor by the slim margin of 25,000. Without realizing it the voters of New York were setting the stage for that unique period of American history marked by the domination of F. D. R.

Even before the President-elect got back from his Latin-American good-will tour in a battleship the Republicans in the "lame-duck" session of Congress began to lay plans for an upward revision of the tariff. The Ways and Means Committee of the House of Representatives began hearings early in 1929, with Hull warning the majority against retaliations by foreign governments if American rates were jacked up any higher. He demanded that witnesses at the tariff hearings be put under oath, in the conviction that paid lobbyists would undoubtedly moderate their claims with the threat of prosecution for perjury hanging over them.

Washington was swarming with representatives of special interests who said their principals wanted the tariff raised on almost everything. A list of the commodities which, according to their testimony, could not be produced in the United States in competition with "foreign products made by pauperized labor" included skeletons, stained glass, asbestos shingles, art objects, furs, straw hats, cigar wrappers, toothbrushes, buttons, textiles, gypsum, fats, cotton, casein, antique furniture, copra, flaxseed, handkerchiefs, glass, meat products, metals, edible oils, jute, onions, peanuts, leather, imitation pearls, canceled United States postage stamps, livestock, lumber, wool, toys, silk, paper, rugs, and shoes.

Under all this pressure Hoover announced that he would summon a special session of Congress, as soon as he was inaugurated, to meet on April 15 to consider "limited changes of the tariff." Most of the Republicans understood that only agricultural items would be up for revision, as it was a fixed policy of their party that farmers who could hardly give away their wheat and other overproduced commodities would be helped by raising the tariff against imports of like products. The farmers of the country had, in the main, never recovered from the depression of 1921, when war prices for food products collapsed and caught so many of them with mortgages and other commitments contracted in the belief that boom-price levels would last forever Hull's picture of the farm indebtedness amounting to $10,000,000,000 was by no means exaggerated.

Just as the special session was to meet, stocks took an ominous fall, probably premonitory in character, and call money rose to 15 per cent. Phenomena of this character, however, only strengthened the protectionists in their belief that American economic life must be protected against all competition from abroad. One of the authors of this thesis was J. R. Grundy, president of the Pennsylvania Manufacturers' Association, who had an open sesame to the majority side of the Ways and Means Committee.

Representative Hawley of Oregon, chairman of the Ways and Means Committee, introduced the bill on which the Republicans hoped to build, and Hull flew to the attack. On May 11 he submitted a minority report charging that the Republicans always "practice embargo or prohibitive superprotection, unfairly distributed, with purely incidental concern for international trade and markets for our surpluses," and referring to "continuous and corrupt political partnership between tariff beneficiaries and dominant Republican leadership."

He followed this, two days later, by delivering on the floor of the House the most exhaustive tariff speech of his career, occupying more than an hour of the time allotted for general debate on the pending bill. He had been building up the speech for weeks because he felt that the United States was approaching a crisis and that tariff restraint might prove the turning point of a reaction toward what he considered a more nearly normal economy for the nation.

Hull attacked not only the pending tariff bill but the whole theory of protection. In particular he attempted to point out what he considered to be the fallacy of protection for the American farmer. He told the House that 334,000,000 acres of land in the United States were planted, in 1928, to crops valued at $7,000,000,000, which enjoyed nominal tariff benefits or none at all, while only 5,500,000 acres were planted to crops valued at $443,000,000, which actually got some benefit from tariff protection. The conclusion he drew from these statistics was that, under any system of tariffs designed to protect the farmer against foreign competition, only an infinitesimal percentage of American agriculture could benefit, by the very nature of American production, consisting so largely, in acreage and value, of commodities such as corn, wheat, oats, barley, rye, cotton, tobacco, and fruits, of which large surpluses were exported every year and which had nothing to fear from competitive imports.

Today the prices the farmer has to pay are 65 per cent higher on the average than before the war [he told the House], while the prices he gets for his products are only 28 per cent higher. That is the range between his income and his outgo after seven years of copper-riveted tariff protection, guaranteed to place agriculture on an economic equality with industry.

Hull claimed that the general tariff rates, which the Republicans were trying to boost, were already higher than those of any country in the world except Spain and that the United States stood twelfth among the nations of the world in per capita exports and only fourteenth in per capita imports. He gave the tariff indices of a few countries, by way of comparison, as follows: Spain, 40; the United States, 37; France, 30; England, 5; The Netherlands, 6 or 7.

Replying to Republican contentions that the Treasury's revenues had been substantially increased as a result of raising tariff rates in the Fordney-McCumber bill of 1922, which was then in effect (the Republican argument left the inference, of course, that further increases in rates would bring greater revenue to the Treasury), Hull declared that the added revenues had been collected, for 75 per cent of their total volume, on only twenty or thirty luxury and largely non-competitive items. Such imports would continue to come into the country over any tariff barrier, so long as rich people wanted them and had the money to pay for them, Hull pointed out, so that they operated as luxury taxes rather than protective tariffs. He maintained that no showing could be made, on the basis of an analysis of customs receipts, for the theory that high protective tariffs produce revenue, reverting to his original thesis that a protective tariff, in order to be effective, had to be prohibitive in height. He said:

Our present tariffs are already framed not only to protect the weakest and most inefficient industry in this country but the most inefficient individual business in that industry. They are framed to protect overcapitalization, watered capital, inefficient management, obsolete and antiquated machinery and plants, and also to protect against freight rates across our 3000-mile continent.

This is an anomalous, not to say amazing, situation in the greatest, richest, and most efficiently productive country in the world. No questions are asked to these phases of industry when tariffs are demanded. The only question, as a rule, is "How much do you want?" The utter lack of importance of an industry, or its lack of justification as an economic or business proposition, is never inquired into as a rule. Most other countries demand a showing of efficiency in these and all other essential respects before granting tariffs indiscriminately.

This pampering of inefficient industries was repugnant to Hull, who had always seen business stand on its own feet in the hills of Tennessee during his young manhood. He was to see, and to deplore even more strongly, the totalitarian plan of nurturing artificial industries solely because war was planned. This factor, fortunately, he did not have to combat in his debates with the Republicans in 1929. The national defense plea for keeping alive an industry or an individual business which could not pay its own way by its own efforts was not then fashionable in the United States nor, indeed, anywhere in the world outside of the Soviet Union.

Hull's time ran out, but John Nance Garner, who was in charge of the Democratic side's time on the bill, was only too glad to yield him an additional thirty minutes. Garner felt, as did most of the Democrats in the House, that the attack on the Republicans could not be in better hands. And they were right. Hull was putting into his speech the knowledge and experience of a quarter of a century—the factual approach which could be supplied only by a man of his assiduity and earnestness. The Democrats lacked such champions as much as did the Republicans.

There was hardly an occupation in the United States, industrial or agricultural, on which he did not touch and for which he did not quote the appropriate statistics to convey what he thought the protective tariff did for them. He was particularly insistent on his theory that high American wages are justified by the high productive capacity of the American workman and that the American wage level does not operate to the disadvantage of the American industrialist to a point where the differential must be represented by a protective tariff. He quoted statistics to the effect that every dollar spent in wages in the United States in 1925 brought about a net production worth $2.50, while a dollar invested in wages in Great Britain brought a net production of only $2.14.

Putting it another way, Hull said that the average industrial wage paid that year in the United States was $1280, compared to $513 for Great Britain, and that the value of production added by the average wage earner in the United States was $3194, compared to $1096 by his British counterpart. He translated the same comparison into horsepower added per employee during manufacture in the two countries and reached almost the same comparative conclusion.

How fundamental is this gulf between the protectionist majority and the liberal-trading minority in the United States is attested by the fact that Hull, as Secretary of State, had to go through these same arguments again, in substance, three times after he became Secretary of State, in trying to convince Congress of the advisability of adopting his reciprocal foreign trade program. The cataclysmic economic experiences of the decade following this 1929 speech, culminating in a second world war, failed to shake the convictions of the ultra-protectionists that their way is best.

Hull's vehement opposition went for nothing, and the House adopted the Hawley bill, sending it along to the Senate despite the many unsatisfactory features it was acknowledged to contain. The House Republicans felt they had done the best they could with a difficult situation. Their leaders were apparently unprepared for the deluge of demands for protection which they received from all segments of the national economic life once they had decided to revise the agricultural tariffs upward.

The fight was only beginning, however. The Senate Finance Committee, of which Senator Smoot of Utah was chairman, decided to investigate the entire schedule which the House had passed. This gave an opportunity for those lobbyists who had been disappointed in the House to reopen their arguments and for the opponents of all tariff revision to present their cases afresh. An alliance was formed between the agricultural interests, represented by Senators Borah and Capper, who wanted agricultural tariffs raised but no others, and low-tariff Democrats such as Senator Harrison. This coalition was pledged to join forces against the boosted rates on industrial products.

Protests from thirty-eight foreign countries were lodged with the Finance Committee over some or all of the rates established by the House bill, according to that measure's enemies, although Senator Smoot denied the accuracy of their statement by announcing that only twenty-five protests had been received, and those from interested parties.

At any rate, the spirit of retaliation had been aroused abroad, as Hull had predicted it would be. In London, Lord Beaverbrook started his ultimately successful campaign for a system of Empire preference, which was formally negotiated at Ottawa in 1932. The Labour party protested this plan, demanding a high protectionist tariff for Great Britain, even against products of the Dominions. For once the Conservatives agreed with the Labour party and urged high tariffs as a lesson to the United States.

President Hoover, who had been concerned over the promotion of better relations between the United States and the other leading nations of the world, was distressed at the venomous resentment which greeted his tariff tinkering but decided, on the advice of his legislative leaders, to stick by the Republican guns on the theory that the storm would blow over without serious consequences for the country.

It began to look as if an estimate made by Hull more than a year earlier had been about true. On that occasion he said:

There is no hope of any real improvement in our relations with other nations except through the substitution of new and different political forces at Washington. The statement has become universal that for six years our government has had no definite or adequate foreign policy.

Under our slipshod and piecemeal policies we have drifted and muddled along until our moral influence has vanished utterly. Unless our interests are still more to suffer, this nation must speedily adopt a constructive foreign policy embracing intelligent, practical, and systematic cooperation

There are many ways of sane cooperation to promote better understanding, friendship, good will, peace, a justice consistent with our Constitution and traditions. An unbiased and educated public opinion can be confidently relied upon in the future to deal wisely and adequately with all new foreign problems involving our rights, duties, and responsibilities arising under New World conditions.

By the time Congress decided to recess for Christmas, on December 22, all was confusion and it was impossible to predict what was to come of President Hoover's attempt at "limited charges of the tariff."

Not only Congress but the whole nation was bewildered. The stock-market collapse which started in October had swept away not only paper fortunes but the lifetime savings of small people throughout the country. The black experience had shaken the confidence of the entire public, investors and non-investors alike, in the stability of the economic and monetary fabric of the country and of the men who headed it.

When market quotations for all securities began to slip backward from their tremendous peaks early in October, the financial writers blamed the phenomenon on a bear pool operating under the direction of Jesse L. Livermore and predicted that prices would re-establish themselves as soon as the raid was over and the lunatic fringe, operating on margin, had been squeezed out. Roger W. Babson, Prohibitionist presidential candidate in 1940, was the only recognized authority who insisted that stock-market prices were due to go much lower.

On October 23 stocks listed on the New York Stock Exchange lost $4,000,000,000 in market value and those over the country were marked down by $6,000,000,000, according to contemporary estimates. But by the twenty-sixth brokers' letters to their clients were urging them to buy in again, as the worst was over. On the twenty-ninth, which was described as the most disastrous day in the history of Wall Street, listed values took another loss of $10,000,000,000, and on the thirtieth the brokers redoubled their advice to buy at once before prices bounced upward.

In Washington the Democrats, including Senator Robinson of Arkansas and Senator Tydings, blamed the Republicans. The Republicans, including Senator Robinson of Indiana, blamed the Democrats. Some Democrats blamed the tariff uncertainty surrounding the Republican revision efforts. W. R. Hearst called on President Hoover to issue a reassuring statement to the American public. Only Senator Capper was unmoved, saying the farmers were not worried about anything in Wall Street.

Hull had long since become discouraged over the state of the nation. He reached the decision, during the summer, that he would serve only one more term in the House of Representatives and then retire to practice law in Carthage. Why he made the reservation about the one more term, he does not now remember. At any rate, circumstances arose to change his decision.

Senator Tyson died, and Governor Horton appointed William E. Brock, a candy manufacturer of Chattanooga, to fill his place. The appointment was good only until the general election in the autumn of 1930, when, under Tennessee law, a senator would have to be chosen by the people to represent their sovereign state until the new Congress came into existence on March 4, 1931.

Hull had always wanted to serve in the Senate, but the confused situation presented him with a dilemma. He was not interested in serving only from December 1930, when the "lame-duck" session of Congress would convene, until the following March, and yet if Brock were elected to the short term he might easily be a successful candidate for the full term as well. The election to both offices would be held in November, and the Democratic primaries in August would choose the party nominees for both races.

After attending Senator Tyson's funeral in Knoxville, along with practically all the other political figures of Tennessee, Hull went back to Carthage to think things over. It had been apparent to him that Governor Horton was going to appoint Brock, with all the attendant complications that appointment would bring into the political picture.

After consulting with some of his political advisers in Nashville and in his own district, Hull made up his mind. On September 2, 1929, he announced to the Nashville correspondent of the Associated Press that he would be a candidate at the Democratic primary the following August, almost a year away, for the senatorial long term to begin on March 4, 1931. He merely said that his efforts, if he should be elected, would continue to be devoted to the cause of peace.

He apparently did not mean political peace in Tennessee, for the announcement threw all political calculations out of joint. In those days important candidacies in the Democratic party were decided quietly in conferences among the acknowledged, though often publicly unknown, leaders of the different sections of the state. A certain nicety of geographical distribution was observed. Senator Tyson had come from Knoxville, so that his successor, under the accepted rules of the game, should come from eastern Tennessee, of which Chattanooga formed the western boundary. The perennial senior senator from Tennessee, Kenneth D. McKellar, came from Memphis, and that seemed to cinch the place for a representative from the other end of the state.

The succeeding months brought anxious consultations among Tennessee democracy. Their upshot was that Hull would be too strong for Brock to oppose in the race for the full term, even though Hull's nomination and election would give both senatorial seats to western Tennessee. Accordingly, when the August primaries were held, the Democrats found that they could vote for Brock for the "lameduck" term and Hull for the long term, although Hull was opposed by Andrew L. Todd and Dr. J. R. Neal. Brock and Hull both won the respective nominations, Hull reporting that he spent $10,000 on his campaign.

The result of the primary, which was considered tantamount to election, was greeted favorably on the national political scene. The New York *Times*, which had so often viewed with alarm Hull's advocacy of income and inheritance taxes earlier in his career, congratulated Tennessee on selecting "a conservative over a radical." The "radical" reference was aimed at Dr. Neal, who had advocated original and startling taxation schemes, calling Hull a jellyfish for merely wanting to boost the two forms of taxes he had always stood for. The paper's editorial writer deprecated Hull's "dry" stand but found comfort in the fact that the prospective senator had once expressed himself as "skeptical" about prohibition. All things considered, the writer thought that Tennessee had nominated, and would elect to the Senate, "one of the most studious and statesmanlike of her politicians."

By electing Hull, it was pointed out, Tennessee would do much "to raise the Senate level of industry, intelligence, and gentility." An indirect rebuke to Mr. McKellar was added in the form of a hope that Tennessee would "give Mr. Hull an equally high-grade colleague." If, as it appeared, the paper was exhorting the Democrats of Tennessee to retire Mr. McKellar, it was doomed to disappointment, for the veteran senator from Memphis survived innumerable factional quarrels to be returned to the Senate in 1934 and again in 1940.

In the general election in November the general forecasts were borne out, as Hull defeated without difficulty his Republican opponent, Paul Divine, for the six-year term and Brock won the honor of serving during the short term of the expiring Congress.

By the time the senator-elect for the long term was ready to take his seat the depression was running full blast, not only in the United States but throughout the world. His gloomiest forebodings had come true. He prepared a parting warning for his colleagues of the House of Representatives in the form of a statement which Representative Marvin Jones of Texas asked to have inserted in the *Congressional Record* and which was printed on February 16, 1931, three weeks before he took the oath as senator.

He demonstrated that the United States had increased its exports in 1929 by only 6 per cent over their level in 1913 and had lent $15,000,000,000 to foreign countries in the process. Stimuli such as foreign loans, sudden booms in new industries such as the automobile, installment selling, and the other panaceas of the twenties could not permanently stave off the unemployment and misery which must ultimately result from unsold surpluses of the commodities the United States could best produce, he continued.

During the time that these ineffective remedies were being tried, Hull charged, the Republican party had been boosting tariffs and stimulating the choking of international trade that produced the very unsold surpluses which lay at the root of the trouble, not only in the United States but throughout the world. To him the remedy was simple. The country had only to turn out the Republicans in 1932 (which was done) and to revert to the traditional economic life of equal opportunity to all, with the protective tariff banished as rapidly as possible.

Whether or not his Southern Democratic colleagues realized it, Hull was addressing them more in sorrow than in anger. One of the principal factors contributing to the discouragement which had made him decide, a few months earlier, to retire from public life was the double-dealing of which so many of his Southern friends were guilty when it came to tariff legislation.

There was a recognized technique for it—recognized, that is, by everybody but Hull, who never had any traffic with it. John Nance Garner was one of the leading exponents of the procedure, and an explanation of his votes and activities will make the whole situation clear. Mr. Garner had, in his Texas district, a number of breeders of angora goats. They were interested in promoting high tariffs on angora wool or any substitute therefor and made their wishes unmistakably clear to Mr. Garner.

As an old-line Democrat, Mr. Garner could not countenance a protective tariff. On the other hand, these influential constituents were breathing on his neck. So he arranged this conflict of political philosophy as follows:

Taking the practical point of view, he would realize from a count of noses that a protective tariff was about to be adopted by the predominantly Republican House of Representatives. Accordingly, he would fight like a wounded tigress to get a protective tariff on angora wool and its substitutes written into the bill and would then vote against the bill, secure in the knowledge that his Republican opponents could muster enough votes to pass it. In this manner he would keep his record clear in the matter of protecting his constituents and yet would follow the old Democratic party line by being on record against a high tariff bill.

There were many such Democrats in the House all during Hull's career, and Garner's reasoning is cited only as an example which became well known through repeated performance and repeated gibes from the Republican side of the aisle. The Vice-

President-to-be and other representatives who found themselves in a like dilemma reasoned with themselves that, much as they were opposed to tariff protection for anybody, as long as it was going around their constituents might as well get their share. Had they been able to defeat all protective schedules, they would argue to themselves and to Hull, they would have voted them all down. Being practical men, as they saw it, they were unwilling to see the manufacturers of the North become the only beneficiaries of whatever Congressional logrolling was going on.

This form of political complaisance was repugnant to Hull and did not improve on closer acquaintance as the years went by. More than any other single factor it brought on the spirit of defeatism which made him decide to renounce his Congressional career before the senatorial vacancy came into sight. It occurred to him that there might be less field for this sort of thing in the Senate, since each pair of senators represented a larger segment of the nation's economic life than did any single representative. Such a conclusion, if it was his conclusion, is open to a certain element of reasonable doubt, for often the two senators from each state merely roll up into a single parcel the protective tariffs desired by all the inhabitants of their state and then trade with other senators on that basis. The sugar senators, for example, will form a compact with the wheat senators, the citrus-fruit senators, and the dairy senators to vote en masse for all the protective tariffs covering those commodities. The proof of the very practical existence of such a system is the fact that men soon come to be known, in the press gallery, as wool senators, beef senators, cotton senators, or by some other nomenclature which suggests Mussolini's corporative state more than the form of government the Founding Fathers thought they were establishing for the United States.

Hull expounded this thesis in the first important speech he delivered after taking his seat in the Senate. The occasion was a Jefferson Day dinner at Cleveland on May 8, 1931. He accused the Republican administrations of Harding, Coolidge, and Hoover of having failed, since 1920, to solve a single major problem in the country's national life and of having "brought upon the American people the blackest period in all peacetime." In a burst of prophetic oratory he told the dinner guests that, because of this inability of democratic government to cope with the vital problems of the people, "democracies are crashing in every part of the world, although the dictators and despotic rulers, who are being enthroned, still retain, in many instances, the empty forms and names common to popular government in order to mislead and placate the masses."

This must have been a reference to Benito Mussolini, because Adolf Hitler had hardly become of enough importance to arouse such a sweeping comment, although his ideas followed exactly the line Hull deplored, as may be gleaned from a reading of *Mein Kampf*. On this occasion Hull called to the attention of his listeners the existence of this form of economic compromise, as illustrated by tariff votes, with the warning that it sounded the knell of the two-party system without which he believed, as did Jefferson, that the democratic processes of the United States could not live. In other words, when low-tariff Democrats started to vote high tariffs on the commodities in which they were interested, just because other producers might get some benefits on their own production, there was no longer any difference in economic principle between the two parties. They merely differed in degree, in personal selfishness.

Taking Jefferson as the symbol of the greatest good for the greatest number and Hamilton as the symbol of special privilege, Hull said that the United States was three fourths Jefferson and one fourth Hamilton in theory but three fourths Hamilton and one fourth Jefferson in practice. The mission of the Democratic party in the forthcoming presidential election of 1932, as he saw it, was to reverse the ratio in practice and to restore the reins of government to the partisans of the Jeffersonian doctrine.

Behind this apparently abstract discussion of the political future facing the Democratic party lay a considerable substratum of practical intraparty politics. This is often true of Hull's public utterances, all of which should be read with as much knowledge of the background and immediate problems as possible. He has an apocryphal way of imparting the homely political truths he has on his mind.

At this juncture Hull was trying to point out to the Democrats, who had been out of office for a dozen years, the way to sure victory. In the previous February, Hull had joined forces with

Senator Morrison of North Carolina and Senator Connally of Texas in a move to head off an outright wet plank in the Democratic platform for 1932. The Northern Democrats, under the leadership of John J. Raskob and Jouett Shouse, who controlled the machinery of the Democratic National Committee by virtue of their offices as chairman and executive chairman, respectively, were bent on putting the Democratic party squarely into the fight on the issue of repealing the Prohibition Amendment, since it was known that President Hoover would be the Republican party's candidate to succeed himself and that he would favor keeping prohibition.

Hull and his Southern colleagues, however, mindful of the inroads Hoover had made into the Solid South in 1928, thought it best not to antagonize the Southern drys by a repeal plank when the Democrats had, ready to hand, a natural issue in the spreading economic depression. They carried their fight to the floor of a meeting of the Democratic National Committee at the Mayflower Hotel in Washington on March 5, at which Senator Robinson of Arkansas supported them in an impassioned speech. They lost that particular cause, but they popularized the idea of blaming the spreading economic distress on the Republicans and their tariff policies during the twelve years they had been in power.

The enactment of the Smoot-Hawley Act, as finally drafted to embody all the compromises and boosts that the conflicting interests of its backers could imagine, had brought an element of added confusion to the already chaotic economic picture. The Chamber of Commerce of the United States had denounced its high rates, and the National Association of Manufacturers had gone on record as opposed to all further tariff tinkering.

Governor Franklin D. Roosevelt of New York denounced the new tariff as one of the most important factors leading to the world-wide depression. The Republicans in Congress charged that the Democrats wanted only to reduce tariffs on products from Republican states. Suggestions ranged from boosting the Smoot-Hawley rates, on the one side, to summoning a world free-trade conference to meet in Washington on the other.

President Hoover tried to find the middle road. He took advantage of the "flexible" clause of the law to lower duties on felt hat bodies from 40 cents a pound and 75 per cent ad valorem to 40 cents a pound and 55 per cent; on finished hats from 40 cents a pound and 75 per cent and 25 cents each to 40 cents a pound and 55 per cent and $12\frac{1}{2}$ cents each; and on edible gelatin valued at less than 40 cents a pound from 5 cents a pound and 20 per cent to 5 cents a pound and 12 per cent. At the same time he became interested in the movement which eventually led to the World Economic and Monetary Conference which was to meet in London in the spring of 1933. Strangely enough, neither of these vigorous moves appeared to stem the awful downrush of the depression in the United States and elsewhere.

Affairs dragged along their tragic course. The depression passed from its economic and financial stages into a psychological situation. Unemployment and want struck so savagely at so many of the population that the cry began to go up that the nation was doomed. Capitalism was finished. Complete and utter bankruptcy was inevitable, and chaos could be the only result during a lifetime, and only communism could finally rise from the ashes of the civilization then burning to pieces. So far as can be judged, the country's public morale had never before reached such a low point.

By the spring of 1932, however, there were the normal stirrings of political interest which always precede a presidential campaign. The Republicans nominated Herbert Hoover to succeed himself on a "dry" platform, and the Democrats assembled at Chicago to select an opponent for what looked to be one of the surest victories a political party could demand. The prospective ease of the forthcoming electoral fight brought forth a multitude of would-be Democratic standard-bearers. It was one thing to carry the torch in a hopeless situation such as had faced the party in the three preceding presidential elections, but it was quite another to snap up the nomination in an apparently sure year.

The convention maneuvers which brought the ultimate nomination of Franklin D. Roosevelt have been too often recounted to be repeated here. Hull took little part in them. He and his "dry" Southern colleagues realized that they were outnumbered on the prohibition issue, so he expended his principal efforts toward incorporating some form of tariff revision in the Democratic platform as a pledge for whatever individual the convention might select.

He played only a minor part in the succeeding campaign. Not being up for election himself, he was not obliged to stump even a portion of his own state. Roosevelt's sweeping victory in November, however, suited him down to the ground and left him highly hopeful that the state of the Union and the world might be improved once again under Democratic auspices. The pessimism and defeatism which had filled him in 1930 had disappeared, and he was casting about in his own mind for ways and means by which he might use the changed political situation to advance the ideas he held so dearly.

CHAPTER XII

The New Prime Minister

THE COUNTRY AT LARGE took heart at Roosevelt's election in 1932. Some 23,000,000 voters preferred to change horses, as opposed to the 16,000,000 who wanted to stick with Hoover. As American presidential elections go, this was a decisive popular victory. Translated into the Electoral College's return of 472 to 59, it took on the appearance of a landslide.

In retrospect it is easy to see how the reaction against almost four years of hard times and against the apparent hopelessness of the future produced a reaction against Herbert Clark Hoover and that any opposition candidate would have defeated him under the prevailing circumstances. However, such an estimate oversimplifies the situation which then confronted the electorate.

On that election night in November 1932 I invited an old friend to dinner, intending to take him on to Times Square to watch the returns amid all the excitement induced by those gigantic crowds of ordinary people who congregate there on such occasions. My dinner guest was George Fite Waters, the sculptor, who had lived in Paris almost continuously since 1915. I myself had just returned from ten straight years in Europe.

We were certainly not representative citizens as we pushed our way through the crowds toward Broadway that night, and yet we were both seized with a great apprehension. During the quarter of an hour it took us to elbow through the throng on the side street we came to the conclusion that all hope for the United States was lost unless Roosevelt was elected. We based this on no knowledge whatever of the Democratic candidate's capabilities but rather on a theoretical blueprint of the workings of democracy, under which the power of the individual voter is much greater in the negative, or veto, sense than it is as a positive measure. In other words, we reasoned that he exercised his franchise more potently and directly when he threw out an incumbent because of discontent rather than when he re-elected an officeholder because he was satisfied or resigned. Since we could see no reason why the voter (neither of us had been qualified to vote in the election) should seek to retain the condition for which poor Mr. Hoover stood as the outward and visible sign, we concluded that the American voter would have lost his punch unless he reacted vigorously in support of Roosevelt.

Senator Hull felt largely the same way as he awaited the election returns in Carthage. He had gone back home from Washington soon after Congress adjourned late in July and had taken a modest part in the campaign. Not being up for election himself, he was under no particular obligation to do so, but he made two or three speeches "for the ticket" at local mass meetings. It was obvious that the Democratic national nominees would carry Tennessee despite Hoover's victory four years earlier, and Hull's speeches were made for the record rather than for any political effect they might have.

The all-time low of Hull's own political psychology, which had been reached three years before when he decided to retire from public life, had been caused to a large extent by the defeat he had suffered at the Democratic convention in Houston in 1928. Al Smith and his allies had succeeded in writing into the platform, over Hull's almost singlehanded objections, a protective tariff plank which, to him, constituted complete apostasy for the Democratic party.

Al Smith had been overwhelmingly defeated in 1928, but this time things were different. Through the preconvention days of 1932 Senator Hull had been probably the closest Congressional adviser Governor Roosevelt had. The two men's acquaintance and friendship was of a political, rather than a personal, character. Hull had known the governor as Assistant Secretary of the

Navy during the eight years of the Wilson administration. Later, when Mr. Roosevelt began his periodic visits to Warm Springs, he often stopped over in Washington and invited Mr. Hull to call on him to discuss politics.

From 1925 on, Hull was convinced that the future welfare of the Democratic party lay in reducing the influence of the right-wing New York branch, typified by John W. Davis, Alfred E. Smith, and the others, and in restoring the party to its traditional position of representing the agricultural and laboring elements of the country. Whether he instinctively felt that Franklin D. Roosevelt was a potential ally in this undertaking, or whether he believed he could best maintain contact with New York Democracy through this medium, Hull kept in touch with the future governor and President at every opportunity.

With this background Hull had attended the Chicago convention and had found the atmosphere completely changed since Houston. He had outmaneuvered the Smith-Raskob forces by electing Senator Tom Walsh chairman of the convention instead of Jouett Shouse, whom they were backing. He had taken an active hand in drafting the economic planks of the party platform and they met his tariff views.

Thus, on the night of November 8, he felt happy and confident. The American voters would certainly turn the Republicans out, he told himself, and the Democratic administration that would profit by that revolt would be one which he intended to support as worthy of the Democratic tradition.

He had listened with scorn to Herbert Hoover's campaign utterance in New York on October 31, almost at the close of the campaign, warning that any reduction of the protective tariff would bring about a situation where "the grass will grow in streets of a hundred cities, a thousand towns; the weeds will overrun the fields of millions of farms if that protection be taken away."

With the same disdainful incredulity he had read the attacks made on Roosevelt by William J. Donovan in his campaign against Herbert H. Lehman for the governorship of New York. Mr. Lehman, who had been Governor Roosevelt's lieutenant governor, was the prospective bearer of the Roosevelt mantle in New York State, and Mr. Donovan felt he must attack the principal rather than the agent in the New York race. This is the same "Wild Bill" Donovan who became one of President Roosevelt's most trusted unofficial observers abroad in the early days of the European war.

Two days after Roosevelt was elected the stock market rose from two to five points. The public reaction was beginning to follow the path Hull had believed it would, and he hurried back to Washington to get ready for the short session of Congress to meet early in December. This was an old custom of his, but under these circumstances it seemed doubly imperative. There was every prospect of a turbulent session until President-elect Roosevelt should take office on March 4, backed by an overwhelmingly Democratic Congress. President Hoover, by his veto power, could prevent any important legislation from passing, because the Democrats could not hope to muster anything like a two-thirds majority of both houses to override him on any partisan issue.

Hull consulted with his old friends in the House and in the Senate as fast as they reached the capital. He had always found that he could accomplish as much in the fortnight or so preceding the opening of a session of Congress as he could in all the session itself, as the members with whom he had dealings were as yet unoccupied with committee work and the other routine activities which are so exacting when Congress is actually sitting. He found that, on the whole, they were content to coast along until the Democratic administration should assume power in its own right the following March, building what record they could to the glory of the Democratic party and the confusion of the Republicans.

But the first important issue that arose was non-partisan in nature. Sir Ronald Lindsay, the British ambassador, and Paul Claudel, the French ambassador, called on Secretary of State Stimson and informed him that their governments were in urgent need of relief from their war debts to the United States. It was an unfortunate moment to bring this thorny question to the fore, but things were going badly in Europe and domestic political pressure was being exercised on the debtor governments.

President Hoover was in a quandary. His unofficial moratorium of the previous June had served to tide the vexing question over the election, but now he had to face the issue as a lame-duck President. He invited his prospective successor to confer with him on the course to be pursued, alarmed at the outburst of public opinion which followed the reopening of the question. For several days there was no comment from Albany, where Governor Roosevelt was cleaning up his affairs in preparation for a long vacation. Finally Mr. Roosevelt agreed to an informal talk with Mr. Hoover, with the public reservation that "in the last analysis the immediate question raised by the British, French, and other notes creates a responsibility which rests upon those now vested with executive and legislative authority."

On November 19 Senator Hull entered the controversy in Washington to the extent of issuing a statement to the press in which he said that the question of the war debts must be lumped with the other "monumental difficulties which must be surmounted in the early future." He was convinced that the state of the war debts was merely an aggravated symptom of an advanced case of international economic malaise and that the cause rather than the effect of the malaise must be treated.

Close as Hull had been to Roosevelt in the days of 1932 preceding the Chicago convention, he had had no direct contact with the nominee and President-elect since the convention had adjourned. Senator James F. Byrnes of South Carolina had become Mr. Roosevelt's liaison officer in Congress, and the President-elect himself was surrounded by a throng of advisers, most of whom were strangers to Hull or were men for whom he had little regard.

They included a few of his old friends, such as Senator Key Pittman of Nevada, Bernard M. Baruch, and Senator Byrnes, but most of the intimate circle was made up of relative strangers to him. There was the Columbia University group, headed by Professor Raymond Moley, Professor Rexford G. Tugwell, and A. A. Berle, Jr. There was the Albany group, including Justice Samuel I. Rosenman, Louis McHenry Howe, Mr. Roosevelt's personal secretary, James A. Farley, and Edward J. Flynn. There were close friends associated with New York City, such as Basil O'Connor, Mr. Roosevelt's law partner, Henry Morgenthau, Jr., General Hugh Johnson, Joseph P. Kennedy, and others. And, above all, there was Mrs. Roosevelt.

These advisers began to winnow the requests, both discreet and brazen, for Cabinet appointments. By early January it was reported that the President-elect was confronted with a list of 160 aspirants for the eleven posts in his Cabinet. Although Mr. Roosevelt had announced right after the election that he would not name his Cabinet until late February, public conjecture ranged far and wide, as it always does when there is an incoming administration in sight.

Senator Hull did not think of himself as a possible Cabinet appointee. Neither did the early guessers. The names that were tossed about were such possible choices as William Green for Secretary of Labor, Felix Frankfurter for Attorney General, Frank O. Lowden for Secretary of Agriculture, J. C. O'Mahoney for Secretary of the Interior, Carter Glass for Secretary of the Treasury, Alfred E. Smith for Secretary of anything at all. The President-elect and his advisers kept their counsel, and the public guessing was almost entirely wrong except in the case of James A. Farley, who, it was conceded, would be Postmaster General, in line with the tradition that this post goes to the winning candidate's campaign manager to consolidate the practical side of an electoral victory.

It was obvious that Mr. Roosevelt realized he had a job on his hands to unite the Democratic party behind the program he had in view, of which glimmerings were visible as a result of his activities as governor of New York, and that his Cabinet appointments would be made with the view of reassuring as many elements of the party as possible. When he came to Washington for his first informal conference with outgoing President Hoover, little more than two weeks after the election, he transacted little or no political business among his own potential followers and relied on Raymond Moley to be his chief adviser in the parleys at the White House.

By the beginning of February, however, a few political writers had begun timidly to tout Cordell Hull for Secretary of State. The Tennessee senator himself had received reports from political friends that his name was under consideration and, at first thought, he did not like the idea. He felt that his long legislative career was only beginning to come to fruition with the prospective advent of a completely Democratic Congress. He believed

that his best service to the country and to the party could be performed on the floor and in the cloakrooms of the Senate.

Roosevelt himself brought matters to a head by offering Hull
the post on a second trip to Washington on January 19 or 20.
The President-elect, having completed his term as governor of
New York, was on his way to a vacation in the South and
stopped in the capital to consult Democratic Congressional
leaders and to confer a second time with President Hoover
(again with Moley as his principal adviser) on the question of
the war debts.

He learned from Speaker Garner, who was to be his Vice-
President, and other veterans at the Capitol that there was not
the slightest chance of putting through the lameduck session of
Congress, which would last until the day of his own inauguration the following March 4, any legislation which bore the stamp
of his approval or which appeared to be a head start on what he
intended to do. Any such project would either fail of passage in
the Senate or be vetoed by President Hoover, they told him, ad-
vising him to call a special session to meet soon after his own
inauguration.

In the midst of these conferences Roosevelt found time to ask
Hull in to see him and to invite him to be Secretary of State.
Hull said he would take the matter under consideration, and the
two men parted without any clear understanding of what their
relations were to be. There was beginning to germinate in Hull's
mind a feeling that the portfolio of State might afford him a
far·vaster opportunity for forwarding his ideas of economic peace
than he would ever have in Congress, but the germ was nourished in such a culture as to prevent him from talking the question out with Roosevelt then and there. He needed more time
to judge the situation.

It had begun to look to him as if Roosevelt was going to be
so totally concerned with domestic politics, through the political
alignments he was making with noted partisans of radical
change, that the new President would have little time or inclination for directing external developments. Like most members of
Congress, Hull had hitherto regarded the Secretary of State with
a tolerant amusement as a sort of dignified figurehead who went
to banquets and conversed amiably with ambassadors. The whole

State Department, as a matter of fact, appeared more comic than important to the rugged sons of the soil who were accustomed to battle for every slightest issue with the strategy of local politics.

On the other hand, there were portents that relations between nations were going to become such that an application of this same strategy might benefit the United States and the world. Hull had been greatly alarmed at the adoption of the Ottawa Agreements for preferential tariffs within the British Empire the preceding autumn. He saw in them, and in other manifestations in the foreign economic field, the spread throughout the world of the ideas he had abhorred and combated during his entire public life in the United States. Perhaps it was time he gave battle on a broader field, he told himself, if he could only be sure that he would have a free hand to do so.

His political friends in whom he confided, especially those in the Senate, advised him against taking it. There was a good deal of grumbling in the Senate over reports that Roosevelt intended to raid its membership to the extent of grabbing four senators for his Cabinet.

When Roosevelt left Washington after the January conference with Hoover he went on an inspection trip to the Muscle Shoals area in Alabama under the guidance of Senator George W. Norris of Nebraska, who wanted to get him interested in the idea that was to burgeon into the Tennessee Valley Authority. Senator Hull and a few other members of Congress who represented constituencies in that part of the country were invited to go along. Nothing Hull saw on that trip, apparently, influenced him for or against the Cabinet proposition, and he returned to Washington still in a state of considerable doubt.

The President-elect went on from Muscle Shoals to Warm Springs. During the two or three weeks he spent at the Georgia resort Mr. Roosevelt received many visitors, most of whom were Democratic hopefuls with politics and jobs on their minds. Their number did not include Hull, although his name must have come up in many a conversation. Mr. Roosevelt became more and more convinced that the Tennessean was the one man in the country who, as Secretary of State, would reassure Southern Democracy against the already visible influence of the Northern left-wingers who were so much in evidence and who would, at the same time, command respect if not enthusiasm abroad.

From Warm Springs, Roosevelt continued his vacation to include a fishing trip off the Florida coast aboard Vincent Astor's yacht, the *Nourmahal.* It was on his return from this trip, at Miami, that the madman, Joseph Zangara, took a pot shot at his party, mortally wounding Mayor Anton Cermak of Chicago.

It had been arranged that Senator Hull and two or three others would meet the train of the returning President-elect at Richmond and make the trip to Washington with him. During the course of that short ride Hull accepted the Secretaryship of State. He had resolved all his doubts and had come to the conclusion that this was the best course, although scarcely a close friend agreed with him. Even then, however, he and Mr. Roosevelt reached no agreement as to Hull's future role, although he himself had decided that he would have nothing to do with the domestic political experiments he saw brewing and that he would devote his whole attention to the establishment of durable peace in the world, built on foundations of prosperity and equality of opportunity. He wanted to test out the thesis he had expressed as follows in 1931:

"The world today, under American leadership over the last ten years, is in a virtual state of economic war. There can be no real progress toward confidence or peace nor permanent trade recovery while retaliations and bitter trade controversies rage."

His acceptance on the train between Richmond and Washington took place on February 17, 1933. The next day, in the capital, he had his first serious conference with Raymond Moley who of course knew of the development although it had not been publicly announced. Hull, on his side, understood that Moley was to be made Assistant Secretary of State, with no routine duties in the State Department, and that he was to continue to act as political and economic adviser extraordinary to the President. Hull took this to mean that Moley would have nothing to do with the State Department, and that first conference passed off pleasantly enough, so far as could be judged.

Newspaper reporters asked Senator Hull what he had discussed with Mr. Roosevelt during the train ride.

"We talked of the speeding of business recovery in a sound

and practicable way," was all Hull would say. "Mr. Roosevelt is going into every phase of the economic situation. He has very definite ideas in mind."

It was not until the twenty-first that Mr. Roosevelt officially announced Hull's appointment and acceptance. At the same time he announced the appointment of William H. Woodin as Secretary of the Treasury. Hull's appointment was well received by the public. Newspaper editorials praised Mr. Roosevelt's sagacity. In the Senate the paean of praise was led by Senator William Edgar Borah, an old ally of Hull in anti-protection tariff fights. Norman H. Davis, Frank L. Polk, John W. Davis, and other middle-of-the-road Democrats joined in the chorus.

The Associated Press, trying to dig up the last ounce of news about the appointee for the information of its readers, discovered the marks he had left in the records of the National Normal University at Lebanon, Ohio, forty years before. The institution had disappeared, but some authority had preserved its archives. The Associated Press correspondent reported that Hull had scored 90, 95, and 100 in debating, 95 in elocution, 100 in rhetoric, and 60 to 75 in everything else.

Now that the die had been publicly cast the Secretary-designate set to work to prepare himself for his new task. There remained less than two weeks before he would take his oath of office. He talked at length with Henry L. Stimson, the retiring Secretary of State. He conferred with Rexford G. Tugwell, Norman H. Davis, Sir Ronald Lindsay, the British ambassador, Paul Claudel, the French ambassador, and with most of the keymen in the State Department. This was the sort of apprenticeship to which he was accustomed—dealing with men rather than intangibles.

On the other hand, the atmosphere was full of intangibles. The country, as a whole, was atingle with excitement over the imminent change of administration—a pleasurable sensation for some, a feeling of apprehension for others. Rarely in the history of the country had the wheels of politics stood so nearly still, awaiting the impetus of a new driving force. Those who feared and those who hoped shared equally the conviction that something positive was going to happen, that the relentless and merciless chain of depression, or of "deflation," was to be broken, for better or for worse. If a whole nation of 125,000,000 souls can stand still at a crossroad, the United States was doing so.

Inexorably, however, the history of the species marches on, even though individuals imagine there is a blessed breathing spell. The events of the world refused to relapse conveniently into innocuity while the United States paused to put a new runner into the relay race of destiny. The days immediately preceding President Roosevelt's first inauguration were fraught with developments of the first magnitude, and no one in the country was more fully alive to them than Cordell Hull.

The acceleration of trends in both domestic and foreign affairs was amazing. It was as if the whole world's stage were being set for the entry of Franklin D. Roosevelt and his company of players. Those three or four weeks leading up to the moving ceremony of March 4, 1933, saw the planting of the seeds of almost every harvest the world was to reap under President Roosevelt's period of responsibility.

In the domestic field the Governor of Michigan declared what was called a bank holiday, and his example was soon followed by several others, including the Governor of New York, who succeeded Mr. Roosevelt. There was relatively little quarrel with this kind of temporary solution, so desperate were cases, and yet it was dimly realized that such steps acknowledged some kind of a permanent failure in the nation's financial structure. Roosevelt was to attempt to cope with the failure by various means, and only the historian of the future can tell whether he did so wisely or not.

As for the rest of the world, it was busy infecting itself with the fevers of war and conquest from which it has suffered ever since. A prophetically pathetic note was sounded by the British delegation to the Arms Limitation Conference in Geneva when it proposed a discussion among the leading air powers of the world "to examine the possibility of the entire abolition of military and naval (air) machines and bombing from the air, combined with effective control of civil aviation."

Disarmament by agreement was still being regarded as the world's salvation. Influential groups in Great Britain, France, the United States, and other leading military powers, with the ominous exceptions of Germany and Japan, were calling for

demobilization of fighting forces as the best guarantee that war
would not again ravage the world. Naval disarmament, begun
in 1921, had been carried further as a result of the London
Conference of 1930 and to the relative advantage of Japan.

On land, only the French declined to disarm. They may have
been wrong, as is argued by those who believe that a really conciliatory policy would have prevented the rise of Adolf Hitler in
Germany. They may have been right in principle, only to fail in
carrying their principle far enough into effect, as say those who
believe the Germans, under whatever leader, will always be
champions of violence and conquest by force.

In the air the question of relative strengths was still largely
academic. No nation had any great air strength, as measured by
contemporary standards, and it was only the occasional and
usually discredited expert, such as General William Mitchell,
who dared predict the potentialities of military aviation. In Germany the Ernst Udets and other survivors of the World War
were carrying greater weight with their authorities and were
already well launched in their efforts, despite the limitations of
the Versailles Treaty, to create in Germany the greatest air power
in the world before their counterparts in other nations should be
able to convince their own hidebound general staffs that the
future of warfare lay in the air.

The great puzzle of the epoch was nearing its solution in
Geneva. The League of Nations was considering what to do
about the continued Japanese aggression in Manchuria. One
member of the League, Japan, was violating the territorial and
administrative integrity of another member, China, and the
League was trying to determine what it could do in such circumstances.

The United States, under the foreign policy of President
Hoover and Secretary of State Stimson, had placed itself firmly
on record against Japan. Mr. Stimson had enunciated the doctrine of non-recognition by the United States of territorial acquisitions brought about through force or the threat of force.
The United States had appointed a member to the Lytton Commission, which was charged by the League with an official investigation of the merits and circumstances of this violent dispute
between two of its members. In view of the League's previous

spectacular failures to adjust such disputes, starting with the row between Mussolini's Italy and Greece in 1923, farsighted observers believed it was having its last chance.

The League had been founded to defend the status quo against arbitrary upset. It provided machinery, inadequate though it was, for the pacific adjustment of disputes and for orderly change in relations between nations. At this epoch it was on trial as a practicable means of carrying out what had come to be called collective security. Its earlier shortcomings, especially in the Italo-Greek dispute, were excused on the ground of youth and inexperience and its several minor successes were cited in its favor, but world opinion believed that the League's future would depend on its demonstration of ability to deal with such a major issue as then confronted it.

World opinion proved right, as it embarrassingly does every so often. The League endorsed the Lytton Commission's report condemning Japan and censured Japan as the aggressor in the dispute with China. The only result was that the Japanese delegation withdrew from the League, serving the formal but meaningless notice of two years required by the Covenant, and Japan considered itself free to pursue the course on which it had embarked. The machinery of the League could provide no hindrance, and the League was, in fact, washed up, although it took a few more years for the world to realize it.

The individual who served Japan's notice on the public session of the League Assembly and who led the Japanese delegation from the hall was none other than Yosuke Matsuoka, who, as Japan's Foreign Minister, negotiated the portentous non-aggression pact with the Soviet Union in 1941. In many ways it was highly fitting that this man, one of the few Japanese who thoroughly understood the strengths and, more especially, the weaknesses of the Western world, should have been the leading spirit in the two most resounding slaps Japan gave to Occidental civilization.

The inefficacy of collective security as a preventive against international crime was established for all to see. Mussolini took the example sufficiently to heart to embark on the conquest of Ethiopia, withdrawing from the League in defiance. Hitler rearmed Germany, reoccupied the Rhineland, and openly proclaimed his aims for world domination, withdrawing from the League in contempt. The World War of 1939 started then, although it was not generally realized by the complaisant "winners" of the conflict of 1914.

In Washington, however, there was a certain, though small, understanding of what was happening. It was shared by Senator Hull, who was shortly to take over the office of Secretary of State. In a press statement issued on February 24 Hull deplored "a general letting down, since the war, of moral and political standards by both peoples and governments."

Henry L. Stimson, the Republican Secretary of State who, as Secretary of War, was to become Hull's Cabinet colleague in the third Roosevelt administration, had already enunciated the American doctrine of non-recognition of territorial acquisitions by force or the threat of force. While the policy was apparently a popular one, as applied to the Japanese incursions in Manchuria, few of its partisans or condoners realized that it was to become the keystone of American foreign policy during the most critical period the Republic had ever had to face.

Hull, for one, was willing to go through with it. Stimson, after consulting his titular chief, President Hoover, conferred with him and with the President-elect before issuing a blanket approval of the League's stand in the matter of the Japanese defiance of the League. The whole affair served to throw the spotlight on the hot-and-cold relations which the United States had maintained with the League since the Treaty of Versailles had narrowly failed of ratification by the Senate in 1920.

The rough-and-ready segment of public opinion, chiefly seated in the Middle West, believed that the Senate, by the narrow margin of votes by which the Treaty of Versailles had failed of ratification (on two occasions it obtained a majority in its favor, although never the constitutional two thirds of those present and voting), had decided once and for all that the United States was completely uninterested in developments abroad. For good and all, according to this view of the case, this country had disassociated itself with the wicked machinations of foreign politicians and would, from then on, rely on its own strength and native ingenuity to avoid the consequences of any mortal conflict which might break out in the world.

Both Roosevelt and Hull, however, had been strong League of Nations men. It must not be forgotten that Franklin D. Roosevelt ran for the vice-presidency in 1920 on a ticket headed by James M. Cox of Ohio, when practically the only issue at stake was the League. There were signs that the administration to come would bestir itself in world affairs much more than had its three predecessors.

William Christian Bullitt suddenly came into the news. He whisked about Europe in the weeks preceding the inauguration in a mysterious manner which gave rise to speculation that he was a personal emissary of the President-elect. When Bullitt returned to Washington he went to live at the Carlton Hotel, where Hull had an apartment, and the two men saw a good deal of each other. They built the foundation of a working relationship which was to endure through many years of close association.

At Geneva the principal military powers of the world were trying to reach an agreement on limitation of land armaments. A large party in Great Britain, encouraged by the naval limitations accomplished at Washington in 1921 and at London in 1930, in full sympathy with a large section of opinion in the United States which believed that the only hope for permanent peace lay in effective disarmament, was attempting to force the rest of the world to that same point of view.

The delegation sent on behalf of the United States by President Hoover was headed by Norman H. Davis, a Tennessean and old-time friend of Cordell Hull. One of the first indications Roosevelt gave that he would preserve a large degree of continuity in the nation's foreign policy, after he became President, was his announcement that he would ask Mr. Davis to remain at the head of the American delegation—a decision that was no doubt recommended, at least by Hull.

With the exception of the appointment of Cordell Hull, Mr. Roosevelt's Cabinet selections were received coldly by the professional Democratic politicians in Washington. On Capitol Hill it was disapprovingly noted that three former Republicans were included but not a single Democrat who had opposed Roosevelt's nomination at Chicago. Times looked bad for the professionals who had been out in the cold for twelve years, and the later disunion in Democratic ranks was foreshadowed in a small way by the disappointed comments of the old Southern wheel horses who viewed with alarm the advent of the Tugwells, Wallaces, Frankfurters, Moleys, Corcorans, Cohens, and the other "outsiders," as they considered them.

On the domestic front things were also moving rapidly toward that dramatic first inauguration of President Roosevelt. Congress repealed the Prohibition Amendment, and the several states set to work to ratify the repeal in record time. The Senate prophetically voted to enlarge the powers of the Reconstruction Finance Corporation.

Change was in the air. A new United States was in the making, set in a new world. Cordell Hull was almost alone in his fear that the change might be for the worse instead of the better.

CHAPTER XIII

Prophet without Honor

Tʜᴇ ɴᴇᴡsᴘᴀᴘᴇʀs that led their editions of Sunday, March 5, with the account of President Roosevelt's first inauguration on the previous day carried in their second-best position, for the most part, an announcement that has more than justified the news judgment of their editors in the succeeding years. The second most important story that morning was the news that the National Socialist party had won 44 per cent of the seats in the Reichstag as a result of the German elections. Frederick T. Birchall, cabling from Berlin to the New York *Times,* permitted himself to depart sufficiently from the Olympian detachment the *Times* usually preserves to interpolate the following into his account of the elections:

"Just as two and two make four, so suppression and intimidation have produced a Nazi-Nationalist triumph. The rest of the world may now accept the fact of ultra-Nationalist domination of the Reich and Prussia for a prolonged period with whatever results this may entail."

These results are now apparent, but the news which the journals dished up so prominently to their readers on that Sunday morning had little or no effect on the American public. The name of Adolf Hitler was not mentioned very often in the various news dispatches sent from the German capital. Old President

Hindenburg was believed to be in thorough control of the situation, and hundreds of thousands of American newspaper readers had never heard of the Austrian-born corporal who was to bring the whole world to war and who was to find one of his most implacable foes in the person of the American President whose inauguration was forced to share journalistic honors with the beginning of Hitler's rise to supreme power in Europe.

On behalf of the American public it must be recalled that its members had immediate problems of the gravest concern on their hands at home, and it is easily understood how they failed to comprehend the full meaning of the German political situation or to be greatly interested in it. Their new President hinted at the possibility of new dangers abroad in the world in his inaugural address when he enunciated the Good Neighbor policy which became the foundation for his subsequent dealings with foreign nations.

In the main, however, President Roosevelt stuck to the domestic crisis in his inaugural speech, assuring the nation that all it had to fear was fear itself. The fear to which he referred was economic dread, heightened by the three years of uncertainty and distress through which the nation had already passed. As Mr. Roosevelt was preparing to ride to the Capitol to take the oath of office on that Saturday morning, insiders in Washington considered it practically certain he would close all the banks in the country as soon as he took office.

It was believed in some New Deal circles that private hoarding of gold was responsible for the banking crisis, and there was talk of imposing a prohibitive tax on gold privately held. The new Secretary of State, Cordell Hull, turned his attention to this proposal in the first statement he made to the press after the Senate had confirmed his nomination along with the rest of the Roosevelt Cabinet. Hull was against the proposed tax.

"The main thing right now is to allay the unreasonable and unreasoning fear in the public mind," he said, in paraphrase of the President's earlier reassurances at the Capitol. "That in itself would be a long step in the direction toward restoration of confidence."

Mr. Roosevelt moved swiftly toward dealing with the banking crisis, although he took a few hours longer than observers had predicted. It was the next day, Sunday, before he announced, after conferences lasting almost all night with Secretary of the Treasury Woodin, that no bank in the United States would be allowed to open on Monday. The announcement was received with calm and almost with relief by the public. Some foreign diplomats in Washington hastily cabled their home governments that this step would doubtless bring on a revolution, misled by what the reaction to such a state of affairs would have brought in their own countries.

The "bank holiday," as it was euphemistically called, lasted until March 13. During the six banking days when the doors were closed examiners swiftly assessed the position of every bank in the country, and only the sound ones were allowed to reopen for business. The others were put into a process of orderly liquidation, and most of them eventually repaid their depositors every dollar they owed them. The special session of Congress, which President Roosevelt called to meet on the Thursday after his inauguration, passed legislation validating the Chief Executive's actions.

The whole affair was a heartening beginning for the New Deal. To most Americans it promised the end of compromise and shilly-shallying on the part of the government in the face of crisis. It appeared that the innate good sense and will of the people to recover would no longer be thwarted through inaction on the part of their elected representatives.

With this first crisis safely surmounted, President Roosevelt turned his eyes to the outside world, where he scented dangers of which the general public was completely unaware. On March 15 he was ready to ask Congress for authority to embargo shipments of arms, ammunition, and implements of war to parts of the world where war threatened. On that same day Arnaldo Cortesi cabled the New York *Times* from Rome that Ramsay MacDonald, the British Prime Minister, would see Premier Mussolini in order to attempt a revival of interest in the disarmament discussions which had been dragging along at Geneva.

Straws were in the European wind. A few days later Guido Enderis predicted in the New York *Times,* cabling from Berlin, that the Reichstag would vote dictatorial powers to Adolf Hitler, the man so few Americans knew. Cordell Hull, looking over matters in Washington, directed his subordinates to make a complete report on German atrocities against Jews. A mass meeting of 20,000 Jews, assembled at Madison Square Garden in New York on March 28, passed resolutions denouncing Hitler's treatment of their co-religionists. It began to look as if it would be very difficult to apply President Roosevelt's Good Neighbor policy to Nazi Germany.

Secretary of State Hull lost no time in trying to impart his apprehensions to the foreign governments with which he now had to deal. As their ambassadors and ministers called on him to pay their respects he declined to let the occasion pass as a mere polite and perfunctory formality. He insisted on discussing the state of the world with these men, and they were astonished at the grasp and understanding the Tennessean displayed. Like most Americans, they had failed to appreciate the remarkable background Cordell Hull had built up through study and concentration on tariff legislation during his long years in Congress. To them, as to the American voter, Hull had stood merely as the symbol of political astuteness on the part of President Roosevelt—a sort of hostage to the old-line Democrats.

Hull told them all the same story. He warned them that the world was moving toward war but predicted that the movement could be reversed if their governments would join the United States in a determined effort to stem the tide. Disarmament must be economic as well as military. The Secretary conceded that his own country had led the way in the race of tariff armaments which had brought the world to the brink of economic war, but he pledged the new administration to a swift and practicable reconsideration of that attitude.

The diplomatic corps with which he had to deal was headed by Sir Ronald Lindsay, the British ambassador, as its dean. Sir Ronald, a huge, shy Scotsman, had had a distinguished career and was a typical British diplomat of the old school, but he carried little weight with the national government headed by Ramsay MacDonald. This was the government which had taken Great Britain off the gold standard, enacted protective tariffs, and fathered the Empire Preference scheme embodied in the Ottawa Agreements. These pacts had been particularly distaste-

ful to Hull, although he said publicly that the British Empire was
only following the example of the United States.

Whatever evaluation Sir Ronald put on Hull's warnings in his
dispatches to the Foreign Office, they appear to have had little
effect. The British ambassador, whose second wife is American,
as was his first, was conspicuously conservative, and practically
his entire American acquaintance was confined to the extremely
rich of New York and Long Island, to whom his wife is related.
It is hardly likely that he attached much importance to the warnings or the promises of better behavior from the simple, forthright Secretary of State.

The other leading diplomatic representatives with whom he
discussed matters were not in much better shape to profit from
the warnings or to make their home governments listen. France
was represented by André Lefebvre de Laboulaye, a cultivated
career diplomat with little knowledge of the United States. M. de
Laboulaye, like his British colleague, had little influence in the
councils of his own government.

Astute Augusto Rosso was the Italian ambassador. He had
served for many years in the United States and eventually married an American woman just before he left Washington to become Italian ambassador in Moscow. By 1933, however, Mussolini had already brought Italy to such a sorry economic pass
that Rosso could offer no assurances on behalf of his own
country.

Cuba was represented by Don Oscar Cintas, a businessman
and a director of several large American corporations. He had
been appointed by the dying Machado regime because of his
friendship with Secretary Woodin. It was vainly hoped in Havana that he might secure financial aid for the tottering Cuban
dictatorship. Hull was advised by Sumner Welles, then ambassador to Cuba, and by Jefferson Caffery, then Assistant Secretary of State, that the Machado government would not last
much longer, and wasted little breath on Don Oscar.

Felipe A. Espil, the Argentine ambassador, had become cynical
regarding American promises of friendship through long years
of service in Washington and New York, during which he saw
the two countries become steadily more irreconcilable rivals in
the Western Hemisphere. Personally he was sympathetic to Hull's

ideas and he trusted the sincerity which Hull and Roosevelt displayed, but he knew in advance he would never be believed in Buenos Aires. Dr. Espil is another foreign diplomat who married an American woman. He listened to what Hull had to say, but the succeeding years only showed how well founded had been his original cynicism. The Western cattle raisers proved too strong for the Good Neighbor policy to reach the entire length of the hemisphere.

The other principal ambassadors included R. de Lima e Silva from Brazil, who left soon afterward for Belgium; Don Miguel Cruchaga Tocornal, who shortly went back to his native Chile to become President of the Senate; Dr. Sao-Ke Alfred Sze, who represented a China already suffering cruelly under Japanese aggression; Don Manuel de Freyre y Santander, the Peruvian ambassador, who succeeded Sir Ronald Lindsay as dean of the diplomatic corps; Don Juan Francisco de Cardenas, who represented the Franco faction in New York during the Spanish revolution and who became Spanish ambassador again as soon as the United States recognized Franco; and Katsuji Debuchi, the Japanese ambassador, who carried little weight in Tokyo and who was recalled soon afterward.

Hull reported to President Roosevelt that there seemed little likelihood of accomplishing much in forwarding the new American foreign policy through diplomatic channels, and the President decided on a more direct appeal to the world's governors. On May 16 he addressed a message to the chief of every sovereign state in the world, containing the proposal that "all nations of the world should enter into a solemn and definite pact of non-aggression; they should solemnly reaffirm the obligations they have assumed to limit and reduce their armaments, and, provided these obligations are faithfully executed by all signatory powers, individually agree that they will send no armed force of whatsoever nature across their frontiers."

This was followed by instructions to Norman H. Davis to offer, at the session of the Geneva Disarmament Conference on May 22, the most far-reaching commitment any government of the United States had ever been willing to make.

"We are willing to consult with the other states in case of a threat to peace, with a view to averting conflict," Mr. Davis said from the floor at Geneva. "Further than that, in the event that the states, in conference, determine that a state has been guilty of a breach of the peace in violation of its international obligations and take measures against the violator, then, if we concur in the judgment rendered as to the responsible and guilty party, we will refrain from any action tending to defeat such collective effort which these states may thus make to restore peace."

This promise was contingent on the accomplishment of effective land disarmament throughout the world. Since that condition was never achieved, Roosevelt and Hull were never called upon to make the promise good. Had they been required to put it through, the effort would no doubt have precipitated another debate in Congress rivaling in bitterness the discussions of the League of Nations following the World War, but they believed at the time that they had the country behind them.

Another avenue for quick personal action was at hand. In 1932 the Lausanne Conference had decided that the nations of the world should meet the following year for a discussion of economic and monetary problems growing out of the world-wide depression. The committee on agenda, on which the United States was represented, had selected London as the place and June as the month for the conference to meet. Hull was vitally interested in the projected gathering, as he hoped there might be an opportunity to put into international cooperative operation the principles of commerce which he had so long espoused.

Partly on Hull's recommendation and partly because of his sense of the dramatic President Roosevelt invited some of the leading commercial countries to send representatives of appropriate rank to discuss with him in Washington the scope which the forthcoming conference might safely be expected to cover. The foreign governments took the hint, and on April 5 Arthur Krock announced in the New York *Times* that Great Britain would send its Prime Minister, Ramsay MacDonald, to consult with the President. Not to be outdone, the French government appointed Edouard Herriot, who, though not then a member of the government, had been a staunch advocate of French payment of the war debt to the United States.

The situation quickly got out of hand, as practically every nation on earth demanded to send a representative to take part in these supposedly important preliminary conversations. A procession of visiting statesmen passed through the portals of the White House, issuing solemnly meaningless communiqués at the conclusion of their allotted visits. Germany sent Dr. Hjalmar Schacht, the economic wizard who could keep a great nation in operation on wampum for money; Italy sent Guido Jung; China sent T. V. Soong; Argentina threw into the breach Ambassador Le Breton from Paris; Canada dispatched Prime Minister Bennett; Japan, Brazil, Chile, Mexico, and others hastened to get in under the wire.

As a result, the preliminary discussions, which might have been useful in forming a sort of informal steering committee, degenerated into a vaudeville show. Even those countries which felt unable to send special emissaries to wait on President Roosevelt insisted that their diplomatic representatives in Washington be apprised of the momentous happenings which were indicated.

Actually nothing of importance resulted from these early talks. While Mr. MacDonald was on board his ship in mid-Atlantic, hastening to answer the Rooseveltian summons, the President announced the suspension of gold exports under authority newly granted by Congress. This was notice that the United States intended to enter the proposed monetary and economic conference under the same rules that would govern the other principal participants, but the British public took it as a direct affront, and Mr. MacDonald's mission was doomed before he ever landed in New York.

Hull took only a formal part in the discussions with the various foreign experts who wove in and out of the Washington scene. Apparently he was not as discouraged by them as was President Roosevelt. As later events disclosed, the President became convinced that the London gathering would be nothing but a stage show at which the United States would be maneuvered into underwriting Great Britain's losses in the depression, through some trick of currency stabilization, if he were not careful.

However, preparations for the conclave went forward. Things were going well on Capitol Hill for Mr. Roosevelt, so far as concerned domestic affairs, but Congress was already showing traces of that *intransigeance* in foreign policy which plagued the President through three terms. The arms-embargo scheme that he had proposed as a method to throw the weight of the United States against budding wars had proved a boomerang. The House of Representatives adopted it in an acceptable form under which the Chief Executive could exercise a large portion of discretion in deciding when and where it should be applied. In this form it might have proved a diplomatic weapon in the President's hands. But the Senate struck out the discretionary provisions, and the administration decided to let the whole matter drop.

A similar fate overtook Hull's plan to secure Congressional authority for tariff bargaining with foreign nations. It was deemed that the time was not ripe, and the administration decided to put that matter over for another year. Besides, it was argued, Congress should not attempt to enact any kind of tariff legislation until it was clear, through the deliberations at London, what the other trading nations were prepared to do.

The White House announced the composition of the United States delegation to the London Monetary and Economic Conference, with Secretary Hull as its chairman. The other members were James M. Cox, whose running mate in 1920 had been Franklin D. Roosevelt; Senator Key Pittman of Nevada, chairman of the Foreign Relations Committee; Representative Sam D. McReynolds of Tennessee; Sam D. Morrison, a Texas Democrat, and Senator James M. Couzens of Michigan, the sole Republican. It was an odd collection of delegates, and it is safe to assume that Secretary Hull had little voice in choosing his associates for the memorable venture. The delegates were obviously selected for their political rather than their philosophical value.

The technical skill was to be supplied by a large staff of experts in various fields. Their ranks included Professor Raymond Moley; Dr. Herbert Feis, the State Department's economic adviser; James P. Warburg; George L. Harrison, governor of the New York Federal Reserve Bank; J. E. Crane, its vice-governor; Dr. Oliver M. W. Sprague, former Harvard professor who had given up his post as adviser to the Bank of England to become adviser to the Treasury Department in Washington, and many others who were either attached officially to the delegation or hung modestly on its outskirts.

The staff work was plotted so that Warren Delano Robbins, a cousin of President Roosevelt and a veteran career diplomat, would act as liaison man between the White House and the delegation offices in London during the early part of the conference, and Raymond Moley would take over this function later, after the conference was under way. The President gave every indication that he intended to hold a tight rein over this conference, for which he apparently felt considerable responsibility because of the ballyhoo resulting from the ponderous preliminary discussions in Washington.

The delegates sailed on two different ships, for reasons that were never wholly clear. The combined delegation, consisting of the six delegates, their forty-three advisers, secretaries, and stenographers, and thirteen relatives of members of the party all reached London in time for the opening session on June 14.

Neville Chamberlain, who was then Chancellor of the Exchequer, made the principal speech welcoming the delegates. He had just announced to the House of Commons that a "token payment" of $10,000,000 would be made the following day to apply on the interest and principal of the British debt owed to the United States Treasury. This was generally, and rightly, considered in American financial circles to be the tip-off that the European debtors intended to get all possible easing of their American liabilities out of the conference as a quid pro quo to any counterproposals the United States might have to offer.

Secretary Hull addressed the gathering on behalf of his delegation. He warned the other delegates that international commerce could not rest at its existing low ebb without causing increasing friction among nations. This was his diplomatic way of saying that Europe was headed toward war unless it could straighten out its economic life on a basis which would make for enduring peace. He offered a resolution that the conference conclude its labors eight weeks thence, for he had already begun to harbor misgivings over the unwieldiness of the gathering.

After the formal opening the delegates settled down to the unspectacular, behind-closed-doors kind of maneuvering which characterizes all such conferences. Work was subdivided as much as possible. Governor Cox performed his assignments hard and conscientiously. Senator Pittman had little interest in anything except his plan to raise the world price of silver for the benefit of the Nevada miners. Mr. McReynolds had his wife and a debutante daughter with him and haunted the American Embassy to see that the proper credentials for a royal garden party and for the royal enclosure at Ascot were forthcoming and that his wife and daughter were presented at court. Senator Couzens was faithful but drew no important assignments. Mr. Morrison almost read himself out of the party by inquiring of newspapermen at a press conference, "Who *is* Beneš?"

Hull, however, found himself in a familiar atmosphere. The London Monetary and Economic Conference was little more cumbersome or difficult to deal with than a new Congress. He set to work with about the same technique he had used so successfully on Capitol Hill. He sought out the men who impressed him as the probable leaders among the crowd of amazingly able delegates who had been sent to London even by the small nations. In the early stages he dealt principally with Ramsay MacDonald, Neville Chamberlain, and Leith-Ross, the British economists, and Jung, the Italian expert he had met in Washington.

Before the conference had even opened Montagu Norman, governor of the Bank of England, and Clarence Moret, governor of the Banque de France, had begun conversations exploring the possibility of some kind of far-reaching currency stabilization. As Hull and his colleagues came into contact with the European delegates they found that currency stabilization was generally considered as a necessary first step before anything could be done about world trade.

Hull believed this view of the case amounted to putting the cart before the horse, and he had President Roosevelt's full backing in that estimate. According to the American thesis, currency instability was merely a symptom reflecting the unsettled condition of international trade. If that trade could be started flowing again through its normal channels and in normal volume, the different currencies in the world would automatically fall into their appropriate grooves in relation to one another and stay there as long as trade continued abundant. This was so completely the official American view that the United States delegation offered, on June 22, two resolutions—one to renounce any attempt at temporary currency stabilization by the conference and the other to raise world prices of prime commodities through cooperative action of the interested governments.

In the meantime complications were arising at home. The time had come for Raymond Moley to proceed to London to take on his part of the liaison work then being performed by Warren Delano Robbins. President Roosevelt was cruising off Cape Cod in the schooner *Amberjack* when Moley decided the time for his own departure had arrived.

The Assistant Secretary of State left Washington in a great hurry and boarded a navy flying boat at New York to alight beside the *Amberjack* for one last consultation with the Chief on June 20. He got back to New York on June 21 and sailed on the *Manhattan* with Herbert Bayard Swope, former executive of the New York *World,* as an unofficial adviser. Moley told the ship news reporters that he was merely going to London to make himself useful and to serve "as a means of contact between the administration here and the delegation."

This explanation, however, failed to quiet the speculation which had been aroused by the dramatic airplane dash to the side of the *Amberjack*. Diplomats in Washington cabled their foreign offices that Moley was bringing some new and important proposal straight from the President himself and advised that their delegates in London move slowly and cautiously until they could find out what the new angle was. Their advice was unnecessary, as things had already slowed to a walk in London. Delegates went through the motions of conferring perfunctorily, but it was obvious nothing would happen until Moley reached the scene.

By the time Moley got to London, on May 27, President Roosevelt and the *Amberjack* had voyaged as far as Campobello Island, off the coast of New Brunswick, where the Canadians were enthusiastically welcoming the new Chief Executive as an old-time neighbor. The Roosevelt family had spent many summers there.

The American dollar, at the same time, was gyrating in movements which brought dismay to the conservative elements among the delegates at London. Mr. Roosevelt, for his part, was represented as believing that the dollar still stood too high in relation to other national currencies and that no stabilization effort could as yet be made without disadvantage to the United States.

Moley, upon his arrival in London, took over all negotiations with the European gold bloc, presumably in accordance with the President's wishes and views. Hull bided his time while his ostensible assistant talked to the monetary experts and sent secret cables direct to the White House for transmission to the President. Hull agreed with the Chief Executive to the point that he did not believe currency stabilization was any panacea for the world's economic ills, but on the other hand he was not unalterably opposed to the adoption of some highly generalized stabilization plan (possibly like the tripartite agreement eventually worked out between Great Britain, France, and the United States) if the lack of such an agreement would stymie all progress along more important lines, as it then appeared would be the result of an adamant refusal by the United States to consider such a proposal.

Being thus in the middle of the road, he could only coast along until his own chief had made up his mind. Moley, as a result of his independent conversations, reached much the same conclusion and negotiated an informal declaration of intent to return to the gold standard under more or less vague future conditions. This he cabled to the President, and Mr. Roosevelt promptly rejected it. When the news of this rejection got around the conference, by grapevine, the consensus of opinion among the delegates was to the effect that the gathering might as well disband. This view was intensified on July 3, two days later, when Secretary Hull read to the delegates a formal rebuke sent by Mr. Roosevelt with instructions to present it to a plenary session. This unprecedented verbal spanking administered by the chief of one state to the representatives of some sixty other states contained most of its psychological punishment in the two opening paragraphs, which read as follows:

I would regard it as a catastrophe amounting to a world tragedy if the great Conference of Nations, called to bring about a more real and permanent financial stability and a greater prosperity to the masses of all nations, should, in advance of any serious effort to consider these broader problems, allow itself to be diverted by the proposal of a purely artificial and temporary experiment affecting the monetary exchange of a few nations only. Such action, such diversion, shows a singular lack of proportion and a failure to remember the larger purposes for which the Economic Conference originally was called together.

I do not relish the thought that insistence on such action should be made an excuse for the continuance of the basic economic errors that underlie so much of the present world-wide depression The world will not long be lulled by the specious fallacy of achieving a temporary and probably an artificial stability in foreign exchange on the part of a few large nations only. The sound internal economic system of a nation is a greater factor in its well-being than the price of its currency in changing terms of the currencies of other nations.

Here was the early Roosevelt in full cry. Whoever drafted that message for him caught faithfully his sincere indignation and impatience at the soft remedies the conservatives of the world had been trying for many years. Mere tricks of bankers, mere conjuring of stable exchange rates out of the silk hat of an economic conference would not cure the evils of inequitably distributed wealth and goods. At this point the President appeared to be in full agreement with his younger expert advisers of the Columbia University wing who were urging new ventures designed to solve once and for all the ills which had beset the world periodically ever since what they called mercantile capitalism had been slowly and almost invisibly metamorphosed into finance capitalism.

Original thinkers such as Adolf A. Berle, Jr., Rexford G. Tugwell, Charles Taussig, and the other younger men who occupied prominent positions in the backstage determination of administration policy agreed that the economic and financial structure of the world had broken down because it was inherently faulty and that it could not be patched up, so as to run again briefly, by such expedients as suddenly declaring that the world's currencies would henceforth stand in a certain fixed relation to one another. There was less agreement as to the nature of the new departures which ought to be tried first, and the variety of the plans they presented to him planted in Mr. Roosevelt's mind the figure of speech he used so often—that of the quarterback trying a new play if one maneuver failed to gain ground.

Secretary Hull, of course, did not go along with the younger advisers in their belief that a radically new approach was needed. He felt, as a result of his long years of study and experience, that it was not the machine which was faulty but its operators. He felt that the world's productive and distributive capacity could go far, under its own momentum, to correct the evils of which complaint was made, if only it were given a reasonably free chance to function. While he agreed with the President's general thesis that currency stabilization of itself would accomplish no miracles, he might have been willing to concede that it would do no harm provided it were accompanied by more farsighted steps to restore the flow of international trade in ever-increasing volume.

The delegates in London were practically unanimous in saying that President Roosevelt's brusque message meant the end of the conference. In Washington the President must have feared the same result, for he cabled Secretary Hull the following day to use every effort to keep the conclave going. Moley left on July 6, and James P. Warburg resigned as an adviser to the delegation, writing a letter to Hull just as the Secretary was urging the steering committee of the conference not to adjourn the gathering. The members reluctantly agreed to a face-saving recess instead of an adjournment and decided that the closing meeting would be held on July 27. The British insisted that no resolution recommending a unified program of public works, to be carried out as "pump-priming" measures, be adopted by the conference, while in Washington President Roosevelt was fascinated with the beginnings of NRA and the Blue Eagle and with blanketing all postmasters under civil service.

The Monetary and Economic Conference met for the last time, as scheduled, on July 27. Secretary Hull read a message from the White House in which Mr. Roosevelt said that "I do not regard the economic conference as a failure," and added a speech for himself in which he reiterated his belief that economic peace was the only sure basis for world security and damned the nationalistic experiments under way in Washington with faint and indirect praise.

"At this moment the world is still engaged in wild competition in economic armaments which constantly menace both peace and commerce," he warned the delegates, adding, at a later point, his opinion that "indispensable and all-important as domestic programs are, they cannot by themselves restore business to the highest levels of permanent recovery."

There was little doubt in anyone's mind that the conference

had been a complete fiasco and that the unwillingness of the United States to discard the nationalistic practices it condemned in others was the principal reason. Frederick T. Birchall cabled the New York *Times* that the failure was due to the British government's insistence on justifying the Empire Preference plan adopted at Ottawa, leaving the British delegation no common ground on which to meet Hull. This was a factor, of course, but public opinion throughout the world lay the responsibility—approvingly or disapprovingly, according to individual predilections—on the doorstep of Washington.

At the time much emphasis was laid on the personal element involved between Hull and Moley, Hull and Roosevelt, Hull and the other delegates, and Roosevelt and his immediate advisers at home. Looking back at the strange meeting from this distance, it would appear that the conference was doomed by circumstances rather than by men. There was profound difference of opinion among the individuals who took the leading parts, but the world itself was in the grip of the indecisions and crosscurrents which eventually brought on the war of 1939.

The Secretary of State landed in New York on August 5 and was invited to come directly to Hyde Park, where President Roosevelt was resting, for a report and consultation. Moley had already had his say in the presidential ear, and rumors were prevalent that Hull intended to resign. The President and his Secretary of State made no public statement about their meeting, but the White House secretariat was encouraged to let it be known that Roosevelt had expressed the utmost confidence in the actions and policies of his chief Cabinet officer and was anxious to keep him in his post because of the forthcoming negotiations for the recognition of the Soviet Union and the Seventh Pan-American Conference scheduled to be held in Montevideo the next December. Hull went back to his desk in Washington, to stay there until long after he had broken all records of tenure of office by any Secretary of State.

About six months later Moley drew back the curtain of secrecy from the skeleton of the conference to the extent of writing that it had failed because "the world was not ready for tariff and money readjustments until the separate nations put order in their own houses." In an obvious dig at Hull's theories he outlined a form of "liberal internationalism," which was to replace, as he saw it, the "dear old liberalism" toward which one wing of the Democratic party was trying to retrace its steps.

"Everything we use can be created for us here," he wrote in a vein reminiscent of the theories with which Germany and Italy were already struggling. "We have made ourselves substantially economically independent. In a financial way we are becoming more independent of England every day."

President Roosevelt declined to accept responsibility for the conference's breakdown when he got around to writing about it in his book, *On Our Way*, published in 1934. He explained in that book that "this country knew, and all other nations knew, that we were engaged at home in a great program of rehabilitation—a program which called for the raising of values—and that no human being could, at that moment, determine exactly where even a temporary stabilization point should be fixed for the dollar, franc, and pound." He also recalled that "Secretary Hull, with magnificent force, prevented the conference from final adjournment and made it possible, we all hope, for a renewal of its discussion in the broad field of mutual relationships." This hope was not to be realized.

In a book called *The Money Muddle*, also published in 1934, James P. Warburg said that the original instructions to the United States delegation called for moves to promote cooperation among the central banks, government spending as an antidote to unemployment, the removal of exchange restrictions, reorganization of the external debt structures "of some countries" (although this apparently referred to private debts), the formation of creditors' associations to compromise conflicting interests in debt defaults, and the use of gold only as a currency cover and a means of settling international balances, with the precious metal completely removed from ordinary circulation. This last point was partly covered in the "silver resolution" Senator Pittman persuaded the delegates to adopt before the recess, but the other projects were never even formally presented in the confusion that followed the presidential change of heart at home.

More than eight years after his puzzled resignation as adviser to the delegation, when he told Mr. Hull he simply could not expound the monetary principles of Mr. Roosevelt because he

did not know what they had become since the delegates left
Washington, Mr. Warburg expressed to me his still-existing regret that the conference went on the rocks. He said he still considers that it was "the last chance for reordering the economic
structure of the world and arresting the trend toward economic
nationalism, which is identical with the trend toward war."

The most detailed post-mortem examination of the conference
which has yet been published is contained in Raymond Moley's
book, *After Seven Years,* which appeared in 1939, just before
war broke out in Europe. By this time the former confidant and
adviser of President Roosevelt had become such a thoroughgoing
critic and opponent that he placed the entire blame on the Chief
Executive. He dealt kindly with Hull, the man whose ruin he was
supposed to have been plotting.

He pictured President Roosevelt as playing off Hull against
the economic nationalists of the New Deal in an effort to keep
all hands contented. At the time, Professor Moley wrote, he believed the President was merely pulling Hull's leg to keep the old-
line Democrats satisfied that the party was following its traditional
policies under the guidance of the assortment of college professors gathered from the North and the East. He had reached the
conclusion, by 1939, that the President was pulling the legs of
all of them. By piecing together the hitherto unpublished threads
which Moley apparently found in his diaries and notes it is
possible to see how the situation struck those of his persuasion in
1933.

To them it was a colossal mistake for the President to make
any concessions to old-line Democracy. It had no future, in their
eyes. Much of this early cleavage surrounded the political fate
of Norman Davis, a close friend of Hull and a man whom the
new Secretary of State kept urging on the President. Davis had
been too closely associated with the Hoover administration in
various capacities, and he had too many friendly relations with
Wall Street and the bankers to be acceptable to Moley and his
friends.

One of Hull's early triumphs over the New Dealers was his
persuasion of President Roosevelt to retain Norman Davis as
chief of the United States delegation to the Geneva conference
on limitation of armaments. The President, while he was tem-

peramentally and philosophically inclined toward the points of view represented by the Brain Trust, was too astute a politician to cut all ties with his party's right wing until he saw how the New Deal would take.

Moley represented Hull as being too wrapped up in his own ideas to see the essential conflict between his own concepts and Roosevelt's domestic policy. He wrote that the two men were separated by an unbridgeable gulf. No doubt it appeared that way to the Brain Trust, but these enthusiastic amateurs in national political life forgot, or underrated, the possibility of workable compromise between two such experienced vote getters as the men they were condemning to eternal conflict. The proof of their judgment lies in the fact that Franklin D. Roosevelt has lasted longer as President and Cordell Hull longer as Secretary of State than any other two men in the history of the Republic—and they have lasted together.

The most interesting part of Moley's account of the London Conference is his explanation, which he concedes is pure inference, of the President's change of heart that led to its collapse. He starts by explaining in some detail that he himself never expressed himself to the President as being in favor of the modified gold-standard proposal which Roosevelt knocked down with such gusto. There is considerable opinion among other members of the delegation that Moley actually did not favor it. By his own account he merely agreed to forward it to Washington, in his role as official liaison man, without recommendation or condemnation.

On the other hand, he states that he saw no great harm in it and believed that the President would accept it in order that the conference might get on to more important work. According to his analysis, it committed the United States to nothing which would have hindered the domestic nationalistic economic experiments Roosevelt was bent on trying. His evaluation of the proposal was probably much the same as Hull's, as was his surprise when the Chief Executive so emphatically refused to have anything to do with it.

After six years of reflection Moley thought he had found the answer to the riddle. He recalled that Roosevelt's companions aboard the cruiser *Indianapolis* when the gold-standard plan

reached him were Louis Howe, his confidential secretary, and
Henry Morgenthau, Jr., who was soon to become his Secretary
of the Treasury.

For two or three days before the proposal was forwarded by
Moley there had been persistent rumors in Wall Street that he
had agreed to some kind of currency-stabilization plan. That was
at the zenith of the reports crediting him with having been sent
to London with plenary powers to dictate the course of the conference—a state of affairs which he claims never existed.

These reports had caused a sharp slump in stock and commodity prices. The speculators had been busily engaged in promoting what they described to their customers, or victims, as
a "flight from the dollar," urging anybody with any cash to exchange it quickly for an industrial stock or a commodity of some
kind, on the ground that the new administration's monetary policies would undoubtedly lead to an uncontrolled currency inflation of the kind experienced in Germany just after the World
War.

Everybody could remember, they reminded their clients, how
the smart man in Germany in those days had been the "*schieber,*"
usually non-Aryan, who hastened to trade his almost worthless
marks to some dullard for something of real, tangible value before the marks became utterly worthless, often the following
day. The United States, as they represented the situation, was in
the position where the monied man had just about his last chance
to trade his cheapening dollars for wheat, stocks, cotton, sugar,
real estate, or almost anything, before it got to a point where
nobody in his right mind would take dollars.

While this argument made relatively little headway, it was
a marginal factor tending to accelerate the probably normal upward reaction of stock and commodity prices from their incredible lows when Roosevelt took office. The inveterate in-and-
out speculators, discouraged by a steadily downward movement
of prices for three and a half years, were glad to cling to any
straw which promised to restore that up-and-down movement
of prices which makes professional speculation possible and
profitable.

Then, just as the fear of currency inflation was beginning to
take hold, rumors of an international stabilization agreement

in London sent the professionals scurrying to cover, and the movement was generally reversed. The markets were so "thin" at that point that a very little buying or selling, provided it was one-sided, exercised an undue influence on price trends.

Roosevelt and the New Dealers did not care what made prices move upward so long as that movement was steady and uninterrupted. Some of them, including the President, sincerely believed that the country's economic ills could be permanently cured if only every producer got more dollars for his product. They thought that the whole debt situation, including defaulted farm mortgages, municipal bonds, etc., sprang simply from the fact that individuals and political subdivisions had borrowed sums of money in the expectation that the prices they would get from the sale of their products, or the revenues they would raise by taxes, would remain at the same level, measured in dollars. All that was needed, accordingly, was to restore those dollars' levels; everybody would pay off, and the nation's fiscal structure would resume its normal shape.

Others of the President's immediate entourage were less interested in this theory than they were in proving that Hoover and the conservatives had maliciously let the country go to the devil by refusing to take such an obviously simple step as boosting prices. Still others (and their number included Howe and Morgenthau) were anxious that the new President, their idol, should not lose the confidence of the people that was beginning to bud as prosperity timidly peeped from around Hoover Corner.

Moley's theory is that Morgenthau and Howe, terrified at the temporary slump in price levels, convinced the President that anything remotely resembling currency stabilization would intensify the alarming symptoms already appearing and that his whole social and economic program would be jeopardized just as things began to look as if it could be translated into legislative reality. Moley's theory admittedly has little upon which to rest except the fact that Roosevelt was removed from all immediate influences but those of Howe and Morgenthau at the time he sent his scathing message to the conference.

Whether or not it is the true explanation can be told by only one man, and he is no longer even interested. In all probability President Roosevelt would now find it hard, in the light of the stirring events of the intervening years, to go back in his own mind and analyze his motives in drafting that historic rebuke. Also, he would probably consider them highly unimportant.

Looking back at them, one is forced to admit that their importance lay in the effect they might have had on Cordell Hull and the foreign policy of the United States. To suffer such a grievous disappointment at the very outset of his term of office —and a disappointment which seemed to stem from such cavalier and variable actions by his chief—would have finished a less tenacious and self-confident man than Hull.

As it was, things worked out. President Roosevelt had already sensed the continued embarrassment Moley's presence in the Department of State would cause Hull; he had decided to keep Hull at all costs, and he engineered one of those strokes by which he has so often eased out a former favorite by appearing to promote him. He had persuaded Moley to take an assignment at the Department of Justice to study means of eradicating crime from the nation.

The Assistant Secretary of State enjoyed considerable repute in this field. He had written books and made speeches on crime prevention for years before he came into the Rooseveltian ken. He explains in his book that he knew he was being kicked upstairs but that he also realized the hopelessness of trying to stay in the same department with Hull and that he sincerely believed he could help in the work Attorney General Cummings was just launching with great ballyhoo. Also, his feelings were considerably assuaged by tardy assurances from a group of New York capitalists that they would back him in starting the magazine *Today*.

What with one thing and another, Hull was not too downhearted when he returned to his desk in the State Department, and he set to work with a will to erase the bitter memories of London. He found that President Roosevelt had encouraged an old friend and classmate, Undersecretary of State William Phillips, to start negotiations with the governments of Brazil, Argentina, and Colombia for the mutual reduction of trade barriers along the lines of Hull's favorite theories. In effect, the reciprocal-trade-agreements program was born, although it was not to have Congressional baptism until the following year.

The Cuban crisis was at its height, and President Machado was forced out by the army, led by Sergeant Fulgencio Batista, a week after Hull talked to Roosevelt at Hyde Park. The challenge of restoring the island republic to some semblance of law and order, which Hull knew could be done only by intelligent cooperation—not intervention—by the United States, excited his interest.

In addition, the forthcoming Pan-American Conference would give him one more chance to test international sentiment for a return to a civilized way of living—and that on a simpler scale where there would be greater chance of success. The mental and physical resilience for which Hull is noted displayed itself once again, and he took a new lease on life as Secretary of State.

He waited just long enough to greet Maxim Litvinoff, when the Soviet Commissar for Foreign Affairs arrived in Washington on November 7 to urge recognition of his country's government after sixteen years of being ignored, and sailed for Montevideo on November 11, leaving the details of the Russian conversations in the hands of his old friend and fellow Democrat, R. Walton Moore of Fairfax, Virginia, whom he had persuaded Roosevelt to name Assistant Secretary of State.

Hull was outward bound on another great adventure in converting the world to sanity.

CHAPTER XIV

The Real Good Neighbor

THE PAN-AMERICAN WORLD into which Hull made his first exploration in 1933 was unknown territory to him. His long years of study and research during his Congressional career had made him thoroughly familiar with Europe—its personalities, its structure, its politics. But those studies were concerned with fiscal theories—such things as taxation, tariffs, budgets, and the like. In these spheres there was nothing to learn from the other American republics, and Hull's researches had not brought him into firsthand contact with the part of the Western Hemisphere to the south of the United States.

When he sailed for Uruguay on Armistice Day, however, Secretary Hull was convinced that a completely new set of economic, political, and cultural relations between the United States and its hemisphere neighbors was essential for the welfare of the New World and of the whole world. His experience at London had convinced him that the turnabout for the world, which he realized must be achieved to avoid chaos, would have to develop from regional beginnings. The bulky unwieldiness of the gathering of representatives of sixty-odd sovereign nations, with different and often conflicting national aspirations, had increasingly impressed him in retrospect, after his first disappointment over the inglorious role played by the United States had faded.

The twenty-one republics of the Western Hemisphere made up an ideal group to attempt the formulation of a common policy, so far as political considerations were concerned. With the exception of Bolivia and Paraguay, which were locked in the throes of the Chaco War, they were at peace among themselves and intended to remain at peace. There was the further common denominator that none of them intended to get mixed up in any foreign war and that they would probably act together to repel aggression against any part of the Americas by a non-American power, although this topic was still in the vague conversational stage.

There, however, the promising terrain ended. On the economic and cultural sides huge gulfs separated many of them from one another and from the United States. With the exception of the United States the republics were not (and are not today) highly industrialized. They were producers of prime materials and, as such, had not yet felt the urge toward protective tariffs as a part of their national economic lives. They had learned the lesson of tariffs only to the extent that many of them imposed high customs duties on imports as a means of securing the revenue needed to run their governments.

In the main they supported themselves by growing coffee, wheat, beef, mutton, wool, and mahogany, and by mining silver, gold, copper, and semiprecious stones, selling these in Europe and in the United States and spending the proceeds on automobiles, travel, suits from Savile Row, champagne, and the amenities of life for the top economic strata. While their system was not wholly desirable or praiseworthy, since it operated through extreme concentration of wealth resting on widespread and abject poverty, it had been in effect ever since the Conquistadores had brought the so-called blessings of Spanish civilization to the New World, and it had the merit of being a going concern.

For the immediate purposes of the new regime Hull had in mind, the economic system suffered from certain rivalries inherent in the duplication of climatic and topographic conditions on the two sides of the equator. The extreme of this kind of competition in efficient and indicated production existed in the case of Argentina and the United States. Nationals of both countries produced surpluses of wheat, beef, wool, and mutton. There was

no economic sense in exchanging those products between the
two countries.

Triangular trade was essential if these two nations were to
have any economic intercourse whatever, and even then their
nationals would find themselves competing in foreign markets
with their identical wares. There were also Brazilian wheatgrow-
ers and cattlemen facing the same problem. In the coffee field,
growers in Brazil, Haiti, Colombia, and Venezuela were in competition for the disposition of their products in the world market.
Sugar was a headache alike for Cuba and Peru, faced with the
increasing production of beetgrowers in the United States and
canegrowers in Louisiana, Hawaii, and the Philippines. Cocoa
was a competitive export from Mexico and the Central American republics.

In other words, economic regionalism faced enormous difficulties. It was unlikely that the Western Hemisphere could ever,
in any useful time, adjust its economic life to any scheme which
would have for its foundation the idea of self-containment. The
economic life of the Western world was tied to the necessity of
a peaceful, old-fashioned multilateral exchange of goods and
services—the very thing Hull believed was the only road to peace
and happiness—and the superficial difficulties in the way of
evolving a common pattern only tended to reinforce the possibilities of success, as he saw it.

The cultural aspects of the problem interested him less, although he realized they presented serious obstacles. The fact that
the Brazilians speak Portuguese, the Haitians speak French, the
United States speaks English, and the rest of the republics speak
Spanish did not daunt him. The periodic politico-religious crises
in some countries (notably Mexico) were other disturbing factors. The arrogance of the Argentines vis-à-vis the Brazilians and
the indifferent contempt of the Brazilians for the Argentines
(rather like the feeling the Chinese used to have for the Japanese), the traditional hatred of the Chileans for the Peruvians,
the Colombians for the Ecuadorians, the Mexicans for the grin-
gos, and vice versa, all had their place but struck the Secretary
as essentially unimportant.

The United States delegation which he headed was superior,
for the purposes of the Seventh International Conference of

American States, to the motley assortment of representatives he had taken to London. With the exception of Dr. Sophonisba Breckenridge, who was appointed at the insistence of Mrs. Roosevelt to be the first woman delegate the United States had ever sent to a foreign conference, the delegates were fairly expert in the field. In addition, Secretary Hull had the benefit of the valuable advice of Sumner Welles, who had exchanged places with Jefferson Caffery and was now Assistant Secretary of State, Laurence Duggan, and other career technicians whose knowledge of Latin America is above challenge. In other words, he was starting for Montevideo under far more favorable auspices than had cheered him on his way to London.

The official delegates, in addition to Dr. Breckenridge, who did nothing but interest herself in the feministic problems that arose, were J. Reuben Clark, a Republican, former Undersecretary of State and former ambassador to Mexico; J. Butler Wright, an able career diplomat who was then minister to Uruguay; Alexander W. Weddell, another career diplomat who was then ambassador to Argentina and later became ambassador to Spain; and Spruille Braden of New York, an ardent New Dealer with considerable business experience in Latin America (his father founded the Braden Copper Company in Chile, and the son had married an attractive Chilean girl).

This delegation could not be described as an aggregation of enthusiastic and dissident amateurs such as had invaded London the preceding spring. Its members showed early in the proceedings that they were prepared to act as a disciplined team for the accomplishment of whatever aim the administration had in mind. These aims were circumspectly limited by a White House statement issued just before the delegates sailed and just after they had received their formal instructions.

"Meanwhile, unsettled conditions, such as European commercial quota restrictions, have made it seem desirable for the United States to forego immediate discussions of such matters as currency stabilization, uniform import prohibitions, permanent customs duties, and the like," the statement said.

While this pronouncement had the air of once again reducing the forthcoming deliberations to innocuity, Secretary Hull gave no indication that he felt in any way hampered by it. As things

Secretary Hull with General Pedro Aurelio De Goes Monteiro,
Chief of Staff of the Brazilian Army

*

turned out, he was not hampered, and the curious defeatist declaration can be ascribed only to a dying gesture on the part of the waning Moley faction. Hull did not believe that any of the forbidden objectives could, or should, be achieved at a single sitting of the twenty-one republics, but he could not see why the United States should "forego immediate discussions."

A few days out of New York, on November 17, the news reached the S S. *American Legion* that an exchange of notes had taken place which constituted the restoration of normal diplomatic relations between the United States and the Soviet Union. I sought out Mr. Hull, who was sitting on the afterdeck of the ship enjoying a moonlight conversation with a few friends, and asked if he had any comment I could send to my paper. He said that the resumption of relations was a "natural and timely action" and expressed his gratification that the two peoples "have resumed normal relations and that the preliminary basis agreed upon was substantially that indicated before I left Washington." It seemed to me he was trying to knock down in advance the report, which did circulate afterward, that President Roosevelt had taken the Russian negotiations out of his hands and had dispatched him to Uruguay as an escape.

The delegation arrived at Montevideo on November 28, five days before the conference was scheduled to open. The atmosphere, or *"ambiente,"* as the local press described it, was excited and not too promising. Delegates of several other republics had traveled down on the ship with Mr. Hull and he had tried to cultivate them. It was obvious, however, that the Chaco War, North American efforts to collect defaulted bonds, the threat of intervention in Cuba, and the presence of the United States Marines in Nicaragua would combine to throw a chill over the gathering. Hull hastily took counsel with his political self and decided positive action was needed.

Ten foreign ministers were listed as the chiefs of their delegations, and the Secretary of State thought it would not be beneath his dignity to call on the nine others. The fact that it had never been done before recommended itself to him. Here was a small and probably useful way to signalize that there was a New Deal in Pan-Americanism as well as in the domestic policies of the United States. During those preliminary days Argentina paid the United States the doubtful compliment of adopting a scheme very similar to the NRA, but that was not the kind of New Deal Hull had in mind.

Taking James Clement Dunn, an experienced and capable career diplomat who was serving as secretary-general of the delegation, as his interpreter, Mr. Hull bustled from hotel to hotel, leaving cards for the other foreign ministers and chatting with them in person whenever he found them in. In two days he covered the field. Then he settled back to receive their return calls. The North American political acumen on which he had gambled was about to be put to the acid test.

The prime object of this adventure into personal politics was to break down the hostile reserve of Dr. Carlos Saavedra Lamas, the Foreign Minister of Argentina. The distinguished Argentine statesman, who has since disappeared from public life, was then reaching the height of his career. He was an arrogant, frigid individual whose influence in Argentine governmental affairs was never understood in the United States, even by State Department experts, and perhaps was not understood by the Argentines themselves. He was noted for the profundity of both his knowledge of international law and his collars. He wore, as a sort of badge, stiff linen collars that were specially made for him by some old-fashioned shirtmaker in London and which must have been four or five inches high.

Before leaving Washington, Secretary Hull had been warned that Dr. Saavedra Lamas practically had horns and a tail. He enjoyed the reputation, whether deserved or not, of being at the bottom of every anti-North American cabal launched in Latin America. He was supposed to represent the almost extinct Spanish don element which sincerely believed that Argentina was the leading nation of the Western Hemisphere, destined to dominate it as Great Britain dominated Europe, and that Brazil and the United States were uncultured, easygoing nonentities which would relegate themselves to their proper secondary places in due course. A noted Brazilian, in commenting on this limited segment of Argentine public opinion, once described Argentina to me as "the Prussia of the Western Hemisphere."

Mr. Hull refused to believe that there was any fatal obstacle in all this. He had met and dealt with many another public figure possessing idiosyncrasies as peculiar as those imputed to his Argentine colleague, and he put his wits to work on the situation. By the time Dr. Saavedra returned his courtesy call he thought he had the solution.

He received the Argentine Foreign Minister in his private sitting room at the Parque Hotel, where the United States delegation was quartered. Only Mr. Dunn was with him. After the inevitable amenities had been traversed Mr. Hull launched into a general discussion of the scope of the forthcoming Pan-American Conference, which was to open its sessions the following day. He talked in such generalities that Jimmy Dunn had difficulty, at first, in translating them into sufficiently vivid Spanish to hold Saavedra's attention and interest. The Secretary said that the conference must approve, unanimously, a general program for the preservation of peace in the Western Hemisphere and in the world. The United States delegation, while heartily endorsing such an objective, would prefer to remain in the background, for fear of offending the sensibilities and wounding the prides of smaller countries. He would much prefer that the head of some Latin-American delegation take the lead in urging such a program.

By this time Saavedra's interest was fully aroused. He had drafted a Pan-American peace convention which was a sort of regionalized Kellogg-Briand Pact. He was very proud of this achievement, even though the Argentine Congress had not ratified it and did not do so for many years. Its author, however, was later awarded the Nobel Peace Prize on the strength of it, at the recommendation and insistence of Cordell Hull. The Secretary's remarks at the Parque Hotel interested him strangely.

Mr. Hull saw that he had played out enough line and decided to pull him in. His catch line, which Dunn again had difficulty in translating in all its fine rich flavor, although by that time Saavedra had fully glimpsed where the conversation was leading, ran something like this:

"Mr. Minister, we want this program to be achieved. We want to support it and we will support it. We want the best man down here to put it forward so we can give it our support."

There was a little pause while Dunn translated that much.

"Now, Mr. Minister, if you won't do it, we are going to get the next best man down here to do it."

That clinched it. Dr. Saavedra changed the subject, inquired whether he could do anything to contribute to his distinguished colleague's comfort or welfare in Montevideo, and got up to take his leave. In the process of phrasing the conventional au revoir he assured Mr. Hull that he would be only too happy to push with all his might the program that had been suggested and that he would count on the support of the United States delegation as had been promised.

This small triumph was a happy augury for Hull's debut into Pan-American politics. For the remainder of that conference he had the wholehearted and effective cooperation of Saavedra, the one man who all the experts had thought would throw monkey wrenches into everything the North Americans wanted to do. Saavedra grew so enthusiastic that he urged Hull to reconvene the London Monetary and Economic Conference, promising the full support of the Americas to any program the United States would advance.

The divergence toward Europe, however, was one of the less happy by-products of the new-found intimacy between Hull and Saavedra. Hull feared that the concrete regional benefits that he believed could be accomplished at Montevideo would be lost in a tide of sentimental and impracticable resolutions calling for simultaneous action of the whole world or at least of all Europe. Enrique Buero, the Uruguayan secretary-general of the conference, was an ardent advocate of the League of Nations and did everything he could to orient the whole proceedings so that they would become a sort of regional meeting of the League. Sixteen of the twenty-one republics were then members of the League, so that this sentiment had too much sentimental backing for Hull and the United States delegates openly to oppose, though they knew it would be bad politics for them back home if the idea should go very far.

In his quiet way Hull set up an antidote for this poison in another of his preconference calls. This time the convertee was Gabriel Terra, the President of Uruguay. Although not a delegate to the conference, as Chief Executive of the nation acting as host to the gathering Dr. Terra would see a great deal of the heads of delegations and would exercise considerable unofficial influence if he cared to do so. Besides, he was to give the formal speech opening the deliberations, to which a Cuban delegate was to reply on behalf of the nation which previously acted as host (the Sixth Pan-American Conference was held in Havana in 1928).

In his preliminary talks with President Terra, Hull stressed the importance of stopping the Chaco War if the Western Hemisphere was to pose as a refuge of peace and as an example to the rest of the world. He implanted the idea that the impending conference ought to make some effort in this direction and persuaded Dr. Terra to make such a recommendation in his opening address. There had been a time when both Bolivia and Paraguay had threatened not to send delegations if their enemy's delegates were allowed to sit in the hall, but that difficulty had been ironed out and the conference officials were offering silent but fervent prayers that the two delegations would not, under the traditional system of drawing lots for precedence and place in the hall, win adjoining seats.

There was more to Hull's maneuvering than the mere smoothing of small local prides, so far as concerned the Chaco War. The League of Nations, to which both the contestants belonged, had appointed a commission to conciliate the conflict, but it had accomplished nothing to date. Hull felt that the commission's meticulous and lengthy examination of the juridical bases of both sides' claims, the unending exchange of memoranda, and the other procedures which, in the end, proved the League's impotence to deal with important crises had established the improbability that the only war in the Western Hemisphere would ever be brought to a conclusion through that machinery. For this reason he was anxious to get Dr. Terra, another pro-Leaguer, to launch the movement for a Pan-American solution of a Pan-American conflict in order to test the efficiency of such procedure.[1]

Without following those negotiations through their tortuous course, it is sufficient to say here that the idea worked to the extent that the two contestants agreed to an armistice, on recom-

[1]Secretary Hull was unaccountably missing for several hours one day shortly before Christmas. Ulric Bell, the delegation's press officer, encoun-

mendation of the conference, on Christmas Eve. Sporadic fighting broke out and terminated the armistice a few days later, but the back of the war was broken and peace was finally re-established by a Pan-American Commission in 1936.

There were other elements pulling and hauling at cross-purposes, as is always the case at international conclaves of the old order, and Hull gave much of his attention to mediating differences and mitigating grievances. He was especially desirous that the other chief delegates should take back home to their governments reports that the Roosevelt New Deal meant a new North American approach to the Pan-American problem. He wanted to be conciliatory wherever he could, to stay in the background, to conduct his mission in such manner that the United States would appear to be only one of twenty-one members of a club. He was determined that there should be no attempt by the United States to dominate the conference, as some of his predecessors had done at previous meetings.

He was as well aware as any other practical politician that the very essence of the Pan American Union's structure is only theoretically, and not practically, democratic. It has always suffered from the same fundamentally anti-democratic basic concept which doomed the League of Nations to a dwindling death. This great weakness is the exaggerated importance given to national sovereignty as opposed to representation by population in the Pan American Union. There is something manifestly lacking, so far as effective democracy is concerned, when the representatives of a tiny country like Costa Rica exercise equal voice with those of the United States or the delegates from Haiti command the same voting strength as those from Brazil.

It is an interesting commentary that the twenty-one republics, under the organization of the Pan American Union, vote as equals but assess the expenses on the basis of population. Thus the United States casts one twenty-first of the votes and pays more than half of the expenses.

However, Hull reasoned, this was no occasion to attempt a

tered him as he came into the Parque Hotel, late in the evening, and asked where he had been. He replied: "Oh, I have just been talking to a few fellows." It turned out that the "few fellows" had been the other foreign ministers and President Terra and that Hull himself had drafted the joint telegram which brought the Chaco armistice.

revision of the organic statutes which bound the republics together, no matter how tenuous the thread might be. He resolved
to follow the Pan-American tradition under which all decisions
at formal conferences are approved by unanimous vote. This
means, of course, that an obstreperous minority, sometimes consisting of a single delegation, can prevent affirmative action by
the rest (this has happened not once but many times, and it was
fear of just such a contingency that made the State Department
experts tell Hull to beware of Saavedra), but it also means that
whatever progress is made at each successive gathering is not
likely to be undone at the next.

Even more important, in Hull's mind, was the maintenance
of an appearance of solidarity among the nations of the New
World. It would only create complete confusion, he reasoned,
if any given course were approved by sixteen republics, for example, while five republics refused to have anything to do with
it. Such a situation would hardly produce the genesis of a world
reawakening which he hoped might be started in the Western
Hemisphere.

The cloakroom strategy that he had learned so thoroughly in
the House of Representatives and the Senate was invaluable to
him at Montevideo. He was able to persuade Dr. José M. Puig
Casauranc, the Mexican Foreign Minister, that his radical economic and monetary proposal (including the cancellation of
governmental indebtedness to private investors) ought to be
referred to a committee of experts for further study. He worked
out with Justin Barrau, the chief Haitian delegate, the basis for
a new financial agreement restoring to the Haitian government
control of its own fiscal affairs, thus preventing an anti-American
outburst on the floor of the conference by the dusky delegates
from Port-au-Prince.

Hull was not all sweetness and light in his dealings with the
Latin-American delegates at Montevideo, however. One morning, behind the closed doors of the steering committee's room, he
let loose an impromptu blast against·an intimation that the
United States government was pursuing what was called its old-
time role of collection agent for the international bankers who
had forced unneeded loans on Latin-American administrations.
Without bothering to deny that his government had ever per-

formed such a function, Hull shouted, white and furious, that anyone who accused President Roosevelt of having any untoward relations with international bankers was a deliberate liar and that no nation in the Western Hemisphere need fear any such activities on the part of the United States government as long as Roosevelt was President.

That phrase was to haunt him through subsequent years of Latin-American negotiations. How long was Roosevelt to be President, and what would happen under his successor, the Latin Americans asked of him time and time again. For the moment, however, the impression on the other members of the steering committee was good. The story leaked out only two or three days later through the admiring comments of committee members.[2]

The Secretary's tour de force, however, was a prepared speech, delivered from the floor in public session, in which he pledged the United States government to complete non-intervention in the domestic affairs of the other American republics.[3] President Roosevelt had promised as much in his Good Neighbor policy, enunciated in the first inaugural address the previous March, but the solemn reaffirmation of the commitment, at the first Pan-American Conference since the change of administration in the United States, had a profound political and psychological effect. The delegates began to report to their home governments that the United States really seemed to mean it, and it was only the occasional cynic, at that time, who remarked that this sort of thing would do very well until the Republicans got back into power in 1936.

As a sop to the pro-European bloc Hull finally offered a resolution calling on the American republics to lower their trade

[2]During this particular meeting the voices rose to such a pitch that murmurs could be heard in the adjoining corridor When Hull spoke a dozen South American reporters, who couldn t understand a word he said, unashamedly glued their ears to the doors. We North American reporters, who could have understood him, felt this sort of thing was beneath our dignity and ostentatiously walked out of earshot, only to pick up the story later, gratefully and in pieces as we could.

[3]The heart of this speech was his statement that "the United States government is opposed as much as any other to interference with the freedom, sovereignty, or other internal affairs or processes of the governments of other nations."

barriers and to invite the other nations of the world, through the machinery of the London Conference, to join in the movement. To this resolution he attached a statement of economic principles (which amounted to nothing but a reiteration of his own views), and he succeeded in getting the conference to go on record as favoring them.

This proposal, and Hull's statements supporting it, forced one last flicker from Raymond Moley's political embers. Speaking in New York, the former Assistant Secretary of State denounced the whole idea because it contained the intimation that NRA, AAA, and other New Deal panaceas were nothing but temporary expedients, which could and would be discarded as soon as the economic health of the world improved. Professor Moley declined to be appeased by Spruille Braden's active sponsorship, without apparent rebuke from Hull, of something very like the commodity dollar as the answer to the New World's monetary ills.

The feminists operating on the fringe of the conference caused some amusement and more headache among the delegates, especially those representing the United States. With the exception of Hull and Dr. Breckenridge the North American delegates did not realize how deeply the women's battle reached back into domestic politics. This was especially true of poor Mr. Weddell, who had lived outside of the United States during most of his long diplomatic career and who kept getting into hot water, first on one side and then on the other. Hull kept discreetly in the background and escaped relatively unscathed.

Doris Stevens was accredited to the conference as chairman of the Inter-American Commission of Women, instructed to report on the status of women's rights by the terms of a resolution adopted at Havana five years before. Miss Stevens was (and is) an ardent champion of the theory of equal rights for women, as advocated by the National Woman's party of which she was an early and leading member. She and other experts had labored, during the five years since the Havana meeting, to produce a monumental report covering the judicial codes of the twenty-one republics, pointing out legal injustices and inequalities. The report recommended that the conference start to remedy these matters by adopting (1) a convention guaranteeing equal citizenship rights to men and women in the New World and (2) a treaty pledging all the twenty-one republics to revise their judicial codes to provide completely equal rights in all domains.

Dr. Breckenridge had been planted on the delegation to scotch that very thing. She was the representative of the League of Women Voters (of which Mrs. Roosevelt and Miss Frances Perkins were leading spirits), which favored protective legislation and special privileges for women instead of equal rights. This divergence of view was inherited from an old schism in feministic ranks, which led to the formation of the two branches of the movement shortly after the woman-suffrage amendment to the Constitution was adopted in 1920. Secretary Hull had been acutely conscious of its existence during his Congressional career.

After much backing and filling, during committee consideration of these two projects, Mr. Weddell announced in plenary session one day that the United States felt itself obliged to abstain from voting for or against either one of them. Miss Stevens went into action by cable. The White House and the State Department were flooded with delegations of indignant women. Telegrams poured in by the basketful, to a point where President Roosevelt sent instructions to reconsider. The United States delegation voted for the two resolutions and actually signed the nationality convention. Only four countries signed the equal-rights treaty, so that Hull and his colleagues did not feel so lonely.

In the evening of the day which marked the about-face of the United States delegation Hull saw Miss Stevens in the lobby of the Parque Hotel. He walked over to speak to her.

"You certainly deserve every congratulation," he told her. "If I ever get into difficulty, I'm coming to find you to get me out of it."

The conference finally adjourned on December 26. Its concrete accomplishments, viewed as from today, were far greater than they appeared at the time. On the surface it appeared that just the usual innocuous resolutions had been adopted, including one calling on all the American republics to sign the five inter-American collective peace schemes then in existence. A fragile armistice had been forced on the Bolivians and the Paraguayans, but few thought that that conflict had been terminated. The veterans among the delegates and the hangers-on shrugged their shoulders and said it had been "just another conference."

It turned out to have been more than that, although the results of that humble beginning were scarcely visible for five or six years. It appears now to have been a definite turning point in inter-American relations. Just as a river may change its course any number of times, so these relations may take another sharp turn in the difficult days that lie ahead, but in 1933 their direction veered gradually away from extreme nationalism, selfishness, and suspicion, toward cooperation and the re-establishment of economic peace in the world. For this change Cordell Hull was largely, if not wholly, responsible.

President Roosevelt's enormous personal popularity was just beginning in Latin America. The rank and file of the people had not yet awakened to the fact that great changes had come to the United States. Their political leaders were still prone to regard the overturn of the Republicans as merely another of those rare upsets which had managed to put the Democrats in power only three times since the Civil War. It took the earnest, patient, and confidence-breeding persuasion of the Secretary of State, in his personal contacts at Montevideo, to start the word spreading among Latin-American chancelleries that something big had happened to the North and that it would bear hopeful watching.

The effect of this second personal adventure into foreign negotiation was good on Secretary Hull himself. It restored his faith not only in his own ability to deal with men of foreign language and customs just as well as he could deal with men of his own country, but it satisfied him there was reason to believe that rational conduct on the part of the world's delegated leaders might yet avert the calamity which seemed so close.

He was not too sanguine, but he was far from being as downhearted as he had been on his return from London. He still believed that Europe was doomed to an indeterminate period of hardship, and at times he feared it would never rehabilitate itself in his lifetime. On the other hand, the young countries of the Western Hemisphere could conceivably group themselves into a nucleus around which the rest of the world could gather in sensible, pacific relations, provided the imminent collapse could be staved off. The principal obstacles he saw in the way were the self-seeking stupidities of the men in high places and the dangerous indifference of the masses, but these factors had always been present when he had dealt with public affairs at home. Despite them, he had found, the democratic process has the faculty of slowly, painfully, and inefficiently achieving the greatest good for the greatest number over a sufficiently long period of time.

The Far Eastern crisis had not yet begun to interest or trouble him very much. That part of the world had received as little of his exhaustive study as had Latin America before his voyage to Montevideo. In his Congressional labors there had been no occasion to consult Chinese or Japanese taxation practices, fiscal theories, or tariff structures. There was nothing to be learned in that quarter, whereas Europe was in an almost continual ferment of experimentation, radical departure from accepted laissez-faire theory, and awakening social consciousness during the quarter of a century he had labored in Congress to bring some of these ideas to his own country.

Even though he had by no means achieved the breadth of view which the developments of the next few years were to bring to him, Hull was then totally at variance with the real New Dealers because he could not bring himself to look at the problems of the United States through the wrong end of the telescope. He could only envision their solution as part of a general world betterment. Whether it liked it or not (and it did like it), the United States had to be a part of the world which surrounded it. The devil-take-the-hindmost proposals which seemed to be gaining President Roosevelt's ear would never work, he was convinced.

The theorist may criticize Hull now, as a few did at the time, for his failure to recognize the revolutionary social and political ideas which were abroad in the world and for placing too much confidence in the economic determinism on which he based his program for world rehabilitation. He may be retroactively blamed for not realizing that these politico-social forces would overpower, at least temporarily, the rationalism he was preaching. Almost anyone, it may be argued, knows what human beings ought to do in their own, and in the collective, interest, but none of us can guarantee that they *will* do those things.

A critique of this kind, which is, in effect, an elaboration of the idea that Hull is a hopeless dreamer and mystic, too good for this world, impractical and rather tedious, fails to take into account its own fatalistic basis. Whatever else may be reproached to him, Hull is no defeatist. The present parlous condition of the world is due in large part to the fact that too many men, during the past twenty years, took the view that nothing could or should be done about anything and, latterly, that real or fancied ills can be remedied only by running bayonets through unoffending young men's midriffs.

That last night in Montevideo the conference machinery broke down, as it is wont to do. Many of the delegations, including that of the United States, had booked passage on the night boat for Buenos Aires. Their luggage was aboard, along with the minor personnel, but at sailing time the principal delegates were still solemnly parading to the rostrum of the Palacio Legislativo to affix their signatures to the various resolutions, declarations, etc., that had been approved. The river boat had to be held until midnight for them all to get aboard.

In Buenos Aires, Secretary and Mrs. Hull went to stay at the American Embassy, a magnificent, rococo, breath-taking structure in the early Metro-Goldwyn-Mayer style of architecture located on the Avenida Alvear. On the second night of their visit Ambassador and Mrs. Weddell gave a state banquet in honor of President Justo and his cabinet, all of whom appeared in full diplomatic uniform, although the outside temperature was hovering around 100. The President and his retinue stayed on until eleven o'clock and then took their leave.

After the commotion of their departure Mrs. Hull found herself standing with Mrs. Weddell. She remarked to her hostess that she had never been so hot in her life.

"Oh, we can cool things off now," said Mrs. Weddell, beckoning to her butler. "We can get them to open those bulletproof shutters."

This was not the Hulls' first disillusionment about the pacific stability of South American democracy. In Montevideo, at a Christmas Eve ball given at the Corasco Hotel by the Brazilian delegation, President Terra had invited Mrs. Hull to join a party of guests in a stroll along the moonlit, palm-bordered beach which is the pride of the Uruguayan capital. Hastily prompted by resident American friends, Mrs. Hull contrived to evade the invitation, although she had no idea why her compatriots were so urgently insistent. Only a few weeks later Dr. Terra was severely wounded in an assassination attempt.

From Buenos Aires, Mr. and Mrs. Hull left for a tour of the lake country, accompanied only by four or five close friends, while the rest of the delegation stayed behind and made the crossing to Santiago de Chile by the trans-Andean Railway. The Secretary was tired, and he felt that five or six days of leisurely touring, out of easy touch with the telephone and the telegraph, would help him. The late Spanish hours of Uruguay and Argentina fatigued him. Accustomed to leading a simple, home-centered life, with meals served at the old-fashioned Tennessee hours, he did not thrive on the midnight banquets and receptions that had been showered on him.

He and Mrs. Hull still look back with pleasure on that interlude, short as it was, in the busy life he has led for so many years. Traveling by train, steamer, and motorcar, they made the same crossing of the Andes that had delighted Theodore Roosevelt on his trip of recuperation following the disappointing rigors of the Bull Moose campaign in 1912. By train to Bahia Blaínca and Bariloche, thence across Lago Todos Los Santos, past Osorno, an extinct volcano that some travelers say is more beautiful than Fujiyama, across the Chilean frontier at Puelo, where the hotel proprietor proudly showed them Theodore Roosevelt's signature on his register, they reached Santiago finally in the private railroad car of the President of Chile.

The voyage back to New York from Valparaiso, aboard a Grace liner, gave the Secretary a good deal of time for reflection, interrupted only by the official Peruvian banquet at Lima and the official Colombian banquet at Buenaventura. While his aides labored over drafting the report that he would have to submit to President Roosevelt, Hull gave himself over to pondering the future. He had just experienced quick, kaleidoscopic views of the state of mind of European and Latin-American politicians. He had found this state of mind not unlike that of the politicians in the United States. He was forced to ask himself whether this kind of mentality would be good enough to survive the crisis he saw ahead.

Already there were looming across the political horizon of Washington the twin clouds which, by their threat of storm, prevented the United States from lifting a finger to forestall the European war and from reaching a timely decision after it had broken out. They were the clouds of economic nationalism and political isolation—no larger than a man's hand, as Hull's ship steamed northward in the Pacific, but pregnant with promise of trouble to come.

CHAPTER XV

Economic Peace

Back in washington, Secretary Hull set about carrying out the commitments he had made in Montevideo. His efforts and the relatively meager results of the Pan-American Conference had attracted a favorable press from those individuals and newspapers who were interested in Pan-American affairs and had inspired no hostile comment from the others. Hull wanted to press on to something concrete, some gesture on the part of the United States that would attest the sincerity of the oratorical advances made in Uruguay, while this atmosphere still prevailed.

His dramatic promise that the United States would not intervene in the domestic affairs of any other country so long as Franklin D. Roosevelt remained in the White House had been prompted by the knowledge that all Latin Americans believed the United States would send troops to establish order in chaotic Cuba. They believed this not only because such action would have been thoroughly consistent with previous North American policy but because there existed a contractual treaty right under which this could be done. This was the so-called Platt Amendment to the basic convention signed by both nations to govern relations between them.

At Montevideo, Hull had promised the Latin-American delegates, publicly and privately, that his government would not invoke this provision of the treaty. By now he had resolved that the best thing to do was to abrogate it in a new treaty with Cuba. On his voyage home from South America he had spent a day ashore in Havana during the impromptu fiesta that the public staged in honor of United States recognition of the provisional government of Colonel Carlos Mendieta. He had been much impressed by the apparent popularity of the Mendieta regime with the general public and even more by the evident relief felt in all Cuba that tranquillity could be restored without an occupation by armed forces of the United States.

During the revolution leading up to the flight of President Machado, and during the troubled days that immediately followed, the State Department had counseled against intervention, but intervention was very close on several occasions. American warships were kept on patrol just outside the limits of Cuban territorial waters, easily visible from shore, for months. They were ostensibly stationed there for the purpose of rescuing American citizens if their lives were endangered during the confusion, but older, more conservative Cubans were unpleasantly reminded of the so-called Army of Pacification which was stationed in Cuba in 1906 and 1907 under almost identical conditions.

The pressure for intervention came from Americans who had business interests in Cuba and especially from those Americans who lived there. Even today there is a substantial segment of responsible opinion among some of the best-informed Americans who have the closest ties with Latin America to the effect that the United States must force its immediate neighbors, including Cuba and Mexico, to keep order. This opinion is largely, but not wholly, dictated by self-interest, and it is shared by a few Latin Americans. These last, however, usually change their tune when they and their friends want to throw out some corrupt government and revert to the usual thesis that the United States must keep hands off.

Hull set to work on a treaty abrogating the Platt Amendment and got it through in time for ratifications to be exchanged on May 29, a little more than four months after he returned from Montevideo. The favorable repercussions from this step were heightened in August, when the last of the American marines were removed from Haiti after an occupation which had lasted seventeen years and when an arrangement was reached to terminate the American receivership of customs of the Dominican Republic. Whatever the American businessman may have thought of these developments, the New Deal in Pan-American-ism was in full tide.

These adventures in the Latin-American field, interesting and desirable as Hull considered them to be, were of relatively minor importance when contrasted with the ominous trend of world affairs in general. Hull was fully alive to the dangers inherent in the withdrawal of Germany and Japan from the League of Nations, the defensive alliance between France and the Soviet Union, Hitler's crusade against communism, the brush between Italy and Germany following the assassination of Chancellor Dollfuss of Austria, and Mussolini's evident intention to annex Ethiopia by force.

The Secretary of State saw that only the most prudent and far-seeing leadership could possibly avert another orgy of killing in the world. The germs of general war were in the air and there was no prophylaxis in sight. He believed that the United States could furnish the leadership and the prophylaxis, but he realized full well that the United States, by and large, was uninterested in assuming the task and the obligation. President Roosevelt agreed with him in both assumptions, and they decided on a compromise course which, like most compromises in matters of extreme urgency, was not good enough even though it may have been the best that could have been accomplished at the time.

The broad outline of the foreign policy of the United States was to be as follows: The country would take the lead in breaking down the excessive trade barriers which were causing increasing friction throughout the world and would endeavor, even at some sacrifice, to re-establish the measure of general prosperity which would mitigate against war. At the same time the country would fashion a policy of non-involvement in war, in response to a genuine popular demand, on which it could fall back in the event the economic approach failed.

The defeatism involved in this course was more apparent than real, so far as Hull was concerned. It is still impossible to fathom how far President Roosevelt believed the first leg of the course would carry the nation or how far he thought it would be possible to follow the chart of non-involvement once the course was changed. It can only be said that he supported Hull to the utmost in the attempted economic solution and that, two years after the European war broke out, he was still hoping publicly for non-involvement.

This curious foreign policy of 1934 represented to Hull nothing more than a practical political arrangement which would tend to rally to its side the maximum of popular support. His long years in American public life had taught him that the successful politician makes concessions. I am using the terms "successful" and "politician" in their best sense. We all remember the definition of a statesman as a dead politician. In the light of recent developments it would appear that we in the democracies must rate as a statesman a *successful* politician.

There is nothing in the world more completely ineffective than a defeated American office seeker. Any American officeholder who is compelled by law to submit a periodic report of his stewardship to an electorate is painfully aware that his defeat in an election is not only an embarrassing personal experience but constitutes a public repudiation of his policies. This is true even though the electors may not have had in their minds any specific policy in voting him off the public pay roll. His successful opponent will labor the inference that the breeze of public opinion has veered to an opposite quarter.

This is probably a weakness inherent in democracy, as the totalitarians are so prompt to remind us, and yet it is difficult to see how it is to be avoided under the representative system of government. The senator and the representative, to speak only of the national legislature, are elected to mirror the wishes of their electors rather than to express their own views in the terms of votes on pending legislation. In nearly every case, of course, a senator or a representative knows that his electors are divided on the issue and he tries to reflect the wishes of the majority of them. If he is usually successful in this guessing contest, he is re-elected time after time. If he is uniformly a backer of wrong horses, he is soon retired to private life.

The Founding Fathers, in their Constitutional wisdom, willed it that way. With all its manifest disadvantages as a system, the scheme has brought happiness and prosperity to a greater number of people over a greater number of years than any other which the human mind has yet devised. Its disparagers can never answer that argument.

In any event Roosevelt and Hull were caught on the horns of the dilemma presented by representative government. Any foreign policy they might devise must, of necessity, be implemented by acts of a Congress which was particularly susceptible to whims of public opinion. Although both houses of Congress were overwhelmingly Democratic, the majority members included many nominal Democrats who had ridden into office on the coattails of the New Deal, some of them by a very narrow margin of votes. Congressional districts which had returned Republicans ever since the Civil War had revolted and sent to Washington unknown potential statesmen who had no other virtue than blanket endorsement of Franklin D. Roosevelt and blanket condemnation of Herbert Hoover.

Voters in such Republican strongholds as Ohio, Kansas, Illinois, and other states of the Middle West were totally unconcerned with foreign affairs when, in the autumn of 1932, they turned out the Republican incumbent in favor of a Democratic unknown. They were registering a protest against the merciless spiral of domestic deflation which President Hoover had decided to follow to its logical conclusion, and no one in the country was more aware of this electoral psychology than its Democratic beneficiaries in Congress. To ask them to make a radical departure in foreign policy from the traditional isolationism of their constituents was to invite them to commit political hara-kiri, as both the President and Secretary of State were aware.

President Roosevelt's Good Neighbor policy, which intimated an interest by the United States in what was going on in the outside world, and his record of having been associated with Woodrow Wilson's aspirations toward American membership in the League of Nations had brought about the formation, or renaissance, of a number of "peace groups," headed by professional pacifists, many of whom had been in trouble during the World War. They had endowed themselves with high-sounding names such as the Women's International League for Peace and Freedom, the Council on the Cause and Cure of War, the League for Peace and Democracy, etc. Like most organized pressure groups, they exercised an influence on Congress far outweighing their numerical strength. In other words, they succeeded in imposing the will of a strongly organized minority on an uninterested majority, just as did the Prohibitionists of seventeen years earlier.

Here, for once, Hull's long political experience was a drawback. From the very inception of the movement which led to the enactment of the ill-advised "neutrality" laws by Congress, he attached undue importance to the representations of these organizations' ostensible spokesmen. He impressed on President Roosevelt, who was already deluged with similar estimates by the distaff side of his personal and official families, the high vocal quality of the organized opposition which would greet any attempt to orientate American foreign policy in the direction of influencing world events—i.e., open prevention of the general war which was staring the world in the face. Hull felt that the nation's official foreign policy must be tempered to the shorn Democratic lambs in Congress who would have to face a perhaps resentful electorate the following autumn in seeking a return to Washington.

Politically speaking, his qualms were well founded. Congress had just authorized one of the strangest ventures in public policy which the country has yet seen in the form of the special Senate committee to investigate the munitions industry, under the chairmanship of Senator Gerald P. Nye of North Dakota. There was practically no munitions industry in the country except the manufacture of ammunition for small arms (shotguns, target rifles, etc.), but Mr. Nye had read *Merchants of Death* and had decided to annihilate them.

He was a new, unknown senator from an unimportant state and a member of the minority party. His election as chairman came about only because some of the committee members belonging to the majority party failed to appear for the organization meeting and because no one else wanted the chairmanship. Also, he had been co-author, with Senator Arthur H. Vandenberg of Michigan, of the Senate resolution authorizing the investigation.

However, no belittling of Mr. Nye and his qualifications or of the committee's antics can detract from the importance its hearings assumed in the formulation of the American foreign policy of that fateful epoch. The North Dakota senator proved to be a dynamic chairman and dominated the proceedings. He started out to prove the thesis that the participation of the United States in the World War (he did not serve in the armed forces) was forced by the "international bankers" to protect their loans and by the munitions makers so that the war would be prolonged and they could sell more of their lethal products. This was just the crackpot sort of theory which would, and did, appeal to the befuddled leftist groups of the country, and Senator Nye was shortly deluged with highly profitable lecture engagements to appear before these organizations and tell them more.

It was established early in the hearings that there was no American munitions industry to investigate, and Mr. Nye frankly abandoned the ostensible purpose of the investigation in order to probe into the origins of American participation in the World War. He searched the diplomatic correspondence of the State Department, introducing allegedly damaging excerpts into his committee's record at times convenient for evening and morning paper release. He summoned practically every living American who had had anything to do with the formulation of major government policy in 1916 and 1917.

The big moment was saved until nearly the last. He summoned all the partners of J. P. Morgan & Company who had been in the firm at the entry of their country into the war. They sat solemnly in a semicircle before the committee and answered questions individually or collectively, as they saw fit. Tom Lamont tried to cushion their replies to the supposed bent of public opinion, but Mr. Morgan himself would have none of that. He would glare furiously when Mr. Lamont attempted to elaborate, and soften in the process, some of his forthright replies. On one occasion Mr. Nye asked Mr. Morgan whether he still believed the United States had acted in its own best interest in entering the World War to prevent the defeat of Great Britain by Germany. Mr. Morgan snorted and answered to this effect:

"Certainly we did the right thing. We would do it again today if we had to."

Mr. Nye did not pursue that line of inquiry.

The so-called investigation went on for months and months. The record of the hearings covers as much paper as the Encyclopaedia Britannica. Old-line Wilson Democrats in Congress writhed as there was steadily built up a picture of their beloved leader depicting him as a weakling, a hypocrite, a liar, and a corrupt tool of Wall Street. They denounced Nye and his committee from the floors of Congress, but they were powerless to turn back the tide of opinion which set in, especially among younger people. Much of the sentiment heard among leftist college students and professors at the outbreak of the European war in 1939, to the effect that it was a pity Germany had not won the World War and that Great Britain was once again planning to use the United States as a lifeguard in another imperialistic adventure, had its beginnings in the half-baked comprehension of these youths of the half-baked conclusions of the committee.

In the main the other members of the committee were a little ashamed of their organization's antics, but they were afraid to speak up. Over the long period of its activities, and through the medium of its ad interim reports, the committee succeeded in implanting in much of the public mind a profound distrust of any administration's conduct of foreign policy. Any President, according to the straw man it built up, and especially a President of Franklin D. Roosevelt's persuasion, would use every possible guile and wile to entice the United States into foreign wars. Only the eternal vigilance of the people and their stern refusal to give the President any leeway whatever could save them from involvement in the first war that came along, Messrs. Nye, Vandenberg, LaFollette, and others preached to the multitudes.

As this distrust was being carefully built up President Roosevelt and his Secretary of State were studying the recommendations of Charles Warren regarding legislation to be proposed to Congress to define a neutrality policy for the United States. Mr. Warren had been Assistant Attorney General in charge of enforcing the nation's neutrality laws in 1914, 1915, and 1916, and Mr. Hull had asked him to make a study based on his experience of those earlier years but taking into consideration changed world conditions. Mr. Warren, with the assistance of the legal staff of the State Department, had been working away quietly for several months by the time the Nye committee got under way.

The central theme of Mr. Warren's findings was that any legal basis for a neutrality policy must be exceedingly flexible in order to permit whatever administration was in power to deal with unexpected crises. He decided that any attempt to outline in advance a course of conduct from which the country's Chief Executive could not depart, no matter what sudden or surprising events turned up, would have the effect of stultifying any influence the United States might try to exert toward the preservation of peace. This philosophy was the basis for all of Mr. Roosevelt's subsequent attempts to get discretionary clauses written into the neutrality laws.

The isolationists in both houses of Congress were determined that a free hand was the one thing the President must not have. They were prepared to discuss on their merits any proposal the administration might bring forward to prevent involvement in war, provided it was a plan which would go immediately and automatically into effect the moment war broke out anywhere in the world. They were particularly insistent that the President be forbidden to "pick the aggressor" (a phrase which became hackneyed through repetition) and that all policies laid down by law be applied equally and in the strictest impartiality to both, or all, contestants in any war.

They were less interested, at the outset, in the details of any possible neutrality legislation than in the maintenance of these principles. On the other side of the issue, the President and Mr. Hull were convinced that any such rigidity would make legislation not only futile but dangerous. Hull has a very strong sense of the Constitutional responsibility and discretion vested in the President in the conduct of foreign affairs. Mr. Roosevelt obviously did not quarrel with this interpretation of the basic law of the land, and they decided to put off recommending any course to Congress until opportunities seemed more favorable.

At best, Hull reasoned, any legally defined neutrality policy would only prescribe the nation's conduct after war had broken out. To him there was an inherent defeatism in merely putting his country on record as to what it would do when other nations of the world fell into the awful chasm of war. He wanted his country to do something more positive—something to prevent this war which the isolationists, as well as everyone else, feared so much.

His weapon closest at hand was the reciprocal-trade-agreements program which he had persuaded Congress to authorize in the spring of 1934, over the protests of the protectionists and isolationists, although these schools of thought did not rally nearly so many votes as they were to do later when the straight-out question of war policy was to be debated. After all, most of them reasoned, the United States would not get into war by lowering its tariffs. Besides, low tariffs had been standard Democratic doctrine for the Southern Democrats during their entire political lives, and now that the Democrats were in full control of both branches of Congress they felt they ought to do something about it.

Hull's great satisfaction over the Congressional victory seemed at first to be thoroughly justified. A number of trade agreements were negotiated with foreign countries and proclaimed in effect by President Roosevelt. The law described these arrangements as executive agreements, instead of treaties, so as to exempt them from the Constitutional requirement of ratification by the Senate. Hull had impressed on the New Deal draftsmen the importance of avoiding President Taft's pitfall in attempting reciprocal tariff reduction through treaty methods with Canada, when small blocs in the Senate logrolled to insure that the necessary two-thirds vote would never be available for the approval of any single treaty.

As the law was adopted, it gave the President authority to negotiate agreements to lower American tariffs, in return for compensatory commercial advantages to American exporters by the other party to the pact, provided that he lowered no tariff by more than 50 per cent of the existing rate and provided that he added nothing to and took nothing from the free list. The power to negotiate was valid for three years.

It was the large degree of discretion granted to the President which rallied the isolationists to the opposition. They had viewed with alarm the huge grants of power voted to the President by Congress in the first days of the New Deal, and they feared that the trend would be dangerous to their desire to circumscribe the Executive's conduct of foreign affairs so that he could not involve the country in war without the positive action of Congress. However, as events turned out, their fears, as well as those of the protectionists, turned out to be groundless. The trade-agreements program was pushed forward cautiously, and no serious harm was done to the domestic economic fabric by the time the Euro-

pean war brought to an end all hopes of economic reconstruction along the lines Hull had in mind.

Notwithstanding the jolt the war gave to his hopes, Hull still
believes that his trade agreements served a useful purpose and
that their utility will be increased many times when the world
at last gets back to peaceful solutions of its difficulties. He embodied in all of them the principle of non-discrimination, which
he believes is the touchstone to prevent war. Through the medium
of the "most-favored-nation" clause he took care to guarantee
that the United States would accord to the commerce of every
other nation in the world as favorable treatment as it was granting
to the particular nation with which it was negotiating.

At first glance this procedure appeared to many critics to
nullify the trading value of the whole program. How could the
United States, it was argued, expect any other country to make
any considerable concession in return for a lower tariff rate that
would be shared by every foreign competitor in the American
market? This doubt even extended to the White House at one
point and led to another bitter fight, later in the same year, in
which Hull emerged victorious with yet another political scalp
at his belt.

In explanation of his pet theory of international trade relations, which dated far back in his own philosophy, Hull pointed
out that the early trade agreements would be made to cover
foreign products of which one nation was the sole, or principal,
supplier. For example, the duty on champagne could be cut 50
per cent without benefiting any country except France, although
the form of "most-favored-nation" treatment could be preserved
vis-à-vis other nations. Thus Finland could enjoy the same tariff
cut on champagne any time its nationals began to manufacture
champagne and ship it to the United States, although all concerned knew such a development was highly unlikely. This same
principle, differing only in degree, ran through all the trade
agreements.

In this way there was built up the beginning of a sound, economic restoration of world trade. In return for American tariff
favors Hull sought and obtained foreign concessions, first for
American farm products, because of the huge surpluses that lay
in warehouses throughout the country, and then for American

specialties in the way of manufactured goods. While American commerce with the whole world increased as the depth of the depression was passed, the nation's trade with those countries which had negotiated agreements mounted more rapidly than the average, both in value and in scope. The best thing about it all, from Hull's point of view, was that these desirable ends had been achieved without causing any international friction, because there had been no discrimination against anyone.

Germany alone, of all the trading nations of the world, felt itself unable to grant "most-favored-nation" treatment to the United States, and Hull eventually withdrew from Germany the generalization of the benefits of the trade-agreements program. For a short time Australia was in the same category, until a merchant-marine squabble was adjusted, but the German situation was irremediable and furnished a glaring example of the dangers of the totalitarian economy to the world's peace. Dr. Hjalmar Schacht, the German Minister of Economics in those days, pushed by Chancellor Hitler to achieve the almost impossible task of making Germany economically ready for war at a time when the country had practically no financial or commercial resources, had been compelled to wheedle, cajole, or force neighboring nations into trade arrangements giving them exclusive privileges in the German markets in return for exclusive outlets for German goods—the barter system, in short. By this time all German economy was so dependent on this system that it could not renounce it merely for the luxury of staying on good terms with the United States. The spread of that system, however, under the grim spur of military necessity, was one of the reasons for the outbreak of war in 1939, by Hitler's own admission.

In the spring of 1934 things looked better to Hull. He was so pleased with the triumph of the trade-agreements program that he was moved to eulogize the whole New Deal in a speech accepting an honorary LL.D. degree from William and Mary College in Williamsburg, Virginia. He told the collegians that Thomas Jefferson, if he were President at the time, would "resolutely deal with realities, as in the instance of the Louisiana Purchase, by vigorously pursuing a program of emergency relief, basically like that now in operation," adding that the Roosevelt program "represents championship of human liberty, human rights, and humanity itself." That was the lifelong liberal speaking. The Constitutional lawyer in Hull led him to append the indirect prophecy that "it has not been disapproved by the Judicial Department," in a context which implied he expected it would be disapproved by the august Supreme Court, as indeed much of it was. Also, he could not help calling attention to the dangers lurking outside our own gates.

"We are obliged to feel deep concern," he said, "that across the water, notwithstanding the terrible havoc and wreckage wrought by the war that began twenty years ago, and notwithstanding that the inventions of science will make future wars more terrible, there is so much reason for the gravest apprehension."

The apprehension became even graver when, on August 2, 1934, President von Hindenburg died, leaving the field wide open for Adolf Hitler to become Germany's Fuehrer and self-appointed apostle of the New Order that the rest of the world has been so strangely unwilling to embrace. Had Von Hindenburg lived a few more years, it is barely possible that he could have kept control of the German moderates in sufficient degree to ward off the program of conquest to which Hitler was already committed—vide *Mein Kampf*. Hull appreciated the implications of the aged field marshal's death, though his alarm was shared by few of his countrymen.

In October 1934 Hull got into a controversy with the Agence Havas, the official French news service, which sounds at least slightly premonitory when one looks back upon it. For several months the Secretary of State had been receiving reports from all over Latin America that the Havas news about the United States, which had wide circulation in that part of the world because of the low rates at which it was offered to Latin-American newspapers, was predominantly of such a nature as to represent this country in a bad light.

Stories of particularly revolting crimes were sent at great length. The divorces and even less savory antics of Hollywood stars were featured. Inflammatory speeches by irresponsible senators and representatives (especially the representatives of the cattle states denouncing the bare mention of admitting Argentine, Uruguayan, or Brazilian beef under any conditions) were cabled in such treatment as to intimate that they represented the over-whelming opinion of the country. The constructive side of the administration's Good Neighbor policy, as it affected Latin America, was ignored.

Finally Hull came to the conclusion that Havas was conducting a studied campaign to belittle the United States in Latin America. Since the agency enjoyed official status he felt he had the right to ask an accounting from the Ministry of Foreign Affairs in Paris, which he did, making his protest public to the American press at the same time. The French government, of course, gave him every assurance that no such policy had the support or even the connivance of high officials and told him that the underlings of Havas who had been guilty of such bad taste and judgment would be soundly reprimanded. Hull then issued a statement in which he rather grudgingly accepted the official explanation and agreed that the campaign had been the work of subordinates.

Washington newspapermen, for the most part, believed that the official French explanation was true, for it was difficult to imagine any purpose that would have been served, from the French point of view, by systematic vilification of the United States in Latin America. It occurred at a low ebb in Franco-American relations, when most Frenchmen still resented President Roosevelt's refusal to ask Congress to cancel the war debt and when they were still smarting under the stinging rebukes administered by Edouard Herriot for the French default. It was generally believed that the campaign was designed and executed by a few individuals who were still disgruntled over the debt question.

At the same time the Washington correspondents could not help having a quiet chuckle or two at Hull's encounter with the French press. He had been on the receiving end of many such complaints from the German Embassy concerning speeches and newspaper articles denouncing Hitler, and to these protests he had always replied that free speech and free press were guaranteed in the United States by the Constitution itself. He invariably ended these little homilies to Dr. Hans Luther, the German ambassador (who eventually lost his job because he could get no more satisfactory replies for the Fuehrer), by a complete disclaimer of responsibility on the part of the Federal government.

Hull's replies to the Germans were, of course, well founded in fact, but they must have sounded as empty to the Wilhelmstrasse as did the French disavowal of responsibility to the State Department. However, there was the difference that the Agence Havas was supported by government funds and was avowedly an official machine for the dissemination of news. The French government had the responsibility, which it conceded by agreeing to reprimand the originators of the scheme, even though it had not actively inspired the anti-American press campaign. In the case of senators, representatives, mayors, newspaper editors, or others who vented their spleen on Adolf Hitler, Hull was really powerless to do anything about it even if he had wished to do so, which is unlikely in the extreme.

No sooner was this little dust-up out of the way than Hull's undercover fight with George N. Peek over the trade-agreements program broke into the open. Peek had opposed Hull's "most-favored-nation" treatment and had advocated exclusive bilateral trading, or barter deals, as the most expeditious way of getting rid of the surplus agricultural commodities which were then the chief concern of the administration's foreign-trade experts. Peek also opposed any reduction in American agricultural customs duties, such as was subsequently granted in the Canadian, Cuban, and other trade agreements.

Confronted by this schism in the high command of his foreign-trade counselors, President Roosevelt performed a typical early New Deal maneuver. He told Hull to go right ahead in his own way and then softened the blow to Peek by appointing him to the more or less imaginary post of Special Adviser to the President on Foreign Trade. Peek, however, did not realize the post was imaginary and began to throw up a good deal of dust in the way of press interviews and statements about the advice he was giving the President, apparently not realizing that the Chief Executive had no idea of following any of it.

Hull, while long-suffering, can stand only so much, and on November 22 he issued a statement completely blasting Peek and his ideas. Washington officialdom drew the inference that the Secretary of State would not have taken such a step without the tacit approval of the President and began to look for Peek's head to fall, as had the heads of Moley and the rest. They did not have long to wait before Mr. Peek found himself bowed out of the official picture and on his way back to his native Moline, Illinois.

Other troubles were brewing on the international horizon, and the biggest cloud lay in the direction of Japan. The Japanese withdrawal from the League of Nations had prompted London and Washington to hold quiet, unofficial talks over the future of the tripartite naval-limitation treaty which bound the navies of the United States, Great Britain, and Japan to a relative strength represented by the ratio of 10 to 10 to 7. The treaty had been drawn to run until 1936 and then to continue indefinitely in effect unless denounced by one of the signatories, who would have to give two years' notice. Thus, if the Japanese wanted to terminate the engagement in 1936, they had to give notice in 1934, and it was this step which the British and Americans believed would be taken.

Although it was realized how inconvenient it would be for the great naval powers of the world to throw away all agreement as to limitation, leaving the door open to unrestricted building competition, the conferees in London decided that it was better to risk such a development than to concede Japan's inevitable demand for naval parity instead of the 70 per cent ratio it then enjoyed by treaty. The decision was one of the early symptoms of the cooperation between the two navies that was to grow ever closer as the world situation became more grave.

Matters worked out as the admirals had foreseen. The Japanese learned of the solid Anglo-American front against parity, and on November 23 Ambassador Saito announced to Secretary Hull that his government wanted to serve notice that it would no longer abide by the terms of the treaty on naval limitation after December 31, 1936. While the step caused some public comment it had been discounted in the press for some time, and it aroused little concern among the people at large.

Representative Carl Vinson of Georgia, chairman of the House Naval Affairs Committee and one of the most enthusiastic Big Navy men in Congress, announced that the United States would now return to the original 5 to 3 ratio with Japan[1] by building

[1]The ratio between the three navies was established at 5-5-3 by the Washington Treaty of 1922. This was modified, on the insistence of Japan, to 10-10-7 in the London Treaty of 1930.

five tons of combatant shipping for every three tons the Japanese constructed. The technicians of the British and American navies, however, knew that it would be highly difficult to know how much Japan would be building at any given point and arranged a close exchange of information among themselves. This was the second milestone along the road of naval cooperation, and Secretary Hull publicly praised the sympathetic and helpful attitude the British officials had displayed during the discussions.

By the time this excitement had died down Hull was scheduled to make a speech before the American Farm Bureau Federation in Nashville, the scene of his early triumphs. He worked hard on it, as he wanted the address to be not only a complete justification of his trade-agreements program but also a source of reassurance to the farmers, following, as it did, so closely on the heels of his defeat of George N. Peek, who had acquired considerable reputation as a friend of the farmer.

President Roosevelt helped him out by speaking to the gathering by telephone from the White House, urging that new foreign outlets be found for American agricultural production— a popular note with the cotton, wheat, and corn-hog farmers. Hull himself suffered from the bad throat which sometimes assails him and had to get his old friend, Judge J. M. Gardenhire, to read his speech for him. The address had been pitched to the cue President Roosevelt supplied over the telephone. It called for the elevation of the total value of world trade from the current level of $15,000,000,000 a year to $40,000,000,000 and promised that if this could be achieved the United States would secure 20 per cent of the added increment, or an annual increase in the national income of $5,000,000,000. It naturally depicted the trade-agreements program as the logical way in which to bring about the desired result.

The busy year ended with Hull somewhat enheartened over the role his country might play in the preservation of world peace but casting an anxious eye at the European and Asiatic pictures. The threat of war was too obvious to be true, in the eyes of most Americans, but their Secretary of State was prepared to take things at their face value in the cause of prudence.

CHAPTER XVI

The First Neutrality Act — The First Misstep

IN A NEW YEAR'S DAY STATEMENT to signalize the arrival of 1935 the Secretary of State told the American public that "the primary purpose of American foreign policy is the maintenance and promotion of peace, both political and economic, throughout the world." This was a bit of wishful oratory on his part—he must have known better. As things were to work out, American foreign policy in the succeeding years was to work unintentionally against, instead of for, "the maintenance and promotion of peace throughout the world." In this same statement Hull took the bloom off his inspiring generalization by citing as the concrete accomplishments of 1934 nothing outside the Pan-American field.

He could only point with pride to the implementation of the principles of Montevideo, including the abrogation of the Platt Amendment, the new treaty with Panama, the withdrawal of the marines from Haiti, and progress on the inter-American highway. The sum total of the accomplishments he listed indicated a modest, to say the most, contribution by the greatest nation in the world to the maintenance and promotion of peace throughout a world which gave every evidence of tottering on the brink of war.

For the isolationists were by this time firmly in the saddle.

They were attracting widespread and outspoken support for their theory that the maintenance and promotion of peace in the world was no business of the United States. The Nye committee had convinced a good many people that Woodrow Wilson's war to make the world safe for democracy had been a befuddled experiment in malicious meddling in the first place and, above all, that it had been a failure. Where, they demanded, is this safe democratic world President Wilson had promised would be the reward of victory? What advantage had accrued to the United States to compensate for the billions of dollars spent and lent, for the thousands and thousands of men killed and wounded?

In their speeches and writings they surveyed the world nearly twenty years after the United States had embarked on its first venture in imposing its own ideals on the rest of the globe—a disinterested venture, they agreed, but one foredoomed to failure. They called attention to Russia in the hands of a dictatorship of the proletariat; Germany under the iron hand of the Fuehrer; Italy living as the Duce commanded; Japan flinging itself in unprovoked aggression against the passive, unyielding bulk of China at the behest of a military dictatorship; and many of the Latin-American countries operating under dictators (the State Department prefers to describe them as ad interim presidents holding office by other than constitutional authority).

There was no blinking these facts, so far as Hull was concerned. He appreciated, far better than did the isolationists, the parlous state in which the world found itself at the onset of 1935. He differed from them, however, in his estimate of what should be the American course in the incipient crisis. He believed that his country could help to promote and maintain peace and to restore the world to sanity, while they took the attitude that the United States could do nothing but withdraw into its shell and let everything else go to pot, trusting to luck to come out right side up when the shooting was over.

It is worth while to examine the isolationist position in some detail, for it was at this point in the nation's history that it began to exercise the influence it ultimately threw against the world's peace and against the best interest of the United States. Also, it was still being loudly and influentially propounded more than two years after the entire continent of Europe, together with much of Africa, Asia, and the Near East, was ravaged by the cruelest war in history, which the United States did not lift one official finger to prevent.

The isolationists were beset by a conviction of futility. The world was in such bad state, they convinced themselves, that no one could possibly do anything about it, least of all the United States. In the first place, their country would only be duped and robbed again if it attempted to cooperate with other world powers in maintaining the peace. There would simply be more defaulted debts, recriminations, and damaged friendships to show for the brave attempt.

On the other hand, the United States, by its peculiar geographical blessings, by its great natural resources, and by the innate good sense and practical idealism of its inhabitants, could be the saving of the postwar world if only it had the intelligence to remain aloof from whatever struggles might break out. For, in the view of the isolationist, there was no middle ground between absolute withdrawal from world responsibility and fatal involvement in war. To them any time the United States lifts its voice in world councils it is building up powerful enemies on the one side and attracting fickle and untrustworthy friends on the other. The only way to avoid this dilemma is to walk alone, they reasoned.

Europe has been fighting practically unceasingly since the dawn of recorded history. That was one of the favorite crushers they put forward to annihilate anyone, like Hull, who ventured to hope that the barbarisms of the past need not be perpetuated throughout eternity. From this incontestable truism they drew the inference that Europe would always be fighting. They added that the ancestors of the Americans now living in the United States came to this country from Europe in order to avoid those very wars and demanded to know why their descendants should risk becoming involved in them again.

The nation, they urged as they still urge, must take no sides whatever in any quarrel. No matter what the individual sympathies of its inhabitants, which they conceded would always be involved overwhelmingly on one side or the other, the government of the United States must not, by thought, word, or deed, help or hinder one combatant over the other. More than that, the government must be prepared to impose on its own nationals limitations of their legal and moral rights in order to prevent provocative incidents. No price was too great to pay to avoid the risk of war.

By holding itself aloof from the world's quarrels the United States would be in a position, at the inevitable close of hostilities, to help bind up the world's wounds and to set victor and vanquished alike on their feet in the hope that they were wiser and more chastened than when it started. Under no circumstances, however, would the United States take any hand in arranging the peace terms or assume any obligation to see that they were carried out. Any such course would smack too much of membership in the League of Nations or of a system of "collective security," a phrase which became practically blasphemy when snarled by an isolationist.

The arguments cited thus far were the more reasonable and plausible ones on which the isolationists built their case. Underlying them, in nearly all rabid cases, was an unreasoning hatred for England. The professional Irishman and his dupes rehashed Ireland's postwar bloody struggles with the Black and Tans, recounted English atrocities in the Boer War, in India, in the Opium War, etc. This was a sure-fire emotional appeal to inject in the middle of an otherwise respectable plea for American isolation. Those who believed that these facts had nothing to do with the present interest of the United States could not controvert them, and the rest accepted them as ironclad evidence that the nation must avoid all participation in world affairs for fear it become involved with perfidious Albion. There was a curious, and completely unintended, fundamental conviction that the United States would always tend to find its own on the same side as Great Britain, as it has for the past one hundred and fifty years.

Hull, like every other rational human in the United States, shared the isolationists' aspirations to keep the country out of war. After all, as President Roosevelt said on a later occasion, asking a man if he wants to go to war will elicit as certainly predictable a response as asking him if he is in favor of sin. The difficulty which the isolationists did not see, and which Hull saw all too clearly, was that the nation which practices isolationism in the modern world will find itself completely isolated, at the mercy of the aggressors, and will lose all voice in the determination of its own fate.

Publicly Hull kept emitting what he describes as "preachments," calling on the other nations of the world to return to a standard of morality at least as high as that of the average individual. He asked of them that they respect their honorable engagements with each other. He said that the German rearmament program could be judged only in the light of Germany's treaty obligation not to raise an army. He reminded the Japanese of their engagements not to violate the territorial or administrative integrity of China. He lost no occasion to put the United States on record as favoring the rule of law and order in the world.

Privately he was convinced, as he told his friends and political cronies, that mere "preachments" would not be good enough if the United States was going to try to prevent a general war. In reply to the isolationists' fear of war he advanced the not unreasonable argument that even the stupid, blundering United States could not get involved in war if there wasn't any war. He argued that the best insurance the country could have against involvement would be to cast its influence, before it was too late, on the side of peace and against war, even if this involved taking the concerted action which was anathema to his opponents.

He must have known he was licked, although he never admitted it. In any event he resolved to bide his time and to waste no strength in swimming against the obviously strong tide. I have heard him, time after time, explain that Great Britain and the United States were not cooperating in the Far East. The American Ambassador would make a protest in Tokyo on Wednesday and the British Ambassador would say the same thing on Thursday, but Hull insisted that this was a pure coincidence. He would concede that the nations might be following a parallel course (their interests were so identical that only idiots posing as statesmen would have done otherwise), but he would patiently work the conversation back to his starting point—that there was no cooperation.

There were occasional encouraging flashes, as when the Senate refused to adopt Huey Long's reservation to the resolution adhering to the World Court. The Louisiana senator and phenomenon had proposed that the United States qualify its membership by declaring in advance that it would respect no decision which it deemed at variance with the Monroe Doctrine. At that, Huey's amendment was defeated by only 46 to 35.

On the whole, however, the isolationists had things pretty much their own way. In the instance cited they managed to block American membership in the Permanent Court for International Justice (the World Court) against the best efforts of President Roosevelt and his Secretary of State.

The only place where the isolationists would consent to the slightest breach in the ramparts was in the field in inter-American relations. They saw clearly enough the interest of the United States in keeping tranquillity and prosperity in the Western Hemisphere, even though they could not agree that this interest extended further afield. Hull took frequent and adroit advantage of this chink in their armor, as he did on January 21 when he apologized to the Canadian government for the sinking of the *I'm Alone,* a Canadian rumrunner which an overzealous coast-guard cutter had chased halfway across the Atlantic and sunk by gunfire when it refused to halt. He promised the Canadians, and made good on it, that he would obtain from Congress the $50,666.50 in damages which had been decreed by an arbitration court composed of a justice from each of the Canadian and American Supreme Courts. Congress raised no objection to the appropriation, but if it had been a British rumrunner and if the British government had been the claimant, the professional Irish members of both houses would have felt impelled to make long speeches twisting the lion's tail and to vote against the bill.

In addition to the long-range unfavorable aspects of the foreign-policy situation Hull was having lesser headaches, as when he had to call off, on January 31, the discussions he had been holding with Alexander Troyanovsky, the Soviet Ambassador, over the possibility of making some kind of debt agreement with the new rulers of Russia to cover the American property they had expropriated in the Revolution of 1917. Hull came to the conclusion that they were only wasting time, as Troyanovsky could get no support from the Kremlin (he was eventually recalled and demoted to a minor position as a research worker in Moscow). The Secretary of State especially regretted the impasse, as the Export-Import Bank had been created for the specific purpose of financing American export trade to the Soviet Union once the debt question was out of the way. He knew Congress would never sanction any governmental credits to Moscow so long as the private debts were ignored.

On the same day that he announced termination of the Russian-debt talks Hull told the Senate Agriculture Committee that the United States should take the lead in convoking another world economic conference in the hope of unblocking international trade channels to the benefit of domestic agricultural surpluses. His trade-agreements program was already coming under fire from special agricultural interests, although only the agreements with Cuba and Brazil had been negotiated. The Cuban agreement made concessions on fresh fruits and vegetables at times of the year when these commodities were supposedly not in production in the United States, but the duty cuts aroused the wrath of the Florida growers, and that indignation exists to this day.

The winegrowers of California became excited over reports that an agreement with Spain was to be negotiated in which the duty on Spanish wine coming into the United States would be reduced. California Republicans in Congress informed the Secretary of State that their winegrowing constituents had the "jitters," and Hull issued the following rejoinder:

"There are ten million unemployed people in this country, with their families making up about thirty-odd million, who have a sure-enough case of jitters under the most embargoed high tariff that has ever been enacted (a reference to the Hawley-Smoot Act, which had been rushed through by the last Republican-controlled Congress in 1930), and I think it might be well to cure that case of jitters before we take up some minor phase. As soon as we can get rid of this major case of jitters we will take up the minor ones."

Lobbyists were finding a new Golconda in the fears that special interests experienced over the trade-agreements program. They undertook, for more or less reasonable fees, to fend off for gullible trade associations any tinkering with the tariffs protecting the particular commodities in which they were interested. Actually, the machinery of the whole program was adjusted to make it lobbyproof, so far as Hull's long experience and ingenuity could make it so, and the ambitious lobbyists were promising services they could not perform.

He had set up a procedure, under the broad authority which the Reciprocal Trade Agreements Act delegated to the President, whereby the negotiations with the representatives of a foreign country were conducted by American technical experts whose names were kept secret. They were not even divulged after the agreement had been consummated. They were career economists and trade experts of the State Department, Tariff Commission, and Commerce Department, for the most part. They were hand-picked to insure that they had no personal interests or hobbies which might influence their cold-blooded consideration of each proposal the foreign bargainers might bring forward, and the whole idea was to reproduce the closest possible approximation of a Yankee horse trade.

The Tariff Commission experts knew, from years of patient, scholarly research, the almost exact impact any given concession would produce on the domestic industry to be affected. They had access to files showing comparative production costs of the various manufacturing nations of the world over long periods of years. They could tell to a fraction of one per cent what portion of the domestic demand was supplied from abroad and what the proportion would be in the event the duty was lowered. They were the watchdogs to protect the American producer.

The Commerce Department experts contributed their exhaustive knowledge, based on years of patient statistical tabulation, of international trade movements, measured by value, volume, and every other possible criterion. They could advise the negotiators on the probable effects of any particular concession, not only on American industry but on the world movement of trade. Even more valuable, they had the file of opportunities for American products in foreign markets with which to guide the negotiators in seeking advantages for American exporters in return for concessions granted.

The Agriculture Department kept the negotiators constantly abreast of the situation regarding the farm surpluses, which it was the first purpose of the program to disperse through orderly trade channels. Whether the American bargainers were to try for concessions on American apples, lard, flour, cotton, or whatever, was determined as much by the American need for getting rid of the commodity as by the capacity of the foreign market to absorb it.

The State Department's own men brought to the joint venture an intimate knowledge of each particular country with which negotiations were in progress. For example, when the Canadians were bickering for their side the State Department sent in John Hickerson, its leading expert on Canadian affairs, to advise the negotiators on the validity of various Canadian claims. They could not have had better or more disinterested advice. The same contribution was made by similar experts to negotiations with other countries.

American producers were invited, as it was announced each time that an attempt was to be made to negotiate a trade agreement with a certain country, to make known to the Committee on Reciprocity Information, which would pass the information along to the actual negotiators, whatever opportunities they saw for their own merchandise in the foreign market under review, outlining the extent of the concession which they desired the negotiators to obtain for them.

The only possible flaw in the procedure (one which was corrected when the act was extended in 1937) was the failure to provide an adequate forum for American producers to be heard in advance of the start of negotiations so that they could register their apprehensions about what would happen to them in the event their tariff protection should be cut down. These expressions would be obviously self-interested and exaggerated in 99 per cent of the cases, but the opponents of the program insisted that the producers should be given the same right to testify in their own behalf as is accorded an accused prisoner in the dock.

In the initial stages of the reciprocal trade-agreements program, however, the only wailing wall for producers who wished to cry before they were hurt was the unofficial forum of press statements by trade-association secretaries or the never-failing appeal to a sympathetic member of Congress to air a complaint on the floor or to insert a statement in the appendix of the *Congressional Record*. None of these procedures produced much effect except to revive in Hull his old-time hatred for all lobby-

ists. On February 10 he issued a blast against the manganese
interests, whose spokesmen were agitating against a projected cut
in the duty on manganese to be included in the Brazilian agreement and to be generalized to the Soviet Union. Both of these
countries are large producers of manganese.

"This propaganda would make it appear that the proposed
reduction of duty on manganese ore from 110 per cent for 1933
to 55 per cent will throw many thousands of American wage
earners out of employment and wreck a nationwide industry," he
said. "The number of wage-earning workers mining manganese
ore in the United States is only a few hundred of a total of nearly
45,000,000 Americans gainfully employed. Despite the tariff
benefits of 69 to 110 per cent paid since 1922 by the general
public, this is the total employment which the industry has been
able to offer to Americans.

"The amount of American production of manganese after all
these years is less than 10 per cent of the amount consumed in
the United States. The other 90 per cent, and more, must be imported as it has been in the past."

The manganese situation was an exaggerated example of the
marginal industry to which Hull especially objected to giving
tariff protection, but there were others that were nearly in the
same fix. Their cries of distress grew noticeably milder after the
Secretary of State lashed out at the manganese miners, especially
since he let it be understood that it would not be the present
policy of the negotiators to reduce protection for industries that
supplied a substantial portion of the national consumption on
terms reasonably competitive with foreign producers.

Much as he decried protection in principle, Hull, as a practical man, was aware that many large industries, employing hundreds of thousands of workers, had built up their structure behind
the sheltering tariff wall and that any sudden dislocation of it
would cause serious repercussions in the domestic economy just
at a time when it began to look as if the low point had been
passed. At the same time he was unable to see why the American
public should pay too much for 90 per cent of its manganese in
order to give a few hundred domestic workers the privilege of
supplying the other 10 per cent. If the manganese miners had
started in 1922 by supplying only 10 per cent of the national

consumption, for example, but had built up their business, under protection, to where they supplied 50 or 60 per cent of it by 1935, he would have placed their industry in the category of those from which protection should not be then withdrawn or diminished.

It was a period when the Secretary of State was treading softly in foreign relations. Hull opposed a resolution offered by Senator Borah to investigate religious persecution in Mexico (prompted by a decree by President Lazaro Cardenas banning religious literature and propaganda from the Mexican mails to combat "fanaticism and religious prejudice" in order to bring about the "spiritual liberation of the people"). He was advised by Ambassador Josephus Daniels that the religious difficulties (which had greatly shocked and concerned the North Carolina fundamentalist) were on the wane and would settle themselves much more rapidly without interference by the United States—a sound counsel, as events proved.

Hull was desirous, above all, of keeping alive in the entire Western Hemisphere a feeling of common concern for the dangerous developments which were taking place in the rest of the world. He told the Canadian Society on February 16, in the presence of Prime Minister Richard B. Bennett, that preoccupation with Western Hemisphere problems must not be allowed to make the two countries lose sight of the crisis in the Far East, which he insisted must be settled on the basis of the 1922 Washington treaties. Ten days later, speaking at Winter Park, Florida, in accepting a degree from Rollins College, he declared that the United States was facing its most serious crisis since the Civil War and warned that "we have today the problem of preserving democracy and at the same time adjusting to modernized conditions our economic safety and our social welfare problems."

This phrase sounded much more New Dealish than Hull really felt at this point. As a matter of fact, he had about run out of patience with the quick and easy remedies that had been tried and found wanting in so many cases. The whole NRA scheme, with its artificial interferences shunting aside the free flow of those economic forces which Hull knew and trusted, had enraged him to a point where he refused to discuss it in public. The AAA principle of curtailing agricultural production, rather than seeking increased foreign markets for American farm produce, impressed him as futile and self-defeating (an estimate concurred in by Secretary of Agriculture Henry A. Wallace, father of the plan, who repeatedly warned farmers it could be only a temporary makeshift).

The pattern of domestic economy which Hull saw the young theorists of the New Deal trying to evolve reminded him too forcefully of the almost identical nationalistic expedients which were bringing the rest of the world perilously close to war. Time and again he called attention to the disease and the remedy, as he saw it, in words such as he used on April 6 in urging on Europe the urgent advisability of "adopting a sound and comprehensive economic program, both domestic and international," if there was to be laid "a solid foundation on which to rebuild stable peace and political structures."

For political relations between various nations were fast reaching a pitch where economic solution would no longer be possible. By July 11 it had become so evident that Mussolini intended to annex Ethiopia by force that Hull conferred with the Washington diplomatic representatives of the nations signatory to the Pact of Paris. This agreement to outlaw war as an instrument of national policy had been signed and ratified by both Italy and Ethiopia, as Hull pointed out in a statement the following day pledging the United States to live up to its engagement thereunder and exhorting the other signatories to do likewise.

On July 24, with war practically inevitable, President Roosevelt had a recurrence of the cautious foreign policy that he and Hull had agreed upon earlier in the year. He asked Congress to reaffirm the neutrality of the United States in the event of war between other nations. The Chief Executive informed Congress that the Good Neighbor policy and strict neutrality in foreign quarrels would govern the foreign relations of the United States. Neither of these keystones of foreign policy was to withstand the tide of public indignation at the Italian aggression against Ethiopia, and it is obvious now that no such pronouncement should ever have been made from the White House.

At the time, however, there appeared to be good and sufficient domestic political reasons to justify the step. More than three months earlier Senator Bennett Champ Clark of Missouri, strong isolationist and England-distruster, despite an exceedingly creditable record in the army during the World War, had joined Senator Nye in introducing a resolution instructing the President to embargo shipments of arms to all belligerents as soon as war should break out. In the interval the Nye committee had started its hearings and the forest fire of "neutrality" had begun to sweep across the country. The imminence of war between Italy and Ethiopia made it appear to its more active members that whatever legislation was to be attempted should be rushed through immediately. The administration, on its side, did not want to be scooped by the isolationists.

As recently as April the State Department had reported to President Roosevelt that it was as yet unprepared to recommend any specific legislation, but by August 17 the late Representative Sam D. McReynolds of Tennessee, chairman of the Committee on Foreign Affairs of the House of Representatives, introduced a neutrality bill which had at least the tacit blessing of the administration. On August 20 his example was followed by Senator Key Pittman of Nevada, chairman of the Foreign Relations Committee of the Senate, although their proposals were not identical. The ill-favored "neutrality" debate, which was to plague the country and accelerate chaos in the world, was under way.

It leaked out that the administration leaders in Congress had determined to ignore the "neutrality" issue and to adjourn the session about the middle of August, as soon as other legislation, desired by President Roosevelt, had been enacted. Senators Nye, Clark, Vandenberg, and Homer T. Bone of Washington, all members of the Munitions Committee, had informed the leadership that they would filibuster indefinitely against the adjournment resolution unless a law was passed to define the course of the United States after the war between Italy and Ethiopia should break out. Senator Joseph T. Robinson of Arkansas, the majority leader, told the White House and the Secretary of State that it would be wiser to yield and pass some harmless measure, because these four young, vigorous men could filibuster for a long time, presenting endless opportunities for undesired legislation to be brought to the floor.

Hull agreed with this estimate of the situation on Capitol Hill. It was before the days when the chambers and offices of the two branches of Congress were air-conditioned, and he could well recall the bad feeling and short tempers generated by prolonged sessions during Washington's tropical summer weather. Hull got the leaders to withdraw from the Senate calendar two Munitions Committee bills which had already been favorably reported by the Foreign Relations Committee (one was drawn to prohibit loans to belligerents, the other to prohibit the issuance of passports for Americans to travel in war zones), with the promise that he would send to the Capitol the draft of a bill that would cover all points the isolationists desired and that would handicap his handling of foreign relations as little as possible.

The debate started in the Senate. Senator Hiram W. Johnson of California, the veteran isolationist who had been so influential in preventing United States membership in the League of Nations, told his colleagues on the floor that "we are not going to be in any war that involves Ethiopia and Italy or that involves any other country beyond our own borders," but the majority felt less certain. Vaguely and restlessly they recognized the Italo-Ethiopian dispute for what it was—the first warning symptom of the general European war which was to come.

After but little discussion the bill was adopted by the Senate and sent to the House, where the Foreign Affairs Committee had been studying for several weeks the more elaborate "neutrality" project introduced by Mr. McReynolds. The committee decided to sidetrack its own fruitless labors in favor of the Senate bill, which the House accepted with one or two amendments. The Senate approved these and Congress adjourned, leaving the following blueprint for the President to follow in case war broke out in the world:

1. He was to proclaim, "upon the outbreak or during the progress of war between or among two or more foreign states," the official neutrality of the United States, and it was to be automatically unlawful thereafter to export from the United States arms, ammunition, or implements of war to any belligerent. He was to define what were "arms, ammunition, and implements of war." Violators of the embargo could be punished by a fine of $10,000 or imprisonment for five years, or both. The President could revoke his proclamation when, in his judgment,

the conditions which had prompted him to issue it had ceased to exist.

2. The National Munitions Control Board was established, made up of the Secretary of State as chairman, the Secretary of the Treasury, the Secretary of War, the Secretary of the Navy, and the Secretary of Commerce. The Board was charged with registering all manufacturers, exporters, and importers of arms, ammunition, and implements of war, and of issuing licenses without which these articles could not be exported from the United States. This step constituted the first peacetime effort of the United States to control the munitions industry.

3. American vessels were to be automatically prohibited from transporting arms, ammunition, and implements of war to any belligerent or to any neutral port for transshipment to a belligerent.

4. The President was authorized to close American ports to belligerent submarines and to proclaim that American citizens traveling on merchant vessels flying belligerent flags were doing so at their own risk.

The law fell far short of satisfying the leaders of the Munitions Committee and their ultra-isolationist companions in the Senate, but they decided to take half a loaf under the circumstances. The provisions seemed to take care of all probabilities that would be presented in the event Italy and Ethiopia got into war, and they felt they could do better at the next session of Congress. They would have been fairly well pleased, they have told me subsequently, if they had succeeded in nothing but the enactment of the automatic arms embargo. That was the underlying principle upon which they wanted to build their whole fabric of involvement-proof legislation.

They were quite right. The adoption of that principle was absolutely essential to their plans. Their procedure could make sense only if the United States forbade arms shipments to both sides alike and built its whole foreign policy around an elaborate pretense that its government and its people had no interest, either sentimental or practical, in the outcome of any foreign war. They have been proved wrong in every separate conflict which has swept the world since that hot summer of 1935 when they first blackjacked Congress into accepting their thesis. Their ranks have thinned as the relentless march of events established the fallacy to which they had dedicated themselves, but some of the veterans are still to be heard advancing the same specious reasoning and taking the same ostrichlike attitude they adopted when they feared the United States might offend the Italian government by selling a few rifles to such unarmed Ethiopian natives as wanted to defend their own independence.

They went on the assumption that the United States could purchase peace by refusing to accept any responsibility for order in the world. Let who want to, or who must, go to war, they said, we will have none of it; we will notify the whole world in advance that we will neither help nor hinder him who gets embroiled.

They believed that their policy might have some value as a war preventive, for they reasoned that a weaker nation might be readier to accommodate its course to that of the stronger if it knew it could get no arms from the United States with which to fight it out. But their main interest lay not in the prevention of war but in preventing the involvement of the United States. Their country must not judge the rights and wrongs of international disputes, it must treat the wrongdoer and the victim exactly alike, if it was to preserve its own peace. Senator William Edgar Borah of Idaho, another pillar of the fight against the League of Nations, praised the new law (with which he really had little sympathy) on the ground that it guaranteed the United States would contract no foreign entanglements (or friends, he might have added).

President Roosevelt signed the bill with the gravest misgivings on August 31, issuing a statement urging its radical revision at the next session of Congress. He dared not, however, risk a test of public opinion by letting it die with a pocket veto after the adjournment of Congress. Hull celebrated its signature by one of his Delphic utterances to the effect that the United States would continue to work for peace—implying, if the auditor wanted to take it that way, that the new law was a hindrance rather than a help in that effort.

And so it was. It stood as an open invitation to every well-armed aggressor in the world to wreak his will on an unarmed, peace-loving neighbor, secure in the knowledge that the neighbor could get no outside help—at least from the United States. It was a particularly insidious form of appeasement, as its implications were not generally understood until the outbreak of the general war in Europe, when it was promptly repealed under pressure of public indignation.

Its enactment had no influence on the outbreak of war between Italy and Ethiopia, which came in October 1935. That die had been cast by Benito Mussolini long before the Congress woke up to what was going on. However, Mussolini's decision was made in full confidence that not only the United States but the other powerful nations of the world would, in the final analysis, condone by inaction the aggression he had in mind. President Roosevelt legally and dutifully proclaimed the neutrality of the United States as soon as the Emperor of Ethiopia announced that the Italian army had started hostilities. The President's proclamation drew a grimly prophetic word of praise from Pierre Laval, then Premier of the French Republic. Laval had already started on his pro-Axis course and was the outstanding champion of French collaboration with Italy.

It was the spirit of the thing that pleased Laval more than the practical impact of the Neutrality Act on the war in question. Even without the handicap of the legal arms embargo the United States could have been of little help to Ethiopia. The whole League of Nations, as well as potent neighbors much closer at hand, failed to halt the aggression, so it is certain that the influence of the United States would have been ineffectual had it been exercised.

There were stirrings of public sentiment in this country against the philosophy, rather than the machinery, of the Neutrality Act soon after hostilities started. It must be remembered that the law dealt only with arms, ammunition, and implements of war. There had been no attempt to regulate commerce in other commodities that are equally vital to the prosecution of modern mechanized warfare.

The League of Nations, on petition of Member Ethiopia, haled Member Italy before it, only to have Italy withdraw from membership. The League then decided to impose economic sanctions against Italy, which was adjudged the aggressor. The British navy was mobilized in the Mediterranean and the situation was tense.

The most effective economic sanction which could be used against Italy would have been to cut off its supply of oil, for which it was wholly dependent on outside sources. Mussolini was using airplanes, trucks, motor ships, and other mechanized equipment on a large scale. He had only a limited reserve of oil in storage. A complete cutting off of oil supplies would have stalled the Italian campaign just as effectively as it would have stopped the Japanese in Manchuria, but the peace lovers of the world could not manage it.

In early November the British told Washington that oil sanctions could not be applied against Italy without definite assurance that American oil merchants would not rush in to fill the orders that would be forbidden to British, Dutch, Rumanian, and other sellers. Hull was in full sympathy with the oil-embargo movement, but he realized he was without any legal authority to tell American oil salesmen where they could and could not market their wares. He started a cautious campaign which might have resulted in an interesting experiment in international law if the whole sanctions plan had not folded up prematurely from other causes.

On November 6 he made a radio speech in which he asked for a more elastic neutrality statute and in which he said the United States must cooperate with other nations of the world to preserve the peace—that it could not unilaterally decree peace for itself alone. A fortnight later, at a State Department press conference, he outlined the "normal commerce" theory which he intended, at that time, to inject into the neutrality concepts of the United States. He wanted to provide his country with an economic weapon to use in the preservation of peace even though the arms embargo prevented it from more direct assistance to victims of aggression.

The United States, he reasoned, could preserve the letter and the spirit of neutrality, in the economic domain, if it declined to expand its commerce with belligerents beyond its normal level, which he defined as an average of the five years preceding the outbreak of war. In the instant case (the matter of oil sanctions) the Hull theory would have operated to back up the collective action against the Italian aggressor. What he was advocating was legislation under which the United States would not refuse to supply oil to Italy but would continue to sell only the 5 per cent of the Italian consumption which it had been accustomed to furnish. Thus, if the rest of the world cut off the other 95 per cent, the Italian war machine would be halted, but not through the direct action of the United States. The odium of the sanctions would have to be leveled at the others, not at us.

This curious compromise of personal desire on Hull's part and his acceptance of the isolationists' domination never made any headway, and it is interesting to recall it now only as an illustration of the confused thinking which characterized those pre-war efforts to crystallize a foreign policy for the United States. It must be remembered that all this time every Italian-American society in the country was passing resolutions denouncing the administration and Congress for even thinking of cooperating in oil sanctions against the mother country. Their activities were another danger signal which the isolationists completely ignored in their proposed blueprint for complete American safety.

Thus the first Neutrality Act came into being to the accompaniment of much the same befuddled reasoning which distinguished for many years the efforts of the United States to thread its way among the shoals of world dangers. It was an early example of the blind concentration on immediate dangers, mostly imagined, to the neglect of long-range perils, fantastically real.

CHAPTER XVII

Practical Pan-Americanism

THE NEW DEAL'S CONCERN with the immediate and unimportant, as opposed to the permanent and valuable, was by no means confined to the field of foreign relations at this epoch. It was a time when the younger and more impatient of Mr. Roosevelt's advisers felt they had lost their early élan. The Congress showed less and less signs of being the "rubber stamp" which the Republicans accused it of being and which the Inner Circle hoped it would continue to be.

There were unmistakable tokens that another election was in the offing. The prospect was welcomed by the real New Dealers, but it was viewed with alarm by most of the conservative Democrats in both houses of Congress. These unhappy members (and Hull would have been one of them if he had stayed in the Senate) regarded the apparent success of the Democratic party with the most mixed of emotions. They were like faithful alumni watching alma mater win with a team of ringers.

During the preceding half-century the difference between Democrats and Republicans, to most of them, had been the immense but not unbridgeable chasm between the Outs and the Ins. The traditional Democrats (almost entirely Southern of origin) coasted along, awaiting those inevitable but brief relapses from Republicanism which blessed the country from time to time. In those brief interludes they gloried in lowering the tariff a little bit and in appointing postmasters in their home towns (a prerogative of which the general public underestimates the political kudos), but they did not expect to revolutionize the nation's course during the occasional four or eight years they might be in the majority.

Since 1932 they had found themselves in unexpected alliance with a group of young intellectuals from the large urban centers who *did* expect to do that very thing. These young men not only wanted to revolutionize the country's political, economic, and social life, but they wanted to do it immediately. It was on this note of immediacy that the two factions parted company. The Southern Old Guard yielded to no man in its concern for the common people, but it was content to manifest this concern gradually, over a period of years. As a politically governing class, these men were sincerely convinced that the permanent gains in national life are those which are made slowly, through a process of trial and error, and they mistrusted the panaceas which the New Dealers invented every few days.

They reminded themselves that they had produced the Federal Reserve System, the Adamson eight-hour day for railway workers, and other real landmarks in the nation's upward and onward path during the brief eight years (only six years in the House) they had had with Woodrow Wilson. Moreover, these social advances had been achieved while the world was at war. After all, they grumbled, given a chance, they could produce satisfactory results by their system of moving one step at a time.

The New Dealers, on the other side, felt that time was lacking. It must be conceded that they had a truer feeling of the urgency of things, of the desperate haste with which the United States must put its house in order in the expectation of worse times to come, than did their political elders. The outstanding exception among the elders was Cordell Hull.

The Secretary of State understood the nation's present dangers and foresaw those to come better than any of the younger men who frequented those intimate White House relaxation periods when Tommy Corcoran played the accordion, but he also appreciated the essential conservatism which has thus far characterized American political life. He was convinced that the get-rich-quick methods of the youngsters would not achieve any permanent good for the country or for the Democratic party.

The more impetuous of the President's advisers were in total disagreement with the step-by-step political philosophy of Hull and the Democratic Congressional conservatives (most of whom had started their political careers as red-hot liberals), and they appeared to be carrying the day at this epoch. They were particularly suspicious of the Supreme Court. Hull and his political colleagues, who had fancied themselves as Constitutional lawyers through most of their lives, felt the traditional respect for the Supreme Court which characterizes the practicing lawyer.

This elemental divergence of view was to precipitate the bitterest fight the Democratic party had gone through since the slavery debates preceding the Civil War. The Democratic party barely survived the ordeal. As a matter of fact, there are many who think it did *not* survive it and that the Democratic party died or committed suicide. This number would not include Hull.

When the Seventy-fourth Congress assembled on January 2, 1936, for its second and last session before facing the electorate the following November, the Supreme Court fight was still a specter of the future. A comic-opera sequence of events had combined to turn the Congressional attention outward for the first two months of the session. Congress was already in trouble with the Neutrality Act it had so complaisantly adopted less than six months before.

Although the measure had been enacted as an admittedly temporary stopgap (the automatic arms embargo, for example, was limited to a life of one year), its brief existence had aroused serious doubts among the partisans on both sides of the primary issue involved. The administration felt that the law had unfortunately and unduly hampered the wise operation of American foreign policy in the hectic days surrounding the outbreak of the Italo-Ethiopian war. The isolationists, on the contrary, feared that the statute was not nearly stringent enough to accomplish their avowed purpose of keeping the United States clear of all foreign disputes.

Despite their best efforts, as represented by the law, the United States had come dangerously close, in their opinion, to being an influence in world affairs when President Roosevelt and Secretary Hull had toyed with the idea of the "normal commerce" prohibition in order to avoid interfering with sanctions imposed by the League of Nations. Not hindering the League, in the eyes of the isolationists, was tantamount to helping it—a course which the United States must avoid at any and all cost.

They were still striving for that academic neutrality which they thought would guarantee the United States against war forever. They felt that a refusal to hamper the League of Nations, in the event it enforced sanctions against Italy, would constitute taking sides against Italy and would thus tend to involve the United States in the war. Where they were shortsighted, of course, was in refusing to admit that hampering the League course was tantamount to taking sides against Ethiopia.

The practical side of the question was that, no matter what course the United States might take, it would favor one side or the other, but the isolationists shrewdly decided there would be less risk in offending Ethiopia than in offending Italy. They advanced the justification that they were seeking to keep the United States out of war and that the danger of war might possibly come from Italy but not from Ethiopia.[1]

Hull saw further than this. In the first place, he did not believe that Italy would make very successful war against the United States, no matter what happened in 1936. In the second place, he saw in the whole situation a flagrant aggression, in violation of treaty pledges, such as would undermine the whole fabric of intercourse between civilized countries. He had felt exactly the same way about the Japanese invasion of Manchuria, the German rearmament, and the German occupation of the Rhineland. These apparently isolated incidents were, to him, the warp and woof of a pattern which would destroy the whole world if allowed to develop.

On the other hand, his practical political instinct warned him that the administration would have to tread warily in its dealings with Congress to escape some sort of legislative strait jacket which would render it completely helpless in dealing with foreign relations. He may have exaggerated the strength of the isolationists, but in his favor it must be said that they gave every evidence of

[1] Mussolini had announced, in a fine burst of Latin oratory, that Italy would fight the whole world if her oil supplies were cut off.

being fully in command of the situation. This apparent strength stemmed from the apathy of a large portion of the membership, particularly in the Senate.

The Secretary of State thought the situation was sufficiently serious to inaugurate a series of conferences with his former senatorial colleagues. He had to deal mainly with the late Key Pittman of Nevada, who was chairman of the Foreign Relations Committee, an attractive veteran Democrat who had managed to keep himself in the Senate for more than twenty years by promoting the interests of the silver miners of his adopted state (he was born in Mississippi and had been a gold prospector and promoter with Tex Rickard in Alaska before he settled down in Nevada). On the side, he had manifested a certain interest in foreign affairs and was, as a matter of fact, one of the best-informed men in Congress on the march of events abroad. But this knowledge was a hobby rather than a compelling specialty.

It was Pittman more than anyone else who fertilized the seed already sprouting in Hull's mind—the thought that the Senate isolationists were in a position to be as embarrassing to Franklin D. Roosevelt as they had been to Woodrow Wilson. Both Pittman and Hull had been ardent pro-League men in the historic fight of 1919–20, and both had mourned the downfall of their beloved leader. They were equally resolved that their new leader would not suffer such an eclipse if they could help it.

Pittman had been highly impatient with and contemptuous of the Nye committee and its hearings. He did not subscribe in the slightest degree to its findings. He had voted for the declaration of war in 1917 and he knew, of his own knowledge, that he had not been actuated by a desire to protect the loans of J. P. Morgan & Company or to prolong the profitable business of the munitions makers. He might have been put to it to define his positive motives in voting to go to war, but he had no difficulty in recalling that they were *not* what the Nye committee said they must have been.

However, by keeping his pulse on the finger of the nation, as all successful politicians must do, Pittman had become convinced that considerable concessions must be made to Nye and his followers. In the House of Representatives, on the other hand, the administration leaders advocated dealing roughly with the isolationists and guaranteed they could deliver the votes in support of any program the administration might put forward. Events proved they were right, but the fear of the Senate served to paralyze the White House and the State Department. President Roosevelt bowed to the judgment of Hull, Pittman, and other seasoned politicians, whether he agreed with it or not (and he probably did agree, as his campaign speeches of the following autumn were to demonstrate).

The month of January was taken up with parliamentary maneuvering. All sorts of bills dealing with the regulation of foreign policy in time of war abroad were thrown into the hoppers of the Senate and the House. They included the highly mandatory proposals of Senators Nye and Clark of Missouri; the vague and not well drafted administration bill which sought to satisfy both sides,[2] and a number of ill-considered projects by individual members, such as the resolution proposed by Representative Louis Ludlow of Indiana to amend the Constitution so that Congress could not declare war until after a referendum submitted to the electorate of the entire nation.

Hull defended his "middle-of-the-road" tactics, as embodied in the administration bill, from the point of view of foreign policy, in discussing the draft before the Senate Foreign Relations Committee.

"It is a very serious period that we are going through," he told the committee. "I do not anticipate any general war. The chances are nine out of ten that there will not be any such war; but it is a serious period, when teamwork here, to the extent that it is consistent, is of the utmost importance . . .

"If we create the impression that we are too extreme in either direction, we can get into trouble—this means either extreme internationalism or extreme nationalism. Some countries might gain the false impression that we will not fight, and we do not wish to run the risk of being imposed upon by reason of any such false impression."

Actually Hull did "anticipate" a general war or at least he

[2] It contained the proviso that "any embargo, prohibition, or restriction that may be imposed . . . shall apply equally to all belligerents, unless the Congress, with the approval of the President, shall declare otherwise"—an example of perfectly meaningless language.

privately calculated the chances at better than one in ten. His testimony to the committee was a good example of the extreme caution, the magnificent understatement, that characterizes most of his public or formal declarations. It is only in private, when he knows his words will not be repeated, that he unburdens himself fully and gives the "off-the-record" listener the benefit of the measured judgment he has developed over the years.

The neutrality fight came to nothing at that session of Congress. Both the executive and legislative branches were too completely muddled in their thinking for any decisive result to be attained. Such staunch New Dealers as Representative Maury Maverick of Texas, for example, plumped for rigidly mandatory legislation to prevent the President from getting into any kind of foreign complication which might lead the country into war, regardless of the effect such a rigid advance delineation of policy might have on the peace of the world. The matter was finally disposed of by a resolution continuing the existing law in effect for another year, thus postponing a decision at the time that was probably vital.

The fact that it was election year had much to do with the Congressional propensity to defer action toward either making the neutrality law more stringent or doing away with it altogether. All of the House and a third of the Senate had to face the voters the following autumn, and many members of both branches felt that their ears were not sufficiently close to the ground or that their fences were not sufficiently strong for them to get into any positive position on this red-hot issue. The public had apparently accepted, without much reaction one way or another, the existing statute, so that it appeared the course of prudence to let it ride until after the elections.

President Roosevelt signed the extension resolution on March 1, realizing full well that this situation would throw the whole question of foreign policy right into the midst of a presidential campaign. However, the Congressional action left him no alternative but to take up the gage. It was a foregone conclusion that he would be renominated by the Democrats, and to many of us it was an equally foregone conclusion that he would be re-elected.

The President and his Secretary of State were confident, but they regretted that the electoral forum had thus been constructed so that the Republican candidate, whoever he might be, would be inexorably forced to champion the isolationist point of view in order to present the appearance of opposition on foreign policy. When the Republicans, assembled in their national convention at Cleveland in June, chose as their standard-bearer former Governor Alf M. Landon of Kansas, a convinced isolationist in his own right, the foreign-policy issue was clear-cut.

Hull, in the meantime, was doing his best to preserve the calm, unsensational treatment of foreign affairs which he had decided was the appropriate accent for the dangerous times. As early as February Senator Pittman had begun his insistent demands for a strong course against Japan. Hull, when questioned about the administration's attitude regarding its Senate floor leader's Far Eastern policies, would neither endorse them nor disavow them.

This was before the Japanese military clique had committed their country to the complete obligations of the New Order in Asia, full partnership in the Axis, and the other expansionist moves that Tokyo subsequently undertook. Pittman's demands for immediate coercive action on the part of the United States to halt the Mikado's men attracted little public support at that time. There was a faction in the navy, made up of officers who had seen considerable service in the Far East, there were missionaries who felt their work in China would be arrested if Japan became dominant, and there were a few professional Jap-baiters in California who agitated for slapping the Japanese down. In general, however, the public appeared content with the appeasement policy the Roosevelt administration followed for so many years, the results of which cannot be evaluated even yet.

Despite his distrust of many domestic aspects of the New Deal, Hull was convinced that Roosevelt's re-election and a continuance of the compromise foreign policy he and the President had evolved were necessary for the continued safety of the nation. He told friends that he would work for the President's renomination when the Democrats met in Philadelphia and that he would stump the country for the ticket if he could do any good. He was selected to open the active campaign for Roosevelt's nomination, which he did in a speech to the Young Democratic Clubs of Maryland on March 5.

In May he made three speeches and gave an interview to the

Foreign Correspondents' Association of New York in which he set the note of his contribution to the Roosevelt campaign. The speeches were delivered before the Chamber of Commerce of the United States, the Academy of World Economics, and the Merchants' Club of New York, and his general theme was that the world's only hope of escaping a devastating war was through the restoration of international commerce, to which he added the declaration that the Roosevelt-Hull program for reciprocal trade agreements was the most feasible method to bring about this restoration.

This sort of thing was to be his principal effort in the campaign, although he did issue an interpretation of the Good Neighbor policy, in mid-September, which created considerable interest in Latin America and elsewhere abroad. He got into a heated debate with Landon over the merits of the trade-agreements program, Landon being a protectionist at heart. But Hull left to the President the defense of the main bastion of foreign policy —the question of what the United States would do in the event war broke out in Europe.

Mr. Roosevelt grasped the nettle firmly in one of his early campaign speeches. Speaking at Chautauqua, New York, on August 14, the President made the implied pledge to keep the country out of war which the isolationists used many times subsequently to plague him. The speech was not nearly so firm a commitment as his opponents have since made it out to be. The nib of it was contained in the following paragraph:

"We are not isolationists except insofar as we seek to isolate ourselves completely from war. Yet we must remember that so long as war exists on earth there will be some danger that even the nation which most ardently desires peace may be drawn into war."

The candidate went on to describe how he hated war because he had seen war at close range. Although this was, and is, a completely sincere aversion on his part, according to his close friends, he may have overdone his effect in the heat of the moment. On dozens of occasions isolationists in Congress and on public platforms have quoted extracts from this speech, in connection with current steps or recommendations of the President, in such a way as to make him appear utterly inconsistent.

Had Hull been making such a speech, or had his advice been asked in drafting it, he would have been less didactic. It is seldom that a speech of Hull's can be dragged up and used against him, although, like all politicians who are frequently on the public record, he is not immune. After he became Secretary of State his innate caution about.leaving on the record observations which could later prove embarrassing became intensified, and his public and official utterances since 1933 follow a remarkably consistent thread.

Just as the presidential campaign neared its climax the Spanish Civil War broke out, lending point to the fears of the isolationists that the United States might get dragged into a general war against its wishes. We have tended to forget, under the influence of the great war to follow, for which the Spanish struggle was only a rehearsal, the intense bitterness it generated. That bitterness spread far and quickly beyond national frontiers and begat class struggle in foreign lands to an extent the Communist revolution in Russia never approached.

For the Spanish war was nourished by religious fanaticism. In Spain the rich and conservative classes were devoted supporters of the Roman Catholic Church. It was their wealth that made the Church in Spain so rich as to be the main support of the Vatican in Rome. When the Spanish Republic, established after many vicissitudes following the departure of King Alfonso XIII, continued to gain strength at the subsequent elections and to attempt reforms, the rich Catholics decided things had gone far enough and that the good old days must be restored by force of arms.

They made General Franco their champion and Mother Church their battle cry. The general launched the Spanish Nationalist party, backed at the outset almost exclusively by Moorish mercenaries who were neither Spanish nor Catholic. The Catholic part of his slogan took root in the outside world, and subsequent developments failed to shake the conviction of good churchmen in Great Britain, the United States, and Latin America that there was only one side to the Spanish issue.

These violent foreign partisans were unshaken when Franco had to solicit military assistance from Hitler, due to the marked lack of enthusiasm of the Spanish for his "Nationalist" movement. If the good Catholics in the outside world had stopped for a moment to consider the dubious (to put the best interpretation on it) reputation of the German Fuehrer for dealing with the Catholics in his own country, they might have wondered how good a bargain Franco was driving. When the great "Nationalist" implored legions of mercenaries from Mussolini, the ex-Socialist who had been in constant hot water with the Vatican ever since he usurped power, their embryo suspicions should have been confirmed. But neither inference bore any weight, and Franco became the world's champion of Catholicism.

The struggle came into the open at a time when Congress had adjourned, leaving what was supposed to be an infallible guide for the administration to follow in case war broke out in the world. The law, carried over from the previous year, provided that shipments of arms, ammunition, and implements of war must be prevented from going from the United States to all belligerents, when two or more foreign nations became involved in war. The law did not cover the situation which had arisen, where a single country fell into the throes of civil conflict.

Unhampered by any specific prohibitions, Hull tried to manage the thorny issue in a common-sense manner. He decided that the so-called "neutrality" policy which Congress had laid down did not apply to the relations of the United States with a legitimate government, with which it maintained normal diplomatic relations, when it was engaged in quelling a domestic insurrection. He declined to recognize the purely paper blockade of Spain proclaimed by the Franco forces, and he decided to collaborate with the great nations of Europe in localizing the war within the borders of Spain. He realized that it might easily spread all over Europe, which was already ripe for a first-class war.

There was every indication that the Spanish war might grow into a general European fight. As soon as the French learned the Italians were helping Franco, they wanted to help the other side. The Russians, learning that the Germans were going to Franco's assistance, rushed to reinforce the Loyalist forces. The British, as usual, were caught in the middle. Their public was badly divided on the merits of the struggle in Spain but was united on the proposition that no general war was wanted.

Out of this dilemma was born the "non-intervention" program which eventually won the war for General Franco. All of the big nations agreed to keep hands off and to let the Spaniards settle their own difficulties among themselves. Hull was persuaded by the British that the United States, in the interest of world peace, must go along with this plan, especially in the matter of refusing to sell arms to either side. He fell in with it, actuated partly by a mistaken belief in the sincerity of the "non-interveners" and partly by the knowledge that Congress would amend the Neutrality Act to cover civil wars as soon as it reconvened in January. In addition, the imminence of the presidential election made it politically wise not to offend the powerful Catholic elements of the country by opposing Franco too strongly.

Like most of the other British appeasement plans, the non-intervention scheme worked badly for Britain—and for the world at large. At the outbreak of the Spanish war the French rushed war matériel, especially airplanes, to the Madrid forces. They were badly needed, as the Franco armies were getting modern equipment of all kinds from both Italy and Germany, in addition to thousands of trained troops, some of which did not even bother to take off their Italian and German uniforms.

With customary frugality the French started by sending to the Loyalists outmoded airplanes which they could no longer use in their own tactical forces, but after a good many of these had been blasted from the sky by superior German and Italian planes the national *amour propre* began to operate in Paris. Good modern equipment was about to be supplied to the Loyalists when the British persuaded the French to come into the non-intervention camp. The Russians had subscribed to the non-intervention agreement with tongue in cheek and supplied what modern matériel they could. High in this list was a Russian-made Curtiss fighter, manufactured under license, which had a marked superiority over the German and Italian planes. It was practically the same plane as the P-36, which is still (at this writing) standard equipment for some of the pursuit squadrons of the United States Air Corps.

The scheme worked out that only the British, the Americans, and the French (the latter grumblingly and against their better judgment) lived up to the non-intervention agreement. The Germans, the Italians, and the Russians frankly wanted to use the Spanish battlefield as a proving ground for their military equipment. In addition, they wanted the political advantage of establishing a friendly government in control of the Iberian Peninsula.

The United States government, up until the time Congress altered the Neutrality Act to fit the Spanish case, was in the unhappy position of refusing all aid to a friendly government seeking to put down an insurrection within its own borders. By unofficial but highly effective means the State Department prevented the Spanish government from spending a penny of its large gold reserves for arms or munitions in this country. Spaniards were flocking to the Loyalist standard, and "volunteers" were arriving in goodly numbers from Russia. In addition, there were brigades of genuine volunteers from France, Great Britain, the United States, and elsewhere, but they all needed arms.

Hull rationalized the administration's doubts and fears in his speech of September 15 before the Good Neighbor League in New York. He observed that "we do not seek or threaten the territory or possessions of others" (paying his respects to the Japanese) and deplored that "in less than twenty years events have occurred that have taken away from international agreements their force and reliability as a basis of relations between nations" (taking in the Japanese, the Germans, the Italians, and the Russians). These unhappy conditions were producing themselves, he said, at a time when the "laboratories and shops are producing instruments which can blow away human beings as though they were mites in a thunderstorm."[3]

Under existing circumstances, he told his listeners, the United States was obliged to formulate its foreign policy realistically, with due regard for things as they were and not as they should have been. This country, he pledged, would support every means for the prevention of war in the world, but it would not "join with other governments in collective arrangements carrying the obligation of employing force, if necessary, in case disputes between other countries brought them into war." The nation must

---

[3] Hull's fondness for figures of speech dealing with thunderstorms must spring from his early life in the mountains. Talking with some isolationist senators during the neutrality debates, he terminated the interview by warning them: "Gentlemen, don't close your eyes like a mule in a thunderstorm."

beware of such commitments, he continued, because of the improbability that "we, by our action, could vitally influence the policies or activities of other countries from which war might come."

"In my judgment," he summed up, in practically the only positive portion of his speech, except for an excellent delineation of his plan for permanent peace based on economic equality of opportunity, "it is not a basic defect of democratic institutions that has led to their decline in so many places, but rather the onset of weariness, fear, and indifference, which can and must be dispelled. These are the heritage of the last war. They must not be permitted to bring on another."

He concluded with the following excellent advice, which his fellow countrymen studiously ignored for the first two years of the war, when it finally came:

"Let us avoid flabbiness of spirit, weakness of body, grave dissent within our own numbers, and we shall have nothing to fear from these storms."

While the speech was intended as a campaign effort, Hull wrote it and delivered it in a manner intended completely to divorce it from partisanship. It attracted widespread comment, both approving and disapproving. The German press lauded it.

With this single exception Hull's participation in the presidential campaign was limited to the defense of the reciprocal trade agreements. He went as far afield as Minneapolis to continue his oratorical feud with Governor Landon and delivered another radio speech or two from Washington, along the same line, before the voters went to the polls. He left it to such administration stalwarts as Secretary of Labor Perkins, John L. Lewis, whose United Mine Workers subscribed $500,000 to the Roosevelt campaign fund, and Governor Earle to shout to the electorate that President Roosevelt *must* be re-elected to keep the nation at peace.

Hull remembered Woodrow Wilson's tragic and undeserved opprobrium resulting from the campaign of 1916 based on the slogan (which Wilson never approved), "He kept us out of war." The Secretary of State knew that mere wishing would not keep the United States out of the war that was impending and he wanted to be connected with no binding promises along that line.

American destroyers were even then putting in at regular intervals to small Spanish ports to take off Americans stranded there, for fear that some of them might get killed, rousing a public indignation which might lead to rash action by the government.

As the election approached, and as its result became more and more a foregone conclusion, Hull's immediate attention focused on a problem close at hand—the state of inter-American relations. Early in the year President Roosevelt had proposed a conference of the American republics, to meet in Buenos Aires on December 1 and to be called the Conference for the Maintenance of Peace. The President's proposal had been based on the happy fact that the twenty-one republics were at peace with each other (the Chaco War between Paraguay and Bolivia had been stopped the previous June) and that there was no visible reason why they should not stay at peace. Under these conditions, Mr. Roosevelt suggested, the New World ought to do something about perpetuating the condition of peace. He and Secretary Hull had been preaching at home that peace is not a negative condition, not the mere absence of war, but rather a positive state of being which must be planned and achieved.

The idea had been well received throughout the hemisphere, and the usual catchall agenda had been prepared. Hull barely waited for the results of the presidential election to be known (he announced that the country's foreign policy would be unchanged and that Roosevelt's re-election would act as a stimulant to the trade-agreements program) before he sailed for Buenos Aires on November 8. He arrived in the Argentine capital a few days before the conference was scheduled to open and made his personal contacts in the same unobtrusive way he had so successfully employed at Montevideo three years earlier, but he remained carefully in the background until the spectacular preliminaries were out of the way.

President Roosevelt had decided that he ought to make a personal appearance at this show which he had staged. He had been unable, since his first election, to pay any visits of state to Latin America, for if he went to one country he would have to go to them all to avoid giving offense. This extraordinary gathering (the regular Pan-American Conference was scheduled to meet only in 1938) gave him a unique opportunity for the very kind of gesture which he knew would be effective and which he knew he would do well.

It was arranged, accordingly, that President Roosevelt would arrive on the cruiser *Indianapolis* the day before the conference opened and that he and President Justo of Argentina would be the only speakers at the inaugural session. The cruiser docked on the morning of November 30, and the President of Argentina was at the dock to greet his distinguished colleague. As President Roosevelt came down the gangplank he stretched out his hand to President Justo and called him *"mi amigo."* Not to be outdone in this exchange of international intimacies, President Justo gave Mr. Roosevelt the *"abrazo"* (the bearlike hug with which Latin-American friends greet each other) while the crowds on the dock cheered to the echo.

That day made history in Buenos Aires. Local newspapermen estimated that one million people lined the streets to see President Roosevelt on the three trips he made across the city (by a different route each time) in the ceremonial coach, escorted by mounted guards in picturesque colonial uniforms. It was a touching spectacle, and President Roosevelt was greatly affected by it. Special trains had been run in to the capital at reduced fares to celebrate the two-day national fiesta the Federal government had decreed. Gauchos came from far-distant points in Patagonia to gawk at this visitor from the North. They stood patiently, ten deep, all day long in the streets until President Roosevelt's final appearance. The Chief Executive had been taken to call on the officials in the Casa Rosada, which houses the Foreign Office and other principal governmental agencies. The crowds in the plaza outside shouted for him until it was deemed wise for him to make an appearance on the balcony. At that point police lines were broken and a small riot ensued as the spectators pressed closer and tried to climb the walls of the building to touch the great man.

My colleague, John W. White, who had lived in South America for nearly twenty years, spent most of that day listening to comments of the crowds in cafés, streetcars, barbershops, and the streets. Late that night he told me that Roosevelt impressed them as a great character, in his own right, rather like an invincible bullfighter. His overwhelming electoral victory of a month earlier had captured the popular imagination. It was as a person, rather than as a President, that he impressed the Argentines.

"Here was a man who could beat the bankers," John White patiently explained to me, as if that should make everything clear. It took a little time for me to realize how far-reaching and unexpected had been the effects of the practically unanimous opposition of the monied people of the United States to the President's re-election.

The President himself was profoundly moved by it all. The following morning he granted one of his famous press conferences to the Argentine newspapermen—probably the first one ever held in Buenos Aires—and promised them he would have the sanitary convention with Argentina ratified as soon as he got back to Washington. This was the agreement which would have permitted properly inspected Argentine beef to be imported into the United States. As matters then stood, all Argentine beef (except canned) was barred because the cattle in some parts of the country were infected. As I heard this sweeping promise I experienced a premonitory shiver. The story caused extra editions of the afternoon papers, with follow-ups and editorials the next morning. Unfortunately that same convention was still unratified by the United States five years after the presidential promise in Buenos Aires.

At the time, however, there was nothing to mar the magnificence of the reception accorded to the North American President. He addressed the opening meeting on December 1, after President Justo had declared the conference open, and sailed away just at sunset, headed for a similar reception in Montevideo.

After this glittering prologue Hull settled down to work. He made his first speech on December 2, following Dr. Carlos Saavedra Lamas, the Foreign Minister of Argentina. Dr. Francisco Castillo Najera, the Mexican Ambassador to Washington, who was a member of his country's delegation to the conference, went on the radio to pledge Mexican cooperation with the Roosevelt policy. Other important delegates issued statements to the same effect, and it looked as if it were all over but the shouting. But Hull knew better. He had already experienced one such conclave.

There was an immediate cleavage of opinion on how far the

Americas should go to band together for their mutual defense. The Central American republics and Colombia wanted a binding treaty committing all the republics to each other's mutual defense. The Dominican Republic wanted a Pan-American League of Nations. The Argentines opposed the whole idea of universal neutrality in the event of an extra-American war and would not endorse the Monroe Doctrine. The North Americans proposed merely that the republics agree to consult together in the event that the peace of any one of them was threatened from within or without, and the deliberations began to adapt themselves to this line of thought.

The conference disbanded on December 27 after its members had signed four principal recommendations. They were:

1. A declaration that a threat to the security of any single republic would constitute a threat to the security of them all, from whatever source it came.

2. A collective-security convention providing for obligatory consultation between the republics when there was a threat of war anywhere in the world.

3. A protocol defining intervention as an unfriendly act.

4. A neutrality convention obligating them all to adopt a common attitude as neutrals in the event war should break out outside the Western Hemisphere.

These inconclusive steps toward hemisphere solidarity were all that could be taken at that time, but they were considerably in advance of anything that had been accomplished at previous Pan-American gatherings. Hull and his associates felt they had made a good start which could be accelerated, if the need existed, at the next regular Pan-American Conference, which was to be held at Lima, Peru, in 1938.

The indecision that prevailed at Buenos Aires was a clear reflection of the state of mind throughout the Western Hemisphere and, indeed, throughout much of the world in those days. It was only in the totalitarian countries that any definiteness of purpose had manifested itself. In the rest of the world the masses and their governors were unable or unwilling to recognize their own best interest, and their actions suffered accordingly.

CHAPTER XVIII

The World on Fire

By THIS TIME the Democratic party was ripe for its inevitable internecine war over the Supreme Court. The storm had been building up for a year, like a thunderhead over the Gulf of Mexico, which starts out as a tiny white cloud and develops into a devastating downpour. The New Dealers had convinced President Roosevelt that the Nine Old Men were permanent obstacles in the way of his entire social and economic program, and the Chief Executive had decided on that direct action for which he is famous.

The New Dealers, for once, were not without allies in Congress. The Supreme Court, by a series of decisions, had invalidated various statutes which were dear to progressive elements outside the ranks of the administration's stalwarts. A year earlier Senator Peter Norbeck, a Republican from North Dakota, had introduced a bill to require the concurrence of seven of the nine justices in declaring an Act of Congress to be unconstitutional. This was only one of many protests against the five-to-four decisions which had marred the Supreme Court's record.

The high tribunal had declared null and void the National Industrial Recovery Act, the Agricultural Adjustment Act, and the New York State minimum wage law for women and children, to name only three out of a procession. They were the three, however, which combined to work up a sizable Congressional allergy for the Court. Representative Ernest Lundeen, a Farm-Labor member from Minnesota,[1] proposed a bill to increase the number of justices from nine to eleven, and Senator George Norris, an Independent from Nebraska, demanded legislation that would require a unanimous decision of the Court to invalidate a law which Congress had voted and which the President had signed. The United Mine Workers passed a resolution asking that Congress curb the high court.

These symptoms of popular resentment against the Supreme Court's highhanded rejection of legislation were visible a full year before President Roosevelt decided to move. Once he decided on the frontal assault, however, the blitzkrieg was on. In his annual message to the newly elected Congress on January 7, 1937, the President said that a more liberal interpretation of the Constitution was essential if democracy was to be successful in the United States.

He followed this gentle hint with a special message to Congress, on February 6, recommending that the membership of the Supreme Court be increased from nine to fifteen by the appointment of new justices to "assist" those members of the court who had passed the age of seventy and who did not choose to retire. This was an obvious attack on the conservative majority of five, all of whom were past seventy, which had so consistently overridden the liberal minority of four.

The message unloosed a tide of proposals. Representative Maury Maverick of Texas, who was in the vanguard of the New Deal on the domestic side, although he opposed the administration's foreign policy, introduced a Constitutional amendment declaring that the Supreme Court could not nullify an Act of Congress. Senator Guy M. Gillette, a conservative Democrat from Iowa, reintroduced the Norbeck proposal, calling for a seven-to-two decision as a minimum for nullification. Senator Key Pittman of Nevada proposed a Constitutional amendment to increase the membership of the Court to fifteen as a permanent matter. Senator Pat McCarran, the other Democrat from Nevada, joined with Representative Hatton Sumners of Texas in

[1]He was later elected to the Senate and was killed in the crash of a commercial air liner near Leesburg, Virginia

bringing in a bill to provide for the retirement of Supreme Court justices at the age of seventy, after ten years of service, at full pay for life. Ironically enough, this bill passed and provided the machinery by which the court was ultimately more completely reformed than would have been the case under the administration's original proposal.

The details of this long, bitter fight, which ended on July 22, 1937, when Senator M. M. Logan of Kentucky, the administration's champion on the Judiciary Committee, moved to recommit the bill and the Senate concurred, 70 to 20, are too well known to rehash here. Its effect on the future of the Democratic party and of the nation are still to be assayed.[2]

The acrimonious and sordid debate had a profound effect on Cordell Hull. He had halfway expected that the Supreme Court would strike down much of the New Deal legislation, as he intimated in his Williamsburg speech of eighteen months earlier, when he said that the New Deal's domestic program "has not been disapproved by the Judicial Department." He did not approve of the policy embodied in many of the invalidated statutes, and he probably shared the constitutional qualms of the Supreme Court's majority. He could not help being miserable over the frontal attack on the tribunal which his whole legal training and experience had taught him to regard as the final bulwark of the American system.

He reached an irrevocable decision. He resolved to retire from all participation in political life and to devote the remainder of his public career to whatever service he could render without taking part in the partisan warfare which had been so familiar and so dear to him. He began to aspire to the American equivalent of the Elder Statesman in Japan, he would tell friends privately and jokingly, but there was no mistaking the profound distrust of ordinary native political methods, in such time of crisis as he saw was approaching, which the Court fight engendered in him.

He had seen the same kind of political chicanery endanger his

[2]Returning from London in the autumn of 1938, just after the Munich crisis, I asked Ben Cohen, who was a fellow passenger, why the New Deal had not accomplished more in the two years since the re-election of President Roosevelt He thought for a minute and then replied: "Perhaps we changed the Constitutional history of the United States."

beloved trade agreements and foist the dangerous neutrality legislation on the American public. He felt that the immediate dangers the United States would have to face were destined to come from without and not from within, and he knew that small-time politics could play no beneficial part in the determination of American foreign policy if the country was to steer safely past the plentiful shoals that already lay on the horizon.

External relations had brought plenty of complications during the time the Supreme Court fight was reaching its bitterest pitch. The Congress, during the first four months of its new session, did practically nothing except debate the extension of the Neutrality Act, as the existing law would expire by limitation on May 1. Its deliberations opened in the midst of a ridiculous, melodramatic incident which would have been funny except for the tragic importance it held for the Spanish Loyalists.

The Neutrality Act of 1936 did not cover civil wars, it was discovered as soon as the Spanish Republic fell to fighting within itself. The combined ingenuity of all the isolationist draftsmen had been insufficient to cover the one actual development which really occurred. All the situations they had foreseen did *not* arise, and the one they did *not* foresee had come to pass. Here was a second irrefutable argument against the attempt to enact, in advance of the event, a policy to cover so complex a subject as international relations, but the administration was unable to make this side of the case convincing to a majority in Congress.

As the existing law stood, on the eve of the new Congressional session, the National Munitions Control Board, of which Joseph C. Green, of the State Department, was active chief, was obliged to issue export licenses to all properly registered dealers and agents except "export or import licenses where the exportation of arms, ammunition, or implements of war would be in violation of this act or any other law of the United States, or a treaty to which the United States is a party, in which cases such licenses shall not be issued."

Since none of these conditions applied, an enterprising exporter had ordered, for the Madrid authorities, a shipment of war materials to the value of $2,777,000 and had secured a license to export it—a permission given by Mr. Green, accompanied by the public statement that he was doing "reluctantly" what the law compelled him to do. The Loyalist government had sent a Spanish ship, the *Mar Cantabrico,* to take the cargo in New York for delivery in Bilbao, and it was being loaded as fast as the manufacturers could supply the implements.

The shipment was to consist mainly of machine guns and ammunition, plus 18 airplanes, 411 fully assembled engines, and spare parts sufficient to assemble about 150 more engines. This appears to be a trifling amount of matériel in comparison with the huge quantities used in the general European war two years later, but it was an important addition to the Loyalist military strength at that time, in view of the relatively small scale of the conflict then. What the Loyalists needed was some modern equipment to counter the supplies being furnished to General Franco by the Italians and the Germans.

Despite the declared intentions of the isolationists to keep the United States from favoring or hindering either side in a foreign war, the plain truth of the matter was evident to everyone else in the country. The effect of letting the shipment depart would be to help the Loyalists. The effect of preventing its departure would be to help the Franco faction. It was another example of the impossibility, in the modern world, of avoiding taking sides in a war. Had there never been a Neutrality Act, perhaps, the United States government could not have been said to take sides. The ordinary usages of international law in regard to contraband and gunrunning would have applied, and the whole transaction would have taken place at the risk of the individuals involved.

Having embarked on the dangerous path of legislating foreign policy in advance, however, the government had assumed a responsibility which was not incumbent upon it and, whatever it did or did not do, it would be favoring one side against the other. This totally unnecessary governmental responsibility was overemphasized by the shrill cries of alarm emitted by the isolationist bloc in Congress as its members entrained for Washington and the new session. According to the burden of their laments the United States would be immediately involved in a European war if the *Mar Cantabrico* were permitted to sail with its meager complement of defense weapons for the Madrid forces.

Congress met on January 5, 1937. A resolution to forbid the export of arms to any faction in a civil war and to void existing

Secretary Hull with Senator Walter F George and Senator
Tom Connally (right) After a Secret Session of the Senate
Foreign Relations Committee on the Lend-Lease Bill

contracts for such export was introduced in both houses on the opening day. Both committees dealing with foreign relations met at once and reported it favorably, so that it came to the floor of both houses on the second day of the session. The Senate adopted it by 80 to 0 and the House by 404 to 1.

Meantime, in New York, the persevering exporter refused to give up hope, even though the unanimous power of Congress seemed to be against him. It was obvious that the Congressional haste could have no other object than to keep the *Mar Cantab-rico* from sailing. Perhaps he had a gambler's hunch that such an unwieldy body as Congress could not act so expeditiously on such a small matter and still be efficient. If so, his hunch was well rewarded.

After both branches of Congress had completed their practi-cally unanimous action (the sole dissenter was a leftist member from Wisconsin who had been born in Corsica) it was discovered that the Senate had recessed before the House had completed its action. This meant that the parliamentary formalities of en-grossing the bill, securing the signatures of the Speaker of the House and the Vice-President, and the final approval of the President could not be accomplished until the next day. In other words, the proposed statute would not be law for several more hours.

By a miracle the *Mar Cantabrico* completed its loading and slipped out of New York Harbor during that night. The port and customs authorities were powerless to stop her, as the law had not been changed and the vessel was completely in the clear under existing regulations. It would be agreeable to record a fairy-story ending in which the audacity and patience of the authors of the venture were rewarded by success, but the fact is that the ship was intercepted by Franco naval vessels in the Bay of Biscay and sent to the bottom a month later.

Secretary Hull was aboard the S.S. *Southern Cross,* returning from Buenos Aires, as these undignified events were taking place on Capitol Hill. He learned enough of the details, even by the meager reports taken down for him by the ship's radio operators, to confirm his opinion that airtight "neutrality" legislation was certainly undesirable and probably impossible. By February 18 he felt impelled to announce that the State Department favored an absolute minimum of mandatory provisions in whatever new legislation Congress might enact in the search for event-proof non-involvement.

He must have known he was voicing a forlorn hope. In the Senate there was a race between Messrs. Nye, Vandenberg, Clark of Missouri, and LaFollette, on the one side, and Mr. Pittman, on the other, to see who could discover more ways of hampering the Executive by prescribing what he must do in times of most delicate crisis. In the House, on the other hand, the administration leadership kept assuring President Roosevelt and Secretary Hull that they would deliver the votes to pass any discretionary legislation which might come to them with the blessing of the White House and the State Department.

The tradition that the Senate must always be appeased by the administration in matters relating to foreign affairs, because it can block, by the adverse vote of only thirty-three of its ninety-six members, any treaty the executive branch may negotiate, carried the day. The administration decided, in the interest of future comity, to take whatever crumbs it could glean from the senatorial table, and the result was a law which stood up only to the point where it was submitted to the acid test of foreign war, when it was radically altered.

At this juncture, however, the tracks were signaled to be all clear for adventures in unrealistic forecasts of the position the United States would take in the event that world chaos were precipitated. The final version of the Neutrality Act, which Congress passed and which President Roosevelt approved, went far beyond the policy that any great nation had ever, in recorded history, felt compelled to adopt in order to keep itself free of the tragedies that were in the making.

To the existing automatic arms embargo, which was the principal feature of the current law, the new edition added the controversial "cash-and-carry" treatment of all commerce with belligerents. The isolationists, still under the influence of the Nye committee's illusion that American commercial and financial interest in the success of the Allies (so that American creditors might hope to get their money) had forced the unwilling country into the World War, believed that the legal requirement of cash on the barrelhead would prevent overextension of commercial credits and similar involvement in another war. Direct loans to belligerent governments or their subdivisions were already outlawed under the Act of 1936, but they wanted to double-lock the door.

The common sense of the administration leaders in the House kept this provision from being utterly crippling, as they insisted that the language be altered to provide that this policy should not go into effect unless the President should find that such a step was "necessary to promote the security or preserve the peace of the United States or to protect the lives of citizens of the United States." This language unwittingly foreshadowed the passage of the Lease-Lend Act four years later, after the country had decided that the cash-and-carry plan would imperil, rather than promote, the security and peace of the United States.

Every time the "neutrality" draftsmen in Congress thought they had evolved a President-proof policy something else in the foreign field would happen to upset their calculations. For example, Great Britain decided belatedly at this point to undertake a mild rearmament program, alarmed at last by the unbelievable military progress of the Germans under Adolf Hitler's tutelage. Senator Nye and Representative Hamilton Fish, Jr., of New York, ranking Republican member of the House Foreign Affairs Committee, hastily collaborated on a bill to prohibit the export of arms from the United States in time of peace as well as war, for fear that this country would aid the British rearmament program and thus offend Germany.

When administration spokesmen pointed out to these gentlemen that they were doing their level best to forward German success in Hitler's obvious aggressive intentions, they indignantly stood upon their personal prerogatives and challenged any imputation upon their personal honor. Mr. Fish had served with distinction in the World War and held a reserve commission in the army (he was on active duty with troops when this was written) and had that advantage over Mr. Nye, who had not served in the armed forces in 1917 and 1918.

What they failed to acknowledge, and what tended to befuddle the issue, was that their opponents were impugning not their personal honor but their judgment. To Hull it was apparent that this country's long-term interest must inevitably lie on the side

of the peace-loving nations of the world and that the United
States would be well advised to make that position clear to the
potential aggressors. The pacifists and isolationists, in their eager-
ness to avoid war at all cost, wanted to advertise to the world
that any international marauder could pursue his depredations
secure in the knowledge that his victim could get no assistance
whatever from the United States.

Like most fallacious philosophical positions, theirs was capable
of superficially plausible defense. In the case of the Spanish Civil
War, for example, they recalled that the United States government had often in the past inherited undignified and unprofitable
aftermaths by trying to sustain some unpopular government
against successful insurgents. They had to go back no further
than 1930, when Henry L. Stimson, then Secretary of State, had
unsuccessfully thrown the weight of North American influence
against a band of insurgents from the south of Brazil, headed by
a man named Getulio Vargas, who remained president of Brazil
a dozen years or more despite this unpromising beginning.

The bickerings of the two branches of Congress over the details
of the legislation resulted in a melodramatic climax which was a
fitting ending for its burlesque prelude. The conference committee's report, compromising the conflicting Senate and House
versions of the proposed law, was presented for the consideration
of both bodies on April 29, when the existing statute had only
three more days to live. The most interested parties were determined that there should not be an interregnum during which
the old law would have expired and the new law would not have
taken effect. In this view Hull concurred. If there had to be such
a legislative policy, he told his friends in Congress, let it be fairly
continuous and let it prevent such scramblings as the *Mar Cantabrico* incident.

The compromise was rushed through both houses that same
day, but it required President Roosevelt's signature to become
law. The Chief Executive had gone on one of his periodic
vacation cruises and was fishing in the Gulf of Mexico. Arrangements were made to rush the engrossed copy to him by navy
airplanes, two of which collided on the surface, the accident de-
laying the delivery to the President until May 1, literally the
ultimate deadline.

In Vienna the Austrian government was already protesting that the Nazis were abusing the recently concluded trade agreement to force political concessions. In other words, the Anschluss had been ordained in Berlin and Berchtesgaden. The Japanese had moved from Manchuria into North China and were preparing the "Shanghai incident" of the coming August which was to usher in the all-out effort to subjugate the entire Chinese people. The Fascists of Italy had completed their conquest of Ethiopia and had proclaimed King Victor Emmanuel to be Emperor of that dubious asset.

The forces of aggression were plainly on the march. Hull was grimly and sadly aware of this to a greater degree than almost anyone in the United States, or in the democratic world, for that matter. On every possible occasion he sought to recall to his fellow countrymen and to the leaders elsewhere that the only hope of civilization lay in curbing the growth of international lawlessness and disorder and in promoting permanent economic peace.

The impression must not be conveyed that the United States was the only villain in the international piece of this critical epoch or that Hull, singlehanded, could have stemmed the tide of the terrific forces which were in the making. He had been right when he told the Good Neighbor League a year earlier that the United States could not "vitally influence the policies or actions of other countries from which war might come." Nor, he might have added, could the United States vitally influence the policies or actions of those countries *to* which war might come.

Anglo-French relations, as well as the domestic political situations of the two nations, were at a low ebb. Their foreign policies had been pulling at cross-purposes ever since the end of the World War, and the fatal results of that hidden but potent friction were already unrolling. In both countries influential opinion was completely at odds over the proper attitude to adopt toward the growing menace of Germany.

In Great Britain there was the "appeasement" wing of the Conservative party, of which Prime Minister Neville Chamberlain was the prototype; the "collective security" bloc with Anthony Eden as chief spokesman, and the small group which advocated immediate strong action to stop Germany's increasingly aggressive measures. Winston Churchill, who became Prime Minister after the war broke out, was the chief prophet of positive action.

The French leaders were split along largely the same lines except that with some of them "appeasement" extended to an actual desire for cooperation—the idea of getting on the band wagon before it was too late. Pierre Laval, Georges Bonnet, and a few high-ranking officers of the army and the navy were those principally mentioned in this category at the time. Marshal Pétain's appointment as Ambassador to Franco Spain, with instructions to keep the newly recognized Spanish conqueror in a good temper, was also discussed at the time as a possible indication that the old soldier was veering toward the Laval camp.

The motives behind the two groups of appeasers were different, but their actions were equally helpful to the Nazis. The British Conservatives were still obsessed by the idea that Britain's foreign policy must achieve a balance of power on the Continent at all costs. They did not want to let Germany go too far, of course, but they were unwilling to join any movement to crush Germany and leave France dominant in Europe.

French appeasers and collaborators were assured by the General Staff that the Maginot Line would protect France against any attack the Germans might be able to make and that France could safely watch the Nazis extend their sway into eastern Europe, peacefully or by force, so long as the French defenses were maintained. There was no need to go afield to stop Germany, it was reasoned, in order to assure French security. That already had been accomplished.

The hesitant elements in both countries had one thing in common, however. They knew full well that neither of them was prepared for any large-scale war. Staff consultations between the armed forces of the two allies were instituted early in 1938, and these talks confirmed the politicians' suspicions.

Hull had no sympathy with the appeasement policy in Europe, although he himself followed a similar course for years with respect to Japan, accepting the counsels of Stanley K. Hornbeck, his principal adviser on Far Eastern affairs. He warned the British and French ambassadors, as well as the diplomatic representatives of the smaller countries lying under the shadow of Nazi menace, that their governments were merely hastening the evil day by their temporizing.

He would illustrate his preachments by homely anecdotes about bullies and bad men in the Tennessee mountains. As a circuit judge he had been threatened many times by such swaggering citizens, who would send word of what they were going to do to him the next time they saw him, in retaliation for some sentence he had imposed on a friend or a relative. Hull told the diplomats that he had always found it to be the safest plan to carry just as big a gun as the bully and to walk right down the middle of the road, neither courting nor avoiding a fight. As a result of this policy he had never had a shooting scrape.

His public statements became firmer in their condemnation of treaty violations, threats, and violence as means of overcoming difficulties in international relations. Their tone was more and more pitched so that the references could apply only to Germany. He was convinced that Germany could be stopped, without war, by a concerted show of opposition by all the peace-loving nations of Europe. Had he been an Englishman, he probably would have sided with Eden in the belief that collective security could be achieved and could be made effective.

But he knew the United States could play no official role in promoting that collective action which might have staved off war, because of the little bloc of isolationists and Britain-baiters, in and out of Congress, whose members insisted that any move the United States might make to prevent war would only drag the country into war. They could not be convinced that the United States would not be dragged into a non-existent war.

Likewise Hull was uncertain of the situation in the President's official family. The Chief Executive was permitting William C. Bullitt, his great friend and Ambassador to France, to make strong public speeches in Paris urging bold and determined resistance to further German expansion. At the same time he was allowing Joseph P. Kennedy, another great friend and his Ambassador to Great Britain, to warn the leaders and public in London that, if they got into war, they would get no help from the United States.

Thus the three great nations which had enough man power and resources to have called Germany's bluff, in the early stages, dallied along the path of indecision and vacillation while the Nazis drove straight toward their objective of European domination by the threat of force if possible and by actual force if necessary. The small nations, with the example of the three great ones before them, naturally decided that it was a time for every man to try to save himself. They were encouraged in their moves toward isolation from each other and from the great powers by soothing German assurances that they would not be molested.

The trade-agreements program, which was the only positive alternative to war which the United States had officially to offer, struck them as too slow and nebulous to be of service in the crisis that was developing. Congress had renewed the President's power to negotiate these bargains in 1937 for another term of three years, but it was obvious that their principal field would be Latin America for the immediate future.

For the Nazis had the democratic world bewildered in the economic as well as the military sphere. They had violated all canons of orthodox economy and had been apparently successful. They had brought Germany to a state of complete readiness for war (the ultimate test of any economic fabric), without gold reserves, raw materials, or foreign exchange. They had made themselves self-contained (or so it appeared) when all the political economists, including Hull, had said self-containment was impossible.

The scholars in the democracies began to see the fallacies and the dangers in the economy of totalitarianism, and some of them began to understand the legerdemain by which the ostensible miracle of German preparedness had been accomplished. To the average man in the street, however, the German situation inspired a certain reluctant admiration. Hitler claimed he had abolished unemployment, while there were still 10,000,000 workless in the United States. There were no strikes or lockouts in Germany, and Hitler made the employers work for the good of the state just as he did the workers.

These palatable bits of German propaganda were readily taken not only in the United States but throughout the Western Hemisphere. The masses who listened to this story could not be bothered to realize that German unemployment had been cured by military conscription and a system of forced labor which would never be accepted in the New World or that strikes and lockouts were sternly forbidden and workmen could not change their jobs or places of employment without the permission of the state.

"After all, that fellow's got something," was a common remark made by the undiscerning about Adolf Hitler. This idea was sedulously distributed by countless agencies in Nazi employ, many of them in the United States and even more in Latin America. The campaign was part of the politico-military strategy which the Nazis had already worked out, along the lines laid down by Hitler in *Mein Kampf,* and which was to prove so successful for them. Its essence was the softening of potential enemy positions from behind as well as from the front. Civilian populations in the democracies were to be kept in a state of continuing indecision by a skillful balancing of threats and wheedling promises.

President Roosevelt and Secretary Hull were not deceived, but the isolationist members of Congress either believed this propaganda or used it to bolster their own arguments—helping Hitler in either event. The constant use of the theme that "we have no quarrel with any country," or that "we can get along with anybody on the other side of the ocean," or that "Europe has always had its wars and always will have them," was effective in attracting popular support for those senators and representatives who felt that the future of the country—and, incidentally, of themselves—lay in keeping the United States inert and uninterested amid the fateful events that were shaping themselves.

Even the annexation of Austria in the spring of 1938, after a campaign of assassination and organized terrorism such as the world has rarely seen, failed to shake their conviction that the United States had nothing to fear. They went even further and said the affair was no business of anyone except the Germans and the Austrians. After all, they recalled, the Austrians spoke German and some of their leaders had wanted union with Germany for years. The Austrian economic and political position had been hopeless from the date of signing the Treaty of Trianon, they continued, and only a rational remedy had been applied to a lingering malady. They regretted the rough stuff, of course, but passed that off as inevitable in all sudden overturns.

At this stage matters had got so thoroughly out of hand that the foreign policy of the United States would have had to go into a state of watchful waiting even without the unsleeping campaign of the isolationists. President Roosevelt was thoroughly resolved, and Hull agreed, that the United States must keep out of involvements and commitments until things had settled down. The break between Chamberlain and Eden, and the successive French cabinet crises, warned them that there was no fixed anti-German policy in Europe to which a parallel policy of the United States could be anchored.

Chamberlain kept assuring the White House that he was fashioning a foreign policy for either pacification or fighting, as Hitler might elect, and that his ultimate decision, one way or the other, would be made independently of any hope for help from the United States. Churchill, on the other hand, sent word to President Roosevelt that the Chamberlain policy was not popular with the British electorate and that Eden would, in the final analysis, stand with the government.

The British were busy trying to liquidate their difficulties with Italy, presumably as part of Chamberlain's attempt to be ready for war or peace with Germany, at Hitler's choice. The plan that was being proposed to Italy (vainly, as it turned out) involved the withdrawal of Italian troops from Libya (whence the French felt they were being threatened in North Africa), in return for which the British would withdraw their battleships from the Mediterranean; the cessation of anti-British radio propaganda, much of which was directed in Arabic at Egypt and the surrounding countries, in return for which the British would recognize the King of Italy as the Emperor of Abyssinia; and an arrangement for British financing of Anglo-Italian trade movements, but with no direct governmental loans involved.

It was on this plan that Eden had broken with his Prime Minister. He and his adherents believed that Mussolini was headed for a fall because of the unpopularity of the costly and profitless Ethiopian campaign and its continuing liabilities. Concessions of the kind envisaged by the Chamberlain appeasers would only strengthen a tottering and inimical regime in Italy, according to Eden's estimate, to which Hull probably agreed, although he was careful to avoid any expression of opinion.

While these feelers were being put forward to Italy the Chamberlain government was considering a series of offers advanced on the part of Germany by Joachim von Ribbentrop, the English-speaking champagne salesman Hitler had appointed as his ambassador to the Court of St. James's. This proposed *modus vivendi* included the following principal points:

Germany would guarantee that it would not invade France or any of the western countries.

Belgium and Holland would be protected by some sort of mutual guarantee by Germany and Great Britain.

The former German colonies in Africa were to be restored to the Reich.

Great Britain was to close its eyes to Nazi advances toward the east.

Chamberlain was toying with all of these ideas in order to gain time, on the theory that Great Britain was not ready, militarily or psychologically, to do anything else. Churchill, on the other hand, regarded this policy as a complete fallacy, because it was obvious that Germany could prepare twice as fast as Great Britain during the appeasement period. The Chamberlain Cabinet was also bolstered by the faint hope that the advertised German advance to the east would be accomplished by trade penetration and propaganda and not by shooting.

The best advice from the British War Office also encouraged Chamberlain to stall for time. Leslie Hore-Belisha, who was then War Secretary, was obsessed with the idea that the German air force could hopelessly disrupt communications and services around London within a few days, scoring a quick knockout. He did not believe that the German air power could contribute in any serious degree to a blockade of the British Isles to cut off food and other supplies from abroad.

The Germans, meantime, were not waiting. The Austrian annexation had hardly been completed when Hitler decided that the Germans in the Sudetenland of Czechoslovakia were being unbearably persecuted. Chamberlain advised the Czechs and the French to permit the "readjustment" Hitler proposed, which involved the annexation of that part of the Czechoslovakian Republic to the growing New German Reich.

Tension was mounting all over Europe, and all professional

armies were ordered to be ready for instant service. By autumn Chamberlain was ready to attempt his last desperate throw of the dice in favor of appeasement. He undertook an air trip to Godesberg and then to Munich, to discuss a stabilization of events with the German Fuehrer. Finally he signed an agreement in the Bavarian capital. He returned to London, stepped from his airplane, firmly clasping his symbolic umbrella, at the Croydon airport, and delivered a message to the British public, which included the following:

"For the second time in our history a British Prime Minister has returned from Germany bringing peace with honor. . . . I believe it is peace for our time. . . . The settlement of the Czechoslovak problem, which has now been achieved, is only the prelude to a larger settlement in which all Europe may find peace."

Sad and sullen Czechs, watching Nazi troops marching down the streets of Prague to give the final *coup de grâce* to the Versailles-born republic, asked themselves what kind of a peace all Europe would find if this was a sample.

CHAPTER XIX

Champion of Democracy

Europe had been closer to war than most of its inhabitants had realized, and the first reaction to the Munich Agreement was one of unutterable relief. This was especially true among the population of Germany, according to the burden of reports from American news correspondents who were still permitted to travel fairly freely about the country. The people of France and Great Britain, after a few shamefaced regrets that Czechoslovakia had had to be sacrificed on the altar of Nazi aggression to purchase peace for the rest of the world, thanked their stars that war had not been forced upon them and turned to their usual way of life.

Strangely enough, the speediest condemnation of Chamberlain's temporizing came from critics in the United States. These attacks provoked bitter comment in London, especially among the functionaries of Whitehall, who wanted to know (and not without reason) by what right the United States was criticizing a decision not to go to war after it had spent the better part of three years impressing on the British that they could expect no help from across the Atlantic if they got into an armed conflict. As is so often the case in these family disputes, both sides were right.

The Secretary of State, having watched the European situation cook up steadily for nearly ten years, knew the Munich

Agreement was no good. During the crisis of the summer of 1938 he had been particularly well informed. He was guided by able reports from Ambassador Bullitt in Paris, from Ambassador Biddle in Warsaw (the Polish capital had been an excellent listening post for diplomatic and political gossip ever since the World War), from Minister Carr in Prague, and from Ambassador Kennedy in London. Not only did Mr. Kennedy have, at that time, the inner ear of the British Cabinet but he was also on close terms with Jan Masaryk, son of the venerable first President of Czechoslovakia, who, happily, did not live to see his country's downfall. Jan Masaryk was Czech Minister in London and had even wider and more intimate governmental connections than did Mr. Kennedy.

Dubious as he was at the alleged settlement Chamberlain and Hitler had reached at Munich, Hull felt he could not publicly express any criticism. He managed to convey an accurate picture of his inner feelings, however, by the carefully guarded language in which he phrased his public comment. It is recommended to the casual reader that he study Hull's public statements carefully if he wants to divine what is really on the Secretary's mind. He will usually discover this by what is omitted rather than by what is said.

"As to immediate peace results, it is unnecessary to say that they afford a universal sense of relief," Hull stated on September 30. "I am not undertaking to pass upon the merits of the differences to which the four-power pact signed at Munich yesterday related. It is hoped that in any event the forces which stand for the principles governing peaceful and orderly international relations and their proper application should not relax but redouble their efforts to maintain these principles of order under law, resting on a sound economic foundation."

In his own office he set his subordinates to working feverishly at all sorts of projects, on the theory that the Munich Agreement would be nothing but the temporary truce it turned out to be. He was especially desirous that the forthcoming Pan-American Conference, to meet at Lima within a month, should set up some concrete system of mutual protection for the twenty-one republics against the general war which he now regarded as well-nigh inevitable, and he knew it would be a hard job to get this done.

He sailed with his delegation on November 25, bound for the Peruvian capital with the most definite project, and the most inflexible determination to put it across, that he had yet carried into Latin America. He felt that the time for polite diplomatic fencing and evasion was long past and that only plain talking and clear thinking could save the New World from the abyss into which the Old World was rushing.

President Roosevelt had selected a strong list of delegates in the main, and the composition of the delegation appeared to please Hull. The President's most spectacular appointment was that of Alf M Landon, the Republican ex-governor of Kansas whom he had defeated for the presidency two years earlier. Governor Landon fell in with the plan with good grace and even managed to laugh at his friends' references to captive kings at a Roman emperor's chariot wheel.

The object of the electoral victor and victim was to make a showing of national unity before the whole world but especially to impress on the Latin Americans that presidential campaigns need not necessarily end up in shootings, as they are so apt to do south of the Rio Grande. Governor Landon carried his full weight of the delegation's routine work and delivered his *pièce de résistance* effectively. This took the form of a prepared speech, given from the floor of the conference, to the effect that the Good Neighbor policy for Latin America would be continued whether a Democrat or a Republican occupied the White House in Washington. Much of the Latin-American frigidity toward that Rooseveltian doctrine had sprung from the suspicion that a turn of the North American electoral wheel which would reseat a Republican at 1600 Pennsylvania Avenue would bring a recurrence of the "dollar diplomacy" practiced by the late Calvin Coolidge.

Landon was quite sincere. Like many Mid-Western isolationists, he had strong mental reservations about Latin America. Men like Senators Borah, Johnson of California, and Vandenberg share this willingness to except the other American republics from their general condemnation of having anything to do with the rest of the world. They looked on this breach in their political ramparts as a logical consequence of the Monroe Doctrine, to which they all subscribed, as they interpreted it. At Lima, Landon's straightforward exposition of his thesis impressed the Latin-

American delegates and was a factor in the success of the conference.

Laurence A. Steinhardt, the United States Ambassador to Peru, was named a delegate and proved to be helpful. Adolf A. Berle, Jr., Assistant Secretary of State, bore the brunt of the negotiations with the other delegations. R. Henry Norweb, United States Minister to the Dominican Republic and a veteran of the Montevideo and Buenos Aires conferences, handled the lesser lights among the Latin Americans and aided his fellow delegates as interpreter. Reverend John F. O'Hara, of Notre Dame University, who speaks Spanish fluently and who spent some years of his early life as a Jesuit missionary in Paraguay, lent the proper Catholic tone needed to reassure the conservative delegates. Kathryn Lewis, daughter of the then president of the CIO, and Dan W. Tracy, of the Electrical Workers Union, who later became Assistant Secretary of Labor, represented the workers of the United States. Green H. Hackworth, State Department legal adviser, and Dr. Charles G. Fenwick, of Bryn Mawr College, looked after questions of international law, and Mrs. Elise F. Musser, a repeater from the Buenos Aires conclave, was the feminist representative.

When the conference got under way, after its formal opening on December 9, 1938, Hull spared himself much of the routine spadework he had performed in Montevideo and Buenos Aires. He spent most of his time in conferences behind the scenes with heads of delegations, seeking to impress on them the urgency of the world situation. He found among the Latin-American delegates the same unwillingness to face facts that distinguished so many of his own countrymen at home.

While there were as many shades of opinions among the Latin-American delegates as would be expected from any representative number of men and women, the school of thought which hesitated at positive action was actuated by a number of understandable considerations. These fell into the following categories:

1. The Western Hemisphere would be well advised to avoid commitments on one side or the other in the event of a European war until it was reasonably clear which faction would be victorious.

2. The southernmost countries of the hemisphere would al-

ways be compelled to jump on any European band wagon because other economies were wholly dependent on European markets and they could never afford to offend a possible customer in Europe.

3. A world revolution toward authoritarianism was under way, and the establishment of the Franco government in Spain, which the United States was even then preparing to recognize, was the first clear indication of a universal trend. The Western Hemisphere must not make the mistake of swimming against an irresistible tide.

4. The racial, cultural, and political gulf between North and South America was too great ever to permit common action, because common motives and aspirations were lacking.

5. There was no real danger of war in Europe. Those who took the other point of view were mere hysterical alarmists.

6. If war should come, it would be swiftly settled and the Americas could profit only by the expanded markets for their raw materials. The peoples of Europe would not stand for a long, devastating conflict.

7. The Latin-American republics could expect no effective aid, economic or military, from the United States if they should decide to enter a "neutrality bloc," which was what Hull was urging.

Hull understood the superficial plausibility of these varying arguments to those who advanced them. He had heard the same line of reasoning pursued in the United States, in Great Britain, in France, in The Netherlands, and in Belgium. He set about patiently to persuade the key delegates against endorsing any of these shortsighted viewpoints, backing his private arguments with facts and predictions that must now sound overwhelmingly impressive to those who heard them at that time.

After a few minor misadventures with the Argentine delegation[1] he was able to bring the conference around to his program.

[1] Dr. José Maria Cantilo, the Argentine Foreign Minister, arrived at Lima as an "observer" and not as a delegate. He journeyed to Callao on a resplendent new Italian-built cruiser which was the pride of the Argentine navy. After listening courteously to everything Hull and the other principal delegates had to tell him, and apparently agreeing in principle with what they had in view, he sailed away on his battleship.

After he had gone it turned out that he had instructed the Argentine

He secured reaffirmation of the Buenos Aires principle that a threat to the security of any American republic would be considered a threat to the security of them all, and this was buttressed by a declaration that a threat of war anywhere in the world would be the instant occasion for a consultation between the foreign ministers of the twenty-one republics. The machinery of an effective Pan-Americanism was set up for the first time.

The deliberations of the conference were followed with closer attention by the foreign offices of Europe than they were in the Americas. The British were planning to secure their food and munitions from Argentina, in the event war should break out and the United States should stick to its course of selling arms to no belligerent. It was planned to build huge munitions and airplane factories at the far end of South America, where it was assumed they would be safe from German bombardment as long as the Royal Navy could rule the Atlantic. The Germans had the opposite interest in the matter, for they hoped that the Latin-American countries would follow the lead of the United States and cut down their trade with all belligerents. The Germans were under no illusion that the British navy would let them get any supplies from overseas, and they wanted to cut down their prospective opponent in the same respect.

For the lines of the war to come were already clearly drawn. Not a delegate at Lima had any doubt that, if war came, Germany would be on one side and Great Britain on the other. The same easy clairvoyance was prevalent in Congress when Hull got back to Washington from the Pan-American Conference and found Capitol Hill about to immerse itself in one of its perpetually periodic debates on "neutrality" legislation.

Owing to a lucky fluke the Neutrality Act was due to come up for reconsideration in 1939 because Representative James Shanley, an isolationist Democrat from Connecticut, had insisted on writing into the 1937 version of the law a limitation of two years on the "cash-and-carry" clause, which he did not favor. The ad-

delegation to agree to nothing without consulting him on the exact text. When the texts of the important instruments were ready everyone subscribed except the Argentines. They had to confess that they could not find their Foreign Minister, who had left the cruiser at Santiago de Chile to take a rest in the Patagonian desert, leaving no forwarding address. It took three days to reach him by telephone, read him the texts, and secure his approval.

ministration, willing at last to face the fact that any further continuance of the automatic arms embargo could serve no immediate purpose except to encourage Germany to precipitate a
general war, decided to take advantage of the automatic review
of the legislation to secure repeal of its most objectionable feature.

Senator Key Pittman again told Hull that the isolationists
were very strong in the Senate and that the desired goal could
be achieved only by stratagem. He suggested that the "cash-and-
carry" principle be extended to cover all commerce with belligerents—trade in arms and munitions as well as wheat and cotton. His political judgment, which appealed to Hull, was that
the administration forces could offer a new bill along these lines,
worded so that no member of Congress would have to vote
directly to repeal the arms embargo.

Once the bill was introduced, however, Pittman found the
going heavier than he had expected. There was violent opposition
in his own committee—the Committee on Foreign Relations. The
isolationists on that committee had been augmented by the addition of Senator Bennett Champ Clark of Missouri, who was
useful not only as another vote but as an adroit parliamentarian
and floor debater. The administration did not want him on the
committee, but the Senate stuck to its tradition of seniority in
awarding him the existing vacancy.

As the session wore on, Pittman became less and less sure of
himself and finally advised that the initial assault be attempted
in the House. On that side of the Capitol the veteran McReynolds
of Tennessee had died and had been succeeded as chairman of the
Foreign Affairs Committee by Representative Sol Bloom of New
York, a jovial Tammany Democrat who had "gone along" with
most of the New Deal and who was a complete partisan of the
Roosevelt foreign policy. Bloom canvassed the situation and reported that he could get the bill through the House.

Discussion was bitter during the committee hearings and, later,
on the House floor. The isolationists were led by Representative
Hamilton Fish, the New York Republican who represented President Roosevelt's Congressional district and who was ranking
minority member of the Foreign Affairs Committee. Mr. Fish
set the keynote for as violent a campaign of partisan bias as has
ever been directed against an administration proposal in the field

of foreign relations, where politics are supposed to be set aside. He found ready supporters among the professional Irish members, the corn-belt isolationists, and the semilunatic fringe of the New Dealers who wanted to put through their domestic utopia before peering into the outer world.

Mr. Fish and his cohorts charged that President Roosevelt wanted to involve the nation in war so as to cover up the failure of the New Deal; that the Chief Executive was a willing tool for the sinister British who wanted the United States once again to save their Empire at its own expense; that Germany was only trying to rectify justifiable grievances springing from the injustices of Versailles; and, most of all, that there wasn't going to be any war anyway. Time after time Mr. Fish got the floor of the House on one parliamentary pretext or another to declaim that the whole war scare was being cooked up by Roosevelt to distract attention from domestic difficulties.[2]

The result of these tactics was a parliamentary frustration which must have delighted the hearts of Adolf Hitler and the other mortal enemies of democracy. Mr. Fish's first lieutenant in the fight, Representative Vorys of Ohio, offered an amendment to the administration bill restoring the arms embargo. Due to lax management on the part of Representative Boland of Pennsylvania, the Democratic whip, this amendment was adopted by a margin of two votes while there were half-a-dozen administration votes in the House restaurant and others were sitting in the galleries with visitors from their home towns.

[2]These positive assertions by Mr. Fish had their amusing sequel—amusing because it came too late in the tragic rush of events to matter. In the summer of 1939, after the adjournment of Congress, he headed the American delegation to the meeting of the Inter-Parliamentary Union at Oslo. En route he stopped a few days in Berlin and was honored, as he no doubt felt at the time, by an interview with Joachim von Ribbentrop, the Nazi Foreign Minister He came away from this talk pale and shaken, issuing public statements to anybody who would listen (and put it on the press wires) to the effect that war was about to break out and calling on the civilized world to prevent it. He wanted the Inter-Parliamentary Union, a harmless body which devotes its time to discussing whether a motion to take up the previous question precludes amendments in the second degree and such important issues, to summon an immediate world peace conference. The self-assured prophet of June forgot in August about the "Roosevelt red herring," as he had described the proposal to repeal the arms embargo, the moment he had the time and the opportunity to face the slightest touch of reality.

The Vorys Amendment was adopted during the second reading of the bill, which is the stage where the House sits as the Committee of the Whole and where no record votes are taken. Had Boland produced three of the many administration supporters who were idling about, not realizing how serious the floor situation was, that would have been the end of the matter. The amendment could not again have been offered. As it was, Bloom demanded a roll call on the amendment during the third and final reading but was beaten by a substantial majority because many feeble members felt they could not be on record as opposing the arms embargo.

The result of the House's deliberations left the administration worse off than it had been when the 1939 "neutrality" debates began. The bill the House had passed contained the arms embargo and, in addition, a number of provisions which had been written in as bait for the isolationists. The principal one of these was the power to the President to define combat areas into which American vessels could not proceed.

By this time Congress wanted to adjourn. President Roosevelt and Secretary Hull were practically certain that war would break out in Europe before Congress would meet again the following January, and they were anxious to rectify the anomalous legislative situation produced by the revolt in the supposedly safe House. In desperation the President summoned a bipartisan legislative conference to meet at the White House and asked the Secretary of State to outline the gravity of world conditions.

Hull explained at length the purport of the reports he was receiving from his diplomatic sources. He tried to demonstrate to his erstwhile Congressional colleagues how the status of the country's foreign policy, if left up in the air as it was at that moment, could only act as one more factor urging Germany to start war at once, before Congress might change its mind again. He felt he was making little headway, and his manner faltered toward the end of his presentation, according to some who attended that fateful gathering, and he knew his plans had received the *coup de grâce* when Senator Borah announced flatly and finally that he knew there would be no war—that he had sources of information which were more reliable than those of the State Department.

It developed after his death that Senator Borah's source for this extraordinary prediction was a planographed left-wing magazine called *The Week,* published by Claude Coburn in London. Anyone in the United States who cared to do so could have subscribed to it for a few dollars a year. Mr. Borah was one of its few American subscribers.

At the time, however, the effect of the Idaho Sage's pronouncement was enough to doom efforts at repealing the arms embargo. Word of it was permitted to slip out discreetly (the White House meeting was supposed to be completely secret and off the record) by isolationists who preferred to believe he was right. Congress adjourned without the Senate considering the neutrality bill. The President and his Secretary of State were left in the position of having been roundly repudiated by Congress on a matter of the highest foreign policy.

In Europe the situation was already desperate, as Hull knew. Mr. Borah's information from *The Week* was not good this time, although that publication has been known to scoop its more conservative rivals on occasion. This was not one of the occasions.

The Polish situation was coming rapidly to its fatal boil. The Nazis had rested long enough after their bloodless conquests of Austria and Czechoslovakia. The timetable called for another move. This time, however, they would have to fight for it. No one in Washington's inner circles was in any doubt that Poland would fight if the Nazis seized Danzig by force. Count Jerzy Potocki, the handsome, cultivated Polish Ambassador whom the public considered merely an agreeable playboy, convinced Hull and everyone else to whom he talked, by the quiet, determined manner in which he insisted, that Poland would stage no bloodless surrender.

All the ostriches of international politics were not in Washington, however. In London the House of Commons voted itself a two-month recess in August, over the vigorous protests of Winston Churchill. A British mission was in Moscow belatedly trying to woo the Soviet Union away from Nazi blandishments.

The lightning struck midmonth, when it was announced that Von Ribbentrop would go to Moscow to sign a non-aggression pact between Germany and the Soviet Union, guaranteeing peace between them for ten years. The pact was actually signed on

August 23, and still Whitehall could hardly believe it. As a matter of fact, it came as a stunning surprise to almost the entire diplomatic world. On the day the first announcement was made I happened to go into the State Department and encountered Count Robert van der Straten-Ponthoz, the Belgian Ambassador, who was waiting to see Secretary Hull. I asked him what he made of the strange development, only to learn that he had not yet heard of it.

"Mon Dieu, c'est le coup de grâce," he exclaimed, pale with emotion, and rushed back to his chancery to cable Brussels without waiting to see the Secretary of State.

His forebodings, of course, were only too well founded. At dawn on September 1 Hitler ordered his armies into Poland. Great Britain declared war on Germany September 3 and France reluctantly followed suit. The most terrible military conflict of history was launched.

President Roosevelt waited until September 5 to proclaim the neutrality of the United States. He sought Hull's advice, as well as the counsel of Secretary of the Treasury Morgenthau and other trusted advisers, in framing its language. Where President Wilson, in 1914, had commanded his fellow citizens to be neutral in thought as well as in deed, President Roosevelt contented himself in 1939 with ordaining the customary admonitions to all Americans "without interfering with the free expression of opinion and sympathy." He summoned Congress to meet on September 21 to repeal the arms embargo and he dispatched Sumner Welles, the Undersecretary of State, to represent the United States at the Consultative Meeting of Pan-American Foreign Ministers which was convoked, under the terms of the Declaration of Lima, to meet at Panama City on September 22.

Hull sent his able lieutenant to Panama with two main projects to execute, and Welles accomplished them both with a minimum of fuss and feathers. The first was the "neutrality zone" proclaimed by the twenty-one republics to extend far enough into both oceans to cover the steamship lanes normally used in commerce between themselves. In this zone the warring nations were commanded to commit no acts of belligerency. The second North American contribution to the emergency was the establishment of a permanent economic committee to sit in Washington for the duration of the war to study means of cushioning its impact on the New World. This organization already has several concrete achievements to its credit.

While these further steps in Pan-Americanism were being decided at Panama, amid a storm of Nazi propaganda[3] directed by the German diplomatic establishment in Latin America, Congress was having little difficulty in Washington in repealing the arms embargo which had given it so much trouble only three months earlier. The arguments of the isolationists, which should have presented themselves in redoubled strength now that the actual test of a general war had arrived, appeared to have lost their savor to a majority of the members of Congress. At last a goodly number, more than half of them, began to see dimly that there was a great evil force loose in the world and that the United States must take some kind of a stand against it—a doctrine that Hull had preached vainly to them for ten years.

Despite certain efforts of the administration to prove its neutrality in the early days of the war, such as Hull's repeated protests to the British government over the search of American air mails at Bermuda, where the Pan-American clippers of those days had to stop for fuel, the isolationists were convinced that official American policy would be overweighted on the side of Great Britain and whatever allies she had. To them such a policy could only get the United States into trouble and might result in actual involvement in the war. Far better, they argued, would it be for the United States to take no official interest in the outcome of the European war, even if this meant assuring a Nazi victory (which, even then, they protested was the last thing in the world they wanted to see—many of them were professional liberals who could not dare appear to condone a totalitarian regime), because this course would minimize the risk of war involvement.

The war across the Atlantic had entered the "phony stage," which did so much to mislead public opinion in the United States, France, and Great Britain. Nothing very dreadful was happening in the early months of 1940 except that it looked as

[3]Otto Reinebeck, the German Minister to all the Central American countries, moved his headquarters to Panama during the consultation and called in from other parts of Latin America some of the brightest young Nazi diplomats to help him. Most of them spoke English perfectly.

The Secretary and Mrs Hull with George Messersmith,
United States Ambassador to Cuba. Arriving at the
Cuban Capitol

if President Roosevelt might run for a third term. By February, John L. Lewis, who had engineered a contribution of $500,000 from the United Mine Workers for the second Roosevelt campaign, had decided to come out against him on the foreign issue. He joined the chorus of those who predicted that Roosevelt was leading the country straight to war.

President Roosevelt sent Sumner Welles to Europe for a quick tour of the belligerent capitals. The purpose and results of this mission were never clearly disclosed, but it was presumed that the President and the Secretary of State wanted an independent estimate of the political aspects of the war at that stage. At any rate, Hull soon afterward put out feelers to the neutral governments to see what part they would take in attempting to bring about an end to the war and in insisting on bases for a durable peace. He announced in March that fifty-five governments had responded to his inquiries, but the matter died at that point.

The isolationists, including Senator Wheeler, began to charge that the President and his Secretary of State had spurred on the governments of Poland, Great Britain, and France to declare war on Germany with promises that the United States would come to their aid as it had in 1917. Hull took this report seriously enough to issue an official denial and to forbid Ambassador Bullitt to appear before any Congressional committee seeking to air this charge. It may have been just a coincidence, but the source of this report was a German white paper purporting to quote documents captured at Warsaw.

In May, after the "phony" stage of the war had ended, Hull modified the regulations issued under the Neutrality Act sufficiently to permit American pilots to ferry American-built airplanes from the factories to the Canadian airports whence they would be flown to England. Up to this point a legal hocus-pocus had been required under which the American pilots could fly the planes to a border airport, taxi them to within a yard of the invisible boundary line, and then hitch up a team of horses to drag them that magical yard. This sort of undignified subterfuge finally became too much for the American sense of humor, and Hull wisely decided to regularize what was obviously the intent of the majority.

This step, coupled with the imminence of the presidential

campaign, seems to have started Colonel Charles A. Lindbergh on his oratorical crusade against any action by the United States to prevent a German victory. By this time the Germans were massing for the march through the Low Countries that culminated in the downfall of France and the miracle of Dunkirk. The rapid spread of the tragedy, added to Italy's tragicomic hasty entry into the war a few days before the French capitulation, in anxiety lest she miss the spoils, had a profound effect on American public opinion and led to President Roosevelt's renomination and easy re-election.

In June, however, before the Republican convention met to nominate Wendell L. Willkie to "meet the champion," as the Republican candidate described the electoral encounter, there was the usual political jockeying within the ranks of both parties by professional henchmen who carried on just as if there were to be two normal party conventions, to be followed by a normal electoral campaign. A good many of the "stop-Roosevelt" Democrats had their eye on Hull as their man. A few state legislatures had endorsed him and he had quite a following in Congress. His backers hoped to get him actively committed to a race for the nomination during the long period when President Roosevelt preserved his oracular silence concerning his own intentions.

This wing of the Democratic party was politically wise. Looking back on the situation from this distance, it is easy to see that Roosevelt could not have been stopped. At that time, however, there is no denying that Hull was the man to stop him, if such a man existed in the country. Of all the outstanding figures of the previous eight years Hull had preserved the admiration and confidence of the public more than any one of them—the President not excluded. The cumulative effect of his forceful but not arrogant dealing with foreign aggressors, his patient but not defeatist advocacy of long-term common sense, and the undeviating consistency of his actions and opinions had been enormous. Lifelong political opponents in the Republican party conceded that they would not be uneasy about the nation's foreign relations with Cordell Hull in the White House.

Gratifying as these assurances of esteem and support must have been to the Secretary of State (for all the apparent distantness of his manner, no man warms more to a sincerely kind word than Hull), he was definitely not interested. His determination of nearly three years' standing to remove himself from the theater of partisan politics was stronger than ever. However, he found himself in an embarrassing position. He could not very well decline publicly the approaches that were put forward to him without appearing to give himself too much importance, but he left no doubt in the minds of those with whom he discussed the subject privately. Finally, on July 15, just before the Democratic convention was to meet, Hull felt able to issue a statement eliminating himself from the contest.

This did not end his difficulties, however. As soon as President Roosevelt decided he would accept the nomination which would obviously be his for the asking, he tried to persuade Hull to accept the nomination for the vice-presidency. All political wiseacres were agreed that this would be a strong combination for the Democrats to offer in opposition to Willkie and McNary.

Like Caesar, Hull thrice declined the crown, although with considerably more sincerity than his Roman predecessor. On the last occasion the President telephoned the Secretary at his apartment at the Carlton Hotel and went over all the arguments again. Hull was as politely adamant as he had been right along. Finally the Chief Executive attempted one of his charming gestures with which he has so often been able to beat down a friendly opponent.

"Let me speak to Mrs. Hull," he demanded. "She will listen to sense."

The lady was sitting a few feet away from the telephone, placidly reading while her husband engaged in this momentous discussion.

"I am sorry, Mr. President," Hull answered. "My wife has a bad headache and has gone to bed."

Soon after the Democratic convention Hull called the second Consultative Meeting of Pan-American Foreign Ministers to meet in Havana on July 21 and decided to attend it himself. The machinery of the call went out from the Pan-American Union, according to protocol, but the initiative was Hull's. He felt that the American republics must take joint action to protect themselves against the Western Hemisphere implications of the conquest of France and the likelihood of a collaborationist government developing there to aid the Germans.

Things went smoothly at Havana, for Hull was sure of himself. He was certain that Roosevelt would be re-elected, that the re-election would constitute an overwhelming endorsement of the administration's foreign policy, and that he himself was committed for the duration of the crisis. All ideas of retirement, such as his wife had been urging on him of late, had completely vanished. He saw the country's problems clearly and he believed he saw the answers.

The Secretary came back from Havana with everything he wanted. The other twenty republics had agreed to a machinery for occupying such Western Hemisphere possessions of conquered European countries as Martinique, the French base in the Caribbean. The occupation, to be sure, was to be made only when any other European power attempted to assert title to such possessions, but, if it came, the step would be a joint one and not merely a unilateral action of the United States which could be magnified by German propaganda in Latin America as "Yankee imperialism." The republics likewise pledged themselves to put a stop to subversive activities by foreign agents in their borders. In return Hull promised substantial economic aid for them all from the United States—a step which this country would have had to take in any event in its own interest.

Hull had already come to the belief that all-out aid to Great Britain would be the surest way to keep the United States out of war. He had no quarrel with the isolationists in their desire to keep the United States from the miseries of military conflict. He differed with them only on the best means to assure this mutually desired result. He felt that he had in his favor the fact that the firm policy he advocated had kept him out of shooting scrapes when he practiced it in his own life riding the circuit in the mountains of Tennessee.

Thus he favored the exchange of fifty American destroyers for the right to construct naval and air bases on British possessions in the Western Hemisphere, and he did not question the political advisability of taking the step in the midst of a presidential campaign. The hesitancies and accommodations which

Secretary Hull Greets Franklin Roosevelt on the President's
Return from the Sea Conference with Prime Minister
Churchill, August 18, 1941

had characterized his thinking during the early "neutrality" debates in Congress were gone. He made two strong and effective speeches advocating Roosevelt's re-election just before the ballots were cast but took little part in the day-to-day campaigning.

Just after Mr. Roosevelt had been named the first American to serve three terms as President, Hull welcomed Admiral Nomura to Washington as the new Japanese Ambassador. Hull and his Far Eastern adviser, Stanley Hornbeck, had not allowed the European debacle to distract their attention from Japan. The Japanese had already established bases in Indo-China, by pressure on the ghost government of Vichy, and were eying Thailand. This could only mean further movement toward the south, including the possible encirclement and reduction by land of Singapore and the conquest of the Netherlands Indies.

The vital interests of the United States in a development of this kind were better understood by the public than the probably more dangerous implications of a Nazi victory in Europe. Even Senators Nye and Wheeler could grasp the inconvenience the United States would suffer if its principal sources of supply of such things as rubber and tin and quinine (the Malay Peninsula) fell into the hands of a militaristic regime in Tokyo.

Hull declined to be stampeded into precipitate action. He believed that war with Japan would serve Hitler's purpose better than any other course the United States could follow, and he believed that war with Japan could be avoided without material loss to this country. The moral embargo on shipments of high-octane aviation gasoline to Japan was already in effect and had worked fairly well. Hull and Hornbeck convinced the President that a gradual tightening of the economic noose, accompanied by periodic proffers of the hand of friendship if Tokyo would mend its ways, would eventually carry the day without the desperate adventure of war. Admiral Nomura was to play an important part in the working out of this policy.

The new Congress, when it met at the beginning of 1941, was badly confused. Its members could not make up their minds whether the voters had or had not endorsed President Roosevelt's foreign policy by electing him for a third time and by returning a Democratic Senate and House. This indecision was immediately displayed in the interminable debates which preceded the final passage of the Lease-Lend Act. Hull whole-heartedly favored this legislation.

The same indecision marked the attitude of Congress in relation to the administration's recommendation that the training period for the army selectees be extended beyond the original year's time which had been approved a year before in the first peacetime conscription the United States had ever attempted. The extension bill passed the House of Representatives by 203 to 202. In all of these vital steps for the protection of the United States the Republican members of Congress voted overwhelmingly against the administration, confirming Hull's opinion that the utility of partisan politics had temporarily disappeared. The questions at stake were such that no disinterested division of opinion could possibly have produced such a preponderance of Republican "noes."

Hull's personal reaction to these manifestations of the democratic process was anything but discouragement. To him the presence of these weaknesses in a democratic country did not betoken, as the authoritarians would have us believe, inherently fatal defects in the democratic system. The superficial vulnerability of shortsighted individuals did not augur the doom of the country. He fell back on his proven doctrine that consistent pursuit of the great ideals common to all men will prevail in the long run. He is as much of a Jeffersonian Democrat today as he was when he ran for the Tennessee legislature half a century ago.

CHAPTER XX

Appeal to the Sword

THE INHERENT ANTIPATHY between totalitarianism and democracy, which Cordell Hull had understood so well and against which he had warned so often, finally brought war to the United States. The vaporings of the isolationists, appeasers, and Axis sympathizers, which had contributed no little to the crisis the nation confronted, disappeared like a morning ground mist under the rays of a strong sun. The Japanese bombers at Pearl Harbor brought home to the entire population of the country the fact that the things for which Cordell Hull stood were very precious —and that we would have to fight to keep them.

The Germans, the Italians, the Bulgarians, the Hungarians, and the rest followed their oriental partner and, at last, the entire world was at war. This final step toward the agony of a defeat from which it will take them generations to recover was their reward for persistently ignoring the kindly, patient counsels of the American Secretary of State. They had mistaken his kindness and his patience for weakness—an error committed a few times previously by individuals whose fate should have warned the Axis diplomats, if they had taken the trouble to investigate Hull's earlier life.

For his own part, he emerged at once as the strongest figure of the Cabinet. A Secretary of State, in time of war, is supposed to take a back seat and wait the restoration of peace to resume his diplomatic trade, but no such role could conceivably be assigned to the veteran fighter from Tennessee. The armed interlude, to him, was a difficult period to be nursed and surmounted, like a setback in an illness, in the inevitable progress of the world to the permanent peace and happiness he could see so well in the future.

Hull by no means underestimated the perils to come in the immediate future. He had spent too many years of careful calculation of the stresses and strains another world war would impose on the fabric of his own country and of the world to fall into the easy jingoism with which many of us disguised our concern for the future. Underneath his preoccupation with the military problem at hand and his stern resolve to see the war through to a definitive conclusion, however, lay a profound confidence that the cause he had championed for half a century was destined to survive against all odds.

The Secretary's outburst of indignation at the diplomatic sophistries the civil government of Japan presented in its note at the very moment the military rulers were ordering the attack on Hawaii was characteristic of him. He believes in straight dealing, and he thought that the Japanese diplomats should have told him and the United States frankly that they and their superiors in Tokyo had failed in their attempts to shape their country's path toward peace. Their insistence on carrying the farce beyond all bounds was what infuriated him.

In the first trying weeks following the outbreak of war with the Axis the American public was more preoccupied with the Japanese side of it than with the graver threat of actual war with Germany. There were critics who assailed Hull for the policy of "appeasement," as they called it, which he had pursued toward Japan ever since the Munich Agreement convinced him war in Europe was inevitable.

These observers failed to think their charges through to the logical conclusion. They neglected to take into account the situation that would have prevailed if Japan had decided upon its attack two years, or even six months, earlier than it did. The subsequent military developments showed conclusively that the precious time for preparation this country gained by temporizing with Japan was worth hundreds of times as much as the tactical

value of the aviation gasoline, scrap iron, and other war materials
which were permitted to be sold to Japan by American nationals
during those days of doubt.

The policy of not prodding Japan to war was not, however, a
Machiavellian scheme in Hull's mind. He was not deliberately
soft-soaping the Japanese civil government to gain time for the
preparation of a crushing military campaign against their country. He sincerely believed that there was a sporting chance that
the moderate elements in Japan would carry the day and that
the military bullies would be summoned back to their own territory by the emperor. Many of the State Department's greatest
experts in Far Eastern affairs concurred in this belief. Others did
not. There was room for honest difference of opinion, and the
fact that the militarists were finally successful in tipping the
scales their way does not brand the official policy as stupid. It
was an even-money bet—which we lost.

The war with Japan was a disappointment to Hull, while the
outbreak with Germany and Italy was a diplomatic anticlimax.
Hull had thought for years that conflict, either military or economic, was inevitable with Germany. He had not taken Italy
very seriously but had realized that Mussolini would tend to follow the same road as Hitler. The Japanese situation, however, he
believed was far from hopeless.

When Hull took over his desk at the State Department the
Japanese had only begun their long career of military aggression.
The invasion of the maritime provinces of Manchuria had been
launched by the fanatical leaders of one faction within the
Japanese army, against the wishes—and even the orders—of the
civil government. There was every probability that the incident,
although then some three years old, would prove in the long
run to be a flare-up of the inexplicable oriental kind with which
Japan's history is dotted. At that period Hull and his aides used
to reply uniformly to all queries about the possibility of trouble
between the United States and Japan about as follows: "There
are no differences between the two governments which cannot be
solved by ordinary diplomatic methods."

Beginning with 1934, however, the Secretary of State started to
work in real earnest on the ambassadors Tokyo sent to Washington. He lost no opportunity to impress on them his conviction

that the United States and Japan had less cause for war than almost any two major powers in the world. He sought to enlist Japan's aid in re-establishing a world order based on political and economic peace, with all international disputes to be settled by rational discussion instead of shooting.

Unfortunately these envoys tended to fall out of favor at home the longer they stayed in Washington. Whatever advice they were sending to Tokyo had to be judged, on receipt, against the kaleidoscopic background of the repeated political shifts in Japan. A cabinet of jingoes would be succeeded by a cabinet of moderates. The moderates would be thrown out by the militarists. The emperor's mystic status, while ostensibly preserved in all its religious significance, constantly tended toward that of the figurehead which King Victor Emmanuel became in Italy. The politicians, who generally favored peace, found themselves ranged against the army and the navy, who wanted war.

By 1937, when the Japanese army moved into China proper and began the occupation of the coastal area, many of our Far Eastern experts lost hope—but not Hull. He redoubled his efforts to convey, through the ambassador, his own and the American conception of the folly of the Japanese course. He hammered home his advice to Japan to follow the road of order under law, rather than the policy of brute force.

The soundness of his advice, from Japan's viewpoint, was not apparent at first. The Chinese, torn by inner division, were unable to offer the magnificent resistance they were to put up later, under the leadership of Marshal Chiang Kai-shek. The Japanese war lords were able to laugh out of court the words of caution offered by the civilian members of the cabinet, most of whom would have preferred to follow Hull's course.

In Washington, Hull came under fire from the guns of the Chinese sympathizers. Missionaries who had been ejected from China came home and addressed religious organizations on the misdoings of the heathen Japanese. Leftish liberals, most of whom also condemned the State Department's policy toward Republican Spain, called for economic sanctions to bring Japan to its knees. Finally Key Pittman, chairman of the Senate Foreign Relations Committee, introduced a resolution calling for a total embargo of exports to Japan. While the measure was never allowed to come to the floor of the Senate, it was a symptom of the growing public impatience with Japan.

All this time Hull was studying the problem from the point of view of long-range policy in Asia. He was convinced that no good would be accomplished by the precipitation of war in the East, especially since the British government could be counted upon for little support if things came to the worst. In any event none of the ideas Hull had in mind would have been served by war, and his entire efforts were bent toward preventing the outbreak of armed hostilities.

The pursuit of this policy involved a difficult job of tightrope walking. The United States had to combine a firm show against Japanese aggression, designed to encourage the liberals and to intimidate the militarists, with a show of cooperation (the avoidance of an economic embargo, for example), so that the militarists would be unable to point to the fatal intransigeance of Washington.

Strictly speaking, this was not a policy of "appeasement," in the sense that the Chamberlain policy toward Germany deserved that term, for it involved no hint of concession on the part of the United States. Great Britain was willing to make any concession within reason to avoid war with Germany. The United States, under Hull's policy, did not intend to concede anything to Japan, for there was nothing to concede, but only wanted to encourage those elements in Japan which were trying to pursue the same path toward permanent peace which this country was trying to follow.

When Japan formally adhered to the Axis in 1940 it became evident that the hope of liberal domination in Japan was fading, and Hull yielded on the question of imposing economic sanctions against Japan. Even then a ray of hope lit up the somber sky with the appointment of Prince Konoye as Japanese premier. Hull was encouraged to recommence his talks, and Tokyo sent Admiral Nomura to Washington as ambassador. The admiral had known President Roosevelt during the World War, he had a wide acquaintance among American naval officers, and his selection appeared to indicate a real desire on the part of the Japanese government to reach an amicable understanding.

The admiral, when it came to talking business, was rather vague. Apparently his diplomatic instructions in Tokyo had gone no further than commissioning him to tell Honorable United States, as politely as possible, to keep its nose out of Japan's business. However, he managed to do it politely enough to string out the discussions for months. Finally, as President Roosevelt and his Secretary of State recognized the uselessness of further palaver of this sort, Tokyo pulled a second rabbit out of the hat in the person of Mr. Kurusu, who left Japan at about the same time as the supply ships and submarine tenders which were to provision the attack on Pearl Harbor. Kurusu reached Washington the middle of November.

Hull was suspicious by this time and warned military and naval officers time after time, with all the vigor at his command, that the Japanese would probably stage a sudden attack to signalize the end of negotiations. At the same time he worked patiently with the Japanese envoys in the hope of a last-minute change of front in Tokyo. He was well aware of the German pressure that was being brought on Japan to precipitate a crisis and resolved not to help the Hitlerian plot by showing impatience or anger.

On that mild Sunday of December 7, 1941, Admiral Nomura called the State Department at one o'clock in the afternoon, Washington time, and asked for an appointment for him and Mr. Kurusu to present his government's reply to the last American memorandum. The appointment was made for one forty-five, but the Japanese diplomats did not arrive until two-five. In the interval between the request for the appointment and their arrival at the State Department the Japanese planes had bombed Honolulu. Hull received them at two-twenty, still without news that war had actually broken out, and settled himself to read the reply they brought to his memorandum of November 26.

In that document, which had not been made public in order to avoid ruffling Japanese sensibilities, Hull had proposed a sweeping plan to ensure permanent peace in the Pacific. It was to be based on a non-aggression pact to be negotiated among the British Empire, the Soviet Union, The Netherlands, Thailand, China, Japan, and the United States. All of these governments were to respect the territorial integrity of Indo-China. This stipulation was the principal one to concern all the powers. The remainder of the plan was devoted largely to the bargain the United States was willing to strike with Japan.

Japan was to withdraw all military, naval, air, and police forces from China and Indo-China and to recognize the regime of Marshal Chiang Kai-shek at Chungking as the sole government of China. Both the United States and Japan were to renounce whatever vestigial rights they claimed to extraterritoriality and concessions under the Boxer Treaty of 1901 and were to endeavor to persuade the other signatories to do likewise.

These were the contributions Japan was to make. In return the United States was to negotiate a trade treaty restoring full commerce between the two nations and binding silk on the American free list. Since silk has always been the principal Japanese export to the United States, the constant threat that an import duty might be applied to it could otherwise have been held over Japan as a constant bargaining menace. Each nation was to "unfreeze" the funds of the other's nationals. They were to contribute equally to a stabilization fund to fix the relation of the dollar and the yen in the international exchanges.

Most important of all, the proposed agreement would have stipulated that no agreement with any third power was to be interpreted so as to conflict with "the establishment and preservation of peace throughout the Pacific area." This obvious reference to Japan's adherence to the Axis was intended to guarantee that the European war would not spread to the Pacific, if the signatories to the proposed pact were sincere.

As he sat reading in his spacious, high-ceilinged, dimly lighted, old-fashioned office the Secretary of State was not long in doubt as to the tenor of the Japanese reply to this proposal. After a very brief introduction, couched in the painfully polite language of diplomacy, the Japanese note called the United States and Great Britain to task for helping China and for inciting the Netherlands East Indies to resist, mentioning the economic sanctions the United States and Britain had put into effect.

"While manifesting thus an obviously hostile attitude," the note stated, "these countries have strengthened their military preparations perfecting an encirclement of Japan and have brought about a situation which endangers the very existence of the empire." It recalled the magnanimous terms of the Japanese

government's memorandum of November 20 in which it had
been proposed that Japan and the United States agree not to
send any armed forces into any regions of Southeastern Asia or
of the South Pacific area except Indo-China (which Japan had already occupied); that both nations cooperate in securing needed
supplies from the Netherlands East Indies (which meant, in
effect, that the United States would have to agree with Japan
about how much tin and rubber it could import); that the
United States restore commercial relations, including the normal
supply of oil to Japan from this country; and that the United
States agree not to "prejudice" the restoration of peace between
Japan and China, which could only mean that the United States
was to abandon China to Japanese conquest and to the subsequent peace imposed by Tokyo.

The Japanese government expressed its regret that these generous proposals had been rejected and said that "the American
government, always holding fast to theories in disregard of realities and refusing to yield an inch on its impractical principles,
caused undue delay in the negotiations," adding that "in view
of the world's actual condition it seems only a utopian ideal on
the part of the American government to attempt to force their
immediate adoption." The last observation referred to the American insistence on pacific settlement of disputes and was a direct
dig at Hull, who was the author and father of the American refusal "to yield an inch."

The note went on to say that the non-aggression pact proposed
by the United States was "far removed from the realities of East
Asia." The reason for the alleged far removal, and the source of
inspiration for the whole communication, was revealed when the
Japanese added that they intended to abide strictly by the terms
of the Tripartite Pact with Italy and Germany in the event that
the United States entered the European war.

"The American government, obsessed with its own views and
opinions, may be said to be scheming for the extension of the
war," the Japanese note charged. "While it seeks, on the one
hand, to secure its rear by stabilizing the Pacific area, it is engaged, on the other hand, in aiding Great Britain and preparing
to attack, in the name of self-defense, Germany and Italy, two
powers that are striving to establish a new order in Europe."

Nothing but condemnation was expressed for the economic pressure which, it was charged, the United States was exerting on various countries to curb their legitimate activities, and the unusual theory was advanced that economic pressure is "more inhumane than military pressure." The non-aggression pact which the United States had proposed was summarily rejected because it embodied the allegedly outmoded idea of collective security and resembled the Nine Power Treaty, which was described as "the chief factor responsible for the present predicament of East Asia." This remarkable estimate of the agreement, which Japan freely signed and even more freely violated, must speak for itself. There is no possible explanation which would appeal to the Occidental mind.

"Obviously it is the intention of the American government to conspire with Great Britain and other countries to obstruct Japan's efforts toward the establishment of peace through the creation of a new order in East Asia," the note continued, ending with the observation that the Japanese government considered "it is impossible to reach an agreement through further negotiations."

Even without the other complications of which Secretary Hull and his interviewers were ignorant at that moment, the note would have constituted at least a rupture of diplomatic relations between the two governments and was close to an outright declaration of war. Hull had expected that his previous note would be unacceptable to Tokyo, by reason of the reports he was receiving in regard to the Japanese political situation. He was not prepared, however, for the brusque and fallacious repudiation of all the ostensibly sincere searches for peace on which the Japanese had pretended to embark.

When he had finished reading the note he took off his glasses and turned on Admiral Nomura, with whom he had been negotiating much longer than he had with Kurusu. He was white and tense with that fury for which he is noted when he feels he is being bullied or tricked.

"I must say that in all my conversations with you during the last nine months I have never uttered one word of untruth," he burst out at the admiral. "In all my fifty years of public service I have never seen a document that was more crowded with infamous falsehoods and distortions—infamous falsehoods and distortions on a scale so huge that I never imagined until today that any government on this planet was capable of uttering them."

The Japanese took their leave as best they could, and Hull went to the White House, to receive the news that war had come at last.

The American reaction was automatic. President Roosevelt delivered a brief, almost colorless, war message to Congress the next day, and that body adopted a declaration of war with only one dissenting vote—that of Representative Rankin of Montana, who apparently felt she must uphold her previous record of having voted against the declaration of war against the Imperial German Government in 1917.

Secretary Hull knew that the Germans and the Italians would follow the Japanese lead as a matter of course. He had long realized, and had stated publicly many times, that the conflicts in the East and in the West were part of the same comprehensive movement of world conquest and domination. He had tried the same tactics of persuasion on the German and Italian ambassadors, in the early days, as he had practiced with the Japanese envoys, but he had given up hope much earlier, in the realization that Hitler and Mussolini were hopelessly committed to the imposition of their designs by force. He had openly and repeatedly warned the people of the United States that they could hope for no peace or security in a world where aggressors were running at large.

Ever since the sad spectacle of the Munich Agreement in 1938 Hull had been convinced that, whenever it suited Hitler's purpose, Germany would wage war upon the United States as a part of the general movement of world conquest. Thus he was neither surprised nor especially indignant when he got word that the German Chargé d'Affaires and the Italian ambassador both wanted to see him early on the morning of December 11.

When Dr. Hans Thomsen, the German chargé, called at the State Department at eight-twenty on the morning of December 11 Mr. Hull sent out word that he was otherwise engaged and asked Dr. Thomsen to see Ray Atherton, chief of the European Division, who found time to receive him at nine-thirty. The German representative merely informed Mr. Atherton that his country considered itself at war with the United States and went into a discussion of the minor practical details that accompany such momentous occasions, such as what to do with his embassy staff and similar questions.

Dr. Thomsen knew that his call was purely a formality. An hour earlier Mussolini, speaking from his balcony in Rome, had announced to the usual crowd of Fascists gathered below that Italy and Germany were at war with the United States in defense of Japan. Hitler was speaking to the Reichstag and, as Dr. Thomsen was cooling his heels on Pennsylvania Avenue, was trying to get to the point of his address, which was the declaration of war. All of this was well known throughout the State Department and the nation, for that matter, so that Dr. Thomsen's formal announcement did not create any undue excitement.

When poor Don Ascanio dei principi Colonna, the Italian ambassador, arrived at the State Department at ten-thirty he was without news from home. Like any private citizen in the United States, he had heard the radio announcements that Mussolini had declared war on the United States, but his Foreign Office had not bothered to send him any instructions. He was referred to James Clement Dunn, Political Adviser on European Affairs, in whose office he inquired about the status of himself and his embassy staff, etc. In the course of their routine discussion Mr. Dunn took occasion to inform the ambassador that the American government had long expected Germany to carry out its threat against this hemisphere and that it was fully foreseen that Italy would obediently follow the same course.

As soon as Congress met at noon on the eleventh it found before it a brief request from President Roosevelt that war be declared against Germany and Italy. The two resolutions were adopted without a dissenting vote in either house, Representative Rankin contenting herself this time with voting "present." The President signed the resolutions at three-five and three-six the same afternoon, without ceremony.

Amid the heartaches and disappointments the war's early days brought to Americans there was one uniformly gratifying and cheering turn of events which was especially heartening to Cordell Hull. This was the attitude of the other twenty republics of the Western World. Nine of them declared war on the Axis within a few days of the attack on Pearl Harbor (Costa Rica actually declared war on Japan before the United States did), and the others severed diplomatic relations or took such other dispositions as to establish their intention to adhere to existing solidarity pacts for the defense of the Western Hemisphere.

Here was the final fruition of Hull's painstaking creation of a practical Good Neighbor policy. He laid the cornerstone at Montevideo in 1933 and built it up, brick by brick, through the conferences at Buenos Aires, Lima, and Havana. Even at Montevideo, Secretary Hull had sensed the possibility that one day the whole New World might have to stand together against an attack on the liberty and fundamental philosophy which was the common meeting ground of the nations composing it. To him this possibility, which grew into a probability as the years passed, transcended the petty differences of language, customs, culture, and economy which then bulked so large in inter-American relations. He made it one of his particular tasks to spread this gospel among all the Latin-American leaders he met in his travels or encountered in Washington.

This was a more difficult job, during the eight years preceding the outbreak of war, than it appears now that war is upon us. In addition to the obstacles which have been mentioned there were political and diplomatic difficulties with which the Secretary of State had to cope. In some of the Latin-American countries unconstitutional governments were in office, liable to expulsion by the same revolutionary process which had brought them to power. In other Latin-American capitals extra-American influences were strong and tended to work against the idea of Pan-American solidarity.

Great Britain, Germany, Italy, Spain, Portugal, France, and even Japan, in a small way, had their spheres of influence which each of them sought to exploit for their own benefit. Mistakenly or wisely, the representatives of all these nations strove to impede that complete Pan-American understanding for which Hull was working. For different, but supposedly compelling, reasons they flattered, threatened, and cajoled the existing authorities in some of the Southern republics into a state of mind where they were prepared to give only lukewarm, if any, cooperation to the proposals emanating from the New Deal in Washington.

Thanks to the basic common sense of the North American

viewpoint, as expounded by Secretary Hull, the threats and
cajoleries receded to their true proportions the minute actual
war threatened the hemisphere. The critical situation appeared
in its true perspective, and the republics rallied to their real self-
interest. Even the most reactionary of officials in Latin America
could see that an Axis victory would do no good for him or his
own interests, even if he were not concerned with the long-range
interests of his country at large.

The advent of war found Secretary Hull in excellent physical
condition. For some months before the outbreak he had wisely
decided to delegate more and more detail work to his staff, saving
himself for the big questions which he knew must present themselves in the near future. He had broken, to some extent, his
lifelong habit of staying at his desk all day and much of the night,
weekdays and Sundays. Mrs. Hull had finally persuaded him that
he would be more effective for the big, important decisions if
he stayed away from the pettier business with which any Cabinet
officer can so easily swamp himself.

The occasional hours and, sometimes, days which he devoted
to relaxation at home or to vacations at the near-by resorts he
likes brought their reward when war came. He maintained his
characteristic calm, and the tremendous, concentrated events
did not make him lose his poise. His usual vigor, mental and
physical, seemed to be enhanced.

President Roosevelt and Secretary Hull made an excellent
team to direct the American effort in a second world war. In the
first one Roosevelt had been Assistant Secretary of the Navy—
close to the fighting forces. Hull had been an influential member
of Congress, enjoying the confidence of President Wilson and his
Cabinet, and had contributed no small part of the legislative and
fiscal policies which brought eventual victory. This combination,
by the fortuitous operations of democracy, was available to the
United States in its hour of greatest need.

Hull was called on to contribute more counsel, in this greatest
of all wars the world has ever seen, than a Secretary of State is
normally expected to give in wartime. This sprang from the
nature of the war itself. The totalitarians invented the concept of
total war, and their onslaughts could be countered only by total
defense on the part of the victims of aggression. Fortunately for

the United States, the diplomatic end of its war effort was in the hands of a man who had gone through the nearest thing to all-out war which his country had previously experienced and had learned many practical lessons about the capabilities and limitations of belligerent democracy.

He brought to President Roosevelt's Cabinet meetings, and to the smaller strategy conferences on which the Chief Executive leaned so heavily, the calm influence and extraordinary insight into international affairs which were his heritage from a long experience. Once again his unwillingness to be diverted from the ultimate goal by immediate compromise was of value to his country. From the first day that President Roosevelt sought his advice on the conduct of the war Hull devoted himself not only to the tremendous immediate problem but to the ultimate task of winning the peace which was to follow the end of hostilities.

A mere review of the broad questions which faced President Roosevelt, in addition to the immediate military problems, serious as they were, demonstrates why any Secretary of State in those days would have been obliged to sit in with the army and navy on almost every major question. No tactical commander could make any long-range policy decision without taking into account the international politics of the Soviet Union, China, Spain, Portugal, Unoccupied France with its Caribbean dependencies and West African possessions, Turkey, Sweden, and the fathomless intricacies of the Middle East. Military leaders quickly appreciated the value of Hull's encyclopedic knowledge of these affairs, even when they differed with the conclusions he drew.

In addition to these domestic values Hull possessed, more than any other contemporary individual, the quality of being able to put into effect the decisions reached regarding external cooperation, by virtue of his term of office of nearly nine years at the State Department. In the absence of any unified military command to direct the operations of all the anti-Axis armies, navies, and air forces, it was necessary to proceed from step to step by agreement among the civil governments of the allied nations. That is to say, most of the anti-Axis belligerents were united by the desire to defeat the immediate enemy but were divided by differing and occasionally conflicting immediate war objectives.

Hull tended to become more and more the catalytic agent needed to precipitate the military chemical reaction of the forces lined up against the Axis and its satellites. Something of the kind was sorely needed, and the democratic side was blessed by the presence and qualifications of Cordell Hull. If, as he is confident, ultimate victory comes to his standard, Hull will be equally invaluable in helping design a permanent structure of peace which will permit the world to recover from the devastating effects of two universal wars within a generation.

There is no human slide rule by which can be measured the value of an apparently great man at the height of his career. Decades, and perhaps centuries, after his death historians will weigh the contribution Cordell Hull has made to his country and his times. A faint preglow may have been afforded by the declaration of peace aims which President Roosevelt and Prime Minister Churchill evolved after their battleship conference "somewhere in the Atlantic." The insistence that all nations, victors and vanquished alike, must have equal opportunity of access to the riches of the world might have been lifted bodily from the speech Cordell Hull made to the House of Representatives in 1919.

As a contemporary estimate of Hull's human qualities during the trying days he has traversed as Secretary of State, I can find no more heartfelt tribute than that made by Sumner Welles on December 28, 1940, in the course of one of those periodic rumors that he and his superior were at odds.

"I think it would have been humanly impossible for two people, over a period of eight years, to agree more consistently and thoroughly than Mr. Hull and I have done. There has never been the slightest important difference of opinion between us, and so far as I am personally concerned I think it would be impossible for any man in my position, who has been so closely associated with the Secretary—who has had the opportunity of being associated with a man of his extraordinary moral courage and consistency, and I think an almost unique intellectual integrity—to have anything except very deep devotion for him."

Like Sumner Welles, most of us will not attempt as yet to pass any judgment on Hull beyond the unanimous tribute that he possesses "almost unique intellectual integrity." Casting an eye about the world horizon as this is written, it is difficult to discern other men about whom this might be said. The rest could be counted on the fingers of a single hand.

Hull has passed most of his threescore years and ten in useful service to his country and to the world. His rank in history will depend on the fate of democracy, for he has been one of its most ardent champions. If democracy should fail and disappear at this critical point in its history, he will be forgotten as a minor prophet of an unimportant illusion in the development of the human race. If democracy emerges triumphant from the tempering furnace, he will be hailed as a major prophet whose words have lighted his fellow men to hope and progress.

Index

CPSIA information can be obtained
at www.ICGtesting.com
Printed in the USA
LVHW041039071020
668174LV00004B/158